Sue Shephard was born in London. Afte spent most of her career working in televi... and directing documentaries, and later Cl... a wide range of educational series. She al... programmes *Food File, Grow Your Green*... Grigson, and three series about food and ... whom she co-wrote the book *United Tastes of America*.

Sue now lives in Bristol in the south-west of England, with her writer husband and two grown-up children.

Praise for Sue Shephard:

'An entertaining, charming and fascinating little book which reminds us that the story of food preserving is the story of civilisation itself. This is a well-researched book full of wonderful information: it is one of the very few books I would have loved to have written myself, though I doubt I'd have done it half so well' Clarissa Dickson Wright, *Mail on Sunday*

'We are not used to placing the humble pickle or conserve at the forefront of human progress. But the more one reads of *Pickled, Potted and Canned*, the more true it appears . . . This is a fascinating and well-researched book, seething with anecdotes and information' *Sunday Telegraph*

'Sue Shephard's book is not only a classic, it is perfectly riveting' *Country Life*

'This remarkable book is full of bizarre stories which not only divert and entertain but yield many illuminating insights into social history . . . The story encompasses accidental discovery and hit-and-miss experimentation, romantic tradition and glorious gluttony, graphic starkness and the downright disgusting' *Daily Telegraph*

'Absorbing and detailed' *Express*

'Sue Shephard's book tackles the whole history of food, from ice-houses in China four thousand years ago to Mr Birdseye and his innovations. What might seem a limited subject is revealed as an alternative way of looking at the fluctuations in civilised society' *Literary Review*

'*Pickled, Potted and Canned* embraces food science, social domestic history, and the national agendas of leaders down the millennia striving to keep up the morale of armies marching on their stomachs, to sustain fishermen and explorers on the high seas, and astronauts voyaging into space' *Financial Times*

'Before your next trip to the supermarket, read Sue Shephard's *Pickled, Potted and Canned*. The shelves will look quite different once you discover why the invention of the sausage was essential to the conquests of Imperial Rome and how Carnation Milk fuelled the Klondike gold rush ... a delightful collection of stories' *New Scientist*

'*Pickled, Potted and Canned* is full of stories – some mouthwatering, others repulsive . . . All the right ingredients are here – an excellent idea, some great stories and diligent research' *New Statesman*

'Food preservation isn't all about jam making. Bloody revolutions, failed expeditions, lingering deaths and even bottled urine experiments fit in here, as Shephard puts her subject in a historical and social context' *Focus*

'This is a good, meaty read which is also suitable for dipping into at any point'
The Scotsman

'This book will enlighten and amaze. It does exactly what it says on the tin – going from the dried meats of the Native Americans to the "tubed" food which is squeezed directly into the mouths of astronauts . . . Food for thought indeed'
The Big Issue

Pickled, Potted and Canned

THE STORY OF FOOD PRESERVING

Sue Shephard

HEADLINE

First published in 2000
by HEADLINE BOOK PUBLISHING

First published in paperback in 2001
by HEADLINE BOOK PUBLISHING

10 9 8 7 6 5 4 3 2 1

ISBN 0 7472 6207 1

Typeset by
Palimpsest Book Production Ltd
Polmont, Stirlingshire.

Printed and bound by
Clays Ltd, St Ives plc.

HEADLINE BOOK PUBLISHING
A division of Hodder Headline
338 Euston Road
London NW1 3BH

www.headline.co.uk
www.hodderheadline.com

In memory of my father
who died while I was writing this book
but who supported me all the way

Contents

Acknowledgements

One of the nicest outcomes of writing this book was to be welcomed into the fraternity of the Oxford Symposium on Food and Cookery, which is held every year at St Anthony's College, Oxford. Here I met academics, writers, cooks and other experts from all over the world and made many friends. Papers covering various Oxford Symposia and conferences on food history held in Oslo and Leeds have been invaluable in my researches and are listed in the Select Bibliography. I am grateful to the authors of all the papers that I used and especially for help given to me by Prof. Richard Hosking, Philip Iddison, Helen Saberi, Dr Michael Abdalla, Jaakko Rahola, Andrew Smith and Peter Brears. I am particularly indebted to Jennifer Stead and C. Anne Wilson for their huge knowledge of English food preserving and for their encouragement. My thanks, too, to Oded Schwartz and my good friend Dorinda Hafner.

Researching a book of this nature meant many hours spent in libraries where I was generously aided by enthusiastic librarians. I would like to give special thanks to librarians at the British Library, the Science Museum Library, the Bristol Public Library, the University of Bristol, University of Reading and Leeds University libraries, the Library of the American Museum in Bath, the National Maritime Museum, the Institute of Food Research in Norwich, the Gloucester & Sawyer Free Library in Massachusetts and the incomparable London Library. I would also like to thank Tessa McKirdy of Cooks Books for obscure and second-hand publications and Tom Jaine of Prospect Books for help with symposiasts' papers.

I am very grateful to Dr Norman Cowell for allowing me to use his Ph.D. thesis and to Dr Stuart Thorne for his assistance and for the information in his valuable book on food preserving. My thanks to Rob Hewett for giving me access to his history of the Hewett family.

I am indebted to Dr Keith Farrer OBE, my food science adviser, who with great tact and courtesy helped me with my untutored science. Similarly, I am immensely grateful to Matthew Parker, my book editor, for his energy and clear-sightedness as he unravelled structural tangles and helped me to make sense of it all. I am lucky to have found so much support and encouragement from my publisher, Heather Holden-Brown, and my agent, Jane Turnbull.

Last, but by no means least, my loving thanks to my husband Ben for our long walks as we struggled with the demons in our own respective books and to my children Louisa and Joe for their forbearance in living in a household with no regular income and two scribbling parents.

Preface: The Longest Journey

A journey from seasons of plenty into the empty seasons or across unknown, inhospitable lands or over the broad and violent oceans, requires sustenance where there is little or none. Every journey demands planning and provisioning . . . even that longest journey of all.

In 1800 some archaeologists working in Egypt found a large jar of honey. They opened it and found that it tasted perfect even though it was thousands of years old. As they greedily dipped into the jar, they found some hairs, and when they tipped all the honey out, they discovered the perfectly preserved body of a small baby.

In funeral rites, the dead were often given a supply of honey to enjoy as they set out for the afterlife. Honey denoted immortality, and from Neolithic times onwards, the Aryans, Sumerians, Babylonians and Cretans buried many of their great men (and women) in honey. Alexander the Great had chosen to be embalmed in honey when he died in Babylon in 323 BC.

As the journey into the afterlife was considered the longest and most important, the Egyptians took the preserving of the body and the provisions necessary for that journey very seriously. Originally the bodies were dried in the hot, dry sands of the desert, but, in later dynasties, the commonly held belief that contact with air somehow caused putrefaction led them to wrap the bodies very tightly in linen bandages. Although they had the right idea, this was not very successful until they tried first removing the internal organs. Eventually they were able to understand the basic requirements needed to preserve a corpse adequately, if not always perfectly. Herodotus, writing in the fifth century BC, tells us that the embalmers removed all the organs, except the heart, which was believed to be the centre of understanding. The body cavity was given a thick coating, both inside and out, of a powdery salt known as natron, of which there was a plentiful supply left by evaporation around oases in the Egyptian desert. The salt drew the water out from the tissues and dried the body cavity, which was then packed with linen and sewn up. After it was treated with ointments, spices and resins, it was firmly wrapped in bandages. This elaborate and expensive process was reserved for the wealthy and powerful. Their tombs were filled with furniture, chariots, symbolic items, precious jewels and ornaments and a large supply of preserved food provisions including stocks of garlic and onions carefully wrapped in bandages like a guard of pungent little mummies.

In 1972, in China, a tomb was uncovered containing the body of a noble woman of the Han period (202 BC–AD 220). Her body was remarkably preserved and among the rich burial remains were generous quantities of foodstuffs to take the woman and her husband, who was entombed with her, on their infinite journey. Preserved in bamboo cases and pottery vessels of various types were rice, barley, red lentil and millet. Fruits such as pears, jujube and plums and the remains of carp, bream and perch, hare, pig, deer, sheep and ox, duck, chicken and pigeon were also found along with lotus root and root ginger and numerous spices. Archaeologists also came across hundreds of inscribed bamboo slips giving information about cooking and methods for preserving such as salting, sun-drying and pickling. It is not known who was supposed to read these and prepare some heavenly meals.

Millennia-old prehistoric insects have been discovered beautifully suspended in amber and perfectly preserved mammoths have appeared out of the permafrost, their tusks now being sold as a substitute for elephant ivory. In 1799 a Tungus hunter found the first frozen mammoth in the ice in Siberia, its last meal of grass and pine cones still conserved in its stomach. William Buckland, who, in the early nineteenth century, was an Oxford professor of mineralogy and later Dean of Westminster, once served his unsuspecting dinner guests meat from a frozen mammoth. 'Dear friends,' he announced, 'you have just eaten meat one thousand years old . . .'

Other humans and animals have been returned to us in a wide range of preservatives. Men and women, victims of sacrifices, have been dug out of peat bogs, and the perfectly salt-preserved corpses of miners have been found buried in tenth-century Alpine salt mines. Nearby were discovered their picks, their knapsacks filled with blocks of salt and earthenware pots for evaporating and moulding the salt into slabs. A frozen man recently appeared out of a glacier with his 'ploughman's lunch' still in his skin bag. Last, but by no means least, if only for his journey home from Trafalgar to a proper burial, came Lord Nelson preserved in a barrel of brandy.

Two frozen woolly mammoths discovered in 1934 in Northern Russia

The Egyptian word for preserving fish by salting and drying was the same as that used to denote the process of embalming mummies. Indeed, every one of these ancient traditions for preserving humans and animals for the afterlife finds a parallel in the known principles of food preservation: drying with salts and spices; preserving in honey or brine; freezing; sealing in airtight wrappings or containers or in natural media such as amber, alcohol, formaldehyde; or burying in cool, wet bogs full of boracic and other acids. The principles are remarkably simple, but the traditions that have developed around them, whether complex or rudimentary, give extraordinary insights into the histories, cultures and the ingenuity of people in their fight to survive and to progress.

Introduction: Shelf Life

Food preserving helped make it possible for our nomadic ancestors to settle down in one place and build agrarian communities where they could live in reasonable confidence that they would not go hungry through the variable seasons and the many other difficulties that nature might throw at them. Food preserving also made it possible for some of our ancestors to travel, taking their food with them as they journeyed over long distances to explore unknown places, confident, if they could find no fresh food, that their portable provisions meant they would not starve.

Preserved foods have played a significant role in our social and cultural history and it is arguable that without the ability to preserve food, man might have been forced to continue his wanderings as a hunter gatherer, following migrating herds and foraging for seasonal foods. A preserved harvest to feed people through the winter also allowed the slow evolution of the social and cultural complexities that owning and storing secure stocks of food and having long periods of seasonal leisure brought in their train. It encouraged the growth not only of arts and technologies, but also of social stratification, slavery and endemic warfare. Without preserved food man might not have been able to send out large armies and naval ships to explore new lands and seas and conquer new territories. There might have been no great expeditions into the unknown, no great discoveries of navigation and science by men such as Vasco da Gama, Magellan, Drake and Livingstone. There might have been no creation of the trade routes along which knowledge and culture was exchanged. The Poles might have remained unreached, rivers uncharted, mountains unscaled and the moon unvisited. None of the greatest achievements in travel, exploration and survival could have been possible without the increasing ability to preserve and carry food into places where

Kublai Khan, the Mongol Emperor, distributing grain in a time of shortage in the thirteenth century

none was available. Even now, men and women still take up impossible-sounding challenges to cross oceans, deserts and ice, and still plan to live on preserved provisions, albeit using the latest in science, technology and nutritional knowledge.

Few people in the developed world have to worry about hunger any more. Yet the first thing everyone does when a crisis looms is to rush out and panic buy, stockpiling great quantities of preserved foods. It is this same instinct that drove our ancestors to find ways to keep supplies of food ready for all eventualities throughout the year. But then, unlike today, they spent a great deal of their time worrying about where the next meal was coming from and most of their energies in producing, storing, preserving and cooking their food. Abundant autumn crops of fruits and nuts and great quantities of fresh young summer vegetables all seem to come at once, for this is nature's way of ensuring the successful reproduction of each species. Short of stuffing themselves in the summer and autumn and starving for the rest of the year, ancient peoples had to find some way of cheating nature and turning these gluts of good things into food that would be available for eating all the year round.

Though the severity of the climate might vary, at least the rhythm of the seasons was predictable. Our forbears also had to find ways to provide against less predictable disasters such as diseases that ravaged them, their crops and their livestock. In some parts of the world they also had to suffer long periods of drought, flooding, freezing or tropical heat and invasions from aggressors and scarcity of food during the long, dark years of war. For many people the threat of famine from any of these causes remains a grim reality.

In the small, isolated, self-sufficient communities around the ancient world, people began searching for ways to preserve life by preserving food. What they found, with their extraordinary ingenuity and powers of observation, was a variety of ways in which they could harness the elements and use the natural chemicals around them to halt the inevitable processes of food decay, even though they had no scientific way of explaining how or why something worked. They developed different methods by combining drying, salting, smoking and fermenting. Each community evolved techniques best suited its climate, its food supplies and its particular needs and culture. In the northern regions, for example, where the harsh winters made it almost impossible to find fresh foods, the people dried their food in the cold Arctic air, cured their bacons and hams in the smoke hole over the hearth and once they discovered salt, they pickled and fermented fish, meat and vegetables. The nomads of North Africa and the Slavic regions, who had no places to store food but plenty of daily milk supplies from their travelling herds, found ways to keep it by drying it or fermenting it into yoghurts and cheeses carried in bags slung from their saddles. In the Middle East, surplus catches of fish, meat and fruits were laid out in the sands or on their rooftops to dry in the baking sun to keep for many months. The gradual discovery of the preserving powers of heat and cold, salts, sugar and spices, vinegars and alcohols and, later, airtight seals and containers slowly transformed the way people ate and influenced their developing culture and lifestyles.

Food preserving did not simply keep food safe for eating, it also changed the texture and taste of foods, sometimes in a way that seemed revolting to people not accustomed to it. In some African and South Pacific countries, the powerful high flavour of rotted, fermented foods was much appreciated. The use of different food preserving techniques around the world helped form national cuisines and taste preferences. Scandinavian and Russian people love sour tastes, while in eastern Europe, sharp vinegary tastes became popular. All over the world, poor people subsisting on dull monotonous, cereal-based diets were able to make highly flavoured preserved sauces, pickles and relishes to pep up their meals. Preserving also rendered some foods more palatable and processed some inedible, even poisonous plants into safe and digestible nourishment.

Preserving methods created interesting new kinds of foods which entered the traditional meals of different cultures: succulent smoked hams, spicy dried sausages and sweet cured bacon; chewy dried fruit that seem to taste of sunshine, jams and marmalade and rich sugared fruits and nuts. Milk was transformed into thick salted butter and hundreds of kinds of matured cheeses. Varieties of strong dry breads and biscuits were developed to eat with cheese and potted meats. Delicate gravlaks, pink smoked salmon and salt cod became ingredients for classic national dishes. The need to preserve food to survive may not now be so important, but the desire to eat the foods and enjoy the unique tastes that preserving has given us is as great as ever. As Alan Davidson wrote in his book *Mediterranean Seafood*, 'tastes once acquired are often retained when the reason for acquiring them has disappeared'.

We know a lot about how people lived and ate and about their food preserving traditions around the world from the many travellers who, over the years, were useful observers as well as themselves being consumers of preserved food. Men such as Herodotus, the Greek geographer and historian who in 460 BC journeyed throughout Turkey, the Aegean, Egypt and Persia 'never tiring of his interest in other men's customs, religions and techniques', including food preserving. The eighteenth-century Chinese magistrate, Li Hua-nan travelled all over China talking to the local people about their food and cooking. He was especially interested in food preserving methods and how they helped ward off starvation. The merchant Marco Polo travelled from Venice to the Chinese court of Kublai Khan in the thirteenth century marvelling at the strange new foods and exotic cuisine. Later came those with a more political agenda such as William Cobbett and Daniel Defoe. Men were not, of course, the only travellers. There were many women, equally famous for their wanderlust and derring-do, who travelled alone in far-flung places. The first known woman traveller to record her journey was Egeria, a devout Christian from Rome who travelled to the Holy Land in AD 383. Many others followed, though the majority of those now famous were Victorian women – Freya Stark, Gertrude Bell, Mary Kingsley, Marianne North and Isabella Bird.

For travellers, food had to be light, compact, long lasting and nutritious. Different cultures from all over the world have nourished their travelling compatriots with varieties of dried meat, dried bread or biscuit, dried fruits and fermented dairy products. Sea travel presented much greater problems for people sailing out of sight of land with no possibility of replenishing provisions for many months. Storage space on wooden ships was limited and the conditions were often quite unsuitable for keeping foods.

Preserving large amounts of food quickly before it spoiled required the help and co-operation of everyone in the community. Until the eighteenth century, few households in northern countries had enough land to grow hay for winter fodder and by November the farmers had traditionally slaughtered all but the best of their livestock, which they kept back for breeding in the following year. The butchered meat was salted into barrels, laid out to dry or hung up above the hearth to smoke. Neighbours visited each other to assist with the salting, the sausage making, with cutting the cabbage for sauerkraut, preparing the apples for cider making and with fruit drying, churning butter and with cheese making. In many cases, they pooled their produce to make communal preserves, producing great barrels of wine or giant cheeses to be stored in their cellars, or bundles of sun-dried fruits, peppers and tomatoes, which they laid out on the roofs of their houses or hung out in the dry air like washing. Co-operative food preserving helped to strengthen the sense of community and everyone went home with a bit of fresh food to eat and some to put by, their stomachs filled from a good traditional feast to celebrate the job well done. For most ordinary people in the world, these food habits changed very little until the demise of the old traditional food preserving cultures in the 1950s and 1960s. Yet when people are uprooted and forced to move as settlers or refugees to a new land, it is their food traditions, including their preserving methods, that they cling to and continue to celebrate in their new homes. This is especially true in the USA, where the numerous 'ethnic' cultural communities are turning away from their initial assimilation as Americans and rediscovering a pride in the culture and cuisine of their origins.

Life for us in recent decades has moved and changed so fast that it difficult to appreciate how slow progress in food development has been in the past. In describing the history of food and food preserving since prehistory, it is very easy to get lost in time. Great events in history certainly affected everyone's lives — invaders, settlers and travellers brought new kinds of food and influenced cooking and tastes, particularly amongst the wealthier households. But for the majority, the basic traditions of food supply and preserving did not greatly change for centuries and so neither did their diet. Their cooking pots were filled, if they were lucky, with much the same unchanging ingredients, which varied only in type and quantity, as they struggled to survive through the unyielding seasons and natural or man-made calamities.

Wealthy eighteenth-century households could afford fresh food but still relied heavily on preserved provisions

Each family strove, in its own particular way, to preserve the products of the July orchard for the January larder. Every man's ambition was food for himself and his family; every woman's rule was 'waste not, want not'. For the vast majority of the population, wherever they lived, as rural peasants or urban workers, it was satisfaction enough if their bellies were filled.

Life could be greatly improved, however, if they managed to preserve for more than their own future needs. A surplus of preserved food could be kept by until there was enough to be taken to market to be sold or bartered for tools, pots, vital salt supplies and other necessities. As populations increased and moved from the country to work in the towns and cities far from the main sources of fresh foods, the need to find foods that were cheap and plentiful and could travel well became even more pressing. Religious dietary laws in Europe forbidding the eating of meat on certain days resulted in a huge demand for fish in the towns and cities inland. Fish was very perishable and had to be preserved quickly. This led to a burgeoning trade in salted and pickled fish, which encouraged authorities to increase already crippling taxes on salt and sugar. Meat was often moved 'on the hoof'. But fresh meat was always very scarce and the rural poor rarely saw any meat apart from the few animals of their own that they kept to be salted, dried or smoked at home in the autumn and winter months.

During the eighteenth and nineteenth centuries, some of the food supply problems arising from the move from an agrarian to an industrial society were eased by great improvements in agriculture and food production. New fertilisers gave higher crop yields and the introduction of mechanised farming, the production of winter fodder for livestock and the development of industrialised food processing in mills, breweries and food factories increased the availability of affordable food. The causes of dietary diseases such as scurvy, rickets and beriberi were not then properly understood but their association with a diet dominated by certain preserved foods was recognised. The British navy, in particular, which had doubled in size during the Napoleonic wars, was still suffering from its inability to deal with the problem of scurvy, its ignorance of vitamins and its inefficient victualling with so much salt food and hardtack. Armed forces throughout Europe and the colonies were desperate for a solution.

Spurred on by these demands for change, scientists and inventors began to make great strides in understanding the biological causes of food deterioration, in improving people's diets and in the creation of new methods of food preservation. The invention of heat processing and canned foods, which could be transported everywhere, kept almost indefinitely and could feed rich and poor alike, changed food preserving for ever. Refrigeration and freezing transformed the fishing and meat industries and the ever wider ownership of fridges and freezers since the 1950s has meant a whole new range of foods could be preserved and stored in the home. Railways and faster shipping meant that both food and people could be transported quickly and more efficiently. New preserving methods meant that food could now be imported and exported in huge quantities, and the economies of a number of countries were transformed. If food could be satisfactorily preserved for long storage and freighting it was now valuable for international trade.

By the 1930s food in Europe and America was becoming big business and a vast, new range of exotic, previously unknown foods began to appear in our shops. Despite the poverty and hunger of the 1930s, many people could begin to vary their diet more and radically to change their cooking and eating habits. The old traditional processes that had served so well and become part of the culture and daily life of communities all over the world gradually gave way to new industrialised food processing. This process is still continuing in many parts of the world and irradiation and other methods of the future are still being tested and explored.

The word 'preservative', along with 'additive', has got itself a bad name in recent years. The developed world has become obsessed with healthy diets, organic foods and the 'sell by date'. Public fears of additives and preservatives, genetically modified crops and irradiation, have sent many people back to so-called organically grown fresh products and to some of the old 'natural' traditional methods of preserving from the past. In America, in particular, they are now adapting old ways to more convenient, modern techniques so they can enjoy the gourmet pleasures of 'home-made' smoking, bottling, pickling and jam making. This is partly out of a desire for foods with real taste and quality and partly from a wish to return to a simpler world where, despite the poverty, hardship and simple diet, the food was at least home produced and one knew where it came from, how it had been processed and what was in it.

The science and technology of food production will continue to be of major concern. Whilst science has enormously improved both the safety and quality of our food today, consumer fears about the introduction of new kinds of processing and packaging, particularly when it seems to profit the food industry rather than the consumer, continue to be voiced (though malpractice and food adulteration is an ancient problem that has worried people since classical times). But we should also always remember that throughout history food preserving has provided cheap, plentiful and varied food supplies for a vast number of people where there was otherwise hunger and malnutrition. We should be just as concerned about our capacity to feed every mouth in the world's continually exploding population. We are still a long way from achieving this, but food preserving will certainly continue to play a vital part.

> Each climate needs what other climes produce,
> And offers something to the general use;
> No land but listens to the common call,
> And in return receives supplies from all.
> The general intercourse, and mutual aid,
> Cheer what were else a universal shade.
>
> William Cowper (1731–1800)

Nearly everything we eat today has been treated in some way or another in order to prolong its life as a safe, transportable, saleable and storable food. On returning from our local stores or supermarket laden with our week's food supplies, we start by unpacking quantities of food that we have selected from the freezer cabinets. We will also put away tins of cooked vegetables, meat, tuna and sardines in oil, fruits in syrup and concentrated soups. We might also have bought bottles of vegetables pickled in brine or vinegar, olives and sun-dried tomatoes in oil, sauces and mayonnaise. We will 'put up' on the shelves jars of chutney, jam and marmalade; and into the store cupboard will go packets of dehydrated, extruded or freeze-dried products such as soups, milk, vegetables, coffee, cocoa, tea, sauces, custards and gravy, as well as cubes of concentrated stock and tomato paste in tubes. We will have stocked up with packets of dried pasta, rice, pulses, nuts and dried fruits such as apricots, prunes and raisins. We may even have bought fresh products such as meat, bread, milk and butter which we will 'preserve' for later consumption in our own fast freezers at home.

If we are fortunate we may also have visited a local delicatessen stocked with delicacies and specialities from many different countries that have been preserved in the old traditional ways, which offer real flavour and quality over the often rather bland and packaged convenience foods that we have put away in our freezers and store cupboards. We can choose succulent and tasty luxuries such as Scottish smoked salmon, Italian dried salami, German smoked sausages, bloaters and kippers from Yarmouth, hams and olives from Spain, salted Baltic herrings and English sweet cured bacon, French potted pâtés and the best matured cheeses of England, France and elsewhere. A cornucopia of delicious, exotic sounding foods, beautifully preserved using modern methods to produce improved versions of the ancient flavours that were once the food of the poor rural peasant. Few people today really know what these old preserving traditions were, who practised them and how they worked. It seems a great shame because the facts and the stories surrounding them are so fascinating:

> An understanding of what food is and how cooking works does no violence to the art of cuisine, destroys no delightful mystery. Instead, the mystery expands from matters of expertise and taste to encompass the hidden patterns and wonderful coincidences of nature. How remarkable it is, when you come to think in such terms, that heat has such fortunate effects on the flavour and digestibility of plant and animal tissues, that roast and meringue are two different outcomes of the same process, that wheat proteins have just the right balance of properties to make raised bread possible, that bread, cheese and yoghurt, beer and wine are all the result of controlled spoilage! Science can enrich our culinary experience by deepening its significance, by disclosing its connections with the rest of the world.
>
> Harold McGee *On Food and Cooking: The Science and Lore of the Kitchen*, 1991

Everything we eat has itself lived as some form of either plant or animal life. As soon as it has been slaughtered or plucked from the stalk, branch or soil, our food starts to deteriorate. Although not necessarily immediately harmful to us, this seriously affects its value as a nutritional or edible food. The food chain is competitive and if we don't quickly take advantage of a food, something else will. Foods that benefit us are also very attractive to many of the millions of minute micro-organisms that proliferate in water, air and soil. Their significance was not properly understood until late in the nineteenth century when Louis Pasteur published his 1861 paper showing that micro-organisms were everywhere in the air. He had drawn some air, taken from different places, through very fine guncotton filters. When the filters were later dissolved in a mixture of ether and alcohol, tiny spores were found. Pasteur then drew air through a guncotton plug into a flask containing a sterile infusion. When the plug, which was now full of the airborne spores, fell into the flask, the infusion rapidly became putrid. Pasteur had finally shown that putrefaction is caused by airborne micro-organisms.

Until then, people had believed that decomposition was a spontaneous event caused, in some unexplained way, by exposure to air. This crucial mistake was to hamper the development of food preserving techniques right up until the time of Pasteur's discovery. Micro-organisms had in fact been seen but not understood much earlier. A Dutch optician Antonie van Leeuwenhoek saw what he described as 'living animalcules' through his home-made microscope in 1665. In 1774, an Italian priest, Lazza Spallanzani, had tried to disprove the theory of spontaneous degeneration by destroying bacteria on foods by heating them in a sealed flask. But, in a pattern repeated throughout the history of food preservation, no one was really listening enough to make the right connections and people continued successfully to preserve their food from decomposition using empirical, and on the whole, scientifically correct methods without feeling the need to understand why they worked.

Despite their inability to see or know about micro-organisms, people had, since the earliest times, observed the results of their activity. They would have seen food rot, and they began to practise a variety of effective methods of cheating these unknown creatures of their feast, developing techniques best suited to their own particular environment, using the elements and natural chemicals available. Amazingly, they also discovered how to create favourable conditions for some micro-organisms so that they were actually beneficial in preserving certain foodstuffs – bacteria for yoghurt (lactobacilli naturally present in milk) and yeasts (from the bloom of the grape) for bread, beer and wine – in a process broadly known as fermenting.

There are different kinds of micro-organisms which decompose food but most need certain common conditions in which to grow successfully, namely a warm, moist environment held on the slightly acid side of neutral and a supply of oxygen. (There is, however, a class of bacteria called anaerobes, which grow in the absence of oxygen and in food preserving these must be destroyed at all costs. *Clostridium botulinum*, the cause of botulism, is the best known of these and the most dangerous.) The aim of most preserving methods is to remove these conditions in order to either destroy or inhibit the offending micro-organisms already in the food. It is also very important that micro-organisms should be prevented from re-entering the food after it has been processed. Effective packaging and storing preserved foods is therefore also important.

A wide variety of techniques were developed to create an alien environment for harmful bacteria. Since there are few processes that can achieve the removal of all the bacteria-friendly conditions, people soon began combining the different methods, using a selection of natural elements and conserving media. Whatever people had was put to use, whether it be the heat of the sun, hot and cold winds, hot sands, cooling soils, fire and smoke, salts, sugars, spices, herbs, acids, oils, airtight containers or beneficial yeasts.

The development of the art of preserving was most likely a long and slow journey of trial and error, and also of taste. The idea of using combinations of different processes such as drying, airtight packaging and low temperature would have been adopted to produce a food that would survive better than that produced by just one method. The fact that they were often complementary or that one ingredient helped to counter the negative effects of another was perhaps also a lucky accident. Nevertheless, the ability of our ancestors to observe, adapt and 'cheat' nature never ceases to astonish.

CHAPTER ONE

DRYING
Meat and Fish

Pemmican so extended the fur trade's field of operations, in an era when canoes and a man's feet were the most practical means of transportation, that every beaver stream in the West became accessible to trappers who stayed away from base for many months.
Evan Jones, *The American Heritage Cookbook*, 1964

Long before the immigrant settlers and gold hunters had started to fill the American West in the mid-nineteenth century, mountain men – backwoodsmen, trappers, hunters, explorers and adventurers – were living their own very singular lives in the old northwest. They are now figures of romance and legend, wild, solitary men who lived on their wits and travelled light.

Amongst them were trappers who would spend many months in the forests and mountains hunting for beaver whose tail skins were particularly valuable. Once a year they would meet up at the traders' fur markets, described as the 'annual season of supply, trade and saturnalia'. These were wild fairs where mangy hunters would jostle with keen-eyed traders and wary Indians. The trappers sold their skins, got drunk on the proceeds, reprovisioned and headed out again, leaving fabulous descriptions of their adventures in the 'hard country', with tales of bear fights, Indian attacks and terrible starvation.

Many did, indeed, perish from hunger, especially in the winter if their small provisions had gone and there was nothing to hunt. Travelling on foot or by canoe over vast distances, the trappers could take few supplies even though they would often be away from base for many months. There was talk of cannibalism, of men bleeding their horses and drinking the blood like Masai tribesmen in Africa, of trappers who ate the ears of their pack mules and boiled anything made of leather — saddles bags or whips — for a grisly broth.

But these frontiersmen soon came into contact with the native inhabitants of the region and learned about pemmican, one of the best portable foods ever devised. Pemmican had been made for centuries by Native Americans to sustain them as they moved through the great mountains, lakes and forests of Canada and North America. It is made by thinly slicing lean meat, usually from one of the large game animals, and drying it over a fire or in the sun and wind. Some tribes were said to have tied the meat to the tops of the women's bundles so that it would dry out in the sun and wind as they walked along. When the meat is completely dried it is pounded to shreds between two stones and mixed with an almost equal quantity of melted fat, lard or bear grease, some marrow from the bones and a few handfuls of wild cherries, service berries or cranberries. It is then packed into rawhide sacks, tightly sewn up and sealed with tallow. Pemmican's name came from the Cree Indian word for fat, and its high fat content makes it a valuable source of energy and warmth in the often freezing temperatures of the region. Hung from a belt or saddle pack, it will sustain the traveller for huge distances in the worst kinds of conditions.

This adoption of a local preserved food, perfected over centuries using local resources to overcome particular hazards, fuelled the penetration of the harsh but lucrative interior of Canada. North American furs were soon traded as far as Russia and China. By the end of the seventeenth century there were well-worn trade routes west of the Great Lakes and in 1793 the fur trader Alexander Mackenzie became the first European to cross North America from coast to coast. He was sustained throughout by pemmican.

Pemmican remained an essential supply for numerous far larger-scale expeditions in later years and was also used on army manoeuvres in remote regions. Different tastes and varieties developed. Sir John Richardson, the Scottish naturalist who explored Canada in 1826, found that he preferred his pemmican meat slowly dried over an oak fire and then mixed with first-grade currants or sugar instead of wild cherries or cranberries. Pemmican is still made and eaten in America by campers, travellers and adventurers but it does not now contain the bear grease and crushed fruit that made it such a uniquely nutritious food. It seems strange that the original Native American pemmican is almost never mentioned in the diaries and records of migrants on the Western wagon trails. The simple and inexpensive combination of powdered, easily digested meat, high fat content and vitamin-rich berries might have protected them from scurvy and saved many lives. Despite the fact that they often took mountain men as guides during the summer months, the godly and respectable migrant seemed reluctant to eat Indian and wild man's food, sometimes with disastrous consequences.

The value of the meat in pemmican was in its drying, which concentrated and preserved it, making it portable and lasting. Drying is probably the earliest and simplest way to preserve food and it is possible that man was drying food even before he cooked it. As a hunter-gatherer living on the African continent, he might well have hung a piece of meat, perhaps the remains of a wildebeest kill, in the branches of a thorn tree, and discovered when he later returned that the meat had shrunk and dried out under the baking sun. He might have noticed that it had not been invaded by insects and their maggots in the way he knew they attacked dead animals left rotting in the shade. Hungry enough to take a bite from it, he would have discovered that the meat was more 'chewy' and the flavour more concentrated. Since it seemed good, he would have shouldered the meat, finding it easier and lighter to carry back to camp. Perhaps the others were not so enthusiastic about this old meat, so he stored it away and when the hunters failed to return with fresh meat, he brought it out and found it was still edible.

In other places, people walking through a parched landscape would find that fruits such as figs and dates, blown from the branches of trees, fell deep into the hot sands and were dried out. They tasted very sweet and were good to chew. In the desert, locusts and dead snakes were found dried, and were eaten. By lakes and along the coasts, fishermen buried some of their seasonal catch in the hot sand or hung it up to dry. Accidental discoveries became repeatable activities and as hunter-gatherers gradually settled down to agrarian pursuits, they began to develop ways of making their surplus food produce keep for when it was most needed.

At first, dried meat, fish and fruits would simply have been eaten raw and dry – the saliva and chewing in the mouth would have moisturised and softened the texture so that it could be swallowed and digested. As soon as liquids could be held in containers, such as skins, bladders and, later, clay and iron cooking pots, dried foods could be soaked back to almost their original state and used in stews, soups, compotes and other increasingly sophisticated dishes.

There is evidence that as early as 12,000 BC, Egyptian tribespeople on the lower Nile dried fish and poultry using the hot desert sun. Areas with similar hot and dry climates found drying to be an effective method of preservation. The ancient Babylonians, whose culture reached its apogee in around 1690 BC, made a concentrated paste from pounded dried fish which they crumbled up into their pottages. These practices survived invasions and the fall of empires. Herodotus, writing in the fifth century BC, describes how the Egyptians and their neighbours still dried fish in the sun and wind and then stored them for long periods.

In some inhospitable regions, preserving was vital for survival. A commander of Alexander the Great's during his campaign from Macedonia to India in 334–323 BC, noted the importance of drying to the natives of the coastal area of Baluchistan in modern-

Catching, sundrying, smoking and curing salmon in northern Europe in 1555

day Pakistan. Much of the fish catch was eaten raw, but the larger and tougher specimens 'they dry in the sun till they are quite sere and then pound them and make a flour and bread of them; others even make cakes of this flour. Even their flocks are fed on the fish, dried, for the country has no meadows and produces no grass.'

Indeed in almost all areas of the ancient world, this simplest form of food preservation was practised from the very earliest days. In China they dried snake, duck and a wide variety of sea foods such as shark's fin for soups, dried sea cucumber, abalone and shrimps. Recent evidence has shown that from as early as 10,000 BC potters in parts of Japan were making cooking pots and storage jars and hunted, fished and gathered a variety of foods such as meat, fish and shellfish for drying.

In each country the methods and materials reflect the local conditions and food supplies. When Europeans arrived in the New World in the sixteenth century, they found long-established drying traditions. Henry Hawks, writing in 1572 about Mexico, then known as New Spain, noticed that 'they have a great store of fish in the South Sea and many oisters . . . the people do open the oisters and take out the meat of them and dry it as they do other kinde of fish and keep it all the yeare; and when the times serve, they send them abroad into the country to sell as other fish'. Today, off the west coast of India, fishermen still haul onto the beaches from October to January vast catches of a small fish called 'bummalo'. Much of it is hung on racks on the beaches to dry in the hot tropical sun to form the local speciality confusingly known as 'Bombay Duck'. The end product smells like fish-glue and tastes like well-worn socks. It was exported everywhere that Indian restaurants had become popular. Sadly it has been banned by the EC which regards both the waters it swam in and the beaches it dried on as health hazards and deem the crunchy, strong, fishy tasting sticks unsafe for Western stomachs.

Most fish can be quickly dried by first splitting and gutting it but meat must be cut up into thin strips across the grain, which increases the drying surfaces and exposes the cut veins so that they drain more quickly. Nevertheless, larger pieces of meat can also be dried. In Afghanistan, for example, a practice survives whereby a fat sheep is slaughtered in the autumn and the wool sheared off, leaving the skin and a thick layer of fat underneath. Then the entire carcass is simply stretched out and hung up on a rack or in a tree to dry. This dried mutton has a very distinctive 'sheep' taste and is used to make a special pilau called 'landi pilau'. Similarly, in Tibet whole pigs are boned and the meat removed leaving a carcass that is mostly fat, which is sewn up and put in a cool place to cure and keep almost indefinitely.

In some regions, especially where it is cooler and damper, meat is 'pre-prepared' for drying with the use of weights such as stones or heavy boards to speed up the initial removal of moisture. Beating, squeezing, weighting, even jumping on the flesh help break down the fibres, releasing and pressing out the juices. All kinds of meat and fish are often first salted to aid the drying and in some cases cooked or marinated before being exposed to the air. The Berbers of North Africa originated a highly specialised dried meat they called 'khli' whose roots go back to time immemorial. It is made using meat marinated in coriander, cumin and garlic and is now very popular in Fez, Marrakech and in Algeria where it is now known as 'khadid'. Traditionally made once a year in vast quantities, it will keep for up to two years.

In other areas excellent drying conditions alone have sustained the practice of drying to the modern day. The dry mountain air in Switzerland is ideal for producing marinated and dried joints of beef called 'bundnerfleisch', which are hung out in a special little tower called *la tournalette*, while in the Italian Alps, where every valley boasts a sweeter, purer air than the next, they still dry tender fillets of beef called 'bresaola', which are dried until they acquire a rich, dark red colour. The flat, whitewashed sun roofs of houses in the Balkans, North Africa and the Middle East offer a quite different environment for sun drying food. Dried octopus and small fish-like smelts, used in fish couscous dishes, are still sold in the souks of Tunisia.

In South America, where there has been a plenitude of meat for hundreds of years, simple drying traditions survive, at least amongst the poor. The Native Americans on the arid southern borderlands sun dried venison and buffalo and one can still find dried beef in the form of 'tassajo', which is made with strips of meat dipped in maize flour, dried in the hot sun and wind, then tightly rolled up into balls to be carried easily on journeys. The modern American 'jerked beef' is derived from thin slices of air-dried meat called 'charqui'. This originated in Peru and was used to preserve excess game after large hunts, though later beef was more usually used. Charqui, a vital food for the Western pioneers, was often broken up and crushed between large stones and then boiled before eating. A German traveller in the Americas in the sixteenth century described it as looking like strips of thick pasteboard and being about 'as easy to masticate'.

From the beginning of the sixteenth century, the world was opened up to Western empires by explorers and traders. Colonists and settlers trying to survive in unfamiliar environments soon investigated local food supplies. They also needed to learn from local people about traditional ways to preserve foods. In South Africa the Dutch farmers spreading out from the Cape into the vast remote hinterland were largely self-sufficient, their diet consisting of meat from their cattle or game, a coarse bread made from their own hand-crushed grain, lard, butter and home-made cheese. The Bantu taught the men how to dry their meat in a way the Boers called 'biltong', to pound millet and to make porridge and beer, and the women learned about spices and pickling from the Malay slaves working in Cape Town as domestics and cooks. When the English took control of the Cape, the Boers found themselves subjects of an unsympathetic imperial power. As their grievances grew so did their resolution. 'The obvious way, the long way of habit, was to trek, to get away . . .' In 1836 all along the frontier lands the Boers got ready. The women prepared provisions, dried fruits and made preserves. They salted and pickled fish and vegetables, filled bags of meal and bought tea, coffee and sugar. Biltong and 'boerwors' (their cured sausage) were hung from the cross-pieces of the wagons. They took with them their herds of cattle, what provisions they could afford and household goods they could stow, along with ammunition and guns, ploughs and spades, and bags of seeds. As livestock was too precious to eat, the trekkers consumed wild game, which they hunted as they moved along the trail. They shot buck, eland, kudu, zebra, even lion. When a particularly large beast was killed they would make camp and turn the meat into biltong. The meat was cut up, salted, rubbed with crushed coriander seed and then hung in strips between thorn trees or strung between wagons as they moved on, drying until it was as hard as a board. The fat was rendered down to make soap, wax for candles and grease for the wagon axles, the skins were salted, dried and kept for tanning to make shoes, harnesses and whips and for weaving in strips for beds and chairs. Some biltong was pounded into a powder and eaten on bread and those who could afford sugar added a little to the curing mix.

When the Boers finally settled down they made a richer farm biltong. The strips of meat would be rubbed every day with a mixture of salt, pepper, saltpetre, crushed coriander and fennel seed, moistened with vinegar and hung up in a dry, draughty place between rubs until the outside was wind dried. The meat was then tied in cheese cloth and hung in a chimney to smoke. Some farmers still take biltong into the fields, cutting slices with a sharp pocket knife to enjoy the soft chewy 'tender garnet red meat inside and the taste which is deliciously spicy'.

Dried meat and fish are actually higher in nutritional value than fresh, despite the loss of certain vitamins. As the South African writer C. L. Leipoldt states in his *Belly Book*, 'Generally speaking dried food is more concentrated and therefore more valuable, pound for pound, than when fresh, and is especially suitable when a high-protein food is wanted.' For this reason, dried food, particularly meat, has been vital for both people and armies on the move since ancient times, establishing from the very beginning a pattern that sees the demands of the military shaping food preservation techniques right up to the modern day. Traditionally, invading forces had to rely for the most part on plundering what they could find and this practice during warfare continued well into the twentieth century. Special foraging parties would go ahead of the troops either to steal or buy food from the local populous. Needless to say, this was not a very reliable way to feed an army on the move if the territory was unfriendly, unpopulated or barren due to extreme climate or other hostile conditions. From the very beginning preserved, portable foods were always going to play a vital role.

Large-scale troop movements were commonly accompanied by

another army of provisioners with portable flour mills and baker's ovens, armourers, sutlers, and other craftsmen and servants employed to service the soldiers including the female camp followers who were never far behind. But speed and surprise was the secret of successful invasions. Troops unencumbered by wagon trains loaded with heavy equipment and quantities of food provisions moved far quicker. Individual soldiers carrying their own provisions made a more effective raiding party and it is not surprising that since weight is the overriding consideration for soldiers on the move, lightweight dried foods were always preferred.

Each country developed its own speciality. In ancient China, large-scale military campaigns were well supplied with dried meats and various kinds of special dried grain foods. According to Yen Yu, in the first century AD, the soldiers sent to fight the Hsiung-nu 'barbarians' in the desert lived on dried provisions and water and each soldier carried a carefully calculated daily ration. There are detailed reports, also, of Hungarian soldiers fighting in Italy in the fourteenth century carrying pouches of dried powdered beef, and orders survive from the fifteenth-century Polish king, Ladislaus Jagiellon, that his troops should be well supplied with dried fish and meat. Russian soldiers from the same period chewed on chunks of elk meat that was dried in bread ovens and carried tightly packed in bags.

Inevitably, dried food became for many armies an essential piece of military planning. Soldiers of the Roman Empire travelled enormous distances and the logistics of supply had to be very sophisticated. Military garrisons, from the Mediterranean to Britain and from Asia Minor to North Africa, built huge granaries and warehouses that they filled with requisitioned hard cheeses, dried fruit, *carnaria* (meat racks) of cured meats and baskets of salt fish hung up in the airy roof space. Bakehouses produced quantities of biscuit from grain supplied from Sicily and central Europe where serious shortages, as a result of military demands, were commonly suffered by the local people. *Amphorae* were filled with all kinds of foodstuffs including olives, honey, preserved plums, figs and dates, lentils, beans and rice, and sent from one end of the vast empire to the other.

As the powerful Danes swept in along the eastern shores of the

British Isles from the end of the eighth century, they built great towered strongholds out on the cliffs, on the heads of river estuaries and amongst the rocks of the wild coastline. These well-fortified and defended raiding strongholds were designed to keep booty, prisoners and, most importantly, supplies. Some had a central 'keep' set amongst a small community of huts, with a spring or well, a fire to cook on and storage and hanging space to keep quantities of preserved foods such as their stockfish and a dried beef, like biltong, made with smoke-dried buck, as well as cheeses, kegs of butter, crocks of whey ferment, dried herbs, cereal and root stores and casks of beer. These towers were thus well supplied against sieges from land or sea and stood ready to re-fortify men after the dangerous sea-crossing in open boats or to provide shelter after their sorties inland. The ragged remains of some Dane towers still stand as reminders of the skill and organisation of some of our ancestors.

The Viking invaders came from a region where conditions had favoured drying as a method of food preservation from the earliest times of settlement in Scandinavia. The long, cold winters had made food preservation a priority, and the abundant supply of fish, together with the cold, dry air, fostered a long and resilient practice of drying fish. Even while still at sea the Vikings crucified their catches of cod in the rigging of their ships to dry in the freezing sea winds until the fish were as hard as planks. In the Lofoten Islands in northern Norway, where the Gulf Stream delivers giant shoals of fish, they still hang sides of cod on high hurdles in the cold, spring air to dry until exceedingly hard and almost indestructible. The Norwegians have successfully exported this resulting 'stokkfisk' (stockfish) for many years. Its name is said to derive from the Dutch word for a piece of wood or stick, on which cod or herring were originally impaled for drying, with up to thirty pieces to a stick. In medieval times, dried fish was so commonly eaten that there were specialist women 'fishsoakers' whose task it was to soften the dry fish before it was cooked.

In countries with a damper, more temperate climate, however, drying had to be carried out in much less favourable conditions. In Scotland they established their own particular traditions of drying fish and meat. In the Faroe Islands, even as recently as the

1940s, the islanders still gutted and cut up their fish and hung it on sticks or hurdles up against the walls of their homes or out-houses in the open air until they were needed, when they were skinned, cleaned and boiled. Like the Vikings in earlier times, 'Some hardy individuals do not trouble to boil it, but merely remove the skin and chew the fish just as it is with obvious relish.' In addition, along the beaches of the Faroe Isles whale-meat would be cut up and laid in great shanks to dry and seal liver was dried and pulverised and drunk with milk or wine to protect against 'fluxes'. Britain and northern Europe enjoyed a much sunnier and warmer climate during the late Neolithic period and the Bronze Age and in Scotland they were able at that time to dry considerable quantities of venison. Even as late as the sixteenth century the Scots still ate raw deer simply pressed between two flat pieces of wood until it was hard and dry.

But as the climate gradually changed, in the north preserving of necessity became more sophisticated. As drying with sun and air became increasingly unreliable in northern communities – particularly in Scotland and eastern Europe – the people began to find other ways to dry their foods. Special drying houses and huts were built in Scotland and on the islands of Skye and St Kilda. The traveller Martin Martin, who visited the islands in 1698, described how the islanders made beehive-shaped 'cleits' of earth and stones arranged to allow a circulation of air where they dried 'fatty sea-fowls' such as the fulmar and the solan goose or gannet, 'without any salt or spice to preserve them'. The geese were kept for the 'space of a whole year' and were then either boiled or roasted. Another much later visitor, Sir William Jardine, wrote in 1845, 'We have eaten them boiled like ham and considered them by no means either strong, fishy or unpalatable.'

Other commentators, however, disagreed. Kenneth Williams toured the northern Scottish islands in the 1940s for his book *Atlantic Islands*, and discovered an ancient method of drying mutton still in use. A whole lamb was skinned, cut open and gutted then spread out flat outside or in a drying house and left to dry for months by which time, he wrote, 'it has a strong flavour and a stronger smell, is the dark red colour of congealed blood, and is like toffee to chew. Its taste is an acquired one, which most

Britons at once decide they can very well do without.'

As well as taste, texture can also suffer from this process. In fact, the very indestructibility of some dried foods made them difficult to reconstitute and cook into something actually edible, let alone nice to eat. Great lengths had to be gone to in an effort to return the moisture to dried fish. A fourteenth-century writer describing some very old stockfish observed, 'It behoves to beat it with a wooden hammer for a full hour and then set it to soak in warm water for a full two hours or more, then cook it and scour it well . . .' It is said that the barges bringing stockfish south towed the fish behind in river water so that by the time it was sold it was softened and ready to cook.

After sinking a fortune in the Newfoundland cod fisheries in 1654, the Marquis de Nointel, Louis de Béchamel, found that the French could not stomach the dried cod that he had shipped across the Atlantic. With his creditors on his back, he was forced to create a white sauce in an effort to make it more palatable. (Béchamel actually developed two versions of his famous sauce – 'Soubise', named after the commander of the French armies and 'Mornay', after a Huguenot family.) An earlier, fourteenth-century recipe recommends that the dried fish be soaked in butter to give it some texture, and then served with mustard to give it flavour.

In spite of these efforts, the sixteenth century saw other methods of food preservation become predominant in central and northern Europe. The damp climate had for a long time made drying outside an unreliable practice and fuel for ovens and drying houses was becoming increasingly scarce. Dried meat and fish, often brought in from elsewhere, was gradually relegated to the food for the poor, and for soldiers' and ships' stores. Instead, people looked around for natural chemicals in the soil, sea, smoke, rocks and plants, that could be used to improve the preserving processes. The most important and earliest discovery was the use of salt. Although drying remains an important stage in many preserving processes, it survives as a preserving method on its own for meat and fish only where it is especially easy or where there is no access to salt. The simplest forms of drying have remained essential to the poorest communities whose staple diet is meat or fish but who cannot afford salt or other, more expensive preserving agents. Countries with little or no natural salt supplies such as Norway, Finland and Japan continued to use air and sun drying until they were able to import salt. The Native Americans, who did not know about salt until the colonists arrived, dried and smoked their food without salt.

Dried fruits and vegetables, however, are a much tastier and more acceptable food and they have remained central to the diet of communities all over the world. Unlike fish and meat, the drying of fruit and vegetables has remained popular partly because of the delicious flavours and textures it produces and partly because in many regions it is still the most effective, cheap and practical method of preserving excess harvests.

Fruit and Vegetables

With the exception of the citrus group, most fruits dry extremely well if left out in the hot sun and dry air. The natural sugars in fruit are concentrated when moisture is removed. This made dried fruit particularly attractive when sugar was not known and honey, then the most commonly used sweetener, was not easily available. Originally fruits were dried until they had a hard, desiccated surface, which acted as a valuable deterrent to insects, moulds and other sources of decay.

Drying is still the simplest way to preserve fruit without the use of sugar. The twentieth century has seen mass-produced raisins, sultanas and currants shipped all over the world from giant processing plants in Australia and California. The hard, dry outer surface has been done away with as the dried fruits are now usually treated with vegetable oils to keep them soft and chewy. Traditionally, though, raisins are made from muscatel grapes from Malaga in Spain, partially dried on the vine or laid on mats in the sun. Sultanas started out as golden brown, very sweet grapes from Turkey and Greece and were known as 'Smyrna' or 'Sultana' raisins. Currants, originally from Corinth, are made from a tiny black variety of grape that has been grown for at least 2,000 years.

Prunes are now also mass produced in California, but demand remains high for the famous 'pruneaux' grown in western France. As they ripen the plums are thinned leaving only a few to fatten and produce a high sugar content. When ripe, they are not picked, but shaken from the tree onto cloths spread underneath. The gathered fruit are put to dry on wattles for several days and turned frequently. They are then finished off in purpose-built ovens for selling, or, for the village, in the local baker's oven. Agen prunes are a delicacy well worth buying to cook in cassoulets and other regional dishes. Many of the locals, however, prefer to turn their plums into eau de vie, a powerful *digestif* traditionally made in the travelling still that goes from village to village. More prunes would then be pickled in the eau de vie to make a satisfying end to a good meal.

Figs and dates are also now produced on a huge scale, and are still a staple for many people living in the Near East and North Africa. We know that the ancient Greeks loved to eat mashed dried figs, mixed with honey and nuts with cups of strong sweet wine. The best figs for drying still come from Greece, Turkey and North Africa. Traditionally they are washed with sea water and dried on the ground in the hot sun. Dates, rich in energy-giving sugar, were regarded by many ancient cultures as sacred. They dry perfectly in the desert sun and can be eaten fresh, dried or ground into meal to make cakes.

The Romans also loved to eat chewy dried fruits. They grew so many varieties that Lucius Columella, first-century author of *De Re Rustica*, declared they were too numerous to catalogue. However, he was able to describe many of the varieties of fruits that were dried, stored in must (the first watery 'crush' of grapes in wine-making) or boiled into a conserve with wine and water. Other fruits such as apples were dipped in wax or clay. Dried figs were particularly popular in Rome, and though Columella considered them to be the winter food of country people, he gives details of an attractive way of preserving them. He suggests treading them out, then mixing them with toasted sesame, anise, fennel-seed and cumin and wrapping balls of this mixture in fig leaves. When dried they should be stored in earthenware jars. Delicious, apparently, with boiled or baked ham.

But in cooler, wetter England, the climate made sun drying fruit so difficult that indoor drying with ovens or fires was the only alternative. Apples, such as Norfolk Biffins, pears and plums could

The eighteenth century stillhouse with its stills and stoves was also useful for drying medicinal herbs and fruit, and later for jam-making

be dried whole over a period of days in cooling bread ovens, but handling them too much meant they burst or split before they were dry. Instead, apples were most commonly sliced in rings, threaded onto strings and then hung up in the kitchen or dried on the stillroom stove. In 1656, John Beale was already complaining of British wastefulness in not preserving the fruits of their orchards and hedgerows: 'Noe plums ever dryed, nor peares, except in few houses.' But fruit growing areas were not cheap fuel areas and despite considerable official encouragement, much fruit was left to rot. Perhaps this explains the later development of the peculiarly English tradition of making marmalades, jams, jellies and other fruit preserves with sugar.

Elsewhere artificial fruit drying became more established. Commercial fruit growing and drying, especially of plums, was widespread in Slovakia, Moravia (now part of the Czech Republic) and Bosnia where, from the Middle Ages onwards, large-scale purpose-built drying houses were constructed. In the mountains of Moravia they were made with stone blocks and in the lowlands with loam and straw. There are many varieties of structure, both simple and sophisticated. Most consisted of two rooms with a fireplace or oven surrounded by drying hurdles in one room, and tables for preparing fruit in the other. In some areas, the stove was set under the drying room with flues and flaps over which the hurdles or wicker frames were set up. Fruit drying on this scale was a time-consuming business and required a number of people to work over long periods preparing, hanging and storing the fruits. It was hard work and was usually done by men, with the stoker virtually living in, in order to keep the ovens going. Plums were dried whole, as were cherries, apricots and apples. These were eaten as an accompaniment to the traditional winter dishes. In some parts of the region dried pears and carrots were ground and sprinkled onto food as sweeteners as late as the 1920s. Sadly these old drying methods have largely died out due to competition from other larger fruit growing areas and because of the fighting in the region, which has destroyed orchards and drying houses.

Apart from the recent passion for sun-dried tomatoes, vegetable drying has seldom been attempted on the scale of commercial fruit processing, but local and home drying survives in Europe, China and Japan. In Scandinavia during the Second World War when there were no sweets, the children chewed on dried strips of carrot, turnip and parsnip. In Hungary and Bulgaria, green beans, mallows and red paprika pods are still strung up on racks or lines on south-facing walls to be sun dried. Ground-dried paprika, introduced by Columbus into Europe from the New World, has become the classic ingredient of traditional Hungarian cooking.

The sight of mushrooms threaded on strings and hung up by the fire or in a warm cupboard to dry is still common in many parts of northern Europe. Dried mushrooms are a wonderful delicacy and home-drying them appears to be a particularly popular activity. In Russia the tradition was to string them up like giant necklaces around the old stove or even on rods above the cooling wood ash which gave them a rich, woody flavour. Nowadays it is more likely to be a hot radiator, which will not produce quite the same aroma and flavour. Louis XIII of France loved their woodland scent so much that he lay on his death bed in 1643 threading mushrooms onto strings for drying. Artichoke hearts, too, were dried in the oven till hard as wood. When needed they were steeped in water for two days and boiled until done, when they 'will eat as well as if fresh cut'. Even yeast could be dried on twigs of a birch whisk or by being painted in successive layers onto a plate or inside a tub until two or three inches thick. In this way it could be stored and then reactivated after several months.

Many varieties of seaweed are dried and are a particular speciality now very popular in the West. 'Konbu' is a thick, wide seaweed used extensively in Japanese cooking. It is cultivated and harvested off the coasts of northern Japan at the end of the summer when it is dried and cut into lengths for sale. Konbu can be shredded, fried, shaved, soaked in vinegar or just chewed like gum. The best soup stock 'dashi', which is central to Japanese cuisine, must be made using freshly shaved konbu. Dried peel of citrus fruit is also used with dried chilli to make a spicy mix, which they like to sprinkle on a bowl of noodles.

Drying fruit and vegetables was not, however, only done for taste. In hard times, few communities had access to meat or fish and preserved crops of local fruits and vegetables were vital to their diet. Chinese peasants, who suffered endless periods of famine and starvation, were relieved in the eighteenth century when they could grow the hardy newly introduced crops of peanuts and potatoes. The sweet potato was steamed and sieved into a paste, which was dried into cakes or strips and stored as a staple winter food. In the bleak, snowbound winters of northern Afghanistan, families of several generations survived until the release of spring, immured in their high-walled homes with stored grains, fuel and dried fruits such as elaeagnus fruit, apricots, peaches, grapes, mulberries, dates and nuts. One still-popular preserved food that helped sustain the Cape trekkers is 'plat perskie' or flat peach – a dried layer of mashed ripe peach rolled or folded up to a convenient shape to be chewed like gum as a thirst quencher.

In spite of the industrialisation of fruit drying, the practice continues on a home or local level remains resilient. Wherever rural life persists, fruit and vegetables are still dried and stored. The Chinese of Szechuan dry spices and bean curd and in the mountains exquisite dried bamboo is stored away for special occasions. In Central America chilli peppers are hung in bunches strung into huge wreaths called 'ristras' outside every pueblo home like flaming red lanterns. Even now, in most parts of rural Europe many kinds of fruits and vegetables are still dried in the bread oven or range after baking when the oven is still warm, but not too hot. Bunches of herbs such as thyme, rosemary, oregano and savory are hung up in barns and kitchens to dry, and one can still see figs, apricots, dates, grapes and plums as well as tomatoes and peppers drying on the rooftops of Middle Eastern and North African houses. On the Greek Islands they thread eggplants, beans and okra onto string and hang them to dry along with bunches of wild greens to keep for the cold winter months. In southern France, Italy, Spain and Portugal, tobacco leaves and cobs of maize are put out to dry with rows of pumpkins of all sizes, shapes and colours on sunny walls and along the roadside. Tomatoes are spread on trays to dry on the flat roofs of outhouses or garages. Greengages and plums are laid on straw mats in the sun and then steeped in brandy, while walnuts, sweet chestnuts and olives are all still put out in the rich Mediterranean sun to help make those succulent regional specialities we enjoy so much.

Pulses

Pease pudding hot, pease pudding cold,
Pease pudding in the pot, nine days old.
Traditional

Until the mid-seventeenth century when potatoes were first introduced, dried peas, lentils, chickpeas and beans were the basic starches in the European diet. For the peasant household, which often lacked any meat, the basic staple was a thick 'pease pottage'. All over Europe, the cauldron or stockpot was kept simmering throughout the seasons with a variable pottage of pulses cooked up with leeks, root vegetables, cereals and the occasional meats. Whatever was available, plus the leftovers, went into the pot, be it a bird or rabbit, or just some cabbage leaves. A piece of salt bacon or fat might enrich the 'stew' on good days. In Spain, the peasants had 'cocido', an 'all-in-one' boiled pottage made with chickpeas or white beans with pieces of salt pork or spicy sausage. English dumplings, originally made with a mix of water and rye flour, were tied in a cloth and hung over the pot to steam. By the Middle Ages, these were commonly made with a mix of dried beans and peas and made a thick, steamed pudding known as 'pease pudding'. To make this, the soaked pulses are tied in a well-greased pudding cloth with some shredded mint, a little sugar and enough room is left for the peas to swell. This 'solid green cannon ball' is suspended over a simmering pot of pork and water. After steaming for about two hours, the pudding can be put on a plate. When pulled gently apart with two forks the pudding falls into crumbly lumps, which are served with the bacon and some bacon broth poured over. A solid, satisfying winter dish.

> Good peason and leekes, to make poredge in Lent
> And pescods, in July, save fish to be spent,
> Those having, with other things, plentiful then
> Thou winnest the love of labouring men.
>
> Thomas Tusser, 1573

If meat was available to the poor, it would most likely be heavily salted, but when dried peas or lentils are simmered in a broth they burst open and absorb much of the salt together with liquid and fat, producing a tasty, nourishing and filling 'mess of pottage'. Most pulses have a tendency to absorb other flavours and it was this chameleon-like quality that became a crucial part of their popularity and versatility. 'Old peson wyth Bacon' is a classic old English dish.

> Take old peson and boyle hom in gode flesh broth that
> bacon is soden in, then take hom and bray hom in a mortar
> and temper hom wyth the broth and strayne home thrugh a
> strayner and do hom in the pot ande let hom boyle. Serve
> forth wyth Bacon.

Pulses are seeds (mainly from the pea family of vetches) that grow inside pods. The discovery that they would keep well when dried probably happened at the same time as people found that they were edible, filling and nourishing. They are rich in dietary fibre and are an important source of protein and carbohydrate. Most varieties will dry naturally if spread out in the sun. In wetter climates they are dried slowly in cooling ovens. Properly stored, they will keep for very long periods.

Because this nutritious food is so easily preserved, pulses have been a central ingredient in the human diet for millennia. Independently all over the world pulses were domesticated and dried for keeping – peas, vetch and chickpeas in the Near East, broad beans and soya beans in China and later haricot and other beans in Central America. Containers of stored lentils have been found in Anatolia that date from the late Neolithic period (6500–5500 BC), shopping lists nearly 4,000 years old from ancient Assyria describe dishes of lentils, peas and beans. A tomb from Mycenaean Thebes revealed the remains of a paste made of lentils that must have been cooked in around 1400 BC. The Greeks even had a god of beans and held a 'beanfeast' in honour of Apollo when a hot pea soup was drunk.

The Romans called pulses *legumen* from *lego* meaning 'to gather' or 'collect'. The later word 'pulse' derives from the Latin *puls*, a porridge of meal commonly made in Roman times, although they also made cakes of meal from dried beans when they suffered a cereal shortage and lentil soup was produced to fortify the legionaries. From Roman times onwards, however, pulses were generally considered to be food for the poor. When cereals were scarce, beans and peas were ground up to bulk out the flour for the poor or even replace it. Europeans of the Middle Ages dried and kept cereals, beans and peas through the year and these served as the staple for peasant households.

The problem with peas and beans is that they are inclined to sprout if not stored properly. The medieval French had a method of frizzling boiled, shelled beans in a heated metal spoon to make 'fèves' or 'frasées'. An English solution, started in the fifteenth century, was to preserve beans by converting them into 'canebyns'. The beans were repeatedly steeped in fresh water, dried on a heated hearthstone or in the oven and then milled by hand to make a rough flour to cook into a pottage with onions, herbs and some bits of bacon. In wealthier homes, canebyns were cooked into a pottage to eat with pieces of meat or sweetened with almond milk and sugar to eat for Lent. Dried peas and beans were common fasting food and a dish known as carlings made from dried peas was eaten in northern England on Carling Sunday, the fifth Sunday in Lent. There are many stories surrounding carlings. According to one, a cargo of dried peas was wrecked off the coast of Durham during a long famine, which was seized by the hungry peasants and saved them from starvation.

Pease pottage was still the English national dish in the seventeenth century when the poor continued to 'bake' their beans and pease in a hearth pot to make their daily pottage. These cooking traditions crossed the Atlantic with the early settlers and strongly influenced colonial life. Along with a 'plain-style' religion and a way of life that was simple and frugal, the British migrants brought with them a tradition of humble, but nourishing meals, made with preserved foods. The women also watched the Native American women cook and learned to make samp and succotash from local dried corn and beans. The three pigs, amongst the first animals to be landed at Jamestown, quickly multiplied, and pork and beans, the mainstay of the European Middle Ages, found new forms and variations in the New World.

For the New England Puritan housewife, making a new home in Boston, it was important on a Saturday to assemble a bean pot to cook all night. This would then last for the next day and with no cooking needing to be done, the Sabbath could be observed. Thus the famous Boston Baked Beans were born. Salt pork and dried beans, the 'heart and soul of Maine', were slowly cooked together, closely covered so that the flavour of the pork permeated the beans as they simmered. Originally it was sweetened with maple sugar, later molasses and mustard were used.

Despite greater sophistication developing in the American kitchen, baked beans remained an important dish. Lydia Child, who published her book *The Frugal Housewife* in Boston in 1829, dedicated to 'those who are not ashamed of economy', believed that the secret to good Boston Beans lay in the quality of the pork. This should alternate fat and lean and make up a substantial part of the dish. Fanny Farmer, whose famous *Boston Cooking-School Cook*

Book was published nearly seventy years later, when Boston Baked Beans were a state if not quite a national dish, wrote that 'The fine reputation which Boston Baked Beans have gained has been attributed to the earthen bean-pot with small top and bulging sides in which they are supposed to be cooked.'

Food writer Gerald Carson recalled some nostalgic childhood memories of the warm, simple style of cooking in a Yankee kitchen: 'Come – move the coffee pot to the back of the range and close the damper . . . The baked beans are waiting for a rendezvous in the earthenware pot – those plump, shiny Yellow-eyes, molasses-dark, their skins fairly bursting with goodness, the slashed salt pork peeking provocatively through the crusted surface. Before the beans have fairly stopped bubbling, lace them with grandma's old-fashioned ketchup. Here's the brown bread, warm, sliced thin, lightly dappled with cow's butter.'

Meanwhile, back in England, King George III was so fascinated by workmen tucking into steaming plates of baked beans as they built the arsenal at Woolwich that he demanded to try some himself. He liked it so much that he declared there should be an annual 'bean feast'. Americans were more taken with this idea than the English, who felt that a feast should be something other than their daily fare. Community 'baked bean days' are still held in many parts of the United States where there are now numerous regional varieties, recipes and methods. Endless arguments rage about proportions of pork to beans and molasses or the best beans to bake, choosing between Jacob's cattle, soldier beans or yellow-eye in New England, and chilli beans, pinto, red Mexican or Hopi beans in the Southwest. Pork and beans, which saved many lives in hard times and during the Depression, are still a controversial subject, as energetically debated as the argument in France about the 'only true way' to make cassoulets.

Thomas Jefferson admired the food of France so much that, while a US envoy in Paris, he made several gastronomic tours of the country. While in France he wrote to his friend Lafayette that if one wanted to learn about food one must 'ferret people out of their hovels, as I have done, look into their kettles, eat their bread'. What Jefferson would have seen in the 'kettle' or cauldron was most likely beans. Haricot beans arrived in Europe from the

West Indies in the sixteenth century, and were soon adopted in place of the broad beans or 'favolles'. As with the American bean pot, there were numerous variations and claims to be the original cassoulet of southwest France. Regional specialities required the inclusion of preserved duck or goose, Toulouse or garlic sausages, lightly salted pig's tail and ears or breast of mutton. The earliest cassoulets were baked in ashes or bread ovens in a specially made, highly glazed, red clay pot called a 'cassole' after the town of Ussel, near Castelnaudary in southern France. The peasants in their 'hovels' who had little or no salt meat, would substitute carrots and turnips, but the most traditional and probably original cassoulet is made with both salted and fresh pork and pork fat.

While dried pulses have declined in popularity, baked beans have remained a regular part of modern diets in many parts of the world. American Heinz tinned baked beans were first introduced into Britain in 1928 as a 'nourishing meal for men returning from work'. Still relatively cheap and nourishing despite the added sweeteners, baked beans remain enormously popular today.

Grains and Cereals

Cereals may have been cultivated and preserved even earlier than pulses and beans. Certainly they were central to the diet of the most ancient communities. As with other foods, different grain and cereal crops were grown in different parts of the world – wheat, rye and barley in southwest Asia, millet and sorghum in Africa, rice in China and maize, or corn, in Central America. From earliest times grains were parched or roasted in order to release them from their inedible hard outer coating and the first farmers would quickly have realised that this scorched grain could be stored safely through the winter without sprouting. What's more, grain that has been parched becomes more absorbent and requires less cooking, and flour milled from parched grain keeps longer and is more digestible. It could be mixed with honey or dried fruit pulp and made into cakes that needed no further cooking and were especially useful for travellers on long journeys.

Getting the temperature right was difficult and archaeologists have often found evidence of spoiled or burnt grain. One ancient and primitive method for parching grain, a technique known as 'graddan', was practised in the Western Isles of Scotland until relatively recently. In the seventeenth century, Martin Martin described how a woman sitting on the ground 'takes a handful of corn, holding it by the stalks in her left hand, and then sets fire to the ears, which are presently in a flame'. She dexterously beats off the grain as soon as the husk is burnt, 'experience has taught them this art to perfection'.

For thousands of years the survival and power of a tribe or country depended on its stocks of grain. Harvesting, processing and storing grain stocks was of huge importance and war was declared only after harvest, when men were available and stocks of grain safely in. One of the earliest records of large-scale food preserving was in ancient Egypt, where it was enormously important to create adequate stocks of dried grain to insure against the failure of the Nile to flood seasonally. Huge quantities of grain were stored in sealed silos, where they could be kept for several years if necessary. Records from 2600 BC show that the annual flooding of the Nile produced surpluses of grain that were stored and kept to feed builders of irrigation schemes and the pyramid tombs. The Great Pyramid of Cheops at Giza was built in around 2900 BC by slaves fed with stores of grain and chickpeas, onions and garlic. Elsewhere stored surpluses were used by ancient leaders to provision the building of other monumental structures or to relieve famine, to protect against sieges or to supply their armies. In China the Emperor Kuan Chung in 800 BC started a long tradition of storing grain surpluses to provide free food for the people during the regular famines. During the long Han dynasty in China (202BC–AD220) 'pei', 'hou' and 'ch'iu', made from dried boiled or pulverised grain, came to play a central part in people's diet. Rice, wheat, barley, millet, even beans were also made into these basic dried grain foods.

In effect, by building huge stores of dried grain, kings or rulers could control the people's primary food supply and even manipulate prices. All over the ancient world, the emergence of civilisation – of social hierarchies, monumental buildings and craftsmen and bureaucrats – depended on the preserving and storing of surplus grain. As these early civilisations expanded, these surpluses could be traded with other groups for luxury goods or raw materials. Detailed record-keeping was required for these transactions as well as to organise the distribution of the grain. From around 3000 BC writing emerged in different parts of the world. In Crete, where from the second millennium BC 'palaces' were built with large food storage areas, many of the surviving fragments of the ancient Linear B language consist of lists of stored food goods, including supplies of millet, barley and wheat. These would be kept in huge jars or 'pithoi', set into the cool earth at the bottom of the 'palace' storehouses, where they were kept at a low temperature and free from insects, airborne moulds and rodents.

In time, drying methods became more sophisticated. In cool, damp Britain the Romans, with typical ingenuity, developed corn or spelt drying areas with flues carrying heat from a fire set below ground in a trench. After harvesting, the grain crops were threshed, winnowed, parched and dried before storing in granaries or in containers kept in cool places. Grain storage has had strategic importance up to the present day. In Malta there are underground grain silos first created in the Middle Ages that had to be revived and re-used during the Second World War.

Where conditions were favourable, other dried grain foods became important staples. In North America corn grains were soaked in lye water and the hulls removed to make 'hominy'. When the hominy is dried and then coarsely ground, it becomes grits, which can still be bought and eaten in many parts of the US. As we have seen, the flat roofs or terraces of houses in the Balkans, North Africa and the Middle East offer a uniquely perfect environment for drying food such as 'byrghel'. Known since the ninth century BC, it is still the most popular, convenient and nourishing staple porridge of the Middle East. It has many names in many countries and as many variations in its preparation and use. It is called 'tzavar' in Armenia, 'burger' in Turkey, 'burguri' in Greece, 'gurgur' in Kurdistan and 'iapsi' in India. Varieties of byrghel are combined with chickpeas, lentils, broad beans, meat, milk, eggs, fresh vegetables or fish in many kinds of traditional dishes including fried meat balls, dumplings, stuffed cabbage, soups, stews and 'tabouleh', a popular byrghel salad that can now be bought in supermarkets.

The hot, whitewashed brick or mud roofs of the Middle East are far too hot to sit out on and sunbathe like the sun terraces and balconies of Europe and North America. But their daytime use as drying places for foodstuffs and laundry is transformed as the sun sinks and the cool evening breezes waft across from the distant mountains. Here, then, the beds and cushions are brought out as cold drinks and snacks are enjoyed. This is the time for relaxing and socialising; it was once also the time in many Assyrian households when special grain foods could be prepared for sun drying the next day. Sunroof drying is particularly vital to the communities of modern Assyrians who claim to be descended from the warrior people of the great empire, but who are now largely Christian peasants living in small, isolated enclaves in Turkey, Syria, Iraq and Iran. Their isolation amongst Muslim people has forced them to be particularly self-sufficient. They used to hide their wheat in covered holes in the floor of their living rooms in fear of attack and theft of their food. Assyrians have a unique and varied cuisine that includes a variety of hard dough products that are sun dried including their own special way of making byrghel. One, called 'ryshtan', is made with unleavened wheat dough shaped into a flat cake and cut into smaller squares which are sun dried, roasted in a frying pan and stored in metal containers. Another is called 'sheiraye', which involves a far more delicate and complicated process requiring a beautiful combination of skill and tradition. Sheiraye is a kind of fine pasta, like vermicelli, known in Arabic as 'sha'riyya'. It is always made by women, who traditionally prepared it by moonlight after supper when the children were asleep. They gathered on the family wooden bed set on the roof of the house in the cool of the night where talk and social activities or *shahro* were enjoyed. Michael Abdalla, an expert on Assyrian foods, suggests that the words *shahro* and *sheiraye* are very similar to *sara*, the Assyrian name for the moon.

Rather as with Italian hand-made pasta, the women rolled the hard, round pieces of dough in the oiled palms of their hands to form long strings, which were coiled up around their left arm and then deftly torn off into short pieces with the fingers of the right. These little strings were laid on straw trays to be sun dried. Sheiraye is usually roasted with some vegetable oil or mixed with byrghel or rice to enrich the flavour. Preparing sheiraye amongst women friends gossiping and singing in the light of the moon sounds magical. Sadly, though perhaps to the relief of some of the women, machines were devised for making sheiraye, and in the late 1950s these circulated from house to house, hauled by oxen or pushed by a man, and the fine art of hand making sheiraye has been lost as a part of those cool, moonlit *shahro* gatherings.

Sheiraye, like the hundreds of other kinds of dried pasta, is thought to have had an Arabic origin. But there have been numerous theories about the true origins of pasta and noodles. The most popular myth is that Marco Polo brought the idea back from his travels in China from 1274 to 1296, where noodles were already common. The word pasta means 'dough made from water and flour', a simple product common to almost any ancient cereal-growing community. The Romans made strips of it and by the tenth century there is evidence that both Arabs and Greeks made

An Italian pasta making business in the sixteenth century. Some to be sold fresh and the rest dried and stored

dried strips of pasta, a practice that spread through the regions of their respective empires. While fresh pasta was traditionally made at home, dried pasta was produced for travellers and for sale. In the twelfth century the geographer Idrisi referred to the existence of a dry pasta industry near Palermo in Italy where 'a great quantity of pasta is made and exported all over, to Calabria and to other Muslim and Christian lands; and many shiploads are sent'.

Another ancient but still important form of pasta, similar to Arab pasta, is eaten throughout the Balkans, Iran and Hungary. It has various names including 'tarhana' or 'trahana'. The dough, made from crushed wheat and yoghurt, is left to ferment and is then rolled into sheets or pellets which are dried in the sun. It is most often crumbled into soups or boiled to accompany meat stews, fish or cheese. Nowadays tarhana is often flavoured with various vegetables or herbs and packets of ready-made dried tarhana can be bought in the shops. It is an ideal portable food for travellers and in the old days bags of freshly made tarhana would have been attached to the horseman's saddle and the rider would 'gallop the pasta dry'.

However, in most parts of the world, grain preserving and storage had only one end product in mind – bread. The oven or hearth used for bread making as well as drying was central to everyone's daily life whether they were nomadic or settled. A supply of fresh baked bread always had to be made. But very few types of bread could be kept for long, so for people who were to travel far from home, a preserved version had to be found.

Hardtack

Hardtack – also known as 'ship's biscuit' or 'pilot bread' – was the staple provision for anyone who set out on a long and perilous journey, be they sailor, soldier, traveller, explorer or migrant. This biscuit was always the largest and most essential component in their provisions. It was the perfect food for both keeping and carrying. Hardtack could be stored in the home over winter to keep against famine or for emergencies and was useful in bulking out the pottages of vegetables and pulses on which most poor rural people subsisted. In addition, as a daily baking was unnecessary, valuable firewood was saved. For travellers, hardtack was light-weight and tough enough to carry on their long journeys over sea or land. Numerous varieties of biscuits and crisp breads have been made all over the world since very early times and modern versions of them can now be found in supermarkets. Usually eaten with cheese, they are also popular with the health conscious and weight watchers of today. The essential point of these biscuits is that they contain neither fats nor moisture and therefore keep for a very long time. Traditionally, they were made from a dough of flour and water, baked and dried to a state of 'immortal' hardness.

The first attempt to make bread cooked over hot stones or in ashes probably produced a flat, unleavened bread which would have been extremely coarse and dry, making it difficult to eat and digest. Gradually there evolved around the world numerous kinds of basic flour-and-water flatbreads in different shapes and forms made with a variety of grains such as maize, oats, wheat, rye or millet depending on their origins. Their descendants can be still found in the tortillas of Mexico, oat cakes from Scotland, chapatis from India, the Chinese 'po', the Ethiopian 'injera', Australian 'damper' and the Scandinavian peasant flatbreads.

Fortunately, people kept on trying to improve on bread-making and it became both an ingenious and creative business. Egyptian bakers can be seen baking nearly fifty kinds of variously shaped and flavoured breads on a mural in the tomb of Ramses III. These succulent and sophisticated breads were made with yeast, milk, eggs, sometimes honey and other rich ingredients. But they were freshly made daily and did not keep. The Romans, needing to find a way of providing their soldiers with bread on the road, produced a type of dried bread or hard biscuit called 'buccellatum'. De Joinville, in his *Chronicle of the Crusades* in 1256, describes how the Sultan of Cairo sent men up the Nile 'who took with them a kind of bread called biscuit, because it was twice baked'.

This is, in fact, what the word biscuit means . . . twice baked. The Greek *paximadi*, Italian *biscotti*, Spanish *bizcocho*, *Zwieback* in German and French *biscuit* all mean 'twice cooked'. In France these biscuits were commonly known as 'biscuits de guerre'. Indeed, throughout history, hard biscuits have been the mainstay of armed forces on land and at sea.

The first baking of hardtack was brief, but it was the long, slow drying out afterwards that evaporated the remaining moisture, making it as hard as a rock and able to last almost for ever as long it was not attacked by damp sea air, rats or the 'blessed' weevils. These beetle larvae would create a pattern of internal perforations in their munching that made it breakable but inedible. Ship's biscuit was so hard that, in order to get one's teeth into it, it had to be dunked in liquid to soften it or broken up into soups of vegetables or pulses. Perhaps it was this necessity that led to the practice of crumbling these hard biscuits into now-famous dishes such as the American chowder as well as many traditional Mediterranean peasant soups of Italy, Spain and Greece, where a barley biscuit or rusk called 'paximadi' is still made in the traditional way.

For centuries paximadi has been a staple food of the Greek people. The biscuit varies from region to region – there are dark and light kinds and some use olives while others are sweetened or scented with aniseed. The original paximadi, though, was made from cheap barley flour twice a year as a practical way of preserving bread for the poor. The leavened loaves of bread were sliced, twice baked and strung up to dry or close kept in tins for up to a year. Paximadi was particularly important in the winter when ordinary barley bread had a tendency to go mouldy very quickly. It also helped to preserve firewood, which is very scarce on many Greek islands. The French missionary, François Richard, wrote from the island of Santorini in 1657, 'The daily food of the people is hard tack made of barley bread . . . They bake bread twice a year. It is so black that when I once showed it one of our priests living in Naxos, he said that in France such bread is proper food only for dogs . . . and he doubted whether even dogs would eat it. Yet children in Santorini crunch it with delight from early morning and they all are in a perfect state of health.' Babies were offered paximadi moistened with water or milk to suck at just as western babies today are offered rusks during weaning or teething. Paximadi is still popular today, especially those made in Crete. Nowadays they are made with a mix of barley and wheat, which makes a lighter and crunchier biscuit that needs no soaking. Elizabeth David tried it and wrote, 'The flavour is good, with an unmistakably earthy tang – anyone who has ever eaten a good barley or Scotch broth will recognise the taste and the aroma.'

The various Scandinavian hard flatbreads, which have been baked and dried since ancient times, are the forerunners of our modern crisp breads. Swedish sour black rye breads such as 'rogbröd' and 'knäckebröd' are similar to a Scottish oat cake. They are made of rye and corn and a hole is left in the middle so they can be strung up in rows and kept dry in the kitchen. The Norwegian 'flattbrød' was made with unfermented dough of barley and oatmeal, sometimes mixed with pea flour or mashed potato. The dough was rolled into enormous round loaves up to two or three feet across and thin as cardboard, and then baked slowly on an iron plate. Scandinavian flatbreads could remain fresh stored on a beam in the kitchen for up to six months.

Jewish 'matzo' or Passover 'bread' is hard and dry, made under very strict regulations of timing and technique to prevent the dough from fermenting. The making of matzo bread is filled with Jewish symbolism for it signifies the unleavened bread of a people on the move. There are other various long, unleavened bread cakes resembling Jewish matzo made in Armenia and the Caucasus. Quickly cooked on a high heat to stop any fermentation, they are then immediately cooled and hung over strings to dry in the sun. The cakes are stored for long periods and can be crushed with hot water and oil so that they swell into a kind of porridge.

Dried meat and biscuit were the universal fellow travellers for anyone venturing into the unknown. Whether on land or the high seas, everyone had their own travelling version of hardtack. American settlers learned to make Johnny or 'journey' cakes and on their Great Trek the Boers made their own 'mosbollietjie' or 'boer-beskuit' made with a coarse flour, fat or butter, some sugar, raisins, yeast made from potatoes or soured dough, plenty of salt and a little milk. The resulting dough was kneaded, shaped into buns, set to prove under the warm bedding in the wagons and then baked – often in a temporary oven cut into an ant hill. When cooked, the buns were cut in half and rebaked into hard rusks that could keep for many weeks. One variety, the 'sur lit', was similar to the Norman-French flatbread called 'surleas'.

In the colourful fairs of medieval France, one could also have enjoyed a popular delicacy called 'nieules' or 'nioles'. Hard, unleavened dough was twisted into ribbons and cooked in boiling water mixed with the ashes of vine shoots, which contain natural potash. This process gave the nieules a savoury, smoky flavour and a dark colour. They were then drained, cut up and dried in the oven till they were hard. Traditionally the makers of nieules were mainly Protestant and after the Edict of Nantes was revoked in 1685, they were forced to emigrate to Germany where the nieule became 'bretzeln', and were made with coarse rock salt instead of potash. In the eighteenth century, another, even greater journey took the bretzeln to America where it became the pretzel.

But for sailors and soldiers the method of making the basic, durable and almost indestructible hardtack or ship's biscuit has not changed significantly for hundreds of years. Always known at sea as 'bread', the production of ship's biscuit is described in detail in the *Encyclopaedia Britannica* of 1773: 'Sea-bisket is a sort of bread much dreid by passing the oven twice to make it keep for sea service. For long voyages they bake it four times and prepare it six months before embarkation. It will hold good for a whole year.' In Bulgaria some villages were obliged to send their men to Istanbul to work in the Sultan's bakeries that provided the army with bread and 'peksimet', a kind of rusk resembling the original ship's biscuits. Provisioning the Spanish Armada was an even greater operation. So much wheat was required for making biscuits that they had to build ovens in Naples where wheat was cheaper and more plentiful. Biscuits were baked six months ahead of delivery to ensure a constant supply and the wretched population of Sicily was reduced either to eating chestnut bread or starving because the huge Spanish orders for wheat took precedence.

In 1650 an officer wrote of Cromwell's campaigns that 'Nothing is more certain than this, that in the late wars, both Scotland and Ireland were conquered by timely provisions of Cheshire cheese and biscuit.' Cromwell firmly believed in the value of 'biscake' for both his soldiers and sailors, and gave orders for the old royal palace at Greenwich to be turned into a biscuit factory. Later, in the eighteenth century, two large bake houses were built at Plymouth and biscuit depots were established at Deptford appropriately called 'Old Weevil'. According to a report made in 1854 by the chemist Sheridan Muspratt, the method of baking the standard ship's biscuits at Portsmouth and Gosport involved a five-man team for each oven and was a marvel of human precision. The turner, the mate, the driver, the breakman and the idleman worked together mixing and kneading the dough in a 'singular and often disgusting method'. The dough was formed into thin sheets and cut into slips by means of an enormous knife; the slips were moulded into smaller biscuit-sized circles. These were then handed to a second workman who stamped them with the number of the oven and the king's mark and after docking (piercing with holes), each biscuit was thrown accurately onto the end of a peel held by another man standing before the open oven door. 'Seventy biscuits were thrown into the oven and properly arranged in one minute, the attention of each man being vigorously directed to his own department for a delay of a single second on the part of any one would have disturbed the whole.' They were carefully graded in size to allow for the longer baking time of those at the back.

While biscuit production continued to be an important business in many ports well into the nineteenth century, sweet and fancy biscuits of all kinds were also being developed and soon became very popular with ordinary people, providing a little bit of luxury for the poor. The Quaker family firm of Carr's are still famous for their Table Water Biscuits which are a thinned down version of their original 'Captain's Thins', which were ship's biscuits supplied to naval officers and quite unlike those issued from 'Old Weevil' for seamen.

During the 1840s, J. D. Carr, the founder, baker and biscuit maker, worked tirelessly as a member of the Anti-Corn Law League because he believed that the terrible poverty in Carlisle where his factory was built was a direct result of the Corn Laws. There was appalling destitution throughout Britain and conditions in the West Highlands was particularly bad. 'J. D.' wrote to the government offering to provide his rye and maize breads free, but transport difficulties meant that the bread would have been uneatable by the time it arrived. Instead he offered the Carr's version of the old ship's biscuit, a coarse, plain biscuit, more palatable than the original and which kept even better now that it was sealed in tins. The Prime Minister, after sampling the biscuit, asked for a 'large pack' to be sent to Windsor where a Cabinet meeting was to be held. The *Carlisle Journal* described with pride and some mirth the picture of the Queen, her Prime Minister and Cabinet, all sitting round nibbling Carr's best ship's biscuits. Happily the biscuits were soon being sent in large amounts to Scotland where they helped to feed the hungry Highlanders.

There were many successive improvements to the basic methods with the introduction of steam machinery, early 'conveyor belts' and biscuit ovens 'built on a new principle' – an endless chain with trays of biscuits passing though a long tunnel. A fifteen-minute bake in a controlled temperature was followed by three days in the drying room. So grew up a vast biscuit industry with names such as Huntley and Palmer's, Jacob's and Carr's of Carlisle, many of whom started by making their own version of the original ship's biscuit and moved on to produce the more refined versions of fancy sweet biscuits sent throughout the British Empire and beyond.

CHAPTER TWO

SALTING
Meat

'And what's going to be done with them now?' asked Ellen.
'I am just going to cut them up and lay them down . . .' and he went
on cutting up the pork. When the cutting up was all done, the hams
and shoulders were put in a cask by themselves, and Mr. Van Brunt
began to pack the other pieces in the kits, strewing them in an abundance of salt.
'Will the salt make it keep?'
'All the year round — as sweet as a nut . . . it will keep everything in
the world if it only has enough of it, and if it is kept dry and cool.'
Elizabeth Wetherall, *The Wide Wide World*, 1852

When the autumn slaughter of the stock was necessary because there was no winter foodstuff, a community that reared and fattened their own pigs and slaughtered them one by one through the autumn and winter months could ensure a small but steady supply of fresh and preserved meat. A household might jealously guard its pig's reputation when it was alive, but most communities, often comprising members of extended families, would assist each other at the pig kill, sharing some of the fresh meat, perhaps taking home a little lard or flitch of bacon so that everyone could eat a little meat at regular intervals through the long, hungry winter months.

Great pride was taken in the family pig. Lovingly cared for and fed with leftovers from the table throughout the spring and summer months, some were even allowed to forage in orchards and woodland for windfall apples, roots, nuts and acorns till they were well fattened, sweet and 'nutty'. By the late autumn or early New Year, every household pig was certain to be the finest – to have the curliest tail, the thickest bristles, rosiest skin and broadest rump. It was bound to be the most intelligent, lively, greedy and, for its brief life, the best cared-for pig in the whole neighbourhood.

There was a similar tradition of pig killing in most parts of the world. The only variation was in the products that were made from it. When the right time had come — when the weather was cool, dry and not too windy and when the moon was in the wane (when pigs were said to eat more) — the knives were sharpened, the cauldrons of water were boiled, preserving and salting jars and tubs were thoroughly cleaned and sterilised and all was prepared. Most important of all, the salt was made ready.

The pig was caught, held down on its side, and the knife plunged in. The farmer's wife held a tub to catch the blood, straining the warm, thick flow through her fingers to prevent it coagulating. As soon as it had stopped kicking and bleeding, the pig was scorched or singed with burning straw until the fine bristles were gone. Next, the soft skin was scraped with a knife or pumice stone and washed over with buckets of boiling water. Still warm, the pig was hung up on a huge hook, head down, its back

In ancient Egypt geese were trapped, hung, cleaned, seasoned and salted and immersed in brine jars

to the wall. Amid clouds of steam, the butcher or slaughterman (known in France as the *tueur*) with a confident stroke cut off the head and removed the brain, which was traditionally given to the farmer's wife. Baskets gradually filled with offal, tripe, ears, feet and cheeks while the skin and intestines were thoroughly cleaned and hung to dry. If a butcher had been called in, he would most probably have had other pigs to kill, but before he left he would be given some cooked brains or fried blood pudding and a glass or three of home-made alcohol, plus a bunch of the best bristles, perks of the job.

The family, relatives and neighbours who had gathered to help then sat around large, scrubbed tables, their hands shiny with fat, busily boning the meat. In the Cevennes mountains in France, famous for chestnuts, silkworms, sausages and 'pig-headed heretics', the people still work hard and eat hard, remembering their not so distant past of hunger, cold and poverty. Heather Willings, who lived amongst them, recalls a way of life twenty years ago which, even now, a few small mountain communities still cling to, where the *fête de cochon* is part of the year-long round of subsistence and struggle, but also a time of comradeship and peasant humour.

> 'We've finished early tonight,' says Henri. 'I think I'll salt the hams, then they'll be done.' He empties a thick pile of salt on to the table, adds pepper, mixes them, then man-handles a fresh, flabby ham down from the shelf.
>
> 'It goes in through the skin much more than the meat,' he explains, rubbing. 'And you need plenty of pepper in the hollows, because that's where the moisture collects when the salt melts, so flies like to lay their eggs there. If you're not careful you can get the ham walking away on its own.'
>
> His audience listens respectfully.
>
> 'It's a good idea to put a handful of gravel in too.'
>
> 'Gravel?' echoes his nephew's girl-friend.
>
> 'That's right. The pepper makes the flies sneeze and they bang their heads on the gravel and fall dead . . .'

Traditional pig killing in Europe is now threatened, like so many good things, by EC regulations. It is still practised in some remote rural areas of France, Italy, Spain, Portugal and eastern Europe where it was once integral to the self-sufficiency of peasant life. In every country and every region where the pig is still slaughtered and processed on the farm, the tradition remains basically the same, while the details and names, the dishes and rituals differ. Common to all of them is the importance of salt.

Salt, the predominant preserver, is used in almost all of the main preserving processes including drying, smoking, curing, pickling and fermenting. Primarily, though, it is used to aid the drying process, especially in regions where the conditions for natural drying are not ideal. The best way to see how effectively salt draws liquid from food is to liberally rub slices of cucumber with some coarse salt. Leave for an hour or two and the surfaces will have become covered with juice 'sweated' out by a process of osmosis. This is the term used to describe the diffusion of a solvent through a semi-permeable membrane until there is an equal concentration of solution on either side of it. Water soluble substances like salt on the cut surface of the cucumber causes water to flow across the cell membranes in the attempt to form a solution outside the cells equal in concentration to the solution remaining inside. If the cucumber is dried using a hair dryer, a warm oven or an airing cupboard, the liquid will evaporate from the surface thereby 'reconcentrating' the salt solution on the surface. This causes further osmosis and the food becomes drier still. This is the simple principle of salting and drying as a combined process.

Salt pork is the ancient and traditional preserved meat of England and much of Europe. The simplest task awaiting the assembled helpers once the *tueur* had left would be to dry salt the legs or hams. 'Dry salting', also known as 'curing' (although that usually refers to a combined drying and smoking process), involves the food being rubbed with salt, often several times, then buried in a container with further dry salt or hung up to dry. The salt aids the drying process and the meat in turn absorbs some of the salt, thus inhibiting bacteria on or near the surface of the meat. This method, the most popular way to keep meat in England up until the Tudor times, was the cheapest but was only effective for short-term preserving. Dry salted pieces of pork would be kept for eating first after the autumn slaughter.

After the pig killing, if some of the meat was required to be kept for longer it would be 'wet salted' or 'pickled'. 'Wet' or 'brine' salting is done by immersing food in a strong saline bath, which is commonly referred to as the 'pickle'. A typical brine would have been made with 3 pints of water, ½lb of coarse salt, 1 oz of saltpetre, 3 oz of sugar with herbs such as bay leaves, crushed thyme and cloves, peppercorns, crushed juniper berries, allspice or nutmeg all tied up in a muslin bag. The water is slowly boiled in a pan while the scum is skimmed from the top. The brine is poured into the crock and left to cool. The meat is added and kept submerged with a weighted board. Many old recipes describe a pickle thick enough to be able to float an egg. A well-flavoured pickle would also contain spices, herbs, sweeteners, vinegars, beer or wine plus other kinds of salts. A number of spices contain antiseptic qualities and are very useful in preserving such as oil of cinnamon, cloves, ginger, white mustard seeds, aniseed, juniper, garlic and chilli peppers as well as some herbs such as dill, thyme, parsley, coriander seeds and tarragon. The essential oils of pepper are also a powerful preservative well known to the Romans who also used nutmeg and aniseed to flavour and preserve meat.

Traditionally, a combination of different salts was used, including bay or evaporated sea salt and coarse rock salt, plus salprunella and saltpetre. The type and quality of salt was important. Modern table salt, which contains additives to make it free running, is quite unsuitable for preserving and leaves a bitter taste. Fine salt seals the meat too quickly before enough has penetrated. The large-grained marine or rock salt dissolves more slowly and permeates the whole flesh giving good results plus a 'fine flavour'. 'Bay' salt from the Bay of Biscay was the favourite, although the large, clear-flaked Malden salt from Essex was thought particularly fine in England where whole grains of salt were known as 'corn', hence the name 'corned beef'.

Saltpetre (potassium nitrate), still used in commercial curing, is also a constituent of gunpowder. It was discovered in the seventeenth century that gunpowder, rubbed into hanging game, appeared to improve the keeping qualities of the meat and it was realised that it had much greater preserving powers than plain salt. In fact saltpetre is capable of killing many bacteria that salt can only inhibit. Salprunella is a reduced form of saltpetre but is more powerful and effective against bacteria such as *clostridium botulinum*, which produces the lethal botulism. Salprunella will also start the 'sweating' process more rapidly and gives cured meat its classic red colour. But its use requires care. Both saltpetre and salprunella are now permitted to be used only very sparingly. Several seventeenth- and eighteenth-century English recipes gave alarmingly high, even poisonous amounts. Too much nitrate turns pickles green, creates a hard texture and gives a dark colour to the meat.

In many cases, including pickled pork, the brine was obtained by packing the food into barrels layered with salt and leaving it until the juices had drained from the flesh into the salt, creating its own pickle. Whenever any meat had been removed the pork brine or pickle had to be boiled up again and left to cool and the pork returned to the pickle with some additional fresh salt in order to kill off successive growths of organisms. The reboiling process had to be regularly done once a month in winter and once a fortnight in summer. Cleanliness and hygiene were as important as getting the chemistry right and most of the recipes from the fifteenth and sixteenth centuries put great emphasis on thorough cleaning. Regular checking of the pickle was another task. If it looked at all suspect the meat had to be drained off, the pickle boiled up, strained through a cloth, cooled and skimmed off, before the meat could be resubmerged in its pickle.

Pickled pork was extremely soft as it was kept under this brine for anything up to a year. It was said to be delicious, melting in the mouth 'like marrow'. It was used in stews, could be sliced thin and fried, or eaten cold with apple dumplings at harvest time. Other parts of the pig could also be preserved in a pickle. Boned and rolled pieces of meat known as collars, were tied tightly in a circle and were 'soused' or pickled. Cooked brawn and offal were also pickled in brine with bran or oatmeal plus some beer or wine vinegar. Country housewives made a simple sousing drink and pickled the head, feet, ears and chitterlings of the pig.

No part of the pig would be wasted: the heart would be cooked, then salted and hung up to dry; the cheek pieces went into the brine crock to cure as Bath 'chaps'; the belly would be salted to go into soups and stews; and the bones would be preserved in brine to flavour soups and casseroles. The fat, too, was a highly valued foodstuff for the European peasant population who worked long hard hours in the cold fields and burned up all their energy. In Hungary, where animal fats have been a particularly important part of the diet, pig fat was often part of the payment of wages and for centuries preserved pig fat was more expensive than other meats. 'May his pig be fat' is an expression still used to wish someone well in business. Traditionally, Hungarian pig fat was preserved in one complete piece and still is in some parts of the country. The pig was opened along its stomach, and the fat around the whole animal was stripped out as one piece from which nothing was removed, not even the edges were trimmed. The fat was well salted and then hung on rods to dry or to be smoked.

In the Caribbean islands, salted pig's tail is still commonly used in many dishes. In French Guadeloupe the *cuisinières* (the traditional matriarchs of Guadeloupe creole cooking) use pig's tail to flavour soups and stews. They like to tell you that the pig's tail is like the penis of the slave owners who often raped or 'took to bed' the young women slaves, and that boiling the tails still provides some sort of revenge.

However, the most important products from the pig were bacon and ham. Once the pig was ready to be butchered, the *tueur* skilfully cut the larger joints to be put aside for salting or, more commonly in France, drying into hams and sides of 'lard' (bacon). Bacon was the cheapest, most popular pork product, and a mainstay of the European peasant diet for centuries. William Ellis, one of many sixteenth- and seventeenth-century English rural gentlemen who produced books on agricultural and domestic improvements, wrote in 1750 that 'Where there is Bread and Bacon enough, there is no Want . . . In the Northern Parts of England, thousands of families eat little other Meat than Bacon; and indeed, in the southern parts, more than ever live on Bacon, or Pickled Pork . . .' Some flitches of bacon were salted and then plain dried while the best bacon was hung in the chimney breast to smoke. Sliced bacon 'collops' were a special English cut of bacon that was fried with eggs, the forerunner of our 'greasy breakfasts' of bacon and eggs. In the past, as we have seen, most home-cured bacon was cooked into a pease or bean pottage.

Commercial bacon production was started as early as 1770

when it is said that John Harris of Calne in Wiltshire, watching pigs resting there on their way from Ireland to London, had the idea of curing them on the spot. Special huge, fat bacon pigs were bred to be killed at any time of year. The meat was cured quickly which meant that it tainted quickly as well. As the quality was not so good, this bacon was sold quickly and cheaply to the poor in country markets. In spite of this, William Ellis considered bacon to be a 'serviceable, palatable, profitable, and clean meat, for a ready Use in a Country house; Ready I say, because it requires not to be kept in a Cellar, or at any Distance from a Kitchen or Chamber, but may be had at all Times of the Year for being cut to broil, fry, boil, or bake; . . . for bacon is so universally traded in, that it may be had at almost any Part of the kingdom; and so serviceable to both Rich and Poor . . .'

Bacon could also be spiced. A recipe from 1864, *The Art and Mystery of Curing, Preserving, and Potting all kinds of Meats, Game and Fish by a Wholesale Curer of Comestibles* for 'superior spiced bacon', suggested taking some pieces of pork 'suitable for your salting tub' rubbing them well with warmed treacle and adding salt, saltpetre, ground allspice and pepper, rubbing and turning every day for a week. The meat was then suspended in a current of air and later coated with bran or pollard and smoked.

Hams

'Are you going to do the hams in the same way?'
    'No – they're to go in that pickle.'
'What is in it?' asked Ellen.
    'Sugar and salt and saltpetre, and molasses, and I don't know what all.'

Elizabeth Wetherall, *The Wide Wide World*, 1852

An ancient legend from the Pyrenees told how one day a pig fell into a salt spring and drowned. When the herdsmen eventually pulled it out they found that the salt meat tasted delicious, particularly the hams. Ham was the luxury product of the pork salting process and most poor households had to sell their hams in order to buy enough salt to preserve the rest of their pork cuts into pickled pork or bacon. Although the English word 'ham' is said to derive from the old English *hamm* meaning 'a thigh', hams seem to have developed as a speciality throughout Europe during the time of the Roman Empire. The Romans loved salty foods and ate salted cheeses and fish, sausages and hams, which they imported from all over their wide empire. They regarded salt ham as so important that the Emperor Claudius and his Senate actually debated whether men could live without salt meat.

Hams are said to have originated in Roman Gaul but the dry salted and smoked Westphalian ham, traditionally made from bear or bear cub, was equally popular in Rome. Throughout the great European forests, lean, free-roaming hogs fattened themselves on acorns and chestnuts before being transformed into succulent hams. Ham-producing centres in Iberia and Corsica, Gaul and the Rhinelands all sent their own regional specialities to Rome. The statesman Cato gives his own Rome-made ham recipe in his *De Agri Cultura*, the oldest surviving complete prose work in Latin. It directs the reader to lay a number of hams in huge earthenware jars covered with half a peck of Roman salt per ham. The hams are to be left, with occasional turning, for twelve days then cleaned off and hung in the fresh air for two further days. They are then rubbed with oil and hung and smoked for two days. Finally, they are rubbed all over with a mixture of oil and vinegar and hung in a meat store where 'Neither moths nor worms will attack it'.

Curing hams can be done with a range of mixtures based primarily on salt with the addition of sugars and spices, herbs and oils. Sugar and honey are also powerful preservers and they have the added benefit of counteracting the hardening effects of saltpetre. Honey or sugar also 'makes the Flesh eat tender, short, and sweet'. Some hams such as the Suffolk are cured in a pickle of black treacle and stout or cider. Others can be first dry salted or brined before drying while many are then also finished off with smoking, with juniper berries, sage, bay and heather, over fires of either oak, beech, pine, hickory or apple wood, or over peat turves, and in some regions over smouldering seaweed. Before hanging, most hams are smeared with oil, pepper or honey to keep out air and insects during storage, sewn into tight coats of muslin or given several layers of whitewash. In some areas hams are buried in a box or barrel filled with wood ash to absorb the remaining moisture then cleaned off with brandy or vinegar and tied in new cloth and hung in a cool, draughty place in the kitchen rafters or an outhouse where they will keep for many months.

The type of pig, its feed and lifestyle and the method used for curing it all play a part in the resulting ham. 'The orchard pig, the moorland pig, the wheat-land pig and the forager pig. Pigs that had character before they were pork' was what mattered, wrote the food historian Dorothy Hartley. The time the meat is left to mature as it hangs high in kitchen ceilings, in airy drying rooms or smoke-houses also determines its final 'hammy' taste. Some hams are cured to be eaten raw while others require cooking by boiling or roasting.

In England, almost every county has its hams, which are less often eaten raw as they are in southern countries. There are the simple heavily dry salted hams such as the Cumberland and the Welsh ham, and the rich Bradenham hams from Chippenham with their coal-black exterior. These are cured for six months under a thick coat of molasses, spices and juniper berries resulting in a sweet spicy flavour. There are also the succulent Devonshire long-cut hams 'smoked or pale dried' and Wiltshire hams, mildly cured from young bacon pigs and not so good for long storage. The mild, pale pink York ham, which is not really from York, is a cure still used by modern suppliers in Europe and the US where it is regarded as one of the finest cooked hams. The York cure includes dry salting and maturing for four months before smoking.

The French, not surprisingly, have numerous excellent regional hams, which are broadly known as 'jambon de campagne' (country hams). These are either dried or smoked. Many of these hams are still made on the farm, mostly by salting and drying. Perhaps the most famous French ham is the 'jambon de Bayonne'. It is smoked to a golden brown colour, has a mild smoky flavour and is always eaten raw.

Italian hams, such as the Parma ham, are amongst the finest raw dried hams. Thin slivers of 'prosciutto crudo', served with warm ripe figs or melon, are irresistible. Great care is taken with preparing this ham, which is dry salted with sea salt during the winter for about a month then wiped clean and hung in huge curing rooms in long rows where plenty of fresh air can circulate around them. The curers must constantly adjust the windows to accommodate the changing winds. If the skin dries too much, or the surface cracks, they must be rubbed with fat and any holes must be filled with a paste of fat and pepper. It takes nearly nine months for a Parma ham to mature, sometimes even longer. A winter cured ham should be ready by the following August, in time to be eaten with the newly ripened figs and melons.

Spain is famous for its huge dried mountain hams, 'jamón serrano', eaten raw, made from the lean meat of the wild Red Iberian pig. These are huge hams cured in the mountain areas near Madrid. The temperature is high, the pieces of meat large, so a quick penetration of salt is essential before drying. The fresh meat is packed into a clean cloth sack filled with crystalline salt and then placed on the basement floor. Friends and relatives visiting the house are expected to pop down to the basement and do a bit of jumping on the sack of meat. By compressing the ham, the drying and salting process is speeded up. Nowadays a case of strong Spanish wine can be used to weight the hams instead. By strange association, in the finale of the film *Jamon Jamon*, the two protagonists beat each other to a pulp using the hard, giant jamón serrano as weapons!

Germany has been renowned for its delicious hams since Roman times though traditionally they are more usually smoked. The Westphalian hams that the Romans so loved are still produced. They are cut from mature pigs, the blood is massaged out and then the hams are first dry salted and then marinated in brine for a number of weeks during which they are repeatedly taken out washed and packed down again for further ripening. Finally, they are hung up to smoke and dry in a low temperature over beechwood sawdust mixed with juniper twigs or berries. The finished hams have a lovely dark chestnut colour with a strong smoky but subtle flavour. Westphalia ham is served in thin slices and eaten raw with bread and butter.

Not surprisingly many of these old, traditional ham recipes travelled with the migrants to America where some have found their own character such as the Kentucky ham. Made from range-fed pigs fattened on acorns, beans, clover and grain, it is dry salted and then smoked over apple and hickory wood and aged for up to a year. However, Virginia hams, often known as Smithfield hams, are perhaps the most famous. These are made from hogs fed on peanuts and are dry salted and heavily smoked. Queen Victoria always ordered quantities of these Virginia hams, which are eaten boiled or, better still, baked with a thick sweet glaze of honey or molasses.

Nowadays most hams are injected with brine to speed up the process. Many are also pre-tenderized and pre-cooked. Commercial smoking processes also leave less maturing time. Apart from the very expensive speciality hams, few hams are now made from wild or foraging pigs or are given the time and care necessary to produce the best quality traditional products. Sadly the vast majority of hams, sitting on their pedestals dressed with paper frills in the delicatessen or pre-sliced and pre-packed on the shelves, will have little of the flavour, texture or the salty, smoky spiciness that so excited the Romans.

Not all of the many different kinds of ham are made from pork. In 1747 Hannah Glasse recommended Welsh or Scotch beef for her recipe for beef hams that required 'the leg of a fat but small beef'. Goat hams were cured in Wales and were known as 'hung' or 'rock' venison, being 'reckoned generally very sweet and fat'. There have been veal hams, goose hams and even badger hams. The smoked 'macon' (mutton as bacon) ham from Cumbria is made from Herdwick sheep and belongs to a long British tradition of using mutton to make hams.

Sheep are also the main animal for eating throughout the Middle East, North Africa and the eastern Mediterranean. In some regions of Turkey they still slaughter a fat sheep in September, de-bone the meat and cut it into lumps which are thoroughly salted and left in a shady place for a few days. Then the meat is again coated with salt and put away in wooden boxes or straw baskets to be kept in a cool place. This salted meat is used in a wide variety of dishes including cooked wheat grain, with stuffed grape leaves or with a kind of ravioli. Similarly, in the mountain regions of Bulgaria where they herd sheep, it is an ancient practice for every household to kill a number of sheep and goats in the autumn. The meat is cut into long pieces, brined and hung on a draughty wall of the house. It is known as 'pastarma' and is a favourite food eaten raw or cooked with pulses.

There are many similar kinds of salted wind dried meat to be found, such as the Armenian 'pastrama' made with beef, described by a nineteenth-century traveller as 'thin, black, leather-like pieces of meat dried and browned in the sun, and with salt and squashed flies'. Turkish 'pastirma' is seasoned with garlic and cumin while 'pasturma' is made in the Balkans from lamb, goat, calf or young buffalo. The more recent and highly popular 'pastrami', eaten in New York Jewish restaurants, evolved from this group of cured meats. It was brought to America by Jews from Romania and other eastern and central European countries, who had the jobs of brewing alcohol for the inns, a task forbidden to other religions, and salting the meats that were served to increase customers' thirst. Pastrami is prepared differently as it is first cured slightly then smoked and coated with a layer of spices, garlic and red pepper. It is also usually boiled or steamed before serving.

Although not as popular and inexpensive as pickled pork, salt beef was a useful standby in many better-off English households. It did, however, require lengthy boiling with hay or bran to get rid of the salt. Alternatively, like pork, it could be boiled in pottages with vegetables and herbs. In medieval times 'green' beef was salted overnight for short keeping while 'hung' beef was smoked for longer storage. Sometimes, in wealthier households, huge rounds of beef weighing up to 20 lb were pickled for three to four weeks. A recipe from 1864 describes a 'Melton Hunt Beef'. This called for a huge joint of prime ox beef to be partially air dried and then rubbed daily with a mix of ground allspice, bruised juniper berries, coarse brown sugar, coarse salt, black pepper, minced shallots and dried bay leaves. Saltpetre, garlic and rock salt were later added and after ten days or so the cook should 'look well to the centre and fat, and setting it up in proper shape, and skewer and bind it firmly'. The meat was wiped and coated with dry bran or pollard and left to smoke for a week using beech chips, oak 'lops' and fern or grass turfs. There were many other variations of dry spiced or Hunt Beef. Some were not smoked but were covered with shredded suet and then given a thick crust made from flour and lard to keep the moisture in and the bacteria out. When cooked, they are said to have had a rich, spicy and mellow flavour. Because of their size and cost, these spiced beef joints (which could also be made with silverside of beef) were often made specially for Christmas.

Elsewhere whatever meat was available was salted for keeping. In Holland they slit geese down the back and salted them with saltpetre and other salts and dried them like bacon. Even seal meat was salted in the Northern Isles of Scotland using the salt ashes of burnt seaweed. It was eaten with a long pointed stick instead of a fork 'to prevent the strong smell which their hands would otherwise have for several hours after'. Meat was the most important food for preserving but as salt was expensive and hard to obtain, only the best cuts of good quality meat were salted. A sick or old animal was considered 'not worth its salt'.

When people had neither salt nor equipment they managed to find ingenious alternatives. Martin Martin, who visited many Scottish islands in 1695, noted that the islanders had found a clever substitute for their lack of pickling barrels. 'The natives are accustomed to salt their beef in a cow's hide, which keeps it close from air, and preserves it well, if not better than barrels, and tastes, they say, best when this way used.' Salt was extracted from seaweed and in many poor regions the acids of various plants – nettle or burdock leaves, dill, parsley, white mustard seeds, stinging nettles and horseradish – were used. Even the salt from sweat was useful, as is seen in the story of Attila, King of the Huns, and his wild and terrible men. The conquering hordes may have raped and pillaged as they rode from the east, but they also took their own meat, preserved and tenderized on the hoof. They cut pieces of fresh meat and put them under their saddles. As they galloped along, the salt from the horses' sweat accumulated under the saddle around the meat. At the same time, the action of the riders bumping up and down on both the saddle and the meat served to press out the liquids and very little air could reach the meat pressed tightly between flank and saddle. When they stopped to rest, Attila and his men had only to sharpen their knives and slice off a piece of delicious gallop-cured meat.

* * *

Salt is to be found almost everywhere in the world in some form or other. The first salt mines are believed to have been in use around the Bronze Age. We know from Herodotus that in the fifth century BC the Babylonians and Egyptians pickled fish such as sturgeon, salmon and catfish, as well as poultry and geese. Sometimes salt was relatively simple to extract, in other parts it was more difficult. Salting was first practised in the Iron Age by the British when it was introduced by the Celts. Sea water was boiled in shallow earthenware dishes until the water evaporated leaving sea salt. This method was still being used after the Romans arrived but they preferred the large-grained marine salt from France that was used to cure hams made by the Gauls. The mod-

Measuring salt in France in 1528 according to royal regulations prior to taxation

ern word 'salary' derives from the Roman salt allowance paid to their soldiers called *salarium*.

People who could not produce enough salt of their own were prepared to pay a high price for it, especially in northern Europe where salt fish and meat became such an important part of the diet. Salt, the 'white gold', became the subject of intensive trading. 'It has been,' wrote Jean-François Bergier in his *Une Histoire du Sel*, 'the reason behind commercial and political strategy, has enriched some and has impoverished others . . . for dozens of generations salt held a position similar to that of oil in our own time.'

As with oil, monarchs and governments were quick to slap heavy taxes on salt. The French got the idea of salt taxes (*gabelle*) from the Normans who took it from the Arabs. France did not abolish salt taxes until 1790 after the courts of Louis XVI had convicted and punished nearly 2,000 people, including children, of dealing in contraband salt. It is not surprising that salt taxation contributed to a number of bloody revolts and caused one of the grievances which led to the French Revolution.

The demand for spices, which were used medicinally as well as for food preservation, also drove a busy trade. By the Middle Ages most of Europe was spice crazy with the Dutch, Portuguese, English and French all fighting to control the sources and markets. In 1600 Queen Elizabeth I gave a royal charter to the East India Company to trade in spices from the East Indies. The Dutch almost immediately formed their own much more competitive and aggressive company and swiftly gained control of the 'Spice Islands' of the East Indies. Many famous explorations were sent out in search of new spice routes and backdoor short cuts to existing ones. When Columbus discovered the New World, he called it the 'West Indies' thinking and hoping that that was what he had found.

The salt and spice taxes were important factors in the decline of salt-preserved food. In addition, the quantity of salt needed to preserve meat meant that even before dietary science developed it was thought to be bad for the health. Explorer Captain Cook complained, 'Hanged beef . . . is not laudable; it may fill the belly and cause a man to drink, but it is evil for the stone, and evil of digestion, and maketh no good juice.' This does not seem to have worried the navy victuallers who continued to order special salted beef called 'salt horse' or salt pork known as 'sea junk', which were neither hung nor dried but left packed in barrels of salt, sometimes for six years until they were all but inedible. Although this was to remain the staple food of navies for hundreds of years, the problems caused by this diet would eventually bring about a revolution in the preserving of meat.

Fish

For many thousands of years, indeed until very recently, fish has provided a particularly cheap and abundant form of protein. The trade in preserved fish has shaped and changed the lives and diet of millions of people. It has been the cause of wars, and of the waxing and waning of national powers; it has created vast wealth and nourished millions of poor over many centuries. The two most abundant and important species were cod and herring, whose numbers seemed infinite, but we now know that they are not.

Fish can be found in the diet of almost every community in the world. Where it was most plentiful, in coastal regions and along rivers, fish could be eaten fresh from the water. But fish will not keep for long, particularly fatty or freshwater fish, so people tried to find ways to preserve their seasonal catches. As with meat, fish was either dry salted or wet or brine salted. Whitefish, such as cod, haddock, hake, whiting and halibut, were traditionally dry salted and then air or sun dried. These fish have a high water content, far more than meat, but if the water is removed, they will remain edible for up to six months, as long as they are kept very dry. After salting and drying, these fish weigh much less and are easy to store and transport and, if preserved properly, they will not lose their nutritional value. Oily fish such as mackerel, salmon, pilchards and herring were wet salted or pickled. This is because the fat in them will oxidise if left exposed to air giving the flesh a rancid flavour.

Salt was used to preserve fish since ancient times, possibly even before meat was cured. The early Mesopotamian civilisations relied on a staple diet of salt fish and barley porridge, and the people living around the Persian Gulf, on the coast of Oman and along the arid coasts of the Arabian Sea, subsisted on dried dates and salted tunny and sardines. Fish curing, depicted in the tombs of ancient Egypt, was so highly regarded that only temple officials were entrusted with the knowledge of the art and it is significant that the Egyptian word for fish preserving was the same as that used to denote the process of embalming the dead. In many parts of ancient China, where the hot, humid climate meant that fish preserving was particularly important; fish were pickled in brine or buried in salt and then sometimes packed in oil.

Trade in preserved fish grew rapidly during the Iron Age period until it became a major business all around the Mediterranean, the mouth of the Dnieper, the Sea of Azov and the Black Sea. Settlements sprang up, often established by Greek colonists, specialising in salting and trading pickled fish, which was sent out in jars all over the Mediterranean and inland into Europe and Asia. The Atlantic was also rich in fish and medieval French Atlantic

In the sixteenth century the blubber of beached whales was chopped up with huge axes and packed into barrels of salt

fisheries created a special delicacy called 'craspois' made from the salted blubber of stranded whales.

Each region developed its own particular gourmet recipe for salted fish to be sold to the rich while dried lumps of salt fish were kept for the poor or eaten by soldiers on campaign. Dried salt fish was nutritious and lightweight and in medieval times enormous quantities of fish were caught off the Dutch coast and salted in order to supply military campaigns. The Count of Holland, preparing for a siege of Utrecht in the summer of 1345, gave huge orders for salt cod, salt and red herring and barrels of preserved eel. In the sixteenth century, tunny – the 'chicken of the sea' – was still being salted around the Mediterranean coast using a method that originated in ancient Byzantium, whereby triangular pieces of fish were packed tightly in layers of salt in stoneware casks. Fresh fish was, however, always more popular and more expensive than salted, even in Roman times, when salted fish became a far commoner food. The Romans brought salting to a high degree of perfection using spices and strong herbs – such as marjoram for conger eel – to flavour their sauces and pickles. They salted red mullet, bream, sturgeon, tunny, eel and swordfish in the numerous ports of Italy, Spain, Sicily and Sardinia, where traders amassed considerable fortunes using armies of slaves. By AD 200 the classical writer Athanaeus could list 200 different ways of preparing and preserving fish, much of which was sent to the far reaches of the empire, where isolated officials wrote desperately to friends and relatives in Rome for more. 'When you come to Byzantium,' begs one, 'bring a piece of salt swordfish, and choose a slice of the back nearest to the tail.'

Salt fish was also widely eaten in Japan and southeast Asia, where the people depend almost entirely on fish for their protein. The Japanese have no natural salt deposits, but around 200 BC it was found that they could produce salt from dried seaweed, which was burnt and the ash dissolved in water from which the salt was evaporated. Although fresh food is always the most sought after, salted foods are still popular in Japan and there is an enormous variety of local cooking and preserving styles to suit the variations in climate and ingredients available. Along coastal and river regions, many kinds of fish, such as shrimp, anchovy, sandfish, walleye or pollack, are dried in the sun, wind or dry night air after being lightly salted. By the Middle Ages salt fish was a central part of most people's diet throughout Europe. Both sea fish and freshwater fish such as lampreys, carp, pike, eels and trout were salted or dried.

Dry salt fish, most commonly whitefish, was widely eaten and was preferred to the unsalted stockfish. Most whitefish are from the cod family and can be fished and salted all year round. Newly salted undried whitefish such as hake, ling, whiting, pollack or haddock were known as 'green fish' (similar to 'green bacon'). Ling is a definite species distinct from cod, but the word was also widely used as a term for salt fish generally. The poorer regions of Scotland and the north of England relied heavily on salt fish right through to the nineteenth century. Along with barrels of salted haddock, turbot, dogfish and plaice, the Scots salted and dried 'sookit piltocks' and speldings, which were 'dipped in the sea and dried in the sun'.

Most Europeans, at least until the Second World War, still kept the tradition of eating fish on a Friday. For many it was more from force of habit than religious observance, a way of having fish once a week on a day you knew the fishmonger would stock up with extra fresh fish. Eating fish during the Lent fast and on certain days of the week was originally a pagan observance that the Christian church adopted as its own, as it so often did with ancient and traditional practices. The Church decreed that certain days, including the whole of Lent, were to be meatless days 'to reduce carnal passions'. Eating fish, which was cheaper and less attractive than meat, was seen as a form of self-denial. By the late Middle Ages, nearly half the days of the year had become 'fysshe' days, but since fresh fish was virtually unobtainable, it had to be dried or salted. Inevitably, some got sick of eating so much salt fish; one fifteenth-century English schoolboy wrote in his schoolbook, 'Thou will not believe how weary I am of fish, and how much I desire that flesh were come in again, for I have ate none other but salt fish this Lent . . .'

For as long as Lent and other fasting periods existed, preserved fish would hold sway in most European homes. The trade in salt fish in the Middle Ages was so extensive that it became quite a problem, blocking the roads and taking up too much warehouse storage space while it waited to be moved. The Saint-Maurice customs post on the St Bernard Pass was reported to be filled with the stench of sacks of salt fish travelling in both directions. So much salt fish was being traded that the storing of salt sardines, anchovies and herrings in bond was forbidden.

Needless to say, the Church or state's rules about eating fish on certain days often had more to do with controlling the supply of food provisions and the economy than with religious scruples. The Romans had long ago ordered fish days to save on short meat supplies. In England in the mid-sixteenth century, eating flesh on a fish day was a serious offence. In 1548, Saturday was declared to be a second meatless day. Fridays and Saturdays, though, were still not enough and a report of 1563 argued, 'It is necessary for the restoring of the Navye of England to have more fishe eaten and therfor one daye more in the weeke ordeyned to be a fisshe daye, and that to be Wednesdaye, rather than any other.'

The arguments raised included the lack of affordable meat, the quantities of fish imported on foreign vessels, the decline of the English fisheries, the desire to increase the navy (which protected the fishing fleets) and the need to encourage shipbuilding of both naval and fishing vessels. Manipulating the consumer in order to create a stronger economy and a more powerful state would appear to have been much easier to organise in those days.

Attempts to enforce additional fish days were later abandoned but the import of foreign cured fish was forbidden and in 1621 James I issued yet another proclamation against eating meat in Lent and on fish days. He admitted that the reasons were not religious but for the 'Maintenance of our navy and shipping, a principal strength of our island, and for the sparing and increase of fresh victuals'.

Controlling and protecting their fishing industries was a major concern for the leading maritime countries such as France, England, the Netherlands and Spain. As the untapped riches of the New World were opened up by explorers and with new shipbuilding technology, the competition for fish became even greater.

COD 'The Beef of the Seas'

O squander not thy grief: those tears command
To weep upon our cod in Newfoundland.
The plenteous pickle shall preserve the fish,
And Europe taste thy sorrows in a dish.

Alexander Pope, 1727

In early June 1650, the tiny fishing port of Olonne, sixty kilo-metres north of La Rochelle, was full of the noise of celebration. In the midst of small fishing smacks in the harbour lay a much larger vessel, almost a hundred tons. It had a dishevelled, exhausted air about it – uncoiled ropes, torn sails, dirty decks – and that unmistakable stench of fish, salt cod. Some fish still hung from the rigging like rigid planks or dried, discoloured bunting.

In the Café des Maritimes sailors and fish merchants were

celebrating with the victorious skipper and his crew of twenty-three men, who, for the second summer in a row, were the first ship to have returned to home port from the rich cod fishing grounds off the coast of Newfoundland, thousands of miles away on the other side of the Atlantic Ocean. Their ship was stuffed to the gunwales with cod and, like the first grouse arriving in London after the 'glorious twelfth', the first 'little hundred' cod to arrive in late June commanded a special price. Paris was waiting for the new fish and the skipper and his crew could expect a valuable bonus.

But whether first or last in, every skipper had to hand over the bulk of his catch to the merchant who had advanced him dried provisions, flour, wine, lines, fish-hooks and the essential supplies of salt. This was the custom at ports along the coast around La Rochelle and Le Havre, the leading Newfoundland fishing ports of Europe in the sixteenth and seventeenth centuries when France dominated the great fishing banks that lay on the edge of the North American continental shelf. On the sandbanks, where the warm southern waters meet the Arctic Greenland waters, there were cod, which in those days were as numerous 'without exaggeration . . . as the grains of sand covering the banks'.

Cod had, of course, been caught nearer to home. In the Middle Ages, cod had been taken in huge quantities from the sea off the Dutch coast and salted. Along with pollack, whiting and hake or haddock, there were plenty of cod off the coasts of Norway, Denmark, Scotland and Iceland that were fished and cured extensively to supply the huge demand for cured fish all over Europe and beyond. In the fifteenth century the first Icelandic 'cod wars' were already being fought, and the English port of Hull owed its prosperity to 'the trade of Iseland – fish, dry'd and harden'd term'd by them Stockfish, which. . . . has strangely enrich'd the town'.

It was Basque whalers who first discovered the new, incredibly rich fishing grounds off Newfoundland. As they chased whales into unknown waters, they came across dense, churning shoals of huge, slow fish that 'one might take from the ocean in basketfuls'. They realised straightaway the importance of keeping the secret to themselves, which they managed to do successfully until nearly the end of the fifteenth century. But of the numerous nationals sent out to explore, chart, discover and claim the New World for Portugal,

England, the Netherlands, Spain and France, few failed to notice the wealth of the fishing and the Basque secret eventually became a marine equivalent of the California Gold Rush.

John Cabot, an Italian explorer charged by Henry VII of England to search for unknown lands, set off from Bristol in 1497 and made landfall in Nova Scotia. He returned to England with stories of boats hauling in great catches of cod off Newfoundland. 'The sea is swarming with fish,' Cabot declared, 'they could bring so many fish that this kingdom would have no further need of Iceland.'

Those with the strongest navies drove out the smaller fry. But having established dominance in some of the fishing grounds, many of which were many thousands of miles from home port, they still had to solve the problem of how to bring the fish back to market in a saleable condition. If catching the cod was so easy, sailing far across the Atlantic to the Banks and bringing the cargo safely home was much more complex. The two main contenders in the race to control the cod trade were the French and the English. Their different methods of preserving the cod would have a profound influence on the course of history in the West Indies and North America.

When the English fishermen moved from Iceland to the newly discovered riches of Newfoundland, they took their existing processing methods with them. For several hundred years the cod and its other relations, the ling, saithe, tusk and haddock, had all been dry salted on board ship in the same manner. Great care was taken as the fish were split ventrally and cleaned of all blood, slime and the black skin inside the 'nape'. The backbone was removed except for a few inches near the tail, which was left to provide rigidity. The fish were then dry salted in stacks about five feet high with salt spread between layers of fish – thirty parts of salt to 100 parts of fish. This stacking with salt was known as 'kenching'. After fifteen to twenty-one days of regular restacking and salting, the salt had fully saturated the flesh and the resulting liquor or pickle had all drained away. The fish was then finished off by drying on return to port.

But the huge distances home from the Newfoundland fisheries meant that enormous quantities of salt were needed to get the fish back in a reasonable condition. The English fishermen did not have large supplies of home-produced salt and so had to continue making their own type of 'green' cod, which required less salt. This was then thoroughly dried on the nearest piece of land before making the journey back across the Atlantic. The increasing need for drying beaches and space for drying hurdles and processing sheds necessitated settlements on the east coast of Newfoundland and later, further south in New England where the winters were milder, the summers hotter and there were equally plentiful supplies of cod.

In contrast, the huge, well-provisioned French ships with their large crews had abundant supplies of salt produced in the salt marshes around Bordeaux. They filled their ships' holds with salt on the outward journey and took enough provisions to be able to stay at sea for up to six months. Many French fishermen also relied on the Newfoundland shore to dry their catch but on the big ships all the necessary preserving for the long journey home could be done on board. Every day the fishermen put out their handlines and caught between 200 and 400 fish. Boys took the enormous fish, up to three feet in length weighing up to 100 lb, to the well-organised processing men waiting at their benches. One man cut off the head and threw it into the sea, a second cut it open and gutted it and a third cut out the backbone and passed the fish to the salter. On some ships they kept the heads to boil into a nourishing ship's stew. The cods' liver was kept for oil, the tongue was pickled to be sold as a delicacy and the swim bladder was dried to make isinglass, once used for making jellies and for fining beer. The prepared fish were arranged head by tail in layers of salt and left for two or three days. New layers of fish and salt were then arranged over the salted ones. And on it went 'until all their salt was wetted' and they returned home fully laden. Because of the plentiful supplies of salt the fish survived the long journey home and the fishermen were also able to concentrate on the larger fish found on the Banks farther from the coast that were too large to dry and needed careful salting. One of these French ships could return with up to 25,000 fish, which would at last be hung out to dry in sheds or the in open air along the warm, dry southwestern Atlantic coast.

The English, meanwhile, had to buy their salt from the Spanish and Portuguese, who were also fishing in big numbers in the early years. But in 1580 Portugal merged with Spain and after the destruction of the Spanish Armada eight years later, both ceased to compete in Newfoundland waters. By the latter part of the six-teenth century, the British navy had secured fishing grounds and was itself being supplied with enormous quantities of dried cod from the Newfoundland fishery. However, the lucrative markets in southern Europe were not keen to buy dry or lightly salted cod. They preferred the superior French variety, which popularly came to be known as 'morue' in France, 'baccala' in Italy, 'bacalao' in Spain and 'bacalhau' in Portugal, where it was affectionately called 'the faithful friend'.

The French may have cornered the quality market but the British method of drying on land had caused settlements to be established and enriched. According to Boswell the 'Sole purpose of the first settlers in New Hampshire was not to escape from reli-gious persecution, but to acquire wealth by fishing and trading.' Boston quickly became a thriving centre for fishing and curing. English fishermen from the Old World were gradually squeezed out as the settlers in the New built a powerful trade. This would soon be turned in a whole new direction.

In the seventeenth century, sugar production in the West Indies was growing so rapidly there was no spare land to grow food for the slaves. The plantation owners relied on provisions sent from the mother countries. In 1738 alone, England sent 16,500 tons of salted beef and pork, 5,000 flitches of bacon and 2,500 tons of preserved tripe to its islands, while thousands of tons of salt cod were ordered to be sent from the New England fisheries. It was thought that the salt cod was particularly nutritious as it provided essential salt replacement for the sweating slaves working in the sugar cane fields under the relentless, burning sun. New Englanders quickly seized the opportunity to sell their inferior cod. At first they sent the 'refuse fish' that was 'salt burnt, spotted, rotton and carelessly ordered'. This 'they put off to the Charib Islands, Barbadoes, Jamaica, etc., who feed their negroes with it'. At the same time, salt cod had also become very popular in West Africa where the New Englanders and Europeans bought slaves.

Before setting sail they filled their ships' holds with salt cod and when they arrived in Africa they paid for the slaves with it. They then shipped the slaves to the Caribbean where they fed those who survived the journey on the remaining cargo of cod. The Caribbean and African markets required salt fish to be dried particularly hard for it to be able to survive the tropical heat. A special hard 'West India' cure was created, which also came to describe the worst quality salt cod – split, over-salted, badly damaged rejects. Having offloaded the new slaves, the ships returned to Newfoundland with sugar molasses, tobacco, cotton, salt and rum, completing their own 'trade triangle'.

As they prospered from this trade, the growing New England settlements drove the French drying grounds farther and farther north into Nova Scotia and the north coast of Newfoundland. In 1763, after nearly ten years of warfare between Britain and France and their respective settlers, France lost Canada and the fisheries but kept its Caribbean islands. By a neat arrangement the New Englanders now sold salt cod to the French colonies of Haiti, Martinique and Guadeloupe, who in turn sold them molasses. This worked fine until the British, fearful of losing control in their American colonies, tried to create stringent trade rules, tariffs and taxes over the settlers. None, however, succeeded in reducing the independent trading with the Caribbean. It was British determination that all New World trade be conducted through Britain that led to the Boston Tea Party in 1773. Ten years later, Britain was forced to recognise American independence. John Adams, one of the American founding fathers who helped to write the Declaration of Independence, described the New England fishery as 'a nursery of seamen and a source of naval power'. Fishing and fighting went hand in hand.

The Newfoundland fisheries continued to flourish. According to G. D. Warburton, an Irish writer who settled in Canada, by the 1840s St John's in Newfoundland was 'the fishiest capital in the world'. He described acres of sheds roofed with cod split in half, laid on like slates, drying in the sun, with ships in harbour 'bearing nearly every flag in the world, laden with cod'. The sparse fields were manured with cod and the people's houses, clothes, furniture, 'satin gown of the mother, and gold chain of the father are all paid for in cod; the breezes from the shore, soft and warm on this bright August day, are rich not with the odours of a thousand flowers but of a thousand cod'. Only the dinner table, he observed with astonishment, was kept sacred from its intrusion.

In fact dry salt fish, with its unyielding toughness and saltiness, was becoming unpopular elsewhere as well. As with fish simply dried, elaborate cooking methods needed to be devised to return moisture to the fish, with the added task of trying to alleviate the overpowering salty taste. In the north of England people would soak salt dried cod in running water, then stew it in buttermilk and afterwards rub it, while still hot, with a dry cloth till it fluffed up like a blanket, very light and white. Another way was to stew the fish slowly in milk and butter thickened with eggs.

Nevertheless, salt cod, sent south from the North Sea since the Middle Ages, established a long tradition in Mediterranean cookery that survives to this day. In the Languedoc, in France, the smooth, creamy 'brandade de morue' is made with salt cod and olive oil so that Elizabeth Luard in her book *European Peasant Cookery* writes, 'The harsh, pale flesh of the northern ocean and the rich, gold fruit of the southern hill-slopes make a perfect union.'

By the eighteenth century in most parts of Europe, however, dry salted fish, like dried meat, was really only eaten by the military, travellers and the poor. But the more pliable, brined fish such as herring, salmon and anchovies remained in common use. Travelling in the opposite direction to the salt cod, pungent salted anchovies and sardines were sent north from the Mediterranean. They are still popular as an ingredient of pizza, salade niçoise and 'pissaladière', and the best are still produced on the French Catalan coast near Perpignan. Freshly caught anchovies must be salted immediately, either whole or beheaded and gutted, and gently packed into large wooden barrels filled with salt and weighted down while they mature for three or four months. Afterwards, the tiny fish are expertly filleted and laid out in jars or cans.

Sardines, really young pilchards, were traditionally brought in around the coast of Sardinia, when there was no tuna, and salted and pressed into casks. Along the Cornish coast vast shoals of pilchards would appear 'between harvest and Allhallowtide'. Every able man would be waiting for their arrival with boats and seine nets to haul them onto the shore. There, the women loaded them into baskets either to be sold immediately in the local markets or, for the majority, to be salted and pressed down into kegs and barrels or smoked for export. Today, small vans still tour the mountain villages of northern Italy selling Cornish pilchards beautifully laid out in their baskets like the petals of a flower.

Along with Cornish pilchards, preserved Scottish salmon was also traded south to the Mediterranean. One tends to think of salmon as being either smoked, canned, frozen or eaten fresh but it was once most commonly salted and pickled in vast quantities. By the thirteenth century the Scots were exporting barrels of pickled salmon as far as Venice. In the north of Scotland, there were 'salmon in such plenty as is scarce credible and so cheap that, to those who have any substance to buy with, it is not worth their while to catch it themselves'. Irish salmon was barrelled in brine and sent to England, and 'powdered' or dry salted salmon continued to be eaten in London until the sixteenth century when salted sturgeon, swordfish and porpoise were still gourmet delicacies for the very rich.

Botargo, a salted fish roe from the eastern Mediterranean first known in ancient Egypt, is another gourmet delicacy still popular in many Mediterranean countries. It is similar to the Greek 'taramás' from which the now widely eaten taramosalata is made. It has long been popular in England and in the seventeenth century Samuel Pepys described eating botargo with bread to serve as a useful blotting paper to soak up a heavy night of drinking. It can be made from the roe of either grey mullet or bluefin tuna. There are different methods for producing botargo depending on the fish and where they are produced. The Sicilians make it with tuna roe carefully removed so as not to break the membranes. The roe are gently laid out on tables and salted and the sacs are filled and irrigated through the duct several times with saturated brine. Next, they are dry salted and weighted with daily changes of salt and increased pressure until the roe are completely impregnated. They are then hung in an airy place to dry. Tuna botargo is made into enormous square-shaped pieces that can weigh up to 7 kg. On the other hand, botargo made with grey mullet roe is much smaller and squashed into thin pieces preserved in a coating of wax. This kind is mainly made in Corsica, Tunisia, Egypt, Turkey and Sardinia, where it is eaten in thin slices with oil, vinegar and ground pepper.

HERRING 'The Wheat of the Seas'

The herring is a lucky fish
From all disease inured,
Should he be ill when caught at sea;
Immediately – he's cured.

Spike Milligan

In historical importance and impact the herring is probably second only to the cod. It is an oily, soft-finned fish particularly perishable when fresh. Unlike the cod, which has no fat and dries well, the herring is difficult to dry as its high fat content would rapidly become rancid when exposed to the air.

Herring come in different guises at different seasons in different places. They are great migratory travellers and, as Jules Michelet described them in *La Mer* 'They live together, hidden in twilight depths'. They rise in midsummer in great masses to spawn, 'crowding in serried ranks, they can never be close enough to each other: they swim in dense shoals, "It is as if the dunes set sail," the Flemich used to say'.

The herring shoals migrated to different coasts through the year and went through various seasonal conditions. Immature herring, caught in the spring, were called 'matjes' or 'matties' ('maiden' or 'virgin') and were most usually lightly salted with the gall bladder intact, a delicacy still eaten in Holland with chopped raw sweet onion and in Sweden with soured cream, potatoes and plenty of aquavit. During their southward migration, the Large or Full herring grew fat and oily, filled with their roe or milt. They were fished in the summer in the seas off East Anglia where hundreds of boats congregated from miles away and many fights broke out. The 'spent' or spawned fish, in poor condition by the time they reached the south coast of England, were used generally for quick smoking such as kippering.

Numerous countries in the north have fished for herring, preserved it in brine or dry salt and traded it with other countries far afield. In the tenth century vast herring catches were brought in along the Baltic coast where they were preserved in barrels of salt and shipped to central and eastern Europe. The inhabitants of the modern-day Netherlands in particular became skilled at sea in their pursuit of the herring and wealthy from trading with it. Amsterdam itself was said to be built upon herring bones, where, Michelet sourly observed, the 'Herring fishers transmuted their stinking cargo into gold'.

By the twelfth century, the French and English were also voracious fishers of North Sea herring, hoisting them out of the sea in vast quantities. By now, fisheries along the Baltic and Pomeranian coasts, though blessed with quantities of salt, brought in such immense quantities of herring that the surplus had to be boiled down for oil. The medieval herring business created other burgeoning trades for people skilled as carpenters, shipwrights, rope makers, net weavers and coopers. Fish women were needed to gill, wash and barrel the fish and hundreds of workers were employed mining or panning for salt and packing and dispatching it. 'The curable herring became the great fish of Northern life . . . the way of life of millions of people has been shaped by the herring,' Jane Grigson wrote in *Fish*.

In the fourteenth century a Dutchman, William Beukels, is said to have invented a rapid method of gutting and salting the 'stinking cargo' on boats called 'Dutch busses', where the fishermen could immediately barrel them in brine. Known as 'kaakharing', it meant that fishermen could venture further away from the coast and stay at sea for longer, which was important if they were to be successful in chasing the unpredictable herring. Although barrelled brined herring or 'white herring' ensured perfect preserving, the barrels were bulky and difficult to transport, so fish merchants and fishermen continued to try various other methods including drying and smoking the brined herring when they were returned to port.

With such seemingly endless quantities of herring to be fished, salt herring became a staple and inexpensive part of the diet of ordinary people. Herrings soused as rollmops in hot vinegar and spices, or pickled in barrels using the same method as that used by the Dutch in the Middle Ages are still an important and popular part of the diet in central and northern Europe. But their bitter, salty flavour was not so welcome in England, or even in Scotland, whose people remained poorer and more reliant on salt fish until early in the twentieth century.

In his book *The North East Lowlands of Scotland*, J. R. Allen described his childhood on a farm in Aberdeenshire. His grandmother bought herrings by the barrel and kept them in the back scullery 'Till everyone complained so bitterly about the smell that they were put out to the workshop'. There, they were accused of turning the tools rusty. 'On a Tuesday afternoon my grandmother took enough to make a dinner and enclosed them in a wire cage that had once been a mousetrap. Then we took them to the nearest stream and anchored the cage at the bottom of a little pool and left it there for a day or two. We then brought home the fish which were first boiled and then baked and served with potatoes and a thick coating of mustard sauce. They tasted to me like old dish cloths full of bones and impregnated with salt.'

Fruit and Vegetables

Salt's dehydrating properties could, of course, be applied to almost any food. Salt was rubbed onto many fruits to speed up the drying; apples or pomegranates, tied together with rushes, were 'scalded in sea water' and hung in the open air and then soaked in cold fresh water overnight before eating. In Japan they salt apricots and eggplant and the Chinese store oranges in salt, a combination considered good for hangovers. Salt and sour fruits such as 'mei', a kind of Chinese apricot, were some of the earliest flavourings used in Chinese cooking which, along with honey, ginger and pickled meats, contributed to their liking for complex sweet-sour flavours. In the first century AD it was written that a Chinese man could live 'like a lord of a thousand chariots' if he had put by 600 gallons of salted beans in his annual store.

This simple way to preserve vegetables was used all over the world. The English cookery writer Hannah Glasse, writing in the middle of the eighteenth century, gave a method for salting French beans in the summer to eat in winter. 'To keep French

Beans all the Year. Take fine young Beans, gather them of a very fine Day, have a large Stone-jarr ready clean and dry, lay a Layer of Salt at the Bottom, and then a Layer of Beans, then Salt, and then Beans, and so on till the Jarr is full, cover them with Salt, tye a coarse Cloth over them, and a board on that, and then a Weight to keep it close from all Air; set them in a dry Cellar.'

In the hot southern regions of the Mediterranean, the Middle East and North Africa, fresh vine leaves are parboiled and preserved in jars of brine to make stuffed vine leaf dishes such as 'dolma'. Great varieties of olives are also soaked in brine until they develop a soft texture and a sour taste turning different colours depending on the type. Appetizers of salted eggplant, turnip, beets, onions, peppers, green tomatoes and cucumbers are very popular everywhere in the Middle East and in North Africa they preserve whole lemons in brine made with lemon juice and coarse sea salt. The lemons are then eaten whole, pith, skin and all.

It is in eastern Europe, however, where salting vegetables has survived on a truly large scale up to the modern day. Red peppers, turnips, cauliflower florets, cabbage, red beet, small carrots and artichokes are all kept in brine. Even some fruits, such as apples and pears, are preserved in this way. As well as being eaten fresh or dried, mushrooms are also salted and pickled in Russia for winter snacks to wash down with plenty of vodka. The freshly gathered mushrooms are wiped over, wedged tightly into a large barrel (or nowadays in bottles or large jars) with blackcurrant leaves, coarse salt, chopped onion, pepper, garlic and herbs. Each of the over forty edible varieties must be salted separately.

The most commonly pickled vegetable, however, is the cucumber. All across Russia and eastern Europe, cucumbers, one of the oldest cultivated vegetables, are preserved in brine. In Poland they are pickled in wooden barrels or glass jars filled with brine, dill, garlic, horseradish and oak and cherry leaves. Oak and cherry are rich in tannin, a strong preservative used to process leather, and it is said that the tanners who worked with cherry and oak bark were so impregnated with tannin that when they died, their bodies were preserved.

It is said that salt pickling vegetables improves their flavour and texture. In most cases, however, the salting of vegetables is only the first step in the preserving process, for the majority of pickled vegetables are put in vinegar.

CHAPTER THREE

PICKLING IN VINEGAR

Salt, Mustard, Vinegar, Pepper . . .
Traditional Children's skipping song

The public bar of every pub in England once boasted a giant jar of onions and another of eggs pickled in waterglass or vinegar, their ghostly, soft whiteness almost luminous in their murky liquids. Pickled onions, like salt, stimulate thirst, which explains their presence along with salted crisps in pubs and bars today.

Although the word 'pickle' is used in many different preserving methods, preserving foods in containers filled with vinegar is always known as 'pickling'. Vinegar is a powerful preservative and is still one of the most commonly used. It works by creating a highly acidic environment where few bacteria can survive.

Vinegar is made through an organic process: when an alcoholic brew made from grapes, potatoes, fruits or grains is exposed to the air, a bacterial reaction turns the alcohol into acetic acid. There is a wide range of vinegars, the oldest types being made from wines from the wine-growing regions and malt from the brewing regions. Where there are plenty of apple orchards, there are also cider vinegars and in rice growing areas, there are rice vinegars. The flavours and colours are both subtle and various ranging from mild, mellow tastes to stronger fruity and spicy flavours. Some vinegars such as balsamic vinegar are made richer by ageing in barrels while others have herbs, spices and sugars added to accentuate the flavour. There were other 'alternative' vinegars such as verjuice, which was commonly used for pickling and flavouring until the nineteenth century. Made from the unfermented acidic juice of unripe grapes or apples, verjuice was used in the same way as vinegar and its milder flavour made it popular in many parts. It could also be distilled and stored for later use. Alegar was another mild vinegar made from sour ale or malt. Wine vinegar, however, was always regarded as the ideal for pickling as it was said to have the best flavour.

Vinegar pickling of all kinds of food suddenly became very popular in the sixteenth century in England when salted foods were losing favour and were gradually being relegated to the food of the poor. When the English farmer's wife had a glut of eggs, she would boil them hard, shell them and pile them into earthenware or glass jars and pour over scalding vinegar well seasoned with pepper, ginger, garlic and allspice. 'The eggs are fit to use after a month' and were quite a treat in the farmhouse kitchen. Similarly pickled were the small, firm 'top' onions, which were the best for the job. Where walnuts were common, the still-green nuts were gathered in July for pickling. An eighteenth-century English recipe directs that the walnuts should first be left to lie in strong brine for a week until they turn black (unless the moisture is first drawn out, it would end up diluting the vinegar and cause the pickle to ferment). After washing the salt off, the walnuts are packed into a jar with whole cloves of garlic, peppercorns and a few cloves. Some vinegar, spiced with nutmeg, Jamaica pepper and allspice, is boiled up and poured over them. They are left to stand overnight when the process is repeated. The jars are finally closely covered and tied down.

Jars for vinegar pickles had to be made from stoneware or glass. Because vinegar is so acidic, it would have dissolved the lead from the glaze of earthenware and poisoned the pickle. Coverings, too, were important and careful corking, tying with bladders or sealing with wax or resin all needed vigilant handling.

Other nuts, mushrooms, fruit and vegetables can all be pickled in the same way as the walnuts. The variations are in the raw materials and in the flavouring of the pickle. Adding sugar or honey produces a more mellow or sweet-sour pickle and adding spices gives it a stronger, additional piquant flavour. Some vegetables need blanching before pickling, others are cooked in the vinegar itself and some need no cooking. By happy chance it was realised that the repeated pouring of boiling vinegar over vegetables not only preserved them better but also made them greener. Pickles were usually left to mature for two to four weeks, though a crisp pickle could go soft after a few months.

The Japanese have always been passionate about their numerous kinds of pickles and relishes and their sour tastes accompany every meal. In Japan they make a variety of vinegars which are always fermented from rice. Some have quite a mild flavour and are not very acidic. Many of their 'pickles' are not strictly preserved foods, but they like to pickle slugs, radish and cucumbers soured in vats of fermenting rice bran, as well as pickling plums and making pickled plum 'jam' – 'sour as Hell's wrath' according to M. F. K. Fisher who, in 1978, spent 'two peculiar and dreamlike weeks' in Osaka at the Tsuji Professional Culinary Institute.

As well as plums, many other fruits such as quinces, peaches, nectarines, lemons, damsons, melons and grapes can be pickled, but unlike vegetables, they are not usually pre-salted. More often they are first cooked in either sugar or vinegar. In China one can find a wide range of vegetables pickled in vinegar as well as boiled peanuts stored in pickle juice. 'Chinese scallion' pickled in vinegar is much loved by children and pregnant women. There is a Chinese tradition that pregnant women crave pickles just as women in the West are said to do. Chilli peppers, both the hot and sweet varieties, which came from South America, swept through the Far East and Western Europe in the sixteenth century and became very popular in mixed pickles, their vivid colours brightening up those giant jars of vegetables one still sees displayed in shops and markets.

In many Middle Eastern households, pickles are still home made or they are bought from special colourful pickle street-booths. They are arranged in large bottles, the contents a medley of crimson, yellow, bright pink and many greens, 'a whole vegetable kingdom of imprisoned cauliflowerets, onions, turnips, cucumbers or green peppers, floating in spiced vinegar'.

Although fresh meat was rarely used for pickling in vinegar, there were many kinds of cooked meats such as brawn and 'collared meats' that kept well in a vinegar pickle. Collared beef could be hung up in a net and dried after pickling. Even an entire half-pig, boned and rolled into a giant collar, could be boiled till tender and kept in a vinegar mix for as long as six months. At the wealthier English tables in the sixteenth and seventeenth centuries, vinegar 'soused' meats were most often eaten cold with salads or as a side dish for dinner. Small birds such as sparrow, larks and squab pigeons were preserved in vinegar until their bones were softened when they were served in china saucers with pickled vegetables. Small pieces of meat as well as pig's trotters and ears were preserved in a spiced Rhenish wine pickle and ox tongues were pickled in wine and vinegar. In the nineteenth century a special 'Tonbridge' brawn was made from pigs kept in the Kentish cherry orchards. The head, ears and feet would be well salted for twenty-four hours and then plunged into the salting trough and weighted down in a good vinegar keeping 'all turned about in the pickle for a week'.

Salted raw meat was sometimes pickled and it was claimed to keep particularly well. Hannah Glasse gives a recipe in her 1747 book called 'The Jews way to pickle Beef, which will go good to the West-Indies, and keep a Year good in the Pickle, and with care, will go to the East-Indies.' The raw meat was salted for a week then packed in barrels and covered in vinegar. A thick layer of oil was floated on top. Raw tripe was similarly treated for shipping to the East Indies.

There is a long tradition of preserving fish by marinating it in vinegar. The word 'caveach', often used in old recipe books, comes from the Arab 'sakbay' meaning meat or fish pickled in vinegar. Brains or tongue could be caveached, but the method was most often used with fish such as cod, salmon, mackerel, smelts, red mullet, sardines, tunny and anchovies. The caveach method is explained by Hannah Glasse in her recipe 'To pickle Mackrel, call'd Caveach'. Holes were made in large pieces of fish into which the seasoning of pepper, nutmeg, mace and salt was 'thrust' with the finger. The pieces were rubbed over and then fried in oil. When cooled, the fish pieces were covered in vinegar and a layer of oil. 'They will keep well covered a great while, and are delicious.' Variations of fish caveach are also eaten in northern Italy, Romania, Turkey and the Balkans and a Spanish and Provençal version called 'escabech' is eaten as an hors d'œuvre. It is bought packed in jars at delicatessen shops and will keep for a number of months. The combination of cooking (or sometimes pre-salting), marinating in spiced acid and close covering in jars sealed with oil is an interesting example of a technique using a combination of preserving methods.

In 1648 during one of the terrible storms that lash the Cape of Good Hope, a Dutch ship, the *Haarlem*, broke up off the coast and two of its officers were washed up in Table Bay. Until they were rescued five months later, the men lived on the abundant, rich indigenous wild foods they found. On returning home they urged the Dutch authorities to establish a settlement there to provision the Dutch East India fleets with vital fresh fruit, vegetables and preserved stores. In 1652 Jan van Riebeeck, a ship's surgeon, went ashore at Table Bay with seventy men carrying building materials, agricultural equipment and sacks of seed. The Cape, the crossroads between the Atlantic and Indian Oceans, soon became known as the 'Tavern of the Two Seas'. The local inhabitants proved unwilling labourers, and so slaves were brought in from Java, India and Malaysia to work in the farms, gardens, vineyards, kitchens and storehouses. Most passing sailors had lived for months on ship's biscuit and salt meat and they soon learned to appreciate the new delights of foods prepared by Malay cooks, such as their dried seafood, spicy chutneys and a special potted pickled fish known as 'ingelegde vis'. The English called it 'curried fish', possibly because of the generous use of spices and seasoning, but it should more properly be called a 'pickled fish curry'. It was so popular that it was exported in great quantities to Europe for the home table.

The Malay were skilled fishermen and as the seas surrounding the Cape were bursting with a huge variety of fish and marine life, they were able to start preserving the fish almost as it came off the line. They split, gutted, salted and dried fish in roughly the same way as was done in many other places but they produced some delightful and exotic dishes from the results. According to the Cape poet C. Louis Leipoldt, whose 1933 *Kos Vir Die Kenner* is the classic Afrikaans cookbook, ingelegde vis should 'only be eaten cold and must be allowed to stand for a week or a fortnight before it is served. It may be packed in jars with a layer of fat on top and will keep for several months.'

This recipe for ingelegde vis is in Leipoldt's English-language version, *Cape Cookery*, and he says that it is the oldest that he was able to find:

> Choose a fairly firm-fleshed fish, such as geelbek or yellowtail; softer kinds, such as stock or kabeljou, will not keep as long. Clean and cut up the fish into equal sized pieces about three inches square; (but do not bone it. In properly made ingelegde vis the bones are so soft that they can be eaten without harm, thereby much increasing the nourishing qualities of the dish!) Fry the fish in lard; strew some salt on them and let them drain while you are making the pickle.
>
> For this you lightly brown sliced onions and a bruised garlic clove, a couple of crushed chillies, a dozen black peppercorns, a tablespoonful of moist brown sugar, and one or two lemons or bay leaves, stirring them constantly till they are well braised. Then add half a cupful of good curry powder, mixed with two cups of good vinegar, and let it simmer for a quarter of an hour. Now add enough vinegar to make the pickle into a fairly thick liquid. Put some of this at the bottom of the dish in which you intend to keep the fish, and put on it a layer of fried fish; cover with more pickle and proceed in the same way till the dish is full.
>
> Mix what remains of the sauce with more curry powder, boil it up with two cups of vinegar and pour this thin sauce over the fish. Put aside in a cool place for several days and serve when required with thin bread and butter . . . Or else pack it in a jar with a layer of fat on top and seal the jar so that it is airtight.

Leipoldt suggests that the dish would be 'greatly improved by the addition of a little tamarind juice', and that it is 'of course much more fragrant when it is made with freshly-prepared curry paste'.

Curiously similar to the Cape Malay pickled fish is one of the most popular English local specialities, 'Newcastle salmon'. Daniel Defoe in his 1727 *Tour through England and Wales* expressed his disappointment to discover that 'Newcastle salmon' in fact came from the river Tweed. The fresh fish was taken by packhorse to Shields, some sixty miles away, where they were pickled with a long-kept secret method. The fish were gently stewed in water, salt and strong beer. After they had cooled, they were put into pots and covered with a pickle of strong sour ale (alegar) and spices and then sealed. Pickled salmon the 'Newcastle' way was said to keep for a whole year and was eaten in great quantity by the poor living in the towns, who also ate pickled oysters, sprats and herrings. Cockles, mussels and winkles in vinegar were also very popular and were sold at stalls in the London markets.

Many local variations of vinegar-pickled herring also emerged, many of which are still popular today, particularly in Scandinavia, where they appear on every smörgåsbord, in open sandwiches or as starters. Rollmop and Bismarck herrings are uncooked varieties of marinated herring that are still sold in jars in supermarkets everywhere. The best herrings for marinating are fat, wet salted fish from Iceland. Typically, they are filleted and soaked in water overnight to remove the salt and then marinated for two days in a mix of boiled water, sugar, allspice, bay leaves, peppercorns and vinegar with some sliced onion and carrot. Sometimes, as in the case of Bratherings, the German delicacy, the herrings are fried before marinating, but more often the fish are hardened instead by the salt and the acid of the vinegar, in the same way that the acid in lemon juice can 'cook' fish to make the South American speciality 'ceviche'.

Many other fish pickles, such as salmon, pike and eel, the recipes for which start appearing in sixteenth-century English cook-books, could not keep for very long. Many of these recipes, however, were for garnishes and condiments to be eaten alongside the staple fresh or preserved foods. Although preserving methods were used, the main aim in many cases was not longevity but taste.

From Garum to Ketchup

Dr Johnson defined a sauce as something eaten with food in order to improve its flavour. An Italian, writing in the 1950s, poured scorn on such an idea saying that it would be difficult to believe that a man of Dr Johnson's intelligence and culture could have

'. . . expressed himself in these terms, if we did not know that Dr Johnson was English. Even today his compatriots, incapable of giving any flavour to their food, call on sauces to furnish to their dishes that which their dishes do not have. This explains the sauces, the jellies and prepared extracts, the bottled sauces, the chutneys, the ketchups which populate the tables of this unfortunate people.'

It is true that very few Italian restaurants are blessed with those red plastic tomatoes filled with ketchup or those sticky, half empty bottles of bilious yellow-brown sauces and chutneys that grace the tables of English and American cafés, burger bars and fish and chip shops. Yet condiments, as they were once called, are a tradition that goes back to the Romans, in Italy!

In fact, because vinegar, like salt, has such a strong and distinctive flavour, it has been an important condiment for people since brewing and wine making were first discovered. The Romans took vinegar on long journeys, where baggage had to be kept to a minimum, to dilute with water as a refreshing drink. Roman soldiers also took it with them on the march. Vinegar is still used with oils and other flavourings to make salad dressing today, but in Roman times bowls of pure strong vinegar were put on the table, in which to dip bread, vegetables, fish and meat before eating.

By this time, the preserving powers of vinegar were already well established. Columella, the first-century Roman authority on agriculture, wrote in his *De Re Rustica* that 'vinegar and hard brine are essential for making preserves'. The Roman epicure Apicius recommended preserving turnips with myrtle berries in honey and vinegar. The Romans particularly loved onions pickled in honey and vinegar. Columella includes a long list of vegetables routinely salted and pickled in vinegar including lettuce, asparagus, sprouts, cabbage stalks, butcher's broom, white vine, purslane and tender little stalks of fennel. Plums, he wrote, might also be preserved in vinegar and his recipe for pickling olives in vinegar is almost identical to the method still used in Greece and some other Mediterranean countries today. Fish were also preserved by pickling using a method learnt from the Greeks. The fish was first fried in oil, then seasoned with bay leaves, salt and spices. Finally, boiling vinegar was poured over it.

Many of the fish pickles were, however, more usually eaten as a relish rather than as a separate dish. The sweet-sour flavour of vinegar pickles was hugely popular in Rome, where virtually nothing was eaten without a sauce or dressing of some kind. To make these, a wealthy Roman spice cupboard contained a formidable list of dried herbs and spices. Dozens of Oriental spices were imported, including pepper, which was the most highly valued. Roman gardens existed only to grow numerous fresh herbs for medicine and flavouring such as rocket, sesame, anise, fennel, parsley, cumin, thyme, savory, mint and oregano.

This Roman passion for seasoning or adding flavour to their foods led them to look further afield for ideas for strong tasting sauces to pep up their meals. The Greeks had the answer. Long before the rise of Rome, they had been using a sauce made from a salt fish called 'garon'. The Romans adopted it and called it 'garum' or 'liquanum' and it became their great gastronomic passion, their favoured seasoning and their 'supreme condiment'. As with ham, a combination of food preserving techniques produced a gourmet speciality. Garum was made with the intestines of mackerel, small red mullet, sprats or anchovies, macerated in salt in jars and left in the sun for two to three months to autolyse, i.e. for the fish's own enzymes to digest the proteins. The acidic concentrated juices, 'self-preserving' in the same way as a vinegar pickle, were drained from this mush, sieved and stored in *amphorae*. Clear and golden in colour, this liquid could also be diluted with wine to make a sauce called 'oenogarum', with oil to become 'oleogarum', or with vinegar for 'oxygarum'.

The Romans set up factories to produce garum and traded it to Gaul and Iberia, where it commanded fantastic prices. Not only thought delicious, it was also a 'keeping' sauce full of essential nutrients. It retained its strong fishy taste almost indefinitely and was so powerful that only a few drops were required, making it particularly useful for travellers. The military made a cheaper version called 'muria', from inferior fish for soldiers to carry in their packs and dilute with water.

Related fermented fish sauces are still being produced in the Far East in vast quantities. In Thailand the most popular variety is called 'nam pla'. In Cambodia it is 'tuk trey', in the Philippines 'patis' and in Vietnam 'nuoc mam', now in great demand in Western supermarkets for making 'Oriental' dishes. Nuoc mam did not, however, find immediate favour with the Western palate. The writer Norman Lewis travelled through Laos, Vietnam and Cambodia in the 1950s trying, as he said, 'to make a sincere effort to throw overboard all prejudices concerning food'. He felt he was becoming quite a connoisseur of nuoc mam, which is always put on the table in a saucer for diners to dip their food into, until he heard it described by a fellow Westerner as 'having an odour resembling that of tiger's urine'. Lewis' 'vintage' description of the process is illuminating. 'Nuoc-mam is produced by the fermenting of juices exuded by layers of fish subjected to pressure between layers of salt. The best result as in viniculture is produced by the first drawing-off, before artificial pressure is applied, and there are three or more subsequent pressings with consequent deteriorations in quality. First crus are allowed to mature like brandy, improving steadily with age. The governor told me that he thought his stock, which he had inherited, was over a hundred years old. All the fierce ammoniacal exhalations were long since spent, and what remained was not more than a whiff of mellow corruption. Taking a grain of cooked rice, he deposited it on the golden surface, where it remained supported by the tension – an infallible test of quality, he said.'

The modern ketchup also originated as a dipping sauce. The name is derived from the Siamese word 'kachiap'. It began as a way to use up the 'pickle juice' in which fish or vegetables had been preserved. Kachiap, in China and Malaysia, was the brine pickle from pickled fish. The idea travelled the spice routes to England where in Tudor and Stuart times, pickled vegetables, herbs, mushrooms and walnuts were regularly used by the well-to-do to accompany dishes or flavour stews. The remaining pickle juice made a piquant seasoning, strongly flavoured by the spices and foods that had been pickled in it. Mushroom and walnut pickle liquors made rich, dark sauces which were bottled up as 'catsup', which came to be regarded as a condiment in its own right. The addition of anchovies, lemon, garlic and grated horseradish made the catsups even more piquant.

In the Berkshire Hills of Massachusetts, just after the American Civil War, Joshua Davenport started experimenting with catsup recipes that the settlers had brought over from Europe. The original American 'love apple or tomato catchups', made with their bountiful supplies of tomatoes, had been rather tart and included

only onions, mace, cloves, nutmegs and black pepper with a little wine. American catsups were 'indispensable with hash, fish cakes and baked beans', but a sweetened catsup was an 'offense against God and man, nature and good taste'.

But Davenport understood the American appetite for sugar and he added two cups of sugar to a gallon of tomato stock and a half-pint of vinegar flavoured with cinnamon, cayenne and salt. He may not have been the first to sweeten a tomato catsup, but he successfully sold his tomato ketchup and today, frankfurters and hamburgers cannot be eaten without it.

An early American tomato catsup

There are plenty of other bottled preserved sauces to choose from on the shelves today that have their origins all over the world. The fiery Tabasco sauce owes its origins to the American Civil War. The recipe for Tabasco sauce is still a closely guarded secret. The story is that a soldier fighting in the Mexican War found some pepper seeds (*capsicum frutescens*) in the state of Tabasco. The plant had pretty flowers that he thought would look nice in his garden back home in Louisiana. On his return, the soldier planted the seeds on the Island of Avery off Louisiana's coast. This was owned by the Avery family who were making their fortune with America's first salt mine, providing salt to preserve the meat to feed the Confederate troops. One version of the story has it that a plantation cook used the peppers to create a hot sauce, which the Avery family exploited commercially after the Civil War had ended. Another tells how when the Union army took the island, the family was forced to flee to Texas until the war ended. Three years later, they were able to return and found their mansion looted and their plantation in ruins. Nothing remained but a crop of Tabasco peppers and some piles of salt. Edmund McIlhenny, a son-in-law and former banker, experimented by crushing the peppers and mixing them with garlic, vinegar and salt. He aged the preserved mixture in barrels, siphoned off the liquid and bottled some in empty cologne bottles. The result was a strong, piquant sauce, which friends and neighbours loved so much that McIlhenny started bottling and selling the sauce and was soon successfully marketing it worldwide.

Along with kachiap, other spicy preserved delicacies were spread around the world by the booming spice trade of the sixteenth and seventeenth centuries. Malay chutneys, such as mango, became popular for livening up the bland European diet. Housewives would give ships' captains their own private orders to bring back quantities of pickles and spices. The famous 'atjar' remained a favourite relish. Atjar is made of a colourful and endless variety of vegetables and fruits – mango, dried peaches, lemons and pumpkins, baby cucumbers, corncobs, young beans and carrots and button turnips. They are cleaned and boiled and preserved in a very strong chilli pickle and bottled to be kept almost indefinitely. They can be nibbled as appetisers or served with cold meats. The Cape Malays also created a condiment called 'blatchang'. Originally made with pounded dried prawns and shrimps, later replaced with anchovies, blatchang developed different complex forms depending on whether it was preserved in tamarind juice, sugar or, later, vinegar. It also has travelled all over Africa and, according to South African writer Laurens Van der Post, it has even been found in a store in Aldeburgh in Suffolk.

When the English lost the struggle with the Dutch for the Spice Islands they concentrated their colonising efforts to the north. Chutneys, thick, sweet and spicy, seem to echo the days of the British Raj. 'Chutnees', sold with labels like 'Major Grey' and 'Bengal Club', were made from sweet mangoes, limes, tamarinds and plantains. The English interest in Indian curries, pickles and chutneys brought home by employees of the British East India Company, sent housewives and cooks hurrying into their kitchens to replicate these exotic foods. New, strong-tasting ingredients were tried out. Lemons, formerly pickled whole in brine and spices were now softened in spiced vinegar and sieved to a fine liquid pickle. To copy a chutney, melon or cucumber was used instead of mango; elder shoots could mimic bamboo shoots when pickled in spicy vinegar. One of the earliest pickles to take off in England was piccalilli. A recipe of 1694 with the title 'To pickle lila, an Indian Pickle' describes a brine and vinegar sauce, flavoured with ginger, garlic, pepper and bruised mustard seed and yellowed with powdered turmeric. In it were put pieces of cabbage, cauliflower, celery and other vegetables.

By the Victorian times, England had hundreds of commercially made sauces, relishes, chutneys, piccalillis, mustards and ketchups. Some of their labels are still on the shelves, others are long forgotten. One of the survivors, Worcestershire Sauce, was 'discovered' when a barrel of special relish, made from an Indian recipe sent in by the customer, was left in the cellar of a chemist shop in Worcester. It was forgotten for many years by which time it was well matured. Made from a well-kept secret recipe, and still bearing the chemist's name of Lea and Perrins, it has become one of the most famous and most ubiquitous of bottled sauces. Some may still remember Yorkshire Relish, Burgess's Anchovy Essence, Quinn's sauce for fish, Harvey's sauces and the imperial sounding Empress of India and British Lion. These were followed later by the similar HP and OK sauces.

Dorothy Hartley describes, in *Food In England* from 1950, a cab-shelter sauce: 'A dark brown spicy sauce made with chopped shallots, garlic, salt, pepper, sugar and mushroom catsup, used to fill the stoppered bottles on the scrubbed tables of the cabbies' shelters in the time of hansom cabs, shaken over steak, chops or London eggs.' Perhaps the most attractive sounding method was a nuns' sauce, made by sisters in a Yorkshire convent in around 1870. The relish was mixed and put in a leadless glazed demijohn and lightly corked. It was left at the foot of the kitchen stairs for a month, and everyone passing up and down to chapel (twice daily) had to give it a shake.

CHAPTER FOUR

SMOKING
Meat

*Many French houses still have a bread oven in the large fireplace,
like English farms. The idea is to hang the joints and sausages, once
cured, above the opening so that the smoke from the fire inside the
oven billows up and around them in a gentle steady waft. This system ensures that the temperature of the smoke never rises above
90°F, at which point the fat begins to melt, and the hams are spoilt.
By burning green branches you ensure plenty of smoke — for extra
flavour burn juniper, pine, sage, bay and heather. Beat the fire
down to keep it smouldering, not burning in flames.*
Jane Grigson, *Charcuterie & French Pork Cookery*, 1967

From the earliest times, food that was not drying satisfactorily
would have been hung over or near the campfire to quicken
the drying. In addition, meat and fish preserved by drying was also
traditionally hung up for safe-keeping under the roofs of huts and
around the smoke hole or chimney. In either case, the smoke of
the fire would have permeated the flesh, partly cooking and further drying it.

There are numerous chemicals in smoke including alcohol,
acids, phenol and other phenolic compounds and toxic substances,
some of which are now thought to cause cancer. These toxic substances, such as formaldehyde, inhibit the growth of microbes,
while the phenols also retard fat oxidation. Smoking is particularly
useful for preserving fatty foods such as bacon and herring.

There are two basic methods for smoking which depend on the
heat of the smoke. When food is 'cold smoked' the temperature
is no higher than 29°C (85°F). The smoke permeates the flesh,
slightly drying but not cooking it, and creates a mild, smoky
flavour. The preservation, however, is only partial and the meat
or fish will only keep for a limited period. Many kinds of cold

smoked or lightly smoked foods are eaten raw such as smoked salmon or smoked fillet of beef.

In 'hot smoking' the heat is raised to temperatures over 55°C (130°F) depending on the type of food. This method partially cooks the flesh, which hardens and turns a dark golden or reddish-brown colour, and produces a more strongly smoked flavour. Beef, venison, game, poultry, smoked trout and buckling are popular hot-smoked products. Originally smoking was combined with salting and drying but modern smoke cures contain much less salt and smoke than the old traditional methods and are much lighter smoked for a more delicate flavour. Smoked foods are now more highly valued for their flavour than for their keeping qualities.

In 1821 William Cobbett outlined in his book *Cobbett's Cottage Economy* the traditional home smoking method, carried out for centuries. He advised that when smoking a flitch of brine-salted bacon, 'Before smoking lay the fitch [sic] on the floor, and scatter the flesh side thickly with bran or sawdust (not deal or fir). Rub it on, and pat it well down upon it. This keeps the smoke from getting into the little openings, and makes a sort of crust to be dried on.' When hanging the meat up, 'Two precautions are necessary: first, to hang the flitches where no rain comes down upon them: second, not to let them be so near the fire as to melt.'

To prevent the smoke becoming so hot that the fat melted, the fire had to be well damped down with smouldering sawdust. Cobbett suggests that 'Stubble or litter might do' to keep it cool enough. Ready access to the right wood was also important. Softwoods such as fir or deal are resinous and can produce a bitter taste. Naturally, in regions where fuel was scarce, smoking was not widespread. Cobbett comments, 'I take it, that the absence of wood, as fuel, in the dairy countries, and in the North has led to the making of (salt) pork and dried bacon.'

Cobbett also discussed the timing for smoking meat, which he said must depend a good deal on the fire's size and constancy. This suggests that if care was to be taken with smoking, someone had to be keeping a watch for much of the time. No doubt for the farmer's wife it was just another chore to attend to as she moved through the day between kitchen, wash house, kitchen garden and farmyard. 'A month may do, if the fire be pretty constant, and such as a farmhouse fire usually is. But over-smoking, or, rather, too long hanging in the air, makes the bacon rust.' The flitch should be perfectly dry but not hard as a board, as no doubt it often was.

Just as important was protecting the meat, after it was smoked, to keep it 'free from nasty things that they call hoppers; that is to say, a sort of skipping maggot, engendered by a fly which has a great relish for bacon'. Frequently fir or other pine wood was thrown on the fire at a late stage in the process to give a resinous or 'tar' coating to deter flies. Smoked meats were also rubbed with pepper to keep off bats roosting in the chimneys who were rather partial to smoked meat. In many homes hams and bacon sides were sewn into muslin or coarse linen bags and lime-washed. In others they were buried in fine clean wood ash in a chest or large barrel or box and kept in sand, which kept out the air thus ensuring '. . . the bacon will be as good at the end of the year'. Nearly 150 years later, Jane Grigson suggests that for those still contemplating home smoking, the old ways are still best. 'Looking romantically back into the mists of agriculture, most people see the farmer's kitchen decorated with head-banging hams, suspended from heavy iron hooks at the far end of the room, away from the heat of the fire, but still dry and contented. And if you have a large kitchen, this is an excellent solution to the storage problem. Although it may be gratifying to glance occasionally at a golden ham, it is really much safer to sew it into a canvas, linen or calico covering, and limewash it three times.'

Many farms would have specially built smokehouses in the farmyard or smoke holes and bacon shelves in the farmhouse chimney. When these weren't available, simple smoke tubs could be made by turning an old hogshead upside down and suspending the meat pieces from hooks driven into the base. A slow fire was lit underneath and the barrel was kept damp to prevent it shrinking. The bung hole made a useful smoke vent. Jane Grigson recommends fitting a smoking box onto the wall above the fire or failing that to take the meat to an obliging local bacon factory.

As well as aiding in the preservation of food, smoking also creates quite new and interesting flavours. Like preserving in vinegar, smoking can transform the original food in quite a radical way, unlike dried or even salted food, which must be rehydrated or soaked back to something like their original form before they can be eaten. Fresh herring, for example can be used to produce such delights as kippers, bloaters, buckling and Arbroath Smokies. The same piece of fresh pork can be transformed into sweetcure smoked ham, spicy smoked sausage or sizzling rashers of smoky bacon.

The main ingredient in the creation of the flavour of a smoked food is the wood or fuel burned beneath it. Green oak sticks, juniper boughs, sawdust or chips of apple wood, birch, hickory and willow bark are favourites, but everyone had their own preferences. In 1750 William Ellis wrote that Dutch or hung beef was best made in the north: 'We in the Southern Parts of England do not prepare hung Beef so well as they do in Lancashire and the North; because they dry it there with the smoak of Turf, which gives the Beef such a very pleasant tang, that it is much coveted and sent for to considerable Distances.'

Dorothy Hartley, writing in the 1950s, came down in favour of oak sawdust for a good cool smoke. She also recommended throwing aromatic juniper berries and herbs onto the fire to give a special and distinct flavour. In her book *Food in England*, she gives an old Rhodesian farm method for sweet smoking hams using wild tree honey, said to be especially preservative with strong permeating powers. The honey had first to be warmed and strained of bits of bark and 'honey bread' or comb. 'Before you kill the pig' a pickle was made with salt, saltpetre, local spices, pepper, allspice and lashings of the honey plus some treacle. The hams were alternately 'put under a snow of dry salt in the salt trencher' during the cool nights and then put into the pickle during the heat of the day. This process went on for some three weeks when at last the hams could be dried and given a good cool smoke with oak sawdust and later some pine to give the meat a dark, slightly resinous cover against flies.

Mutton, goat and venison were also traditionally smoked in some regions, but the staple smoked meat all over the world was the humble household pig. In China, smoking was an important and ancient process for preserving food including pork, duck, eel and a kind of apricot. During the 1750s magistrate Li Hua-nan, travelling around China on business, made copious notes about the local diets and especially their food preserving techniques. Food was in short supply at that time and people were under constant threat of hunger. Pork was always the most available meat for the poor, but even that was expensive, so people found ways to preserve it. They pressed salt pork in a barrel, turning it every five days for a month, before drying it in the wind. Salt with crushed garlic was pressed into slashed strips of pork, which were then marinated in wine vinegar. Next, the meat was smoked over bamboo strips (or metal wire) and sealed in a clean jar. For the rich, noted Li Hua-nan, there was a gourmet equivalent: cypress-smoked Siamese suckling pig.

Sausages

Cows are for milk, pigs are for sausages . . .

As the conquering armies of Imperial Rome marched through Gaul, Britain and Germany, the local people must have been fascinated by the legionaries' food provisions, some of which they had never seen nor tasted before. As well as their small bottles of garum, soldiers often carried strings of dried or smoked sausages.

Sausages made a very nourishing and portable food as well as being a convenient way to preserve, package and store small bits of meat and blood in the home for the leaner months. Sausages were probably a more sophisticated development of haggis and other mixtures of coarse-cut meat, cereals and flavourings that were packed into the skins or stomach sacks of animals. Some sausages were prepared for immediate cooking and eating, while many others were dried or smoked to keep for long periods. The word 'sausage' comes from the Latin *salsus*, meaning 'salted'. The Romans, who loved highly spiced food, ate enormous quantities of spicy and phallic-shaped sausages, which were popularly eaten at pagan festivals. Not surprisingly, the early Christian Church condemned them. The Romans, nonetheless, developed a wide variety, including *pendulus*, a large slicing sausage, and *hilla*, a very thin sausage using the small intestine, rather like today's dried mountain sausages. The first-century Roman gourmet Apicius gives this recipe for the still famous smoked Lucanica sausage from southern Italy: 'Pound pepper, cumin, savory, rue, parsley, mixed herbs, laurel-berries, and liquamen, and mix with this well-beaten meat, pounding it again with the ground spice mixture. Work in liquanum, peppercorns, plenty of fat and pine-kernels, insert into an intestine, drawn out very thinly, and hang in the smoke.'

Pepper, the most popular Roman spice, was a strong deterrent against bacterial growth. The fat and airtight skins protected the stuffing mixture from airborne microbes and the spices and herbs helped to make the meat more palatable and easier to digest. Many of the preserved sausages still made today have their skins treated in some way to keep out bacteria. Often they are brushed with oil and then covered in a mixture of dried herbs, crushed pepper or ashes before being hung high up in the smoke-house or a cool, dry place.

Once it had taken off, the tradition of sausage making in Europe became an important part of meat processing after a kill, using up the leftover bits and pieces. By the Middle Ages, sausage making was becoming more sophisticated and fresh sausages were made with the meat from pigs, chickens, rabbits, sheep, goats and even oysters and horses. This would be mixed with a choice of bread-crumbs, eggs, ginger, mace, cumin, pepper, parsley, rue, bay, berries and raisins, pine kernels or dates and stuffed into intestines which, in England by the early 1600s, were twisted into links and strung up and sold at market.

'In the centre among the ∫heep-pens,' writes a contemporary observer, 'were tho∫e who ∫old in booths or at ∫talls oy∫ters and ∫au∫ages.' But these were not sausages for keeping, and it was advisable to stand to windward of a '∫au∫age ∫tall' because of their strong odours. Because of its damp climate, Britain does not have a tradition of matured or preserved sausages. The bland English sausages sold today would not pass as sausage for the French, Italian or German housewife.

In Italy, by contrast, many types of sausages are preserved. Some are simply air dried for many months in the hot Mediterranean breezes, but many others are subsequently smoked. Whether smoked or dried, they would then be hung up to keep in cellars or cool sheds, or stored in kiln-dried salt, slaked lime, charcoal, wood ash, malt culms, oat hulls or meal. Salted or smoked hams and sausages do not, contrary to advice on modern labels, keep well in the deep freeze and, if they are well prepared, there is no reason to put them there.

The number and variety of sausages and salami that have been dried, smoked or lightly fermented is so great and the names so colourful that it is impossible not to mention a few, just to hint at the mouth-watering wealth of the sausage world. Italy boasts some of the finest sausages of all types including the many famous regional varieties of raw air dried salami. Served in thin, cherry-red slices dotted with white, waxy pieces of fat, they are eaten as antipasto. For travel and snacks there are the thin, hard, spicy straps of 'peperone'. You can also find succulent smoked Italian 'bolognas' and a range of sausages made with pieces of cured meat such as 'coppa' and 'culatello'.

From Spain and the Iberian peninsular come the famous highly spiced smoked 'chorizo' made with red peppers or paprika, many kinds of air dried 'butifarra' including a sweet one and the hard cured 'salchichón'. From Majorca come the orange-coloured, soft but long-keeping 'sobrasada', whilst in Greece they make sun-dried 'loukanika' flavoured with red wine and coriander. In Cyprus the 'paphos' sausage is preserved in lard and in the Lebanon a famous pungent, smoked beef sausage is still very popular.

Many types of French sausages are made for cooking such as 'andouilles' and the blood sausages, including 'boudin noir', which is similar to black pudding. Most regional cured sausages are dried rather than smoked except for the cool smoked 'cervelet' and the smoked 'saucissons' from the Franche-Comté. Coarse-cut slices of dried French sausage, such as 'saucissons d'Arles', are delicious eaten with bread and fruit. Germany claims to be the sausage-eating centre of the world and the passion there for all types of sausage is legendary. These are traditionally eaten with sauerkraut, pickled cucumbers or black bread and washed down with copious quantities of German beer. There are said to be over a thousand types of German sausage ranging from the garlic and cumin flavoured 'Knackwurst', to the air dried 'Rohwurst' and a ham sausage called 'Schinkenwurst', which is cured over the smoke of beechwood and juniper berries. The square-shaped German 'Landjager' is dried and smoked with a hint of cherry wine, the 'Braunschweiger' is hot smoked, whilst the Austrian 'Wienerwurst' – claimed by some to be the original frankfurter – is merely lightly smoked. There are hundreds of kinds of salami from Hungary, Germany and Denmark and from Scotland comes the air-dried coarse venison salami. Norwegian 'reinsdyrpölse' is made with reindeer meat and strong spirits. 'Laap ch'eung' sausages are hung to dry in the cool, breezy mountain air of parts of China where, typically, they have probably been making sausages long before anyone else.

Crushing, smoking and curing food in Aouaria in French Guyana in the early nineteenth century

The Arawaks and Caribs, natives of the Caribbean, dried and smoked meat on green-wood lattices erected over fires made of animal bones and hides. The Caribs called this technique 'boucan'. The Spanish called the green-wood lattice 'barbacoa', which eventually grew into the modern 'barbecue'. This is now hugely popular in Australia and America but has nothing to do with smoking. Smoking does, however, have strong traditions in America, particularly in areas where outside drying was impractical. Until only quite recently, large farms and homesteads smoked the abundant produce reared on their land. Writer Paul Engle remembered his childhood at the beginning of the twentieth century helping on his Uncle's farm in Iowa:

> My job would be the ham. I would gouge holes in it with a steel knife-sharpener and fill them with salt, brown sugar, and a little saltpeter. Then the hams would soak in a tub of brine for a month or five weeks. Taken out and rubbed clean of salt, they were covered with pepper and more brown sugar and hung to drain for two days. The final step

was to put them in the smokehouse over a fire of green
hickory (the smoke itself was so rich I am sure a man could
have lived on it alone). That ham had no water or quick-
curing chemicals in it, just solid meat and natural flavors,
with a juice which, when mixed with milk and maybe a
pinch of flour, was transformed into a gravy with an
authority worth of an appetite honestly earned by hard farm
work in the open air.

Numerous Old World sausages travelled with the migrants to
America where they are still home made and smoked in many
homes. Sausage making was traditionally a job the children could
help with. The intestines would be turned inside out and soaked
in brine all night. The next morning they were scraped clean. The
children helped stuff, twist and cut them and then carried the
strings of shiny new sausages out to the smokehouse. One
American meat packer famously boasted that they used up 'everything but the squeal'. Paul Engle, however, remembers the sound
of fresh sausages popping and crackling in the frying pan. 'Now
listen there, boy,' said his uncle Charlie, 'you can hear the squeal
if you've got good ears,' and he could.

Fish

Around Lake Biskupin in northeast Poland, archaeologists digging
in the 1960s discovered a strange kind of ancient settlement. There
were forty-three peculiar pear- or bag-shaped holes and sixteen
hearths. Professor Z. Rajewski, who discovered the site and dated
it to around the ninth century, believed that it was the remains of
a sophisticated centre for the mass production of smoked fish. At
the bottom of the holes were fish bones and scales and the hearths
were covered with a thick layer of burnt bones and scales – the
remains of fish such as pike, bass, roach, bream and a very big catfish. Professor Rajewski and his team attempted to smoke some
fish using exactly the same techniques that they believed had been
used 1,100 years ago. After scaling and gutting, the fish, which
were mainly quite large, were cut up and soaked in brine for two
hours. Smoking experts who examined the site decided that the pit

was suitable for a hot-smoking process so the fish pieces were first smoke dried over the open hearths in temperatures of up to 100°C (212°F) and then hung on a rod in the holes over a smoke of oak sticks and green juniper. The holes were covered over with wood planks or a straw roof and left for up to two hours. If left any longer, they found that the fish turned tough and lost their necessary fat. The experiment, using authentic ninth-century equipment, produced some tasty golden-brown smoked fish.

In fact more primitive methods of smoking than this are still practised around the world. In many parts of Africa the tradition is for fish to be sun dried and hard smoked until almost burned. Large oil drums are covered at one end with wire mesh. The fish are laid on the mesh and smoked over a charcoal fire. Wet wood shavings are then scattered over the embers, producing a dense smoke. This kind of hot-smoked fish is called 'bonga'. Simple 'smokehouses' made from large old barrels or oil drums can be found still in use in many parts of the world.

In medieval Europe vast amounts of salmon were salted and dried, but in North America the Native Americans, because they knew nothing about the preserving powers of salt, relied on smoking and drying their fish. Catching salmon was laden with cultural significance for the northwest Native American tribes who believed that the fish were undersea people who put on salmon skins to swim ashore and offer themselves as food to the hungry land people who might otherwise starve. If the salmon runs had failed and the winter was severe, then whole villages did indeed starve. Chum and sockeye salmon, which are low in fat and ideal for preserving, were dried and smoked in huge quantities and stored for the hungry months. When freshly caught, some of the fish were barbecued over an open fire, cooked in earth ovens or simmered in pits of water using hot stones taken from the fire. But the huge surplus was filleted or cut into strips with deep knife cuts in the flesh and hung on drying racks exposed to the air. The drying process was speeded up by building smouldering fires made of alder wood underneath the drying racks and the fish were left to smoke for different lengths of time to make either a hot- or cold-smoked fish. To break down the fibres and encourage the drying and smoke penetration, the fish were regularly turned, rubbed and squeezed. After about ten days, the smoked fish were tied in bundles and hung in the rafters over the open hearth.

After the area was 'settled' by the white man, these Native Americans adopted the European method of marinating in brine before smoking, which does improve its preserving qualities. It also meant that the fattier types of salmon could now be smoked. An elder from the Lummi tribe described how his people kept their traditional ways of smoking their fish in a smokehouse whilst adopting the use of salt. 'They didn't wash their fish. They got these ferns from big fern patches . . . they'd carry them down the hill here. Then they'd have big beds of ferns six to eight inches thick. All these dog salmon would be laying there. Then the women, or whoever it may be, would butcher them: Then they'd take a handful of ferns and they'd wipe all this slime off them. Ferns were really sharp. They would clean the fish right off. The fish would be cut open. They sprinkled salt over them and then folded them back up. Then they set them overnight. The next day, they'd hang them up on top of the smokehouse and smoke them.'

The elder explained that they had a reason for not washing the fish. 'They said that when you hung them up they would be too moist and the flesh would tear and drop off. It would create steam and they would be too steamy. The salt would draw moisture out.' He also described how 'They would flop the row of salmon eggs over a group of sticks and they'd dry them too just like the salmon. I liked eating the eggs but they would stick to my teeth, so I didn't eat very much of them.'

Of course, this produced a version of smoked salmon very different from the wonderful delicate mild-cured salmon we eat today, which is cold smoked and eaten raw. Scottish smoked salmon, too, was originally hard and dry. In most Scottish fishing villages, households would have a wooden smoking shed built near the sea called a bothan. There was a hollow in the centre of the beaten earth floor for the fire but no chimney so that the shed would literally fill with smoke. Bothan-smoked fish included haddock, salmon, spelding and herring.

Hard- or hot-smoked 'red herring' were an essential part of the staple diet of poor people during the Middle Ages. Salted herring were hung up and double hard smoked until they turned a dull red. The hard-smoked red herring could be safely exported on the slow-moving sailing ships, packhorses or rumbling carts of the times, to markets far from the cold north seas in which they had lived. It was said that the very strong taste drove away hunger but it could be reduced by an overnight soak and then boiled with potatoes in their jackets for the classic 'Tatties an' Herrin'. But the herring caught off the Scottish coasts tended to be too fatty for successful trade in red cured herring and they were unable to compete with Yarmouth and Lowestoft where the fish arrived in a leaner state.

But there were plenty of other fish off the coasts of Scotland, and other 'smokes' used to produce tasty smoked fish that could withstand the long journey inland to markets of the Scottish and English towns. Amongst them was the 'Bervie', a cured haddock from Inverbervie near Aberdeen. The split and brined fish were heavily smoked with a fire of 'stickly' peat and partly decayed sphagnum moss from the moors, which flamed up and 'cooked' the fish. Bervie smoked fish were blackish-brown from a hard smoke and a particularly dry cure, which meant that they kept very well even in hot weather.

As the railways gradually penetrated into Scotland and transport generally improved, these tough, long-lasting cures became less important and the more delicate flavoured, less heavily cured fish took over. One of the most famous was the Finnan haddock named after the fishing village of Findon where, in the 1820s, the fisher-wives started producing their own home-cured haddock. The fish were gutted, split open and the heads cut off. After a good scrubbing to remove all the blood, the fish were brined with some additional sugar for a short while. Then they were spitted and hung up in the bothan with a carefully watched fire of good hard wood and fir cones to give the best flavour. The villagers packed these pale golden fish into baskets which they gave to the guard of the stage coach which ran from Aberdeen to Edinburgh where the guard had a brother in the fish trade. Finnan haddock became so popular that business grew rapidly.

Along the Moray Firth, fishing villages put up smokehouses and began to produce more sophisticated fish to send to London. Other specialities include the shortlived 'Eyemouths', the hard,

Making Red-herrings.

Huge medieval smokehouses were stacked with rods of herring to be smoked and then packed into barrels

glossy 'Aberdeens', well smoked in kilns or 'lums' with soft grey peat, and the light, golden yellow 'Moray Firths' or 'Buckies'. The famous copper-coloured 'Arbroath smokies' are still made just as they were centuries ago except that they are now smoked over oak wood or birch chips instead of peat. The fish are cleaned but not split, and hung in the smoke in pairs by the tails on little wooden spits or over old whisky barrels.

When prepared in the home, smokies were soaked in the brine pot and hung over the fire or in the chimney to smoke, and kept there easily to hand for the cook through the winter months.

Sometimes they were gently boiled until the skin came off and they were eaten cold or they were cooked in the oven with some butter or simmered in milk. Kedgeree became a popular dish with rice and hard-boiled eggs stretching the fish for a large family. Dorothy Hartley recalls her own memories of 'home smokies':

> It was over an open hearth on the moors that I first saw smokies, ranged in rows, where the open rafters came down against the wall. Here the low roof made a natural fish rack, and against the dark-tinted thatch the gold-smoked fish were thrust endways, in rows like pegs; when the wind came howling through the open door and set the lamp flame aswing, the live shadow would roll around their gold eye-discs, and the light flickering along their gold-twisted sides, would set them to a ghostly swim in the dry tide of the peat smoke.

Further south, towns along the east coast of England had also become famous for their smokeries. Yarmouth in particular developed the 'red herring' during the fourteenth century. 'A red herring is wholesome on a frosty morning: it is most precious merchandise because it can be carried through all Europe. No where are they so well cured as at Yarmouth,' enthused the sixteenth-century Lowestoft-born author Thomas Nashe. Along with salt herring, 'reds' were the cheap mass-produced food of the period, although smoked herring was always more popular than salt. Lowestoft and Yarmouth alone have exported hundreds of thousands of barrels of red herring to Italy, Greece, France and Holland as well as huge quantities sent inland to feed the English. Red herring, like salt cod, were also sent out to the slave colonies. An even harder smoked 'black herring' was also developed, which is still sent to Africa and is said to stand up to any climate, last indefinitely and taste terrible.

The methods used for processing red herrings changed very little. The shipboard salting was washed off and the fish re-salted for two weeks and then washed again. They were then 'rived' or 'speated' on sticks or 'spits' through gills and mouth, twenty-five fish to a stick, and smoked for fourteen days. The smokehouses had open tiled roofs for through-draughts and inside a series of wooden frames reaching from floor to roof, with small transverse beams, called 'loves', over which the sticks were placed in rows. A number of fires were lit on the stone floor using oak chips and these were kept burning for two days. Next, the fish were left to drain for a day and then the fires were relit for two more days and so on for fourteen days until the fish were thoroughly cured. A milder smoke cure giving a sweet, gamey flavour, produced the 'bloater', which was enormously popular around the areas where they were made such as Great Yarmouth but they did not keep or travel well.

In 1843 John Woodger, a Northumberland fish merchant, experimenting in his smokery, invented the herring 'kipper'. 'Kippered' salmon was a process already in use in Scotland in the fifteenth century. The word 'kipper' meant a salmon which had spawned (*kuppen* in Dutch means 'to spawn') and was therefore sluggish and in poor condition (hence the expression 'I'm feeling right kipper'). Thin and low in fat, this salmon, if they bothered to catch it, was simply split and smoked. 'Kippering' could also mean drying, but it was a delicate, smoky fish that Mr Woodger wanted to recreate and he adopted the name for a similar process he had developed with the herring. They, too, were gutted, split down the back, lightly salted and smoked overnight. Splitting before smoking meant less salting was necessary.

The harder smoked, very salty reds gradually died out as refrigeration finally arrived to help keep the more delicate cold-smoked fish such as bloaters and kippers. These were eaten with brown bread and butter and for many years reigned supreme on the breakfast and supper tables of Scotland and England. Until recently, first-class travellers could still get to enjoy the legendary British Rail breakfast kipper.

With the modernisation of fires and cooking hearths, home smoking all but died out. Big old-fashioned chimneys and open hearths were gradually bricked up and coal fires and stoves built in their place. As early as 1821 William Cobbett wrote that 'when there were plenty of farm-houses, there were plenty of places to smoke bacon in; since farmers have lived in gentlemen's houses, and the main part of farm-houses have been knocked down, these places are not so plenty . . . there is scarcely any neighbourhood with a chimney left to hang bacon up in'.

The factory-built electric home smoker, which first appeared around 1965, appeals to gourmet cooks, fishermen and hunters (many home smokers smoke their own catch or will freeze it first until a convenient time to smoke it or wait until neighbours have enough to pool their fish for a shared smoking). Modern smoking machines were also invaluable to small companies setting up in production selling gourmet smoked foods. In Europe and the US these mail-order businesses have proliferated, offering a fabulous range of products from smoked mussels, scallops and salmon to smoked boar, reindeer, duck or ostrich.

CHAPTER FIVE

FERMENTING

There is an old Korean legend about a poor farmer who had only a couple of wilted cabbages left to eat. He took them down to the sea and put them in a pot filled with sea water to wash and freshen them. When he returned a few hours later he found that the cabbages had grown bigger, and instead of a handful of limp cabbage leaves, the farmer now had some hearty-looking cabbage heads to feed to his hungry family. He decided, however, that if only a few hours made them this big, an overnight soak would surely produce even greater miracles. Next day the farmer returned full of excitement and looked into the pot. But he found to his horror that it was half empty. Not realising that it was the salt in the water that had brought about the change, he thought some thief must have sneaked out and stolen his secret. As he thought about how to find the culprit, the farmer took a handful of the reduced vegetable and chewed it. It was, he realised to his astonishment, not only quite different from the usual cabbage, but was also delicious. Thus, it is said, the famous Korean fermented vegetable pickles called 'kimchi' were born.

These kind of stories and legends are testimony to the human ability to observe and adapt, and to discover, through experience, trial and error, how to replicate and control the processes of nature in the fight for survival. As in other kinds of preserving, fermentation would first have been discovered when prehistoric hunter-gatherers found and ate fruit and meat that were naturally fermenting. They would also have seen that some of the foods they brought back to the home and stored began to ferment. As they developed a taste for it, they would have found that fermenting produces many useful changes in food. The flavours of fermented foods were intensified and the food became easier to digest, could keep for a long time, was quicker to cook and also seemed to be good for them. Crushed grains of cereal that became moist fermented as did grapes, figs and honey and later, when herding developed, it was found that milk left in a warm atmosphere soured and fermented. Fermenting created many kinds of new foods and drinks that could be kept to consume at a later time.

The skill and ingenuity of ancient people to harness these natural processes, to add chemicals and flavours and to combine with other processes to create new and beneficial foods never ceases to amaze. As communities became more settled and populations increased, these skills were developed and honed until there were thousands of different kinds of brewing and fermenting traditions in almost every part of the world.

The basic principle of fermenting is to promote the growth of certain micro-organisms on selected substrates, usually some form of sugar – maltose for beer, fructose for wines, lactose in cheese, added sugars in fermented sausages – to produce a desired end product such as alcohol in beer and wine, carbon dioxide to make bread doughs rise, and lactic acid in cheese making and in the curing of sausages. To preserve food, the right conditions for the fermentation – temperature, pH and, where appropriate, moisture content – are selected and maintained to promote the growth of desired organisms so that they swamp the unwanted and potentially dangerous contaminants that may rot or poison foods or spoil the fermentation. Once this has been achieved, many foods will keep very well.

In many types of traditional processes it is also usual to 'boost' or start the fermentation by introducing a batch of some useful organisms or yeasts, what is broadly known as a 'starter' culture. Around 4000 BC when leavened bread was already being made in Egypt, they used dates and figs to create their starters. Herodotus wrote that 'All men are afraid of food spoiling, but the Egyptians produce bread dough which has to be spoiled.' He was, of course, referring to yeasts for starting bread making and brewing beer. Some types of food are injected or rubbed with moulds to produce a special kind of fermentation. Penicillium moulds, for example, which create the blue veining in blue cheese, are naturally present in the caves and cellars where many cheeses are matured. In the past in many parts of the world the most basic kind of starter was created by simply re-using the same container repeatedly without cleaning it so that it continued to carry the fermenting organisms.

Fermentation as a preserving technique was especially valuable in cool, damp climates where drying and associated dry salting and smoking were unreliable and where long, unproductive winters made it necessary for large amounts of foodstuffs to be preserved. Preserving the leaves, roots and fruits of plants through fermentation is a very ancient practice and vegetables are probably the food we most associate with fermenting. There is considerable overlap here between pickling in vinegar and fermenting. The bacterial reaction that turns alcohol into acetic acid to make vinegar is itself a process of fermentation. As we have seen, pickling in vinegar creates an acid environment where micro-organisms cannot survive. For vegetables, fermentation takes the process a step further when, in the right conditions, the foods themselves create their own acids.

For this to be successful depends on the proportion of soluble sugars in the vegetables, the moisture content, the temperature in the first few days of fermenting (15–20°C 59–68°F) and on the exclusion of air. Adding salt (as the Korean farmer did), vinegar and other acids encourages fermentation by suppressing unwanted organisms, as well as contributing to the preservation. Although in Europe vinegar pickling has largely replaced fermentation, some traditions have survived as part of the everyday diet. Virtually all plants can be fermented, but the classic vegetable for preserving in this way is the cabbage.

The cabbage goes back a long way, but the firm, well-packed globe of crisp green leaves we know today is a fairly recent phenomenon. In ancient times the scraggy leaves from the large variety of wild plants of the brassica family were eaten. Cabbage is well endowed with vitamins and was traditionally believed to help counteract the ill effects of alcohol. The Greeks and Romans made various claims for its medicinal qualities. 'It has a powerful nature and a great force,' claimed one Roman writer, who believed it could cure cancer amongst other ailments.

The cabbage is not a sophisticated vegetable. It smells when it grows, it smells worse when it is cooked and when eaten it causes flatulence, which smells worst of all. In one of his satires Juvenal highlighted the differences between a rich patron and his poor client: the patron eats olives with his 'excellent fish' while the client is served cabbage as his 'nauseous dish'. In general, cabbage has always been regarded as a country food or a poor man's sustenance. Russian peasants have always subsisted on rye bread, kvas and soup made from pickled cabbage. By the early Middle Ages, boiled cabbage was one of the mainstays of the north European peasant diet.

The cabbage, though, has been fermented for centuries in many countries, the end result being commonly known as 'sauerkraut'. It is generally believed that sauerkraut was invented by the Germanic people and it was said to be the favourite food of Charlemagne. However, a very similar food was being made in China as early as the sixth century using cabbage, mallow, kohlrabi or mustard greens, melons and pears. These were put in preserving pots with salt, brine or rice mush where they were left to ferment. Men building the Great Wall of China were fed on a sauerkraut fermented in wine. Today in China families still make their own 'paocai' or 'yancai' – Chinese versions of sauerkraut.

Sauerkraut was being made in most rural homes across central and northern Europe until well into the 1950s and it still remains a popular home-made preserve. An early Polish method was to pickle cabbages in special ditches, whose sides were lined with wooden planks. Layers of whole cabbage alternated with layers of cabbage leaves, the top layer being shredded. In some areas of Poland the cabbages were first scalded in boiling water or quickly heated on a bonfire or in an oven. The layered cabbages were then pounded with feet or wooden clubs to release the juices and air bubbles. Later, barrels were used instead of ditches. The cabbages were then covered with a linen cloth and a wooden lid weighted with a heavy stone. Mould was removed from the top of the barrel periodically and the linen rinsed and wooden lid scrubbed. The water was topped up as required. Barrels of freshly pounded cabbage were kept for about a fortnight in a warm kitchen or stable and later transferred to a cellar or larder where they were kept for the whole winter. Sometimes sour or hard apples were added along with caraway seeds and dill. As with simple vinegar pickling, the tannin-rich leaves of oak and cherry could be added as well.

Until recently, an average Polish family pickled several barrels of cabbage during the autumn after the potato harvest. It was a communal activity with neighbours and relatives joining in to help and socialise. At the end of the work they held a party with traditional dancing. Sauerkraut, still extremely important in village cooking, is served as a vegetable with meat dishes or dumplings. In addition, the liquid is dredged from the barrels and used as a stock for soups made with cured pork, lard, flour and flavourings.

This method of preserving the abundant cabbage crop was, until recently, practised all over damp northern and central Europe. In Holland, tubs of sauerkraut were a common sight in the warm living room where they were kept for up to twelve days before being moved to a cool pantry or cellar. Sauerkraut is also a typical Bulgarian dish. There, it is usually prepared in large barrels filled with whole cabbage heads, salted with sea salt. Water is poured over them and sometimes horseradish and maize grains are added. For two weeks the water is drained daily from the bottom of the barrel and poured again into the top so that the salt is evenly distributed. The cabbage is then put in a cool place until, after about a month, fermentation ceases and it can be eaten with pork, beans, wheat groats and rice.

Sauerkraut travelled to the New World with the Germans, Dutch, Moravians, Romanians, Russians and many other peoples for whom this was a staple and traditional dish. It is still made in America in huge quantities using much more sanitary methods and with a generous addition, in some German-American communities, of sugar to please the American sweet tooth.

Cabbage is also the usual component of Korean 'kimchi', although radishes, turnips, cucumbers, aubergines, onions, garlic, chillies, chestnuts, pinenuts and seaweed and sometimes even fruit can also be used. It is probable that the origins of kimchi lie in the Chinese pickles that were brought to Korea in around AD 654 and were modified to suit the local food products and taste. Korean kimchi have a sweet, sour, fizzy taste and are very different from Western sauerkraut. Vegetables are fermented in very strong brine or salt with added spices and fresh ginger and some hot, spicy varieties were later created when peppers were imported in the early part of the seventeenth century. For most Koreans a meal without kimchi would be unthinkable. There are said to be over 180 different kinds, but the most popular is whole cabbage kimchi, which is prepared in large quantities in November for the coming winter. Preparing kimchi at home is still an important annual event. Making a year's supply for a family of five once required at least 100 heads of cabbage, though nowadays the same household living in town may make their own with only thirty heads. Many companies still give employees 'kimchi bonuses' in November to help them buy in all the ingredients for the winter kimchi production. All the family gather to help fill the jars, which are buried under the ground during the winter and are said to smell terrible when opened.

In much warmer regions, where the food supply is not seasonal but where fresh food does not keep for long in the heat, fermenting is also often used to keep foods. The Hawaiian Islands were first settled by the Polynesians in the fifth century after a voyage of nearly 2,500 miles of open sea. They were sustained by 'poi', a paste made from pounded taro root that they had fermented in large pits in the ground. It is still a staple food of Melanesia and Polynesia, eaten with fish, meat and vegetables or with milk and honey. In Fiji, if a young man wanted to marry he was expected to have a number of well-dug food storage pits before he could propose to his girl. Her parents would visit the man's home to inspect his storage pits to see if he was worthy of the marriage. Only if the young man could show that he was able to keep the surplus food from his garden properly would the girl's parents give their consent. Successful food preserving in the Pacific Islands, where the warm wet weather makes food go bad very quickly, was a sign of good husbandry and a good investment. Pacific Islanders have been preserving root crops, bananas and breadfruit in fermentation pits for at least 2,000 years. It was once the most important method of preserving large amounts of surplus food for times of need and for special ceremonies. The devastation caused by a hurricane as it rips through houses, breadfruit trees and fields of crops can take many years to heal. If the breadfruit trees are brought down, the people are forced to harvest all the fruit at once and they must quickly preserve it.

Fermentation pits have to be dug in a sheltered, well-drained place and lined with dried banana leaves with a further lining of green banana leaves or giant taro leaves to protect the food from the soil. The breadfruit, bananas, plantain or roots are peeled and cleaned and laid in the pit. More leaves are laid over the food and weighted down with heavy stones to keep it well sealed from air. After about four or five weeks the pit is opened and fresh layers of leaves are put down. After six to eight weeks, the breadfruit will have fermented and become soft with an acid flavour. Some can now be taken out to use and fresh food can be added. Clean fresh leaves must replace old leaves as they rot or become mouldy. The fermented breadfruit can be pounded into a smooth mixture flavoured with coconut or sugar and shaped into balls, which are wrapped in leaves and boiled or baked in an earth oven. Another way is to spread the fermented food out on mats to dry in the sun. When it has become crisp and dry, it can be stored in tins or pounded into a flour, which is then mixed with wheat flour and used to make biscuits, bread or cakes and other dishes.

Similar food preservation techniques were practised by the New Zealand Maoris and they acquired a taste for fermented food. The 'higher' the food, the better the Maori seemed to have liked it. One traditional favourite was 'paua', a kind of tough abalone, which they buried in the ground for some weeks until it was soft enough to slice like cheese. Alternatively, partially husked maize was tied up in a bag and left in the running water of a stream for up to six months. The evil-smelling mushy grains were then scraped off and cooked with salt in clear water. This 'kaanga-pirau' was then eaten with more salt. Potatoes were similarly immersed, then skinned, mashed, formed into cakes and baked in the ashes of the fire to make 'kotero'. The isolated Maoris had an obsessive interest in food preservation, storage and trade. Sadly, the trade brought them into contact with the outside world where they were rewarded with deadly diseases such as measles, whooping cough and venereal disease and their numbers were decimated.

In many parts of the world food was preserved by burying it and allowing fermentation to occur, resulting in a softened, rot-ted, but edible food. Originally this might have been done to hide or protect food from insects and thieves until the hunter could return for it. In England in the Middle Ages, venison was sometimes buried instead of being hung, but this might have been because it was poached and it was necessary to hide it. Charcoal burners were habitual poachers and often buried rabbits and small game under their ovens where they became 'high'. Retaining its own moisture while lying in the cool, moist ground meant the food would slowly ferment using its own yeasts and enzymes, resulting in a preserved food with a very strong flavour. In China, too, they buried eggs until they were fermented to the point of decomposition, though the story of the 'thousand-year-old egg' is a popular misconception. In some cases the right combination of natural acids in the soil helped preserve the food. European fishermen who worked off the Newfoundland coast sometimes buried their catches of cod, salted and dried, under the turf until they were ready with a full shipload to return home across the Atlantic. It was believed that the soil on these coasts had magical preservative powers. The magic turned out to be borax, which is antiseptic and is found in these areas in a high concentrations. Elsewhere the natural soil acids were given a helping hand. An archaic Slovakian method for preserving venison was to bury the meat in wooden vessels in highly acidic ashes. In the Northern Islands, including those of Scotland and Ireland, underground chambers called 'souterrains' were discovered attached to hut circles containing the remains of animal bones and some grain, either lying loose or in storage jars, while on the floor were layers of charcoal and wood ash. Sir Lindsay Scott, who discovered the chambers, believes that the ash was used to preserve foods, a theory born out by Martin Martin who visited the Isle of St Kilda in 1695. He reported that 'They preserve their eggs in their stone-pyramids, scattering the burnt ashes of turf under and about them to defend them from the air . . . They preserve them six, seven or eight months as above said, and then they become appetising and loosening, especially those that begin to turn.'

Burying and fermenting fish was also a common practice similar to game hunting, it was usual, when there was a substantial catch of fish in waters too far to transport home in one journey, for the fish to be buried underground to keep it cool and safe from predators. In South Africa the Hottentots buried fish in the sand until they were well rotted. However, this kind of fish preserving is most often associated with Scandinavian communities where pike, perch, trout, salmon and other fat fish were traditionally buried in the ground to ferment along with some kinds of cheese and crocks of aquavit, their potent alcohol. In Iceland shark meat was buried in hollows in the sand in carefully layered pieces, close together to keep out the air, and covered with a pile of flat stones to press the flesh down as it fermented in order to avoid air pockets. The Inuit continue to bury and ferment whale, seagulls and wild duck in this way. Fish parts not normally used for human consumption were also buried to keep fermented for hard times. As recently as the 1940s, cod's heads were buried in the Faroe Islands until they became very high, when they were dug up, washed and scraped clean and boiled before eating. Vast quantities of fish were also simply fermented in barrels of brine. Farmers from inland would journey to the coast in the autumn to buy barrels of strong smelling, fermented herring to feed the household through the winter. The stronger the smell, the better the fish, which they ate with potatoes or their dried flatbrød.

Gravlaks (or gravlax) is now a popular luxury food on the menus of high-class American and European restaurants. The name means buried or 'grave' salmon. However, the luxuriously pink, thin slices served up on our plates today have not been buried, although a modern technique of pressing produces a similar result. These very old traditions have survived in many parts of Scandinavia as well as in Iceland. In the past, there were two traditional methods. For the short term they used a mild fermentation; the fish were put into barrels of brine and buried in the ground to keep cool for a few days where they became soured as 'surlaks'. The highly fermented, better preserved method was used for the large summer catches to keep them for the long winter when snow and ice made fishing difficult. Quantities of the raw fish were sandwiched between layers of birch bark and fir branches, weighted down with stones and buried in a hole dug into the ground which, even in the summer, was cool enough to act as a natural ice box. Only fat fish could be fermented in this way such as the Norwegian fermented trout 'rakørret' or 'rakefisk'. This is a great delicacy just as popular today as it was hundreds of years ago. Rakefisk lovers are invited to special rakefisk parties where the stinking, soft, fermented fish is eaten with boiled potatoes washed down with plenty of beer, aquavit and drinking songs.

In Sweden Baltic herrings are fermented into 'surstrømming'. Barrelled up with a small quantity of salt and left to ferment in the warm midsummer air, it is still made and can now be bought in cans. Jaakko Rahola writes that it 'smells so terrible that most people cannot even imagine eating it'. He describes how in the Thirty Years' War, 350 years ago, the Swedish and Finnish soldiers fighting in Germany stopped to have a feast whenever a shipment of surstrømming arrived from the north. Like rakefisk parties, surstrømming feasts still take place today, accompanied by boiled new potatoes and raw onions, preferably out of doors as the smell can permeate a whole house so that it is uninhabitable for many days.

Kegs of butter were also buried in the peat bogs of Scotland and Ireland right up to the eighteenth century. Left in the cool, acid ground, the butter slowly fermented; it was said to need seven years to reach the desired taste. In 1931, archaeologist Professor J. Ritchie found an intact keg of fermented bog butter on the Isle of Skye. He found that it 'Tasted like rancid butter with a slight acrid flavour and a long, acidic aftertaste'. The food historian C. Anne Wilson in *Waste Not Want Not* wondered whether burying butter in this way was primarily a 'desire to provide against famine in a time of glut' or 'a positive wish to turn the butter into what was regarded as a delicacy by changing its flavour'. This question of priority of purpose is relevant to most parts of the world where fermenting is common.

As we have seen, fermenting can radically change the taste of certain foods creating strong, even overpowering, characteristic flavours and smells that many cultures have become habituated to but others find disgusting. The Scandinavian love for fermented fish is no more understandable to an outsider than the Korean passion for kimchi. But taste and necessity gradually developed together into traditions handed down from generation to generation. Now many fermented foods, because of their very distinctiveness and unpopularity with outsiders, have taken on cultural significance and the enjoyment of them and involvement in the rituals of preparation and eating is part of belonging to a certain country or people.

The flavours of many types of preserved meats have been improved by partial fermentation. The passion in England for hanging game before it is cooked allowed the meat to autolyse or ferment slightly, which breaks down its fibres. This makes the meat easier to chew, renders it more digestible and gives it a heightened or 'high' flavour. Likewise some preserved meats, whether dried, salted or smoked, have also undergone a degree of fermentation, which enhances their keeping quality and the texture and flavour of the meat. From the now-lost city of Salamis in Cyprus came the raw, matured 'salame' sausage, which spread through Europe into the wide ranges of salami of Hungary, Italy and Denmark. Brine-pickled meats, traditional bacons and hams became mildly fermented while some dried meats, such as charqui and sausages filled with raw coarse chopped meat like chorizo, peperone and cervelat, have also fermented slightly.

The evolution of different taste preferences around the world – tart, acidic flavours in Russia and eastern Europe, subtle fermented foods in Japan, spicy sour tastes in southeast Asia – can often be traced to their food preservation techniques, particularly in the case of fermenting, which produces some of the most distinctive flavours of all the preservation methods. Fermenting was so important to the Lithuanians that they worshipped a god of pickled food called Roguszys. In many households in northern and eastern Europe, a very early technique of fermenting still survives. Kept by the fireside was a clay pot used for fermenting a kind of sour soup, known in Poland, for example, as 'zur'. It was the practice not to wash this pot so that a small amount of soup was always left carrying the useful bugs to start the next fermentation. After the meal some boiled water was poured into the pot with some flour (oats in the south, buckwheat in the east and northeast, and rye elsewhere). The zur pot was left overnight by the warmth of the kitchen range. In the morning the mixture was sufficiently sour. For special occasions, meat, sausage, bacon, cream and flavourings such as garlic, bay leaf, pepper could be added if the family could afford them. For fasting days, only salt and garlic were added and during Lent it was often used instead of fats and milk.

Some of the many processes for making and then packing katsuobushi in Japan in 1799

To celebrate the end of fasting in Poland, the zur was 'killed' (as a symbol of fasting and of winter) by burying the zur pot, breaking it or hanging it from a dead branch. The distinctive taste is still popular – factory-produced zur is now sold in bottles and there is even a synthetic zur powder that can be bought in the shops.

The Japanese have a wide range of special fermented foods in their cuisine. Perhaps the most extraordinary and quite unique fish product is still in everyday use in Japan. Cured 'katsuobushi' is produced from fish called bonito or skipjack tuna, which are transformed by various processes into something resembling a mouldy chunk of wood. From this hard block of fish, tiny slivers are shaved with a kind of carpenter's plane mounted on a box to catch the shavings. These are regularly used to give flavour and aroma to numerous dishes, soup stocks and dipping sauces. They are also used as a relish or sprinkled on top of cold tofu. The large bonito are filleted and simmered for twenty minutes to set the protein; later the small bones are carefully removed with tweezers. The fillets are hot smoked in a chamber using oak, wild cherry, beech or chestnut wood for six or more hours a day, every day for up to two weeks. The smoke-dried fillets are then put out in the sun for three more days for a further drying. Then begins the process of 'moulding', which removes any remaining moisture; the fish are put into special chambers that are impregnated with the mould *Aspergillus glaucus*. After two weeks, when the mould has begun to grow inside the fish, they are put out in the sun again to kill off the surface mould. This moulding and sunning is repeated over six weeks until the pieces resemble 'well seasoned' small lengths of dry wood. The sound given when you tap one piece against another indicates the quality. The higher the note the better the katsuobushi, which will keep for ever. Nowadays Japanese cooks buy convenient bags of ready shaved katsuobushi, though Professor Richard Hosking believes that the fragrance cannot compare with that of freshly shaved katsuobushi.

In China the most characteristic and traditional way of preserving is by fermenting. There, ritual has developed around the process of creating the important 'starter' cultures. Unlike the usual Western 'starters' taken from previous batches, Chinese starters have to be made from scratch every time and involve a chain of complex operations. From a sixth-century agricultural text, the *Qimim Yaoshu*, we learn that 'Every step is detailed with striking precision. The quantities employed, the best place for each operation to be carried out, even the smallest gestures are minutely described . . . this precision is made possible through a system of "touch stones" based on sense perception.' This has obvious practical roots, for the rigorous methods ensured a micro- biologically cleaner process and guaranteed the best results every time. In contrast to the more primitive European methods, in China everything must be scrupulously clean, the men must scrub their finger nails and 'Pregnant women were not allowed to interfere with any part of the fermentation process as she was herself considered to be in a state of fermentation'.

As elsewhere, many of the Chinese fermented products are now created for reasons other than strictly preserving. The Chinese make numerous tasty fermented condiments such as relishes and vinegars. There are two groups, 'chi', exclusively from soya beans, and 'jiang', which can be made of either vegetables or meat and fish. 'Shih', a salted and fermented black bean sauce first made around 200 BC, was at one time the only relish that the rural population in China could afford, though it was also very popular in the towns. Tofu, a Chinese staple, is a curd made from various kinds of beans and peas, first used in about the tenth century. It is made by adding sea salt to bean milk and was originally intended as a preserved food but was later adapted for use as a coagulent. Tofu was introduced to Japan in the thirteenth century and became popular with the Buddhists as a substitute for meat and dairy products, which their religion forbade them to eat. It is now made and distributed all over the world for sale to vegetarians.

As well as improving flavours, fermenting can transform indigestible and unpleasant-tasting foods into a range of highly nutritious ingredients. Soya beans, for example, when simply cooked are rather indigestible have a poor taste and a 'beany' smell and, like the unfermented cabbage, cause flatulence. But after fermenting with a mould, the soya beans become softer and more palatable, more nutritious and better tasting. The soya bean, rich in proteins, calcium and iron and free of saturated fat, is now regarded as the perfect health food. 'Tempe', a curd 'cake' made from fermented soya beans, is widely eaten as a meat substitute in Indonesia. Soya is possibly the food most often fermented, being turned into a huge variety of products from bean curd to soy sauce. There are numerous varieties of rich, dark flavouring sauces, made from fermented soybeans mixed with wheat, traditionally made in China, Korea, Japan, Thailand, the Philippines and Indonesia. The most famous is soy sauce, now as liberally splashed over Western food as tomato ketchup. The traditional processes for soy sauce production, which originated in China, are lengthy and complex involving many different steps to achieve the right maturity and flavour. Modern production methods are, however, much quicker and the sauce is now also pasteurised before bottling.

Japanese cuisine is characterised by the special flavourings of 'miso', soy and katsuobushi. Fermented soybean products have a 'meaty' savoury flavour, with some more subtle than others. Miso, a thick fermented paste of grain and soybeans, is used as a nutritious and savoury flavouring. The barley or rice is first steamed and when cooled but still warm is inoculated with spores of a mould called *Aspergillus oryzae* and left to culture for two days. Soybeans, which have been washed, cooked and crushed are then added, with the addition of salt and water. This mash is then put into large, deep cedar vats and left while the slow process of fermentation begins. The best miso requires two years during which time the bacteria and enzymes transform the grain and beans into a highly nutritious paste similar in consistency to peanut butter, with a dark colour and a rich aroma. There are many varieties of miso eaten in different regions. Some misos, made with vegetables and whole soybeans are quite sweet and are eaten as a relish rather than used as a flavouring or ingredient. In the early days miso was made by Buddhist monks at the temples and was consumed enthusiastically at the imperial court. By the tenth century it had spread into the provinces when Buddhism became more concerned with the common people who were encouraged to eat a simple healthy vegetarian diet. A peasant meal might consist of rice, barley (or millet for the very poor), pickled vegetables and miso soup. The nutritional contribution miso made to the diet was extremely important.

Probably the

Huge jars of pickles and racks of cured meats were ingredients for this army of cooks preparing a Chinese banquet

oldest, certainly the earliest recorded fermenting technique and universally the most popular is the production of alcohol such as beers and wines and distilled spirits like sake and aquavit. Fermented wine of all kinds plays an important role in Chinese cuisine. Everywhere local 'wines' are made by fermenting glutinous rice, sorghum or millet. In the novel *The Scholars*, written in the early Ch'ing period (late seventeenth century), food and drink are lovingly described and noted. One character tells of a jarful of liquor as 'Made of two pecks of glutinous rice and twenty catties of fermented rice. Twenty catties of alcohol went into it too, but not a drop of water. It was buried nine years and seven months ago, so it must be strong enough now to blow your head off!'

Apart from their obvious attractions, the ancient art of brewing and distilling also had the additional advantage of improving the diet of poor rural communities where every vitamin, mineral and protein was vital to survival. Fermented grains are more nutritious than ordinary cereals and the consumption of kaffir beer is known to have added valuable B vitamins to the poor maize diet in many parts of Africa and helped to prevent the dietary disease of pellagra. Fermented vegetables also retain their essential vitamins and the sauerkraut barrel in poor north European homes would have helped reduce the incidence of scurvy. Unfortunately only a few ships' captains, such as Captain Cook, thought it worthwhile taking supplies of sauerkraut or pickled vegetables to sea.

As well as making food tastier, more digestible and more nutritious, in some parts of the world with little supply or variety of foodstuffs, fermenting can even be used to process foods otherwise inedible or even poisonous. Across Europe in Neolithic times, primitive sour soups were being made from fermented nettles, cardoons, sorrel and the young growth of birch and willow trees. The bitter cassava tuber, which contains cyanide, must be properly treated with a lengthy process of washing, grating, fermenting and grinding until it is finally reduced to a useful flour used extensively in Africa, South America and some Caribbean islands. Fermenting is also used to make edible parts of animals not normally consumed. This is practised in regions where there is great scarcity of meat, in order to use and preserve every last scrap.

Of all the African and Middle Eastern countries, Sudan is said to have the largest number and greatest diversity of fermented foods with as many as eighty distinctly different fermented foods and drinks. In her book *The Indigenous Fermented Food of the Sudan*, Hamid Dirar writes: 'The struggle of man in these regions of the world against death as a result of hunger, malnutrition and famine is so deep rooted that practically all aspects of life of an individual and of a community are completely shaped by this ever-present battle.' With necessity and taste again developing together, the Sudanese now like strong, rancid flavours, particularly in meat. 'Shermout' is made of dried and fermented strips of meat, hung inside the house until it has a very strong 'rotten' taste and sometimes is even maggoty. There is another more primitive method, now only used in remote rural communities, where the mud houses include a special enclosed humid and dark store room called a 'gatee'. Here the meat is hung on ropes to slowly mature. No light must enter 'not even the moonlight'. A quick-dried shermout, similar to charqui, is also made with strips of meat laid on metal trays or palm leaves, or hung on a rope to dry in the sun. Sometimes made with gazelle poached from game parks, the meat has to be hurriedly butchered and dried, including the bones, to avoid arrest.

The scarcity of fresh meat (like most herding communities, the Sudanese rarely kill their animals for food) has meant that the people have discovered ways of not wasting a single piece of a dead animal. 'Miriss' is made from pure fat fermented, mixed to a paste and stored in special fermenting containers called 'burma'. It is sold in the markets of western Sudan where its presence is always well advertised by its foul smell. 'Dodery' is prepared from chopped up fresh bones left in water in the 'burma' to ferment for three days. The liquid is reserved for flavouring while the bones, marrow, fat and tendons are crushed into a paste, mixed with 'combu' (potash) and returned to the burma for further fermenting. The resulting soft paste can be kept in the burma for two months, rolled into balls or sun dried for longer keeping. Shermout, dodery and miriss are all used to make highly flavoured sauces.

High in the Nuba Mountains they make 'Kaidu-digla' or 'bone ball'. Some chopped and dried bones are crushed into a coarse meal, using large stones. Powdered combu and water are added to make a thick paste and formed into balls or fat discs, which are fermented and sun dried. 'Bone balls' will keep for many months and can be reprocessed and used for a variety of dishes. No possible sources for meat go unexploited. The wild rabbit of southern Kordofan is skinned and the offal, head and feet are removed. The remaining carcass is put in a covered jar and left to ferment for a few days. The softened, fermented carcass, called 'jerbi-jerbi', is boiled in water then pounded up with a pestle and mortar into a paste, which is used in a rich meaty soup or sauce with peanuts, sesame or melon seed paste, onions, salt and spices. Other small wild animals such as the porcupine, ant-eater, mountain rodents and wild geese are similarly treated.

Another hunter process for those not on the run from game wardens is 'um-tibay'. It is made from all the bits of a slaughtered gazelle that most might expect to leave for the vultures. The intestines, spleen, offal and bones are chopped into small bits and everything is stuffed into the stomach bag, which is hung on a tree and left to ferment for about three days by which time a very strong smell has developed. This haggis-like package is then buried in hot coals or ashes and left to cook slowly overnight. The next day it is cut into strips and either eaten straightaway or sun dried. Nomads and camel traders who drive their herds to Egypt still use dried um-tibay and shermout on their long journeys. Unfortunately the popularity of these foods has resulted in the severe depletion of the gazelle population. But the skins, hides, hooves, brains, spinal cord and even the urine are all turned to nutritional use by fermenting. Nothing is wasted.

⌒ CHAPTER SIX ⌒

MILK PRODUCTS

The Bedouin were desert dwellers in the arid areas of North Africa, Arabia, Jordan and Syria who once herded sheep and goats, riding their camels across vast stretches of inhospitable, sand-swept desert. Sometimes they stayed in oasis villages where fresh provisions were close at hand but at other times food and water were several days' travelling away. The Bedouin have always held a great fascination for Western explorers and travellers. Lawrence of Arabia is perhaps the most famous, though the first time a foreign traveller accompanied a caravan was in 1503. In 1876, Charles Doughty lived with some Bedouin groups for two years travelling with them into the interior deserts where he experienced the hardships, the famous hospitality and the constant danger of being an infidel amongst Muslim people. Doughty also recorded the Bedouin way of life, unchanged for hundreds of years.

Apart from driving the herds and some occasional hunting or raiding, the men did little of the work. The women made and broke camp, cooked and cared for the children and young animals and did the milking and dairying. It was an extremely hard life, always on the move, sleeping under the stars in freezing cold and riding before a burning sun in the open wilderness. 'Each mother,' Doughty reported, 'is seen riding upon a camel in the midst of the roll of her tent-cloth or carpet, in the folds lie nested also the young animals; she holds her little children before her.'

Like many Westerners, Doughty both loved and feared the desert wilderness. 'Wanderings in all the waste of Arabia, criss-crossed with the old trodden camel paths, there is not any place of the immense waste, which is not at some time visited in the Arab's wanderings, and yet whilst we pass, no other life . . . is in the compass of a hundred miles about us.' He looked out for the dried camel dung, occasional sets of trivet stones of old nomad pot-fires, or other comforting tokens of humanity passing through. In some deserted places he found the little ovals of stones which marked the death of a nomad generations before or inscriptions on rocks in the mountains and caves – nomad graffiti of those who passed by yesterday or a thousand years ago.

Doughty also had a keen interest in the Bedouin diet, which had to be easy to carry and last well in these extreme conditions. Water for men and animals was the primary concern. This was carried in skin bags and guarded ferociously. There would be the occasional game meat such as desert hare, which they flung whole onto the fire and ate, still intact with its fur on. From their small supplies of wheat grain they made a primitive bread known as 'abud' with a dough mixed with a little of their precious water, cooked in the embers of a dried camel dung fire. The main staple, however, was milk from their animals. Where possible, camel milk was drunk fresh and after a hard day's travelling was very welcome. Doughty appreciated the 'sounds of the spretting milk under the udders in the Arabs' vessels. Food for man and health at a draught in a languishing country'. The milk was brought foaming in a bowl, which the children licked up afterwards with their fingers.

But milk is one of the most perishable foods and it is not surprising that a wide variety of techniques were developed in antiquity by nomads like the Bedouin, which would preserve and transform milk into some of the most famous, delicious and most commonly eaten of all preserved foods. For the now less nomadic Bedouin, milk is still their primary trade commodity, and most of their income comes from sales of their clarified butter, known as 'samn'. Some fatty, coagulated milk is churned in inflated goatskins then heated with flour and some cumin and coriander until it is pure fat with no water left. The samn is poured off and stored until they have produced enough to sell in the city markets. A very similar product still made in India is called 'ghee'. A way of pre-serving butter to keep in the Indian climate, ghee also has religious importance because of its purity.

Nomadic peoples such as the Bedouin could not cultivate vines for wine making or cereals for brewing, and many kinds of fermented, or alcoholic portable milk brews were created and greatly valued where the water was scarce or unsafe to drink. The Nordic 'barbarians' who poured into the Roman Empire in the fifth century brought with them a curdled sheep's milk called 'skyr', which they salted and sealed into large containers for the winter. For Icelanders, skyr is still a national drink. Genghis Khan and his Mongolian tribes, who swept across Asia in the thirteenth century, were sustained by another alcoholic sour-milk drink called 'koumiss' or 'kumiss', made with mare's milk from their herds of semi-wild horses. It is still made by the Kazakh peoples of Turkestan, who believe it has great health-giving properties, and it is now an enormously popular alcoholic drink in parts of China.

Nomads from different regions make many fine distinctions about the way koumiss is made and used. According to the thirteenth-century French emissary, William of Rubruck, one method involved the mares' milk, on the edge of fermenting, being poured into a large skin bag and beaten. They used a 'piece of wood made for that purpose, having a knot at the lower end like a man's head, which is hollow within; and so soon as they beat it, it begins to boil like new wine, and to be sour, and of a sharp taste; and they beat it in that manner till butter comes.' Having tasted it, he observed that 'After a man hath taken a draught, it leaves a taste behind it like that of almond milk, going down very pleasantly, and intoxicating weak brains, for it is very heady and powerful.'

'Kefir', a centuries-old, mildly alcoholic sour-milk drink, which also originated with the central Asian nomads, is still much enjoyed in the Balkans and parts of eastern Europe, where it is believed to ensure a long and healthy life. It is made from sheep, cow's or camel's milk fermented with a special starter of kefir grains. These are a mixture of several acid-producing cheese bacteria combined with casein, and look like small yellow seeds. These are soaked in warm water until they have swollen to three or four times their original size when they are put into the milk and left there for a day. Herders and nomads the world over produced similar drinks. Nomadic groups on the Pamir plateau in Afghanistan produce an acidic drink called 'chambat' from the milk of their Bactrian camels. In Mongolia, yak milk is fermented into a kind of fizzy drink and Laplanders produce 'pima' from reindeer's milk.

The Bedouin, too, Doughty reported, would leave their fresh

milk out overnight to sour and ferment. But for a lighter, more portable and durable product, they produced a dried milk, called 'mereesy' or 'jamid'. Easy to carry and quick to reconstitute, it lasts one or two years, only growing harder. It can be ground to a powder and mixed with water or even sugar, dates or flour if they have them. Mereesy is made with the buttermilk remaining after samn preparation and contains the protein and carbohydrate parts of the milk. As described by Doughty, this buttermilk was boiled to a 'hard shard and resembles chalk'. When diluted with water it made a drink 'much to thank God for, in lean times and in the heat of the year, in the wilderness; in the long dead months when there is no milk . . . excellent to take upon journeys'.

But even the nomad tires of the interminable milk diet and Doughty recalled a sheikh calling out to him 'Hast thou not some Damascus Kaak [biscuit cake, like ship's biscuit] to give me to eat? Wellah, it is six weeks since I have chewed anything with the teeth; all our food is now this flood of milk.' Dates were particularly essential to survival in the desert. An ideal travelling food, they dried naturally in the sun, grew prolifically at most of the oases and were cheap. They provided excellent nutritional balance with the milk products. Even the camels ate them for fodder. Sometimes there were delicious fresh dates with their 'sappy sweetness' and their hard berries 'melted to ripeness in the trees, softly swelling under the sun with the genial honey moisture'.

Vegetables hardly featured in the nomadic diet though the women knew where to find some wild plants for food and medicine. They made a kind of cake from samhh, a wild plant with fleshy stems and branches full of brine-like samphire. The grain or seed when ripe was beaten out and ground into a coarse flour. It could be made into a 'wild bread', black and bitter, or a porridge said to taste like camel milk. The flour could also be kneaded with dates and a little samn, into cakes to be eaten raw, 'A very pleasant and wholesome diet for travellers who in many open passages durst not kindle fire.' For really long journeys, the women made quantities of a rich preserve called 'ba-theeth' by heating a mix of parched flour, dried dates and samn and kneading it into a solid mass. It had excellent keeping qualities and needed no further cooking. Like mereesy, ba-theeth could be carried in saddle bags to chew en route.

Long before we were obliged to use powdered milk in plastic cups of tea or coffee on our travels, the Mongols had invented a form of dried milk they could take on the longest journeys and quickly reconstitute when required. Marco Polo, on his travels across central Asia in the thirteenth century, described how the Mongol people made this amazingly simple and portable preserved food. 'First they bring the milk [almost] to the boil' and 'at the appropriate moment they skim off the cream that floats on the surface and put it in another vessel to be made into butter, because so long as it remains the milk can not be dried.' This is because any cream left in the liquid would have quickly turned the dried milk rancid. As we have seen from other dried foods, the removal of all fats is essential for successful preserving. Marco Polo continues, 'Then they stand the milk in the sun and leave it to dry. When they are going on an expedition, they take about ten pounds of this milk; and every morning they take out about half a pound of it and put it in a small leather flask, shaped like a gourd, with as much water as they please. Then, while they ride, the milk in the flask dissolves into a fluid, which they drink. And this is their breakfast.'

Many of the descendants of these fearsome Asian nomads — such as the Kirghiz, Kazakhs and modern Mongols — have now become settled or semi-nomadic but they have nevertheless retained their pastoralist traditions, especially in their food. Like the Bedouin, their diet is frugal, consisting mainly of bread and milk products but, unlike the Arabs, yoghurt is predominant.

Yoghurt is said to have originated with the Aryan tribes who lived on the shores of the Black Sea and in the Caucasus. It has many different names: in the Caucasus it is known as 'matsun', in Turkey and the Balkans 'yogurtlu' (the 'g' is silent). In Iran it is called 'mast' but when it is diluted with water, it becomes a cooling drink called 'abdug'. The health-conscious Scandinavians make 'taetta' and in India they make 'dahi', their own kind of creamy, soothing yoghurt, a wonderful counter to hot, spicy curries. It is also used in many countries as a meat tenderizer. The best yoghurt is made from sheep or buffalo milk, which produces a particularly creamy clotted richness.

Yoghurt is milk curdled by the action of beneficial acid-producing bacteria that convert the lactose (milk sugar) into lactic acid and create a soft curd with a fresh, tangy flavour. Anyone can make yoghurt: simply tip a pot of good-quality natural yoghurt into a litre of warm milk and leave it to stand in a warm place for twelve hours (or in a thermostatically controlled home yoghurt maker) and you will have the same product that has been made in Asia and the Balkans for centuries. Yoghurt is valued throughout the world for its alleged health-giving properties. There are numerous centenarians living in the Balkans who reportedly owe their longevity to a diet of yoghurt and it is known to be good for the digestive system as it destroys many of the microbes that cause infections in the intestine. It is also much more easily digested than raw milk, so essential nutrients such as calcium and phosphorus are absorbed more easily. Yoghurt, whether 'natural' or processed and mixed with fruit flavourings, can now to be found on the shelves of every Western store and supermarket and more recently 'health-giving' fermented drinks originating in the Balkans have become all the rage.

But it took a very long time for yoghurt to become accepted as part of the Western diet. The sixteenth-century French king, François I, was said to have been cured of his depression and neurasthenia by some sheep's milk yoghurt brought all the way from Constantinople, not as yoghurt but as a flock of sheep, that had to walk all the way to Paris. There, they were freshly milked for the king's yoghurt and then died of exhaustion and cold, which seems poor reward for their service. The king recovered but the miracle yoghurt was forgotten again in Europe for many centuries.

Although yoghurt is a form of preserved milk, it does not keep for very long and various ways have been developed to keep it for longer. In Iran and the United Arab Emirates they still sun dry forms of yoghurt pressed into cakes or balls. Sold in the markets, they have a hard, chewy texture and a rather sour salty flavour and are used as an ingredient in a wide range of dishes. In the mountain regions of Lebanon dried yoghurt balls called 'lebne' are preserved in oil and are still an essential part of the local diet.

As well as yoghurts and fermented milk drinks, nomads and other travelling people have made many other fermented and dried milk products. The Turkic nomads of the Golden Horde, from whom many of the Kazakhs, Kirghiz and Tartars are descended, found new ways to use milk during the Middle Ages. Their 'kurt' is made by mixing raw milk and yoghurt and ageing it in a small leather barrel. The mixture is churned to make butter, then the curd is removed and converted into kurt by boiling it down until it is solid and then drying it on a board. While at the boiling stage it can be mixed with thickened yoghurt and salt for a richer product. Kurt can be used in a variety of ways: it is pounded in a mortar and added to soups, stews and porridge or mixed with sweet butter.

Wherever herding is predominant, preserved milk products have been vital parts of the diet. While travelling as a missionary in southern Africa in 1855, David Livingstone found quite another type of milk curd. 'The Bechuanas put their milk into sacks made of untanned hide, with the hair taken off. Hung in the sun, it soon coagulates; the whey is then drawn off by a plug at the bottom, and fresh milk added, until the whole sack is full of a thick sour curd, which, when one becomes used to it, is delicious. The rich mix this in the porridge into which they convert their meal, and, as it is thus rendered nutritious and strength-giving.'

In parts of central Europe large flocks of sheep graze during the summer in mountain pastures far from the villages. Each day's milk is poured into large barrels and salted so that it thickens of its own accord. On the next day more milk is added which also thickens, the process is repeated until the barrel is full and covered with a thick layer of fat. This is called 'samokis' and keeps until the following spring.

Similarly, in the Orkneys and on the coasts of Scotland shepherds made a sour-milk drink called 'bland'. It was traditionally made of buttermilk with hot water added to make a white cheese-like substance floating in a liquid or serum. This liquid, or 'bland', was stored in barrels, where after a time it would ferment into a refreshing, 'sparkling' drink. Sometimes drunk as a substitute for beer or ale on land, right up to the nineteenth century fishermen would also take a few kegs to fortify themselves as they sailed far out to sea in their open boats.

Carrying milk in skin bags slung from pack animals as they moved from camp to camp also led nomadic people to the discovery of butter. The shaking and 'churning' movement of creamy milk resulted in the cream separating itself from the liquid and forming into greasy lumps which could be squeezed together into solid 'pats' of butter. A valuable source of nutrition, especially in colder climates, butter will keep well, though this kind of primitive travelling butter would have been very greasy and rancid compared to the kind of butter consumed in the West today.

The ancient shaking method for making butter spread rapidly and survived in some remote places until quite recently. There is a description of a butter-making party in northern Scotland in around 1870 that beautifully illustrates the simple shaking method of making butter: 'They put cream in the skin of a lamb or the skin of a sheep and they threw it from one to the other . . . by the time it had gone fourteen or fifteen times round the company, you had butter.' The labour-saving plunge churn had, however, developed in Europe by the eighth century and by the Middle Ages butter making had become quite a sophisticated business. Butter kept so well that large quantities were made for market and export. Summer butter was salted down and packed into wooden firkins or tubs to sell in the winter. Dorothy Hartley in *Food in England* explained how to preserve good butter for winter. It had to be extra well washed, pressed dry and packed into clean well-scalded kits (small kegs or tubs). The butter was held in the hand and then 'flung hard' into the kit to ensure a close pack. Each layer was salted and then rammed down with the knuckles of the closed fist to get rid of any air pockets. The shepherds who spent all summer high in the Welsh hill pastures had barrels of dried oat cakes sent up to sustain them. They lived on these oat cakes with butter, cheese and curd dishes all summer. At the end of the summer, the oat cake barrels were filled with butter and brought down to the villages to be sold for winter consumption.

West Country dairymaids were famous for their 'Clowtyd' or clotted cream, made by very slowly heating the cream on a layer of milk until it thickened and had a 'cooked' flavour. It is not strictly a preserved food but clotted cream was popular with sea-going travellers as it kept relatively well packed close into sealed tubs and even now it can usually survive the modern postal service in a thriving Devon and Cornish mail-order business.

* * *

Most people over fifty will recall the childhood pleasure of plunging a finger into a can of thick sweetened condensed milk and slowly licking the lovely, gooey, over-sweet gunge. These cans have travelled to the extreme ends of the world and revived travellers, soldiers and mountaineers. It was particularly popular in the tropics, especially with the Memsahibs in the colonies. Concentrating milk is in fact quite an ancient practice. In India buffalo milk is boiled down to a paste called 'khoa' and used in their rich sweet confections. But it was not until the nineteenth century, perhaps the high-water mark of the marriage of philanthropy, science and innovation, that a way was found to preserve milk almost indefinitely without drying.

In America, news of the terrible deaths by starvation and of cannibalism amongst the Donner Party of migrants, who in 1848 took the wrong route west and became trapped in the mountains over a long, deadly winter, horrified the nation and set Gail Bordern, a local surveyor-land agent on a life-long mission to find new ways to make foods long lasting and portable. One year later, Bordern had already 'made an important discovery'. He had invented a meat biscuit '. . . an improved process of preserving the nutritious properties of meat, or animal flesh, of any kind, by obtaining the concentrated extract of it, and combining it with flour or vegetable meal, and drying or baking the mixture in an oven in the form of a biscuit or cracker'. That summer Bordern gave his meat biscuit to some friends who were also embarking on the long and dangerous journey to California and in 1851 he took samples of it to the Great Exhibition in London, where he promoted it as useful for naval expeditions, long voyages and sieges. It received special commendation by the Exhibition judges, though no one appears to have taken it up for production in Britain.

On his return voyage, Bordern's ship was hit by storms so severe that the wretched cows in the hold were too seasick to produce milk for the babies on board. One immigrant baby died and the pathetic hungry cries of the other infants moved Bordern again, this time to find a way to produce a nutritious preserved milk that would travel and keep without spoiling.

Despite six years of effort and $60,000 of his savings spent, Bordern's meat biscuit business was failing to produce any profits and so he turned all his attentions to preserving milk. He borrowed vacuum pans from some Shaker friends living at New Lebanon NY and started experimenting with a process for making a milk product that did not discolour, did not have a burnt taste and would last for a reasonable time. It seemed a tall order but eventually he felt sure that after much trial and error he had finally found a way of condensing milk that made it keep. Bordern, like so many others before him, did not at the time realise that it was the heating process that had destroyed the micro-organisms in the milk. He was doing the right thing but without knowing it and had produced a pleasant tasting, condensed milk with added sugar to help inhibit bacterial growth. New Yorkers, so long accustomed to drinking fresh milk adulterated with chalk to make it white, molasses to make it seem creamy and water to make it go further, did not immediately see the benefits of Bordern's milk. But he persisted and by a lucky chance he met a wealthy grocery wholesaler on a train who became convinced that the product would sell. He gave Bordern the financial backing he needed to set up his own company, which he called the New York Condensed Milk Co. At first he hawked bottles of his milk from door to door, his sales increasing as New Yorkers gradually learned about how their 'swill' milk was treated and how it came from Brooklyn cows fed on distillery mash. Sales were further boosted with orders from Union Army provisioners and he finally made his fortune selling condensed milk for field rations for soldiers fighting in the Civil War. Bordern created his own Eagle Brand which he exported all over the world in competition with similar British and Swiss products.

Another American concerned with the high number of children dying as a result of suspect milk was Elbridge Amos Stuart, a Quaker grocer from Indiana. He, too, invested his savings to create another new process, an unsweetened sterilised, evaporated milk in cans, which he then sold in enormous quantities to gold seekers on their way to the Klondike. He called it Carnation Milk.

Both Bordern and Stuart were hard-working, caring men of a type that the nineteenth century produced, fired with a passion for success coupled with a genuine desire to see real improvements in people's health and diet. Bordern died in 1874 and his tombstone reads 'I tried and failed, I tried again and again and succeeded.'

Cheese

> Cheese is milk that has grown up . . . it is pre-eminently
> the food of man – the older it grows the more manly it
> becomes, and in the last stages of senility it almost requires
> a room to itself.
>
> Edward Bunyan (1872–1939), *The Epicure's Companion*

In the fifth century BC there lived in Persia a great philosopher and religious reformer called Zarathrustra. He decided to become a hermit so that he could contemplate his moral philosophy free from distractions, so he retired to the desert to be alone and meditate. Legend has it that Zarathrustra survived in the wilderness for twenty years on nothing but water and daily slivers cut from one ancient and gigantic cheese.

Making Gruyère cheese in 1760 involved various processes and equipment including heating, milling, draining, salting, moulding and maturing

The production of giant cheeses has a long tradition. They were usually the hard, long-lasting cheeses such as Italian Parmesan, English Cheddar and Swiss Emmental. Large Holland cheeses were taken on long fishing expeditions and were often described as 'cannonballs'; one ship's records reveal that it set sail in 1675 with 'a great Chesshyre cheese' on board. As early as 1600 there were Cheddar cheeses so large that two men were needed to lift the cheese onto the table.

Large cheeses were most commonly made in communities where milkings were pooled in a co-operative. For sending to market, one large cheese was made instead of several small ones. They were transported on carts to market where they were cut up into portions for sale.

Giant cheeses were also made for festivals and, occasionally, vast family cartwheel cheeses can still be found in remote rural areas. Val Cheke tells a story in her 1959 book *The Story of Cheese-making in Britain* about a party of exhausted 1930s skiers taking refuge in a small inn on the Franco-Swiss border. They were appalled to find the inn was filled with a macabre collection of glass cases containing the preserved corpses of deformed animals and amazed to see, propped up against a wall, an enormous and ancient 'family' cheese weighing between 2 to 3 hundredweight. It was 'blackened by age and hard as horn, like some great wagon wheel without the spokes. A wedge-shaped opening showed that it had been attacked on previous occasions of jollity, and a further wedge was now prised out and every guest received a chip. Washed down with copious draughts of wine and beer, the hardened casein succumbed to the digestive processes of the convivial eaters, and gave no ill effects.'

In 1841 a giant 'commemoration' cheese was made at Pennard in Somerset from the milk of 730 cows. It had a circumference of 9 feet, 4 inches, a depth of 20 inches and it weighed 11 hundredweight. This enormous Cheddar cheese was presented to Queen Victoria as a wedding gift from the patriotic people of Pennard. It was reported to have been uneatable but it was not, however, unbeatable because the Canadians, who have no tradition of cheese making but had successfully adopted processes such as cheddaring, sent an even more gigantic cheese to the 1893 World Exhibition in

Chicago. This cheese, called 'the Canadian Mite', made in Perth, Ontario, weighed 10 tonnes (22,000 lb) and used up 103,000 litres of milk. It was taken on tour, causing quite a stir everywhere until it finally found a home in a London restaurant where it had to be cut open with gardening tools. The customers vowed that the two-year-old monster still tasted delicious.

Cheese is amongst the oldest, most nutritious and best-preserved staples of both peasant and manorial larder and some of the hard cheeses, if properly made and matured could be kept for many years. Perhaps the Archdeacon Denison, when he wrote a letter to *The Times* in January 1887, was stretching things a bit when he claimed to have kept a piece of Cheddar under a glass on his hall table for forty-one years. Despite having become rock hard, the cheese was, he wrote, 'still sweet'. (It is difficult to imagine why the Archdeacon kept his cheese so long and why he kept it in the hall rather than the larder or dining room.)

Cheese was an essential, palatable and popular food in ancient Jerusalem, Greece and Rome. The hard, keeping types of sheep and goat's cheeses were invaluable as robust and portable produce and quickly became important for the export trade. Cheese was also known to be very nutritious, and was especially important to rural people as a source of home-produced protein. The Romans fed hard cheese to their wrestlers and gladiators to build up their strength. At the cheese market in Rome one could find Ligurian sheep's cheeses, the famous 'luna' or moon cheeses from Etruria 'remarkable for their size, each one weighing up to a thousand pounds', smoked goat's cheese (a Roman favourite), cheeses from the Gard, the Lozère, Dalmatia, Savoie and Gaul. Hard, matured cheeses such as Parmesan or Pecorino were made famous by Roman legionaries who flavoured them with pepper. Every soldier carried a chunk of cheese in his knapsack. As it would need to keep well and stand being jolted about over long distances, the legionaries would take hard cheeses such as those from the mountain regions of Gaul, the Alps, the Jura and the Massif Central. Cantal from the Auvergne and Beaufort from the Alps, ancestors of the English Cheshire and Cheddars, were also popular.

The ancient experts, such as Pliny, Columella, Cato and Appicius, all discussed and wrote about the value and merits of cheese and cheese making. They knew that animals fed on aromatic plants gave well-flavoured milk; they wrote about which were the best breed of animals to use and the best methods to apply in order to achieve perfect curdling, as well as giving tips for storage and recipes for cooking with cheese. Virgil in the *Georgics* recommended picking laburnum, sweet clover and salty herbs 'in abundance' to feed to the animals, while Columella showed an understanding of the principles of hygiene, the use of rennet and the subsequent draining, salting and storage of cheese, which they called *formaticum* (hence the French *fromage* and Italian *formaggio*). It was also during this time that cheese presses began to replace weighting on the moulds. Although a great deal of human ingenuity has gone into working out the many varied sequences in the production of hundreds of different kinds of cheese, the basic methods have changed little over the years, and Columella's description might seem familiar to a traditional cheese maker today.

Like sausages, some cheeses are designed for long storage and others are for short keeping or eating fresh. Fresh cheeses are cream or soft curd cheeses made by simply souring the milk. They are not true cheeses and will not ripen if stored. The matured, long-lasting 'preserved' cheeses are ripened using enzymes from rennet and from micro-organisms. The harder, longer travelling cheese also developed tougher rinds to protect them.

As anyone will see who leaves a bottle of milk out of the fridge, the milk soon sours and becomes semi-solid. The solids are the curds and the liquid is whey. All that is needed to make a compact and delicious food is to drain the curds, usually in a mould. In ancient times this would be either a wicker or rush basket, an earthenware pot with drainage holes or a calabash punched with holes. Alternatively, the curds could be simply squeezed or pressed by hand. The drained-off whey was used as a drink for farm workers and to feed the pigs. The drained curd eventually forms the kind of soft curd cheese that will only keep for a while in cool conditions, though some types of curd cheeses are preserved by brining, smoking, drying or bottling in oil. The Armenian 'tchanakh' is preserved in vats of brine as are many curd cheeses made in Georgia and the Caucasus. The Afghanis, who depend on dried fruit from their orchards and cheese from their goats, sheep and she-camels, make 'serat' from sun-soured sheep's milk. The resulting curds are kneaded into balls before being smoked and then dipped in wax to preserve them. 'Bandal' is a well-known smoked Indian cheese of buffalo milk with a special, spicy taste from being smoked over fires made with cow dung. In Nepal and Tibet they make small cheeses from fermented yak milk, moulded between two stones and then wind or sun dried. Some semi-soft cheeses can also have their life prolonged by washing them in brine, beer or spirits and the Swedes make a 'Priest's cheese' that is given a good wash in neat whisky.

But true, long-lasting cheeses require the addition of rennet extract. Rennet, containing the enzyme rennin, is the digestive juice secreted in the stomach bag or vell of suckling ruminants. Possibly people discovered they could eat the solids or 'maw curds', the curdled remains of the last feed found inside the stomach of a slaughtered calf or kid. They may also have noticed that when they carried milk in the stomach bags they used as containers, it curdled faster and became thicker and that the resulting curds kept a good deal longer than milk simply left to sour overnight. Rennet contains natural enzymes that go on working on the curd until it eventually ripens into a semi-solid substance like a big 'junket'. Gradually people discovered that a small piece of the vell was sufficient to transform the curd into cheese and that they were able to preserve the vell for producing rennet. In poor regions, where livestock was too precious to kill for rennet, cheese makers turned to vegetable rennets. It was found that extracts of certain plants had similar coagulating powers to rennet. The sap from a fig or melon tree is still used in the East, while the plant juices from ladies' bedstraw, known as the 'cheese-rennet herb', was also used to coagulate cheese milk giving Cheshire and Gloucester cheeses their yellow colour. Jewish cheese makers in particular, who are forbidden by their *Kashrut* to combine meat and milk, used fig tree sap and ladies' bedstraw. Other wild plants with varying degrees of effectiveness have been mentioned throughout history such as spearwort (which is poisonous), artichoke, teasel, some kinds of thistles and the butterworts. Many cultures used wild plants to curdle their milk. In North Africa the people of the Maghreb added artichoke beard, which had been dried and preserved in jars, and sometimes fig juice was used. In northern Slovakia, dried milk curds used to be mixed with cherry leaves and yeast and left until half rotten. In nearby Bulgaria, wood ants (containing formic acid) or a particular kind of thistle was used. Modern 'rennet' is made by fermentation and is thus a 'vegetarian' rennet.

Although the process is now mechanised, in the traditional way of making Cheddar cheese, for example, the curd had to be broken up or cut by hand or with wooden utensils. The curd pieces remained in the whey, which was heated up while the curds were gently stirred about until the acidity of the curd was judged to be right. In the days when cheese makers used instinct and experience, temperature was tested by dipping the elbow into the whey and acidity was judged by the consistency and texture of the curd. Acidity has long since been measured in the laboratory and may now be controlled by on-line pH meters that measure and record the development of acidity from the beginning. When the predetermined level of acidity is reached, the whey is drained off.

The drained curds now had to be milled, a process once done by tearing the curd by hand and later with hand-turned spiked rollers or 'chip mills'. The milled curd was then salted, cooled and mellowed and finally packed into moulds or 'vatted' where it was pressed under weights. The moulded cheeses were regularly taken out to be scraped, resalted or 'dressed' in cloths. Once pressed, the cheese was put in storage to mature.

Until the discovery of pasteurisation and other modern hygienic methods, cheese making, ripening and storing must have been a terribly hit-and-miss affair. Many of the old techniques were very crude and fraught with dangers throughout the process. Successful cheese making depended on so many factors: the cows themselves and the type of pasturage; the temperature of the milk as it was processed; how the skimming, draining, mashing or breaking of the curd and squeezing out of the whey were carried out; the care given to the salting, weighting and pressing into moulds; the cleanliness of the air and work surfaces; the storage conditions and care of the cheeses as they slowly ripened.

So many factors could prevent successful cheese making. Some could be put down to carelessness, others to bad luck or to conditions beyond the cheese maker's control. The harassed dairy-maid of old was often made the scapegoat for cheeses that went wrong '. . . for some might dry into harsh and arid crumbs, some dissolve in putrefaction in spite of therapeutic herbs, while others rolled off the shelves propelled by the gas of their own fermentation. If they stuck to the shelves in a slimy mass, the dairymaid was to blame for lazy handling. It was her fault if they got grease spots in a hot room, or became covered with mould in a wet one, and hers was the blame if flies "blew", and maggots crawled and when mites reduced the cheese to dust.'

Of all the types of cheese made by dairymaids, village cheese makers, farmers' wives and shepherds high up in the mountain pastures, there was always an element of risk that something, somewhere in the process, might not be quite right. Happily, however, many new characters of cheese evolved from some of these strange mishaps and went on to became much-loved regional specialities.

> Cheese is made of mylke, yet there is sortes of cheese,
> which is to say, grene chese, softe chese, harde chese, and
> spermyse. Grene chese is not called grene by reason of
> colour, but for the newness of it, for the whey is not halfe
> pressed out of it. Softe chese, not new nor to olde, is best.
> Harde chese, is hot and dry and wyll to dygest. Spermyse is
> a chese which is made with curdes and with the juce of
> herbes.
>
> Gervase Markham on English cheese making in 1615

In Britain, simple curd production was probably common before the arrival of the Romans. As in other regions, the simple acidic curdling of milk had gradually evolved into the controlled production of a curd that could be preserved. Real cheese making, which may have been introduced by the Romans, became an important part of Romano-British agriculture. By Anglo-Saxon times, most rural households owned a 'milch' cow or rented one from the farmer. Many also kept a goat or two for milk. In small farm or cottage kitchens or outhouses, cream was separated from the milk, simple cottage or cream cheeses were hung up in muslin to drain and home-churned butter was stored away in a cool place.

Until the middle of the fourteenth century, British farms were self-contained communities of workers, held under the feudal supremacy of the landowner. The 'manorial' system of farming created specialist labourers such as shepherds, dairymaids and cowherds whose jobs were clearly specified and whose concessions and 'bounden duties' were laid down and strictly applied. The dairying season was initially short, though it gradually lengthened until it stretched from early April to the end of November, by which time the cows were dry. Not all cattle were kept through the winter. Because of the lack of feed, most, like the pigs, were fattened up in August for slaughter. Fresh dairy products in the winter were therefore almost non-existent, and butter and cheeses had to be preserved and 'put by'. Of necessity then, northern European cheeses were predominantly of the hard, matured variety ideal for long keeping. Their strong natural rinds, cloth or wax coatings further preserved the scents and goodness of summer to cheer northern palates through the bleak midwinter. Cheeses from the hot, drier Mediterranean regions, where the cow cannot thrive, are made from the milk of hardier sheep and goats. There are thousands of such cheeses made in Greece, southern Italy, Andalusia, Corsica and North Africa. In the remote mountain villages of Spain and Sicily rural peasants still subsist on a diet of olives, bread and goat or sheep's cheeses.

Gradually, as cheeses took on particular characteristics arising from the climate, conditions and traditional processes of their places of manufacture, they acquired their famous names. The best-known cheeses sold at English markets were sent from Cheddar, Cheshire, Shropshire and Banbury, while lower-quality cheeses came from Suffolk, Essex and 'the very worst', apparently, from Kent. Cheese making and selling became big business with cheeses being sent all over the country and shipped abroad to foreign markets. This led to increased production on the farms and communal cheese making on a larger scale, with even bigger cheeses being produced. These famous great cheeses were matured on the farms and could be kept for two to five years according to size. Cheese types were classified by hardness or softness, age and suitability for the tables of the rich and the poor. The growth of urban populations created an increasing demand for tradeable foodstuffs, particularly those that preserved their goodness on the journey to town. Landowners and yeomen farmers improved their farms and increased their output in order to keep up with the demand.

Greater trade in dairy produce, however, often meant that the farm workers' diet actually became worse rather than better. Milk was now far too valuable to drink – it produced cream and best butter for sale and the best-quality pressed cheeses were sent to market for rich city folk. Dairy workers were left with the by-products to accompany their meagre diet of dried beans and peas and salted fish or meat. The skimmed or semi-skimmed milk was made into 'flet milk' cheese, which became an important item in a poor man's food. It was also popular with travellers and seafarers because it was cheap and kept well 'one year under another'. The urban poor, too, were left with the cheaper grades of dairy products. During the eighteenth century, ships brought quantities of butter and cheese to London from Yorkshire and East Anglia. Often this would be in an appalling condition; some butter was described as tasting like 'train-oil thickened with salt'.

However, trade also brought many rural regional cheeses to the public table and the London markets filled with Double Gloucester, Wiltshire and Stilton cheeses and the huge cheeses 'from the meadows and marshes of Essex – noted for their massiveness and thickness'. The huge, hard-keeping Suffolk cheese was not popular, and became known locally as 'Suffolk Bang' because of its hard, horny texture. Samuel Pepys wrote in 1661 '. . . and so home, where I found my wife vexed at her people for grumbling to eat Suffolk cheese, which I also am vexed at'. It was also loathed by naval seamen:

> Those that made me were uncivil,
> They made me harder than the Devil,
> Knives can't cut me, fire won't light me,
> Dogs bite at me, but can't bite me.

While many cheeses took their names from their place of origin, a few claim to be called after individuals and who better than the dairymaid herself, the brighter of whom must have experimented with new ideas. It has been claimed that the famous Stilton was invented by a Mrs Stilton, the head dairymaid on the estate of the Duchess of Belvoir. This unlikely attribution at least shows that dairymaids may have received some recognition for their labours and skills. The more likely story is that a Mrs Paulet of Wymondham made cheeses for her relative, Cooper Thornhill, landlord of the Bell Inn at Stilton in Huntingdonshire, a famous hostelry on the Great North Road popular with travellers going between London and Edinburgh. The

Nineteenth-century English dairymaids were often romanticised, and few dairies would have been as well-equipped as this one

Stilton was so enjoyed that guests were prepared to pay the enormous price of 2 shillings 6 pence a pound for it. Many local varieties disappeared or were absorbed into the name of one county or local cheese. Cheese's importance, however, remained. As Val Cheke wrote, 'For all the changes which occurred over the centuries, cheese as such maintained a unique place in the rural economy, and possessed its own traditional values in the country. A full cheese store meant less privation over the winter months, and a good harvest of cheese made the difference between starvation and survival.'

The giant cheese of Olde England was both a symbol of prosperity and hospitality, and there were many festivals surrounding cheeses, especially the still-famous cheese rolling festivities. In Gloucestershire, cheeses, seen as great, round golden-yellow orbs of goodness and longevity, are still decorated with flowers and carried through the village to the churchyard where they are rolled three times round the church.

By the nineteenth century, science and commerce had largely taken over. Cheese-making factories had sprung up threatening the traditional farmhouse cheese makers. Pasteurisation, mechanisation, refrigeration and steam transformed cheese production and the dairymaid moved out of her dairy and onto the factory floor. Today cheese is 'cheddared' all over the world, especially in Canada, Australia, New Zealand and America.

Processed cheese is made with special emulsifying agents added to a cheese blend. The mix is then cooked at around 85°C (185°F), well above pasteurisation temperatures. The hot and semi-liquid cheese is poured into lined containers, wrapped and sealed. Processed cheese has an almost indefinite keeping quality providing it has been correctly processed and sealed. There are also cheese 'spreads' for sandwiches, flavoured and coloured to brighten up the bland result, which really cannot and should not call itself cheese. As Val Cheke lamented as far back as 1959, 'Gone are the cheesy flavours, hot and strong, subtle, biting and tasty. In their place is the smooth, mild, spreadable product with a flavour little resembling the initial cheese.' No wonder there is now a burgeoning trade in organic and 'real' cheeses made in the traditional way back on the farm.

CHAPTER SEVEN

SUGAR

Sugar and spice and all things nice . . .

*Mixed with fruit and flowers, sugar produces jams, marmalades,
preserves, pastes, and candied fruits in a conserving process which
lets us enjoy their flavours long after the time which nature had
meant them to last.*
Jean Anthelme Brillat Savarin, *The Physiology of Taste,* 1825

On a winter's night in 1797, a terrible storm roared along the
east coast of Scotland. All night as people slept, the wind
lashed the rooftops and boiled up the sea, tearing ships from
anchor and driving those still out in the North Sea to rush for shelter wherever they could find it. A Spanish merchant ship found
refuge in the small harbour in Dundee, its rigging and sails ripped
to shreds. Bound for Leith, the ship had got lost and could go no
further. The captain was
forced to find a quick
buyer for his large cargo
of Seville oranges.

Up wi' the white pots o'
Bonnie Dundee

*An advertisement for Keiller's Dundee
Marmalade with the traditional white
stone pots still in use*

The next day, Janet
Keiller worked as usual in
her grocer's shop, irri-
tated that her husband,
James, had been down at
the harbour so long.
When he at last returned,
he was wearing a beaming
smile. Full of pride in his
business acumen, he
announced to his wife that he had bought, at a cut-throat price, a
whole shipload of oranges. Seville oranges were not unknown in
Scotland. Janet knew about them, in particular she knew that they

were extremely bitter, uneatable and therefore almost unsaleable.

A true Scotswoman, Janet decided to make the best of the situation and, after ordering carts to bring the oranges and summoning an army of helpers, she proceeded to transform the oranges into quantities of her now famous Keiller bitter orange marmalade. This not only saved face for James Keiller, but also made them and their descendants a tidy fortune.

This tale, though largely true, is not, however, the beginning of marmalade. As C. Anne Wilson writes in her thorough and fascinating *Book Of Marmalade*, 'Janet Keiller did not invent orange marmalade. But she contributed to the establishment of the "chip" version as Scotland's very own marmalade.' There were, in fact, plenty of contemporary marmalade recipes for her to choose from, but faced with such an enormous quantity of oranges, Janet probably adapted one that only required the peel to be chipped or shredded rather than one where the peel had to be pounded to a soft pulp in a mortar. She thereby saved herself some work and, by making a less solid preserve, would also have produced more of the white stone pots per pound of oranges and therefore a greater profit.

Orange marmalade making was by this time already a popular practice in both English and Scottish homes (the stricken ship was probably supplying Leith for that purpose). Though it was not eaten on toast or for breakfast, pots of marmalade were already available in a few shops as luxury items, and other fruits had been conserved in sugar for as long as sugar had been available. In fact, the origins of marmalade did not involve oranges at all.

> There are three kinds of honey, that of the flowers, that of
> the dew, and that which flows from a reed.
>
> Aristotle, 371 BC

Long before cane sugar was brought out of India via China and the Middle East and on to Europe and the Americas, people were taking advantage of natural sweeteners to preserve their food. Honey was the most universally used and was already known as an effective preserver of both humans and food. It is itself a great 'self-preserving' food – it will keep almost indefinitely and is one of the best natural sources of energy for man. The Masai warriors of east Africa took no other food than honey on their long expeditions apart from the freshly tapped blood from their cattle. Spiced honey bread, still eaten in France as 'pain d'épices', was made and kept for travel in many countries including ancient China. The sugar and spices helped to preserve the bread and made it a long-lasting, energy-giving food.

Like vinegar, sugar, either as cane sugar or glucose, or in the form of honey or molasses, creates an environment where no living organism can grow. As we have seen, sugar is also used with other preserving processes. Hams are covered in honey to create an anti-bacterial coat to protect them during storage and sugar is also used to counteract the hardening effect of saltpetre. In Rome, honey was used medicinally, to make cakes and sweetmeats, in wine and beer making and as a preservative. The Roman gourmet Apicius described many methods for keeping meat using honey: 'Preserve your meats in mustard mixed with vinegar, salt and honey,' he instructed. Epicurean Romans had a particular favourite – preserved edible dormice in a honey sauce.

Honey was long used for preserving fruits as well, either whole or in a jam. In summer, the Amerindian tribes of Canada made a sweet, dried paste of wild strawberries crushed in pure honey for their winter provisions. Most fruits and vegetables, which contain their own sugar to a varying degree, can be preserved by simply adding more sugar and thus increasing their sucrose content to the point where micro-organisms will be inhibited by the high concentration of dissolved sugars. The earliest kind of jam making, too, dates back to pre-Roman times when fruit pulp was mixed with honey and spices and dried in the sun.

In the first century AD, the Greeks made a preserve, using their abundant crops of quinces, by stuffing pieces of peeled and pipped raw fruit tightly into jars filled with honey. After a year the fruit became as soft as 'wine-honey'. This Greek quince preserve was called 'melomeli' (apple – *melo*, in honey – *meli*). The Romans later reversed the words into 'melimela' and improved the preserve by cooking the fruit in the honey with pepper and spices and sealing the jars to make them airtight.

Quinces have a high pectin content so that when cooked,

preserves made with them would have had a very solid texture. Pectin is a vital ingredient for successful jelly and jam making. All fruits contain varying strengths of pectin; some, like grapes and berries are particularly rich in it and will, after sufficient boiling at the right temperature, gel into a firm set without help. In an early form of jam making the sugar was boiled up to a 'candie height' (115.6°C/240°F) and then beaten until it crystallised into a hard candy. Nuts and raw fruit were dropped onto this and the candy was then gently re-melted until the fruit was slightly cooked, releasing its pectin so that it set but still retained its flavour and colour.

Other fruits, such as apricots, peaches and strawberries need to have more pectin added. Nowadays powdered pectin can be bought while the white rind of citrus fruits is another useful source of pectin and can be thrown in with the boiling fruit. As well as helping the preserve set, the pectin interacts with the high concentration of sugar in the jam to prevent the growth of moulds.

Although for the Greeks and the Romans honey was the preferred sugar preservative, they also boiled down grape-must to make sweet syrups of varying thickness in which to preserve fruit. Another early sweetener was maltose, made from germinated grains of barley, most often used for making beer. In addition, the Persians and Arabs used the sap from a leafless desert plant, the thorn-honey or sheep-thorn, which may have been the 'sweet dew' Aristotle refers to. In the same way, the Japanese raisin-tree or 'tree-honey' produced sweet seeds and leaves while the Native Americans developed a method for extracting the sugar from the Canadian Maple by freeze drying it overnight. The water in the sap froze leaving the sugar deposit, which they then boiled down into the rich golden-brown syrup. This they mixed with bear fat and cornmeal to make a portable and nutritious food, similar to the meat pemmican, that could be taken on their long journeys by foot or in canoes. Corn or maize plants also produce a sweet syrup still used today on modern American pancakes and waffles as an inferior alternative to the more expensive maple syrup. There are several other trees around the world that have sugary saps, which may have been used as sweeteners and preservers, such as the rich sweet palm oil in Syria, the *Eucalyptus gunnii* in Tasmania that gives the

Aboriginals a sweet syrup, and the sap from the little coconut tree in Chile, which is boiled into a thick treacle to sweeten dishes.

Perhaps the most extraordinary and long-lasting sweetener is the biblical manna the Israelites found that saved them during their wanderings in the Sinai desert. Manna is, in fact, the secretion of a small insect that feeds off the tamarisk bush. It is still collected by some Bedouin at dawn before the arrival of the ants who also love it. One man is said to be able to collect 4 lb of this 'Bread of Heaven' each morning. Sealed in earthenware jars, it will keep indefinitely. There is another variety of manna-producing tamarisk in parts of India and a tamarisk grows in Persia where the manna is shaken from the twigs and used to make honey cake.

However, it was to cane sugar that Pliny, the Roman scholar and natural scientist, was referring when he described sugar as 'A kind of honey that collects in reeds, white like gum and brittle to the teeth, the largest pieces are the size of a filbert [an edible hazelnut].' The sugar cane was native to far away India and far too rare in Rome for use as anything other than a medicine. But the north-east coast of India, now known as Bengal, was then called Gur, 'the land of sugar'. There, for many hundreds of years, the cane had been collected and the juice extracted to be boiled down to make a granular substance called 'sand sugar'.

Being the first to use this sugar, it is not surprising that Bengalis are famous for their love of sweets, which 'borders on an addiction'. In Calcutta there are sweet stalls and shops on every street corner, while in homes, sweets are served at the end of every meal including the all-important afternoon tea. The two ingredients of Bengali sweets are milk and sugar. The milk is thickened, either by boiling it down into khoa, or by curdling it with lemon juice or yoghurt to produce channa. Some of the most popular sweets are 'cham-cham', small patties dipped in thickened milk and sprinkled with grated khoa, and 'rasgolla', a light spongy white ball of channa served in sugar syrup. A dark-coloured, fried version is called 'ledikeni' after Lady Canning, the wife of the first Viceroy of India. Bengali cuisine is strongly influenced by the legacy of Anglo-Indian and Portuguese traditions including Portuguese sweets, English custard puddings, marmalades and rich fruit cakes made with quantities of almonds, raisins, dried and candied fruits, cream, eggs and butter. But Bengalis use sugar, spices and local produce to create the most delicate and subtle flavours uniquely their own.

The use of cane sugar slowly spread outwards from Bengal. In the seventh century AD, the Chinese Emperor Tai-Hung sent workmen to Gur to learn the art of sugar refining and by the tenth century camel caravans were carrying the 'sand sugar' north through the empty deserts to Europe. This newly arrived cane sugar was initially regarded as a spice, and in medieval Europe was used principally as a medicine. It was enormously expensive and was therefore only available to the wealthiest households.

Nevertheless, sugar gradually began to be more widely appreciated for its appetising sweetness in sweetmeats, confectionery and desserts while it was increasingly valued also as a preserving agent for fresh fruits. Sweetmeats had appeared on the menu of the most sumptuous feasts and banquets of the Romans, the Athenians and in Byzantium, and the most wealthy and noble households of the European Middle Ages adopted these delicacies for their own tables. These sweetmeats were considered a digestive to clear the palate, as sorbets were to do later, and guests at these feasts would take them back to their rooms to nibble before going to bed. Good hosts even placed little decorated comfit-boxes filled with sugared almonds, pralines, nougats, candied spiced preserves and lemon peel, marzipan made with ground almond paste, egg whites and sugar, and crystallised fruits, flowers and angelica for the delectation of their guests in the privacy of their chambers. It was believed that sugar helped their digestion. Indeed, the high-meat diet may well have caused terrible constipation and sugar is known to 'loosen the bowels'. Unfortunately what was not known was that sugar would also loosen and rot their teeth.

Since sugar was new, rare and expensive it was obviously something to display lavishly at the baroque banquets held to impress royalty and other persons of great importance. These dazzling events were filled with drama, symbolism and enchantment and the discovery that sugar could be boiled up and spun into elaborate decorations and inventive sculptures made sugar the high point of the finest and most talked-about banquets. Ex-Queen Christina of Sweden, when she decided to convert to Catholicism, visited Italy in 1655, where she was treated to unlimited pomp and splendour with glittering displays of exotic dishes and allegorical tableaux-vivants called 'trionfi', all made of sugar and fruit, whose appearance was 'quite natural'.

Sugar has a remarkable ability to preserve many things in a striking, almost life-like state. Candied or glacé fruits retain much of their shape and colour. Fruit, if cooked on its own, tends to break down into a mush because it would normally shrink as the water is drawn out during boiling. But when cooked with sugar, the sugar becomes partly incorporated into the fruit replacing what is lost, so that it keeps much of its shape, texture and colour. Candying, probably developed in the Middle East, is a very slow process of replacing the natural juices of the fruit with the sugar solution or syrup. As in some fruit-drying processes, citrus peel and some hard fruits are first soaked in strong brine or acid solution to draw out some of the liquid before boiling and to encourage the fruit to absorb more sugar. Once candied, the fruits can be 'crystallised' by painting them with egg white and dusting liberally with sugar. Flowers can be preserved through crystallisation alone. Once sugared, the fruit or flower is then left to dry out in a warm, well-ventilated place.

When the Portuguese, through the exploratory voyages of Vasco da Gama, discovered a sea route to India at the end of the fifteenth century, they began the opening up of the East to European maritime traders. Initially, the Portuguese took the finished sugar back home from India and soon Portuguese and Spanish nuns, mixing sacred and profane, prayer and sugar, had learnt to make highly elaborate sweets, some full of symbolism and eroticism, which they sold on a regular basis to help pay their living expenses. Italian nuns, in convents of silence, still make their famous confectionery, which they sell, silently, through sliding doors in the convent walls.

Soon, however, the cane plant itself had been shipped across the world and planted in huge quantities in Europe's new possessions in the west, particularly in South America and the Caribbean. In a remarkably short amount of time after 1500, sugar, while remaining expensive, had become a staple trade commodity throughout much of the world. The tiny Caribbean islands became jewels in Europe's imperial crowns and to grow and process the sugar, millions of slaves were shipped from Africa to work in the cane fields.

Slaves processing sugar cane in a boiling house in the West Indies, 1836

By the seventeenth century, therefore, cane sugar was more readily available and preserving fruit with sugar became an affordable option. Recipes that had previously used honey were easily adapted. In northern Europe hard cakes of spiced quince preserve, considered beneficial to health, an aid to digestion and an effective aphrodisiac, continued to be made in the way learnt from the Romans but with sugar instead of honey. They were packed and stored in boxes and could be sliced and eaten as sweetmeats.

The English had their own particular version that included pieces of warden pear, but seemed to prefer the Portuguese quince preserve. Using their sugar from India and their abundance of quinces, the Portuguese had developed their own speciality, which they had called 'marmelada' (like the Roman 'melimela'). Less spicy than other versions, marmelada had a delicate flavour of rose water and musk. As early as the beginning of the sixteenth century, 'little chests' of marmelada were included in the cargoes of Portuguese merchant ships arriving in English ports. Gradually the same process was applied to other fruits, which then came to be known as a 'marmalade' of pears, damsons or plums. By the seventeenth century some marmalades were made into a looser texture and were potted instead of boxed, particularly in the cases of soft fruits such as gooseberries, raspberries, mulberries and cherries. This type of fruit preserve eventually came to be known in England as 'jam'.

Along with sugar, Arab merchants had brought into southern Europe small, bitter oranges, which were then used to make sharp, sour sauces or tangy, bitter-sweet succade. By the mid-seventeenth century there were recipes in England for various conserves of oranges, which included boiling them whole in sugar. All the methods produced a thick, slicing orange marmalade ready for boxing. Gradually true, softer, potted orange marmalades were being tried out in English households and in 1681 Rebecca Price faithfully wrote down her mother's special 'marmelett of orin021'. This used thinly sliced peel of Seville oranges boiled until tender. Then the peels, plus the pulp and 1 lb of sugar for every four oranges were slowly heated up together: 'so keepe it with continual stirring till you think it be enough . . . it will not be stiff as other marmelett, to be cutt, but must be taken out with spoons.' There were two kinds most often made, a beaten marmalade of orange peel and pulp pounded in a mortar and a clear thick jelly with thin shreds of peel floating in it.

One problem with making these sugar preserves is that when the preserve has set in the jars and been sealed, moisture can form between the surface of the food and the lid encouraging mould. Today we use waxed papers, but in the seventeenth century lady cooks had to seal their stone pots with rounds of handmade writing paper dipped in brandy. The tops were then sealed with pieces of clean dried bladder stretched over and tied down firmly. Writing in 1604, Lady Fettiplace warned of keeping jams in the right conditions: 'If they begin to grow then set them where fire is in a cupboard.'

Marmalade may have changed from a 'brick of fruit' to a 'strong jelly' but it still had not moved from the dinner table – where it was eaten as a dessert with syllabubs, fruit creams and ices – to the breakfast table, to be spread on hot, buttered toast. But the Scots, who traditionally warmed up in the morning with a dram of whisky, gradually succumbed to the new fashion of tea and toast with some marmalade, which had been long believed to be 'warming to the stomach'. Unfortunately for those Scots gentlemen who missed their whisky, it was many years before marmalades were produced with additional whisky, brandy and even rum.

It was said that good marmalade improves with age. Anthony Blunt, who once owned the famous jam and marmalade firm of Elsenham, told C. Anne Wilson how he had once come across some pre-war 2 lb jars of thick-cut marmalade, by then at least twenty years old. He tasted some and found it 'positively ambrosial, proving to his complete satisfaction that marmalade really does improve with age'. Its remarkable keeping qualities meant that marmalade could be sent all over the world, to expatriate Britons and foreign royalty and dignitaries. It was popular sea-going fare and travellers and explorers ensured that marmalade was on their list of provisions. In 1980, a tin of Frank Cooper's marmalade was recovered from the last cabin of Captain Scott's fateful expedition of 1912, still in perfect condition.

Many famous marmalade and jam making companies still prosper and it was most often due to a grocer's wife like Janet Keillor. In 1864 Marion Robertson, wife of another James, a grocer in Paisley, turned their stock of unsaleable Seville oranges into a transparent jelly marmalade which she called 'Golden Shred'. It was so successful that they soon opened a factory. Many may remember the unfortunate collectable gollies in every Robertson's jar, happily now long gone. Four years later, farther north in Morayshire, another grocer's wife Margaret Baxter was making jams and conserves in the summer, when most fruit was available, and orange marmalade in the spring. Margaret's preserving skills soon became famous, creating a thriving family business. From one hardworking generation to another, Keiller, Robertson, Baxter and many other household names have continued to flourish in the production of English and Scottish jams and marmalades.

Many kinds of fruit preserves are made all over the world. Still using the original quince, the dark golden, sweet-scented French 'paté de coing' is popularly made both at home and commercially. Jams are made in the Middle East and the Balkans and eaten as a sweet using a spoon. Traditional hospitality in homes from Turkey to Iran and from Bulgaria to Egypt will mean a spoon of a thick, sticky, very sweet preserve or sweetmeat washed down with a glass of cold water and a small cup of strong Turkish coffee. Nevertheless, making jellies and jams or 'putting up preserves', as our great-grandmothers would have called it, is a peculiarly English tradition. It is one of the last great home-preserving activities that still tempt an English household to buy or gather quantities of fruit, get down the large iron or copper family preserving pan, find Granny's old sugar thermometer, bring out boxes of old jam jars and go out and buy special bags of preserving sugar with 'added pectin' at the shops.

The Women's Institute, village fêtes and church bazaars have all ingrained in us a sense of the special pleasure and value of home-made cakes and jams. Elderberries, blackberries, wild crab apples, rowan and bilberries can still be found along the hedgerows of country lanes but going out together to collect and bring home bowls and buckets of wild fruit has now been superseded by trips to the 'pick-your-own' fruit farms. Abundant supplies of fruit can now be gathered in a few hours and, in a couple of days, plenty can be prepared and boiled up for bottling.

Spiced sweetmeats, sweet preserves and confectionery remained as favourite gifts long after sugar had become cheap and available to even the poorest. These sugar preserves are still seen as symbols of luxury and of celebration. Sweets made at home are carefully stored away in boxes for festivities and special occasions. In France there is a long tradition of giving pastel-coloured sugared almonds to celebrate the birth of a child. In Italy, frangipane or almond marzipan is given as a gift and Greek 'halva' and Turkish 'Delight' sweetmeats are now known almost everywhere.

Christmas and feast days are traditionally the time for giving delicious hand-made chocolates or translucent, glistening crystallised and candied fruits. Stockings are filled with perfect, whole marrons glacé, ginger and pineapple. Jars of brandy marmalades and special jams and preserves with elegant labels, tied in decorative cloth. Under the tree we might find sugared marzipan shapes and preserved flowers dusted with fine sugar, wrapped in wax paper and packed in little wicker boxes.

⌁ CHAPTER EIGHT ⌁

CONCENTRATES

Changes in the technology of food preserving and their far-reaching effects began in Europe as early as the sixteenth century, which saw an increase of activity in food preservation along with a fast-expanding range of exotic new ingredients and new cooking methods. Changing lifestyles, a growth in food trading and longer sea voyages in search of the new foods and spices demanded new preserving ideas.

The Elizabethans were very concerned about food production and preserving. Because of their elementary farming techniques, their food supply was precarious. What's more, the effective preservation of enough food to get them through to the next harvest was liable to failure because their methods were still mostly limited to salting, drying and smoking. These early techniques, despite having sustained people for centuries, had their practical drawbacks: salted foods after a time became too salty to be eaten; smoked or dried foods sometimes became too hard and if the humidity of the air was too high, as it often was in Britain, they soon became rancid. Sun or air drying was only possible in high summer and oven or stove drying used expensive fuel. Moreover, a poor understanding about the preserving processes meant that many people could not be sure about the quality of preserved food nor the length of time that their food could safely be kept.

Most traditional processes were developed by trial and error, and instructions and recipes were passed down the generations by word of mouth. New ideas and discoveries were added on to old, but errors inevitably crept in. As people learned from their mistakes, much food must have been wasted or spoiled, while uncountable numbers must have suffered at some time from food poisoning as a result of inadequate or faulty preserving. The symptoms of poisoning, however, were common to many other ailments suffered in those days and would not necessarily have been associated with what had recently been eaten. As Jennifer Stead indicates in *Waste Not, Want Not*, many early recipe books regularly mentioned the possibility that foods could 'Rot, putrefy, hoar, cloud, rope, sour, corrupt, or go rank, rusty, foisty, musty, mouldy, mothered, tainted, fly-blown or maggoty'. Some offered highly risky advice on how to recover 'tainted' meat or stale vegetables and others recommended strong flavoured ingredients, so that the taste of spoiled food would not be noticed. This gave rise to the myth that the common use of spices was to mask the taste of rotten food. Spice was far too rare and expensive to have been wasted in this way. As late as the mid-eighteenth century, cookery writer William Ellis suggested cooking tainted meat with lots of root vegetables and onions and Richard Bradley gave a hair-raising recipe for preserving old pigeons:

> When your Pidgeons are boil'd tender enough, take them
> from the Fire, and when the Liquor is cold, lay your
> Pidgeons in a large Gally-pot, and pour the Liquor upon
> them, and cover them up close with Leather, and they will
> keep a long time.

Another well-known remedy for rotten venison was to cut off the green bits, bone it and bury it in the earth for up to two days. In her *The Art of Cookery made Plain and Easy*, published in 1747, Hannah Glasse offered a remedy 'To save potted Birds that begin to be bad' that sounds highly alarming.

In Elizabethan times, frugal housekeeping involved the application of inherited knowledge and cultural traditions of self-sufficiency within a rural, strictly seasonal economy. The basic necessities of sustenance still depended on skills in drying, salting and smoking foods. Vinegar for pickles and relishes and sugar for preserving were only available to the better-off at this time. Anything that could be done to increase yields was worth trying and anything that could be done to improve storage was equally worthy. Expanding populations coupled with an undeveloped agriculture and the continuous and relentless pattern of famines and good harvests meant that the preservation of food remained absolutely essential to survival. Preserving skills were vital to every household, rich or poor, and were never more needed than then.

Passing on this knowledge, however inadequately done, was an important way to ensure that the next generation could feed itself. But shifting populations, new techniques, ingredients and preserving agents, meant that oral traditions were becoming ever less reliable. This led to an explosion of books printed during the sixteenth and seventeenth centuries aimed largely at an affluent female readership, and through her the servants and farmworkers she supervised. In many of these books for 'Ladies', preserving, particularly conserving with sugar, went hand in hand with skills in making medicines and cosmetics, and in distilling, cheese making and brewing, and was not regarded strictly as cooking, which is what servants in the kitchen did.

As with Columella, Cato and Pliny in Roman times, it was most often male, educated estate owners who wrote these instructional manuals covering improvements and good practice in food production, preserving and cookery, men who had time and money to spend on pursuing their 'philosophical' experiments. John Partridge, who lived on the land and had first-hand experience of food production, wrote a book in 1573 called *The Treasurie of Commodious Conceits, and Hidden Secrets, Commonly Called the Good Huswives Closet of Provision, for the Health of Her Households*. He was typical of the gentlemen concerned with the Elizabethan problems of agriculture and food. Another was Thomas Tusser, a Suffolk farmer who used rhymed proverbs to guide his fellow farmers in good practice:

> Both salt fish and ling fish if any ye have
> Through shifting and drying from rotting go save,
> Lest winter with moistness do make it relent,
> And put it in hazard before it be spent.

Another gentleman farmer who wrote extensively on growing, cooking and preserving food was Gervase Markham. In 1615 he published *The English Hus-wife*, which claimed to teach 'the inward and outward virtues which ought to be in a compleat woman'. It included instructions on how to bake 'pyes', and make good butter and cheese, as well as how to oversee the preserve making, deal with estate accounts and the servants, mix medicines, weave and dye cloth and brew and bake. It would be some years before the 'compleat' women, who managed to run their households successfully without instruction, wrote these kinds of books themselves.

Hugh Plat, however, was not a country gentleman but a lawyer who became an inventor. He was born in 1552, the son of a wealthy London brewer. He was a 'classic Renaissance figure for whom all knowledge was his province', a dilettante writer of poems and classical anthologies and author of cookery books for ladies. But the climate of this age was not just literary it was also scientific and Plat's love of ingenuity and his eclectic interests led him to try out all sorts of innovations including 'newe and artificiall' ways of preserving food. His inventions included rainproof clothing, a varnish for armour to preserve it from rust, an oil for cannon 'to the same purpose', and a special type of bullet of greater range than that ordinarily used. He published a number of broadsheets describing his scientific or pseudo-scientific discoveries, the most well known being *The Jewel House of Art and Nature conteining divers rare and profitable Inventions, together with sundry new Experiments in the Art of Husbandry, Distillation and Moulding*. In it Plat wrote extensively about his concern with the lack of winter feed for livestock and the ignorance about manures, bemoaning the 'wasteful great muck-heaps'. He also wrote *A Closet for Ladies and Gentlemen, or, the Art of Preserving*. His most popular work, *Delightes for Ladies*, which first appeared in 1608, became one of the most sought-after works on horticulture amongst seventeenth-century gardeners.

In 1596 there was a particularly inclement, wet season resulting in poor harvests and great hunger. Plat was concerned about the food shortage, not only because people might starve, but also because they might riot and make disturbances and so he wrote another tract about how to prevent famine. In it he aimed at no less than to create 'new and artificiall discoveries of strange bread, drinke and food, in matter and preparation so full of rarity to worke some alteration and change in this great and dangerous dearth'.

Plat's interest in alleviating famine spread to concerns about naval victualling and scurvy. He tried to interest the Royal Navy in a number of preserved foods and in 1607 he produced a broadsheet entitled *Certaine Philosophical Preparations of Foode and Beverage for Sea-men*. This listed twelve foods and medicines for use at sea, including a kind of macaroni pasta to be eaten 'in stede of bread'. Although few of his inventions or suggestions were taken up by either civilian or naval authorities, Plat did advise both Drake and Hawkyns on provisioning for their voyages and he did supply Captain Lancaster with lemon juice prepared with his 'philosophical fire'. But he became increasingly disillusioned as the navy largely ignored his advice and failed to order his preparations. He wrote that if his advice received 'Entertainment according to the worth thereof' he would be happy to continue his researches, but if it were rejected he would withdraw his offers of help which, he wrote bitterly, were rarely rewarded. He was, however, later given a knighthood by King James and Sir Hugh continued to use the names of Drake and Hawkyns as advertisements for his food preparations.

Often Plat is verbose and rather vague in detail and explanation. Many of the ideas were neither new nor his own. But he did combine his own experimental experiences with the knowledge of 'divers gentlemen of the best skill and practice'. Had he lived a generation or two later, he might have been a founder of the Royal Society, but in keeping with current fashion, he tried to enhance his discoveries or 'secretes' with an air of magic and mystery. Alongside forward-looking food preservation, he wrote with equal enthusiasm on alchemy, magic and witchcraft. He described as 'philosophical fire' something which was probably no more than a kind of bottling using alcohol. Nevertheless, he had certainly grasped the beginnings of some important new preserving principles such as heat-sealing, fat-sealing, bottling and the concentration of meat.

His 1607 broadsheet aimed at the Royal Navy included the recipe for a broth 'preserved by this fire of Nature from all mouldiness, sowereness, or corruption, to any reasonable time . . . a necessary secret for all sicke and weake persons at sea, when no fresh meats can be had, to strengthen and comfort them'. This 'strong and restoratif broathe' was to be made with meat suet, leg of beef, calves' feet and spices. It was sweetened with 'liquerice' and strengthened with isinglass boiled 'to a great stifness' and then baked and dried into a solid jelly-like 'mouthglew', a sort of glue. This 'portable soup' is the forerunner of our modern stock cubes. His primary aim, though, was to preserve meat without having to use salt.

Almost all new preserving discoveries were derived from ancient ones. As we have seen, foods had been 'concentrated' by removing the moisture since the very beginnings of food preserving. Fruits, some vegetables, soups and milk had often been reduced to a thick syrup or hard block. The Romans knew how to evaporate grape juice and keep it in jars for many uses and since the Middle Ages, regions of central Europe rich in vines have concentrated grapes using a traditional method. The fruit was slowly boiled over a low heat until it thickened then a white hot piece of iron was dipped into the juice to thicken it further into a viscous syrup which was used to sweeten wheat or maize porridge, tea and fruit compotes.

In the really hot regions, many kinds of home-made liqueurs, sauces and compotes were left in the sun to evaporate. Assyrian villagers still make and use in their everyday cooking a form of concentrated tomato paste called 'maye d'bajanat'. Like our modern concentrated tubes of tomato paste, it gives dishes a 'distinct subtle taste and a red colour' and children love to eat it spread very thickly on their bread liberally covered with powdered peppermint.

But the nutritional importance of meat, particularly for invalids, remained undisputed for many more years. Soon, similar recipes to Sir Hugh's for various kinds of pocket, cake or portable soup began to appear. In 1694 Ann Blencowe, an MP's wife, recorded a recipe for a 'veal glue' in her *Receipt Book*. A strong broth was to be made from a leg of veal. It was to be simmered and stirred continuously for seven hours, then left for a few days. The 'settlement' was scraped off and the jelly then 'steamed till it reaches a Glewish substance'. 'You may know when it is done enough by putting a Little by to be cold and if 'twill cut like a soft Cheese it is as should be.' This was then cut into lumps, wrapped in flannel and paper and would 'keep many years'. It was easily reconstituted into broth by dissolving the pieces in boiling water. It is worth noting, however, that the broth from a whole leg of veal would by this method 'not make a piece bigger than your hand'. Mrs Blencowe recommended it as 'of extraordinary service to such as travel in wild and open Countries, where few or no Provisions are to be met with; and it will be of no less Benefit to such families as have not immediate recourse to markets'. In 1747 Hannah Glasse gave two recipes for both 'portable' and 'pocket' soup. The quantities were enormous, for example for portable soup, 'Take two Legs of Beef, about fifty Pounds Weight', 8 or 9 gallons of water, twelve anchovies, large helpings of herbs and spices, six large onions and a dry, hard crust of a 'Two-penny Loaf'. The cost of fuel must have also been considerable as the soup had to simmer for at least eight to nine hours. A piece of the soup as big as a large walnut 'will make a Pint of Water very rich'. Hannah Glasse recommended her portable soup to sea captains and as a welcome gravy to go with cooked salt beef, which tended to be rather dry.

But the benefits of pocket or portable soup were not always appreciated at sea. In 1772 Captain Cook took cases of portable soup on his three-year voyage around the world. The soup, kept mainly for sick sailors, was mixed with pease flour. It was described as being made by boiling and evaporating the most putrescent parts of the meat to the consistency of glue, which may explain why some sailors were flogged for refusing to eat it. However, its capacity to 'keep sound for years together' cannot be questioned. One of these cakes of soup, made in 1770 and believed to have been part of Cook's supplies, is still kept in the National Maritime Museum in Greenwich. It is a small, oblong, flat cake, greyish white in colour and stamped with a broad arrow. It looks just like 'a slab of glue'. Tested in the 1930s by Sir Jack Drummond, it had 'changed very little' although it is not recorded what it tasted like.

In 1848 the famous German chemist Baron Justus von Liebig began to experiment with his 'Extract of Beef'. His first attempt was made whilst he was Professor of Chemistry at Liverpool University when the daughter of a friend was suffering from typhus. Von Liebig made her some concentrated beef juice and, when the child recovered, he published his method, 'A New Soup for invalids', with great claims for its benefit to mankind. He continued to improve on his preparation, which involved immersing raw beef in cold water. When the soluble elements had dissolved they were filtered and squeezed out of the liquid which was then boiled, coagulating the proteins, leaving a clear soup which could then be evaporated over a gentle heat until it left a thick, brown, gooey extract smelling strongly of roast beef. Liebig's tasty and soothing meat extract was designed to be fed to invalids and it was successfully adopted as a treatment for sick and convalescing patients in homes and clinics in place of the old beef tea.

Von Liebig believed that his extract was a 'body-builder' and an important alternative to meat because it contained all the useful components of meat (in fact the fat and fibre discarded by this process contain most of the protein). He hoped also that his extract could be used to feed the 'craving multitudes' of workers who could not afford meat, whom von Liebig referred to as the 'potato-eaters of Europe'. He also promoted its use for soldiers, selling its 'unique nutritional benefits' to the generals in the Franco-Prussian war. But not everyone was impressed. Florence Nightingale, who was sent some extract to try on her patients, wrote in her *Notes on Nursing* that the solid matter that von Liebig obtained by evaporating down beef tea amounted to no more than a few grams and in the course of preparation the protein was largely thrown away. Modern tests show that the extract contained the B vitamins riboflavin and nicotinic acid together with mineral salts, especially phosphates, all of which do benefit convalescent and weak patients and do stimulate the flow of gastric juices and saliva helping stimulate appetite and digestion. But it had no muscle or body forming qualities.

In 1862 von Liebig met Georg Giebert, a road engineer who had been working in South America. Giebert told him about the massive quantities of meat being left to rot in Uruguay and Argentina, where cattle rearing was largely for the production of hides for leather. There was as yet no economic way to preserve or sell the unwanted carcasses except to render them down for fat. Von Liebig quickly saw the potential for his new beef extract and together they formed a company in Fray Bentos, Uruguay to manufacture von Liebig's Extract of Meat.

Von Liebig conducted a vigorous and effective advertising

campaign to sell his new beef extract. Posters boasted that 36 lb of beef were reduced to 1 lb of extract, which provided a nourishing soup for 128 men. Many people believed the eminent chemist's claims that the extract provided the same nutrients as meat but in a highly concentrated, preserved and portable form. It became particularly popular with travellers and explorers. Dr Stanley carried

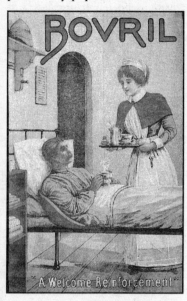

A casualty of the First World War gets a 'nourishing' drink of Bovril

a jar with him to Africa in 1865 and polar explorers Nansen, Amundsen, Shackleton and Scott all took some in their supplies. Isabella Bird, travelling in Japan, cautioned her reader against 'encumbering himself with tinned meats, soups, claret, or any eatables or drinkables except Liebig's extract of meat'.

In 1899 the name Oxo appeared and was later applied to the solid cubes that followed the liquid extracts. Also from the original von Liebig company came Lemco, Bovril and the Brooke Bond Company, which became the parent company name. People eventually stopped thinking of meat extracts and cubes as alternatives to meat and they instead became a convenient boon to cooks in the kitchen, whilst 'Brand's Meat Essence', 'Boots' Liquid Beef' and others joined von Liebig's extract in the sickroom.

Von Liebig claimed to have received no benefit from his discoveries, though the profits from the meat extract business must have made him a very rich man. He was a curious figure who pursued many theories of food science, some right and some wrong. He was certainly an early proponent of organic chemistry and his early work laid the foundations of the knowledge of the nutritive value of the proteins. But he erroneously claimed that muscles were reduced by activity and could only be rebuilt with proteins and he also maintained that all food was antiscorbutic, which delayed the proper understanding of scurvy's causes and cure. He had enormous energy, curiosity and enthusiasm but was also hot-tempered and impulsive; he got into an acrimonious dispute with Pasteur over the action of yeast, which led to the development of a yeast product now known as Marmite, made with surplus yeast from the brewing industry. Sir William Osler once said of von Liebig that there may have been better chemists but none have been more influential.

CHAPTER NINE

PIES, POTS AND BOTTLES

Pies

Very early in the morning, for the greater part of the year, before dawn had even spread some light and colour in the sky, the men and young lads would throw on their clothes, breakfast on bread and lard, snatch up their packs or dinner-baskets and hurry off through the dark lanes and sleepy countryside to the fields. There, they would spend their day working in freezing cold winter wind and rain or, in summer, under a parching hot sun. Meanwhile young children would be shaken sleepy-eyed from their warm beds, dressed and breakfasted, wrapped in what warm clothing they had, and sent off on the often long walk to school with their dinner bags slung on their shoulders.

Before cars and trains had made travel a simple matter of speed and time, the countryside was filled with people making regular journeys on foot every day away from home and home-cooked meals. Everyone was used to carrying some provisions, however small or simple, to feed them during a hard day's work or many miles of travelling.

This food had to be portable, to be able to wait ready-prepared overnight by a warm hearth, and not be likely to spoil in the hot sun. The classic 'Field Fare' described in early literature were cured meats and sausages, dried fish, radishes or raw onion, a pickle or a clove of garlic and some dried fruits. To drink there might be some beer, wine, buttermilk or cooling fermented drinks. Hard bread or biscuit eaten with a chunk of cheese was also a combination that was relatively cheap, kept and travelled well, had a good flavour if made well and was a portable and filling

'Ploughman's lunch' — farmworkers and their horses stopping for lunch in Wiltshire, 1937

combination. A wide variety of hard cheeses travelled in tradesmen's packs, ploughmen's sack or pilgrim's bags and their reputations grew.

By the late Middle Ages, however, another food preserving technique provided a staple food of the fields and lanes of Britain. Filled pies and pasties became the traditional ingredients for a packed lunch and were carried on the road or into the fields for centuries. The Cornish pasty in its original form was popular with Cornish fishermen, fieldworkers and tin miners who carried them in their boats, out to the fields or down the mines. The sturdy, compact crescent of pastry was filled with snippets of meat, onions, sliced turnips or carrots and potatoes and could sometimes have a sweet filling of cooked apple or jam at one end and a savoury one at the other. Pasties are a perfect picnic and travel food: they keep relatively well, they are transportable and, if home made, are delicious.

Versions of the Cornish pasty are still made all over Europe. In Finland there is a tradition of making 'kalakukko'. This is a fish, meat or vegetable pie that used to be served warm, directly from the oven, on Saturday evenings when the family had gathered for supper after their weekly sauna bath. It was also baked for family feasts and special occasions. Described by Jaakko Rahola as a good food for travelling when cooked in a special handy size, it 'made a good day's food for a forest worker and it could be kept for a long time'. There is even a special family travel version with a built-in carrying handle made of wicker, originally developed for the long journeys to church on Sundays. The pies were hung on the branches of a nearby tree to be eaten before setting out for home after the service washed down with their soured milk drink. The thick pie-crust was originally made of unleavened dough using rye, pork fat, water and salt. The most common filling was small fish, dried, salted or fresh, depending on availability. In very hard times it could even be made of salted herring heads, which were removed before eating so only the fishy flavour remained. There are numerous other versions of the pie, with different fillings and different types of crust dough. Instead of fish, cheap stewing cuts of meat, udders and lungs or even squirrel meat has been used. Potatoes were not introduced into Finland until the late eighteenth century, so turnip and cabbage, along with plenty of bacon or pork fat made up the thick, rich filling. Kalakukko is still popular in Finland where nowadays it is served in the home with potatoes and sold in shops as a speciality, neatly sliced to show off the carefully arranged fillings.

Even in the cities, where traditionally many workers went home for the midday meal, some itinerant workers had to carry with them some form of convenience food. Living in the tenements of the Lower East side of New York in the 1830s, early Jewish settlers travelled all over the city to work as peddlars and merchants and they needed to be able to take their own kosher food with them. 'Piroshki', a street food still sold by vendors on the streets of Russian towns and in market places, are small savoury pies made of fried or baked dough surrounding a filling of meat, rice, sauerkraut, vegetables or some combination of these ingredients. 'Knishes' and 'burekas', now eaten as canapés in smart New York parties, were once little Russian pies for journeys and snacks. Small pastry turnovers called 'manti', filled with lamb or goat meat, are still sold in the markets of the Tajik and Uzbek

Republics along with 'pilmeny', a sort of suety manti rather like ravioli. Bunches of pilmeny are seen strung up outside the houses in the freezing Siberian winter where they can be broken off in frozen bits to be cooked when required. Along with Chinese spring rolls and Mexican stuffed tortilla, all these pies originated as ways of protecting food for keeping and travelling.

> 'And there's those who don't know what a pork-pie hat is, there's lots more that don't know what a pork-pie is. It's a very rare thing, let me tell you, a good pork-pie, and I can say so, for I'm one of the few people who can make one, though I say it myself.' Pies made with good lean fillets of pork and 'snow white' lard, best black pepper corns, some fresh made stock and a hard boiled egg. 'It was really very clever, because not only did Aunt Lily have to build the pastry into a tower, she had to fill it with pieces of meat and hard boiled egg, and pour in some gravy and put on a pastry hat just to fit.'
>
> Rebecca West *The Fountain Overflows*, 1957

Preserving food by first cooking or preparing it and then sealing it in a convenient and airtight environment really owed its origins to the invention of the pastry or pie-crusts in England in the Middle Ages. At this time recipes started to appear for 'chewetes' and 'flampoynetes', the latter a raised pie-crust or 'paste of dow' made with wheat flour or rye, filled with a pounded paste of pork mixed with cheese and spices and sealed with a decorated lid of pastry. Poultry, game, venison and fish were also popularly used in many versions of pies. 'Chewetes' were made from chopped pork and chicken baked in a 'coffyn as to a pye smale'. After the pastry case was filled, clarified melted butter or sometimes lard was poured into the crust or 'bread' until it was completely filled. Air pockets where bacteria could breed were eliminated and an airtight seal was created, which helped preserve the contents, though not, it should be said, for a very long time.

Strong pastry crusts of rye or wheat flour made perfect containers in which cooked meat, fish or vegetables could be baked, filled with melted butter or fats and tightly sealed with a lid of pastry. They had the added advantage of being easily portable, with the exception of the quite enormous pies that were often made. The thick, strong crusts were not necessarily always meant to be eaten. They kept the inside moist and the outside clean and their primary functions were as a casing for baking, a 'coffyn' for storing and as a carrying case for transporting.

The cold pie became very fashionable and its portability grew to be quite a novelty. Henry III, who loved Severn lampreys, had some despatched 'in bread' to his court in London. Pies could be made on country estates and sent up to the city, close-packed to prolong freshness, protected by robust walls of pastry to withstand the journey. In the colder months, when the butter seal would not melt, they could keep over long distances. One recipe suggests, rather over-optimistically, that a fish pie would keep for a year provided 'the Butter be not opened, nor craked, that the air get into the fish'.

Many pies were too large for travel and they played a part in the medieval love of display and drama. Huge pies were baked for feasts for the nobility including ones from which live birds could fly out when cut open. The ultimate show of wealth was a pie in which a whole goose was boned and baked in a raised pie-crust, and an even more lavish and exotic Christmas pie was 'stuffed' with a turkey, stuffed with a goose, stuffed with a fowl, then a partridge and finally a pigeon. 'This was then enclosed within a thick raised pie-crust, with hare, woodcock, moor-game and a large quantity of butter.' Christmas pies were sometimes sent as presents but did not always arrive in one piece, despite warnings that 'the walls must be well built'. Nevertheless, the crusts were always very ornate and cooks took great pride in their pastry decorating skills.

These portable pies served as a major breakthrough in storing and transportation of cooked meats safely and without spoiling. As well as handy food for the fields, the pie was a godsend for mothers worrying about an absent child. 'Dear Ned,' wrote Brilliana, Lady Harley, to her son at Magdalen College, Oxford in 1639, 'I have sent you by the carrier a box, derected to you, in which is a turky pie and 6 pyes, such as my lord, your grandfather, did love. I hope to remember you againe in lent . . . I have sent your

tutor a box of dryed plumes . . . tell him it is a Lenten token.'
Sir Edward was only fourteen when he went up to university and
his loving mother was concerned, like all mothers, that he was eating properly. 'I have made a pye to send you; it is a kide pye. I
beleeve you have not that meate ordinaryly at Oxford; one halfe
of the pye is seasned with one kind of seasening, and the other
with another.' She also sent him a 'gammon of backen' and
another 'Lenten token of dried sweetmeats for your tutor . . . The
dried appells are for you'. 'Deare Ned,' she finishes, 'be carefull
of your self, especially be watchfull over your hart.' Sadly Ned lost
his attentive and caring mother soon after, when she died during
the siege of her home by Royalists in 1643.

Pots

Despite the popularity of pies amongst the gentry and nobility, a
move from pie-crusts to a new method known as potting came relatively fast. By the late 1660s, the pastry pie-case, a mainstay of
'pocket foods', was giving way to earthenware pots. These were
stronger, more watertight containers for preserving meats and fish.
The pot would be sealed under an airtight layer of clarified butter, pork or duck fat.

Food to be taken to sea had to be protected from the damp sea
air, and it was best to make it both watertight and airtight. Sir
Hugh Plat, in the same 1607 paper for the navy that described his
concentrated broth, laid out a method of bottling food and making it airtight with a layer of olive oil. Keeping food airtight, using
sewn-up skins, bladders or pie-crusts was already a well-known
preserving art. So too was sealing food in earthenware jars of liquids such as oils and must. Sir Hugh's 'new' method, though
rather confused, seems to come somewhere between these two
ideas and that of sealing cooked foods in solid fats, which we now
know as potting. Sir Hugh later described how potting was first
being done in the sixteenth century:

> Some do use to parboil their Fowl, after they have taken out
> the garbage, and then do dip them in Barrowsgreace [lard],
> or clarified butter, till they have gotten a new garment over

them, and then they lay them one by one in stone pots,
filling the stone pots up to the brim with Barrowsgreace or
clarified butter.

Flavoured with cloves and salt, stopped very close and kept in a
cool place, 'these Fowl will keep sweet a good moneth together'.
Sir Kenelm Digby, an English Catholic whose book of 'Receipts'
was published after his death in 1669, gave five recipes for potted
meat including one 'To bake Venison to Keep' and another 'To
bake Pidgeons (Which are thus Excellent, and will keep a Quarter
of a Year) or Teals or Wild-ducks'. For potted venison, he
instructs his reader to 'Divide a Stag into four pots; then put about
a pound of Butter upon the top of each pot.' The meat was to be
baked overnight in an oven, and after cooling and all the remaining liquid had been drained off, the meat was repotted under a
thick layer of clarified butter. For greater protection, Digby's
recipe suggested that the potted meat was bound very close 'with
a piece of sheeps Leather so that no air can get in. After which
you may keep it as long as you please'.

Many recipes of this period still gave the choice of 'a Pot or
strong Crust' but by 1712 special potting pots were being manufactured on a large scale. In 1738 the Duke of Montagu was sent
a 'Pott of Charr' by carrier, which he declared to be 'the best I
ever eat'. Hannah Glasse, writing in 1747, advised that fish should
be 'Beat to a Paste, put into your potting-pot, and put it down as
close and hard as you can' before sealing it with clarified butter.
She also warned the cook to 'Let your Butter be very good, or
you will spoil all'. Spices were used liberally including pepper,
nutmeg, mace, cloves and sometimes wine or brandy was used to
'moiston' the mixture. Cooks found that meats, fish and cheese
kept even longer if they were first mashed up with butter before
potting. This method has not changed and is still used for making
meat and fish pastes today. Nowadays our potted shrimps or pâtés
have only a fine layer of butter covering the top. In earlier times
there was a thick layer of suet or butter set stiffly over the meat
to exclude the air with some aromatic herbs laid on top to keep
away the flies and help to preserve the contents. Seafood, fish and
birds of all kinds were potted. Pork and beef were cooked before

potting though very occasionally cured meat was potted. In 1750 William Ellis gave a 'Yorkshire Cook-Maid's Way to Pickle Pork', which was to rub pieces of pork with salt, saltpetre and sugar and pot it under fat. 'No way exceeds this,' Ellis declared.

According to Dorothy Hartley, only the best parts of the meat were cooked in pots in this way as it was essentially a 'condensing process used to compress extra food value for seamen and travellers'. Meat, considered the most valuable foodstuff, was always the first food to take advantage of new preserving methods. Luxury potted meats, potted salmon, potted hare and potted shellfish could until quite recently be found around old seaport towns and in some old country inns. In the old coaching days, when gentlemen and ladies travelled at considerable discomfort on heavily rutted and either dusty or flooded roads, the inn must have been a welcome sight despite the variable quality of the food and the service. Many were notorious for the damp bedding, slatternly servants and the landlady, 'a slipshod person in curl-papers' serving food often described as 'atrocious'. John Byng, who travelled around England in the 1780s, often complained about the food. One inn served 'a little miserable stale trout, some raw, rank, mutton chops and some cold, hard potatoes' but even worse was the landlady's 'Fusty old tart of last year's fruit. I open'd the Lid, and closed it tightly down for the next Comer. No Tricks upon Travellers'. In *Tancred*, Disraeli described quite a different spread at the King's Head at Thatcham. 'What a dinner! What a profusion of substantial delicacies! What mighty and iris-tinted rounds of beef! What vast and marble-veined ribs! What gelatinous veal pies! What colossal hams! Those are evidently prize cheeses! And how invigorating is the perfume of those various and variegated pickles!' By Disraeli's day, coaching had become a thriving commercial business and the well-prepared landlord of the King's Head would have known exactly how many customers he might expect and when. But for travellers arriving at a country inn alone and unannounced, the story was quite different. Robert Louis Stevenson, who loved to journey off the beaten track, might have found a small inn if he was lucky, otherwise he would have to find a house or farm that took in travellers as and when they passed by.

The howling desert miles around,
The Tinkling brook the only sound,
Wearied with all his toils and feats,
The traveller dines on potted meat,
On potted meats and princely wines,
Not wisely, but too well he dines.

Even the most hardened traveller dreams of a warm welcome and shelter with a table full of good things. Stevenson's well-fed verse suggests this was one of his better experiences. Potted meats, fish and cheese were popular standbys in inns both large and small. But it was far less easy to produce a meal of fresh food in out-of-the-way places and the innkeeper's wife, who probably doubled as farmer's wife, had to be prepared to put up quantities of preserved and stored food to provide for passing guests. She had to be skilled at salting and smoking the bacon and hams, and at pickling, potting or sousing the meat or fish. The smokehouse had to be hung with sausages, fish and flitches of bacon. The summer milk had to be turned into cheeses and the butter salted down in tubs. Bottled fruits and preserved or fruit cheese needed to be put up, and lemon curds and almond fillings kept ready for a tart or pie hurriedly baked as the unexpected travellers ate their first course. She would also have had to prepare bottled sauces and pickles to eat with the brawns and salt beef, collared tongues, pressed beef and cold boiled hams. Tins of dried biscuits would have been stored and eggs, pickled or waxed, carefully packed away. The root cellar was laid with straw or sawdust and filled with bins and barrels of potatoes, turnips, carrots, apples, pumpkins and other storable foodstuffs. She had to brew home-made ale and even make cowslip wine. On top of all the other farm and housework these small country innkeepers had to be prepared at any time for the sudden arrival of travellers who might stay one night or be snowed in for days.

Demand for potted foods became so great in the eighteenth and nineteenth centuries that it transformed the English pottery industries in towns such as Stoke-on-Trent, Coalbrookdale and Stockton-on-Tees. Potting pots gradually became more refined, made of glazed earthenware, delftware and stoneware, attractively decorated on the lids and sides with themed designs such as hunting scenes, species of fish or historic events. Some of these pots have now become collectors' items. Cheaper glass jars were also brought into service.

The same principle of sealing cooked food in fat so that it was protected from air has been applied in different ways around the world. In the Pacific Islands bamboo is used as a container. In the Solomon Islands, for example, meat or fish is cut up and packed into bamboo lengths of about 3 to 5 feet. Tiny balls of crushed banana leaves are pushed into the open end. Then the bamboo pieces are turned over hot coals until the steam comes out of the ends, a sign that the meat or fish is well cooked. As the food cools the fat becomes firm around it, helping to keep it airtight and a banana leaf is tied over the ends while it is still hot. The sealed bamboo are tied in bundles and stored on a rack over the kitchen fire. If some of the food is taken out, the bamboo must be sealed again with leaves and reheated over the fire. Storing them over the fireplace means that some smoke also permeates the food further helping in preserving it.

The Lebanese make a product called 'qawwrama' from their famous fat-tailed sheep, which are specially fattened for killing at the end of November. They are stuffed rather like geese are in France for 'foie gras', the women pushing food into their mouths until the sheep are so fat they can barely move. The fat is cut from the slaughtered sheep and rendered down in a large brass pan. The lean meat is cut into pieces and pressed to remove the moisture and then fried in mutton fat with seasoning. Earthenware crocks are filled with the hot meat and rendered fat and carefully sealed up with wet clay. Qawwrama keeps like this all winter and is useful for stews and stuffed vegetables.

A fourteenth-century Polish account similarly describes chunks of cooked meat immersed in melted, salted lard and stored in jars for several months in a cool place, still a common practice in some parts of eastern Europe. In southwest France, where almost every preserved food they prepare is now a famous gourmet speciality, the goose still reigns supreme and the word *confit*, meaning 'something preserved', belongs exclusively to that gastronomic region. A confit can be made with goose or duck fat in which the goose, duck or other meat is submerged and very gently cooked, preferably over a wood fire so that the wood smoke can play its part in adding flavour. The meat is then stored in the fat – *sous la graisse* – producing a delicacy that is smooth textured and 'gamey' in flavour. 'Rilletes', another southwestern speciality, are the French equivalent of British potted meat, using shredded scraps of meat from pork, goose, duck or rabbit.

The Atlantic coast off western France was once teeming with sardines, particularly around the town of Nantes. The region, which was later to become famous for its Newfoundland salt cod industry, began a lucrative trade by preserving the sardines in large earthenware jars called *oules*, which were filled with the local melted butter or olive oil from the south and sent to Paris and other cities inland. A popular Spanish version of the French confit is called 'olla'. As part of the pig killing, the pig's loins and ribs are prepared and cooked and then placed in the olla pots and covered with a thick skin of lard or oil.

Potting, essentially a technique which involves sealing cooked food under melted fat, produces a food that is cooked at a high temperature with plenty of fat and very little water. Most organisms are thus killed or entombed in the fat as it cools and solidifies, unable to move or proliferate. The hard 'skin' of fat also keeps airborne contaminants from entering. As a way of preserving food, however, it must have carried many risks from food poisoning, especially in some of the early recipes which recommended pounding and re-potting after some food had been taken, without re-sterilising by re-heating the food. But despite the claims for long shelf life, potted food was mostly a luxury item probably consumed quite quickly in most households. There are a number of potted foods still available in shops today including potted cheese and potted shrimps. Many of these have not been sterilised and sealed under clarified butter in the traditional way and can claim to be potted only by virtue of being sold in attractive pots.

Bottles

While cooked meats and fish potted under airtight layers of fat were becoming popular amongst the well-off in sixteenth-century

Europe, new ways of bottling fruits and vegetables, cooked and uncooked, with or without sugar, were also being found.

Storing and preserving food in airtight containers is an ancient practice, as old as the belief that protecting food from the contaminating air prevented putrefaction. The Romans were very enthusiastic about hermetically sealing food to preserve it, such as in airtight jars of honey, brine, vinegar and oil as well as containers filled with fruit syrups, concentrated must or wine. Mulberries were covered in their own liquor in a 'glass vessel' and stoppered. Pots and lids were coated with pitch and buried mouth down in the soil, and fruit was coated with wax or a mix of plaster clay and oil lees. Hermetic storage was also particularly important for keeping various grains. But although burying food in the ground may have helped preserve it by keeping it relatively cool and free from airborne bacteria, it was not possible to remove part of the stored food without disturbing the rest and almost certainly letting air into the pit. The food stored in this way would not have been conveniently to hand, nor was it movable. By contrast, food sewn into skins and bladders was portable and possibly airtight, but only until it was opened. Most foods carried in this way, such as dried or smoked meat or sausages, would have needed to be first treated by some other form of preserving method.

While cooked meat and fish was kept airtight, sealed in a pot under a coat of fat, in a process broadly known as potting, fruit and some vegetables began to be preserved in earthenware jars and bottles using a variety of liquids that helped to preserve the food as well as keeping the containers free from air. Honey, sugar syrups, brine, alcohol and vinegars possessed their own preserving qualities and were therefore ideal media in which to preserve food in bottles. In fact, fruits and vegetables could be kept in bottles almost indefinitely if they were in heavy solutions of honey, sugar, alcohol or vinegar.

Pure alcohol is an ideal preservative since nothing can grow in it, however a very high proof is required to counteract the acidity of fruits preserved in it and many people feel, reasonably enough, that this is a waste of good alcohol. The technique originated in the medieval European monasteries where the art of distilling was extensively practised. Fruit steeped in bottles of alcohol – peaches and plums in brandy, cherries in kirsch, pears in eau de vie – remain popular favourites for Christmas cheer in northern Europe and the US. In Germany they still make a celebration preserve of layered fruits in alcohol and sugar in an earthenware pot called a 'rumtopf'. New layers are added as different fruits come into season. Fruit syrups and liqueurs are a wonderful way of using surplus fruit and are popular all over the world. The French make 'syrop de cassis' from blackcurrants, and in the Middle East guests are welcomed with spoonfuls of a rich conserve of crunchy nuts, grapes and sliced lemon bottled up in brandy and sugar.

Preserving food in oils is another ancient custom, popular in ancient Egypt, Greece and Rome. Oils do not possess natural preserving qualities but they are a useful alternative to animal fats in hot countries where the fats are liable to melt. There are many different kinds of oil – sesame, sunflower, soya, groundnut and, of course, olive oil – and their different flavours add to the quality of the preserve. Mushrooms, sun-dried tomatoes, aubergines, artichoke hearts, seafood and olives are all delicious and look wonderful suspended in large glass bottles of glowing resin-coloured oil. The Romans particularly liked balls of soft cheese preserved in jars of oil.

Vinegar and brine are both powerful preservative media and there is a huge range of pickled vegetables, already described, as well as some fruits such as spiced oranges or plums, hot pickled limes from the Punjab, and salted lemons from North Africa. The strong acidity of vinegar presented considerable problems before glass was widely available as people used copper and other metal utensils and containers that acid fruits corroded and in which some vegetables turned a nasty green. Glass is an ideal material because it is non-corrosive and can be made heat resistant. Glass jars and bottles of all sorts of shapes, designs, colours and sizes also make attractive transparent containers, showing off colourful displays of the foods packed inside them.

Food preserving, especially bottling, was essential for the European colonists living thousands of miles from home in difficult climates, surrounded by strange cultures and cuisines. Preserved foods sent out to early colonists were no doubt important contributions to their survival and would also help in their cultural survival, a way of keeping up standards and staying in touch with home. Gradually Western preserving methods were adapted by colonial housewives who taught their servants the fine art of English jam making while using local vegetables and fruits to bottle and pickle some exotic-sounding fare for their tropical larders. Bottling also freed farm families from having to rely on the wooden pickle barrels, root cellars and smokehouses to get them through the winter. The robust Kilner and Mason jar (introduced in 1858) was fitted with metal clips, screw tops and rubber rings to keep the contents airtight. These were enormously popular right up to the mid-twentieth century both in rural and town households for preserving surplus of fruits and vegetables such as tomatoes, sweet corn, berries, peaches, relishes and pickles.

It was this process of preserving food in sealed containers or bottles that proved to be the jumping off point for the preserving revolution to come. The arrival of the airtight glass bottle or jar and the 'cooking' of food within it were major turning points in the move from empirical traditions to scientific processes. True to form, it was some time before anyone seemed to have either understood the effects of this process or to have grasped the potential benefits it might have brought.

From its arrival in the West in the sixteenth century until well into the nineteenth century, sugar remained an expensive luxury that even wealthy households kept under lock and key. Preserving fruit as sweetmeats or jams was enormously attractive to the sweet tooth of the rich everywhere, but if fruit could be preserved without sugar . . .

There are some kinds of fruit which are very acidic and require much less sugar or heating to preserve them. The key example is the gooseberry. The earliest known recipe for gooseberry bottling was in *A Book of Receipts according to the Newest methods* published anonymously in 1680. 'Gather gooseberries at their full growth, but not ripe. Top and tail them, and put them into glass bottles, put corks on them but not too close, and sit them on a gentle fire, in a kettle of cold water up to the neck, but wet not the cork, let them stand till they turn white, or begin to crack, and set them till cold, then beat in the corks hard, and pitch them over.'

In 1705 William Salmon's popular *The Family Dictionary* gave a number of fruit-bottling recipes including one for gooseberries.

This similarly described heating the bottles but specified that the corks should be loosely put in the 'jars', which were at that time wide-mouthed containers. When the fruit was cooked, the corks were to be knocked further in and sealed. In 1727 Eliza Smith gave an almost identical recipe in her *Compleat Housewife* but used 'bottles', meaning they had narrow necks so that only small fruit such as gooseberries and cherries could be pushed through. Richard Bradley in his recipe of the same year advised that the cook should buy special wide-mouthed bottles, 'Quart Bottles that are made on purpose with large wide Necks'. Hannah Glasse's 1747 *The Art of Cookery Made Plain and Easy*, consisting mostly of recipes taken from earlier works, included the same recipe for bottling gooseberries as Eliza Smith and Richard Bradley, who themselves may well have copied theirs from William Salmon. Copying recipes from other authors does not seem to have been regarded as plagiarism in those days; it is not so well tolerated today though it is still known to happen. The recipe, as it appears in Glasse's book, is this:

> To keep Green Gooseberries till Christmas.
> Pick your large green Gooseberries on a dry Day, have ready your Bottles clean and dry, fill the Bottles and cork them, set them in a Kettle of Water up to their Neck, let the Water boil very softly till you find the Gooseberries are coddled, take them out, and put in the rest of the Bottles till all is done; then have ready some Rosin melted in a Pipkin, dip the Necks of the Bottles in, and that will keep all Air from coming in at the Cork, keep them in a cool dry Place, where no Damp is, and they will bake as red as a Cherry. You may keep them without scalding, but then the Skins will not be so tender, nor bake so fine.

This startlingly modern process would not seem out of date to anyone who bottles fruit today. It would have produced a sterile, preserved fruit without the addition of preserving sugar. Yet no one understood the principle nor was able to recognise the importance of the recipe, which sits unremarkably on the page alongside many other fruit recipes, its huge, revolutionary potential unseen for another fifty years.

CHAPTER TEN

NAVY BLUES

Joining his first ship was a day every seaman or boy would always remember, whether he had been 'pressed' into service, was a volunteer or had been enlisted as a boy by his family to learn seamanship as a captain's servant.

As the ship was loaded and made ready for a long voyage of discovery or for naval service, every hand would be busy lifting, hauling, hoisting and stowing, greasing, swabbing and furling. There was little time or care to give a frightened newcomer. Young Frederic Chamier, only twelve years old, stood nervously on the deck of the thirty-six-gun frigate *Salsette*, dressed proudly in the new uniform that had so dazzled his family and the servants at home that morning. He watched nervously as his large chest of precious possessions – clothes, food and the little luxuries his mother had tucked away for him – was hoisted aboard to the cries of derision from the master's mates.

'Why! Does this youngster think the ship was made for him?'

Chamier, who had never been aboard a ship before, was horrified by the noise and smells on the main deck. As he remembered in his book *The Life of a Sailor*, published in 1833, 'Ye gods, what a difference! I had anticipated a kind of elegant house with guns in the windows; an orderly set of men; in short, I expected to find a species of Grovesnor Place, floating around like Noah's Ark.' What he saw instead were 'the tars of England', without jackets, shoes or stockings, rolling brine-filled barrels of salt pork, beef and fish down into the hold. Following these came casks of beer and rum, kegs of butter, huge cheeses and sacks of flour, oatmeal and dried beans and peas. A vast quantity of hardtack was also taken down the hatches into the hold. Through one porthole came coal, at another they brought down wood to fuel the galley fires.

It all seemed like the chaos of Hell. 'Dirty women, the objects of sailors' affections, with beer cans in hand, were everywhere conspicuous: the shrill whistle squeaked, and the noise of the boatswain and his mate rattled like thunder in my ears; the deck was dirty, slippery and wet; the smells abominable; the whole sight disgusting.'

The small boy's picture-book world of jolly Jack Tars, the glory of Nelson and his great fighting ships, their billowing sails filled, speeding before the winds as they swept into battle with France, was shattered. 'For nearly the first time in my life, and I wish I could say it was the last, I took the handkerchief from my pocket; covered my face and cried like the child I was.'

Despite being thrown in at the deep end and being expected to eat and sleep with the ordinary crew, the conditions young Chamier had to endure as a captain's servant were considerably better than for the majority of seamen. But he never forgot what he saw as a child in the galleys and mess rooms of those huge wooden vessels, powered only by wind and muscle. His book, written when he himself took command of his own ship, is filled with graphic accounts of life and food at sea.

The provisioning of ships' crews had to be carefully calculated. Quantity and cost were the primary considerations for any navy and quality, variety and nourishment seem to have come a very poor second. A seaman serving on a ship in the reign of Henry VIII was thought to require a daily diet of 1 lb of biscuit, 1 lb of salt pork or salt beef and 1 gallon of ale. Spanish ships of the Armada, sent out by Philip II in 1588 to assert his claim to the English throne, were loaded up with thousands of barrels of biscuit (in every navy considered to be the most important food ration), one barrel of ship's biscuit being roughly equivalent to 225 lb. They also took hundreds of barrels of salt pork, salt fish and hard cheese, plus pickled vegetables, oil, vinegar, rice, pease, oatmeal and kegs of salt butter. For the ordinary seamen, this monotonous and unpalatable diet would continue for many hundreds of years. The ship's diet for a naval seaman, entirely made up of preserved foods, remained virtually unchanged in quality, quantity and variety. A Tudor sailor would have eaten roughly the same amount as his descendants serving in Nelson's navy 300 years or more later.

Sailors' mess table in Nelson's navy. The table was slung between two guns on the gundeck

The captain and his officers ate reasonably well while stocks lasted and they could take some of their own private supplies but the ordinary seaman's catering arrangements were extremely primitive. In home port the men could buy some available fresh provisions and on arriving in foreign ports they were surrounded by bumboats selling fruit and other fresh foods. Nevertheless, naval ships, in desperation, were known to hijack passing fishing boats returning home fully laden and raid their hold for fresh fish.

It is worth remembering that armies of the time were just as poorly provisioned. The Welsh chronicler, Elis Gruffydd, was serving in 1545 in Henry VIII's army based in the garrison at Calais. His unit was called out to intercept a French force but their response was slow and sullen. Unpaid, the soldiers had been forced to take food from the King's storehouses, '. . . where it had been kept too long. The bread was hard and baked with corn and meal which had lost its taste and savour, and the salt beef stank when it was lifted out of the brine, the butter was of many colours and the cheese dry and hard . . . which made the soldiers miserable and reckless.' But as well as having sporadic access to commandeered or bartered fresh food, at least an army was not faced with the particular problems of staying at sea for long periods.

Until the mid-nineteenth century, sailing ships were built of timber and their wooden hulls absorbed water. This may have made them more buoyant but it also meant that they were terribly damp. Since the principal method of preserving food was by drying, taking it to sea presented special problems. Stowed away in the lower decks below water level, stores of dried peas and ship's biscuit rotted as well as being attacked by weevils and the inevitable ship's rats. Salt itself is absorbent and salted foods such as 'barrel beef' and pork were also likely to spoil if they were not properly stored. Only food preserved in barrels of brine or vinegar were completely protected but these were bulky and heavy in vessels already loaded to the gunwales with men, sails and rigging, cargo, guns and ammunition. Naval commanders concerned with speed and merchant ships' owners with profits would always cut back on food supplies before anything else.

Pork and beef were heavily salted for use at sea. Often, though, the meat was put straight into the barrels of brine without a pre-salting to drain off the blood and fluids, which then soured the pickle. It was known by sailors as 'barrel pork' or 'sea junk' and it required lengthy soaking (which it rarely got) before being cooked, often in sea water as fresh water supplies were rationed. This practice was vividly described by the seamen's missionary E. J. Mather in his book *N'orrard The Dogger* when he went on a fishing trip in the North Sea to get first-hand experience of life at sea. Although it was men's souls he was concerned with, he also knew how important their comforts and conditions were. For him, cooking on board seemed a curious business.

> Not many minutes had elapsed before the cook . . .
> emerged from the companion and approached me, holding
> with a very mysterious air, a small net to which a stout line
> was made fast.

'What have you in that net?' I enquired.

'It's the salt beef for tomorrow's dinner, sir, and I'm going to lash it to this cleat, so as it may tow under the vessel's stern to take the salt out.'

'But if that is for to-morrow's dinner, where is the beef for this evening?'

'Why, here it is,' said he, hauling on board another small net similar to the one he had just cast over the stern, 'it has been astern of her since this time yesterday.'

'You see, sir,' chimed in the fourth hand, 'that 'ere beef gets uncommon salt when it's bin in the harness cask for six weeks, and we're obliged to get some of the brine out of it, or we couldn't tackle it nohow.'

'And so you find that the best way to extract the salt from the beef is by towing it in the salt sea.?'

'You're right, sir; that's how we're forced to do it.'

This was all new to me, and my curiosity being excited, I followed into the cabin to see the end of this novel style of cooking.

A huge pot was boiling furiously on the fire, and what with the smell of fried fish still remaining from breakfast, the stale fumes of tobacco, and the heat from the nearly red-hot stove, the atmosphere of the cabin was quite unbearable. The cook promptly removed the lid from the great sauce-pan, and popped in his net of salt beef. It struck me that the water looked very peculiar, so I asked.

'Is that fresh water, cook?'

'No sir, it's sea water. We can't afford to use fresh water; we only carry enough for drinking.'

The cook produced a large tin dish and a sack, which, he told Mather were the 'taturs, sir and that's the pudden'. The whole lot went into the saucepan of beef and sea water. Mather found the pudding rather heavy, the meat terribly tough and very salty, in spite of its twenty-four hours' soaking. It looked, wrote, Mather, like a wedding-cake, 'Being encrusted with dry white salt within a few moments of its removal from the boiling sea-water'.

The result was that the salt burned the sailors' lips and mouths making them dreadfully thirsty for the ship's scarce water supplies or their rations of grog. Sometimes producing even this meagre meal was beyond the provisions. The 'sea junk' and salt beef, also known as 'salt horse' (which it sometimes was), often became rancid, hardened beyond reconstituting or was attacked by maggots. The ship's cheese, usually the very hard Suffolk or Essex variety made from the thinnest skimmed milk, sometimes became so tough and dry that sailors carved buttons from it. Salt fish became soggy or mushy. Fats went rancid, beer went sour, the water putrefied.

But they had to make the best of it and many of the ship's cooks created a unique naval 'cuisine' with dishes such as 'lobscouse', ship's biscuit crumbled into a stew of salt meat, and 'burgoo', possibly derived from the Middle Eastern byrghel, made with oatmeal 'grits' cooked into a porridge or gruel containing 'gobbets of salt horse'. 'Sea pie' was made with meat and vegetables layered with crumbled hardtack. Dutch seamen made 'dunderfunk' (thunder and lightning), a sort of cake of soaked biscuit, mixed with fat and molasses, baked in a pan. 'Midshipman's crab' was an exciting concoction of pickles, salt beef, biscuit crumbs and crumbled hard cheese with galley pepper made from soot and ashes. The officers had a rather more interesting variety of ingredients to play with and they could make their own 'figgy-dowdy' with this recipe:

> We take ship's biscuit and put it in a stout canvas bag.
> Pound it with a marline spike for half an hour.
> Add bits of pork fat, plums, figs, rum, currants.
> Send it to the galley, and serve it up with bosun's grog.

Grog was named after Admiral Vernon, nicknamed 'Old Grog' because of his grosgrain cloak. He made the mistake of trying to dilute the seaman's allowance of a half pint of neat West Indian rum. Their daily allowance of 8 pints of beer, however, served as an important part of their calorie intake. Unfortunately the beer quickly soured and went off. On long voyages they drank watered wine which helped reduce the bacteria in the ship's putrid water supplies. The favourite drink, however, was 'flip', a mix of beer and brandy or rum, sweetened with sugar and heated with a hot iron. A 'small chirping Can of Flip' was the only warm drink enjoyed by naval sailors until around 1800 when they were allowed hot cocoa and tea.

Navy cooks were privileged old salts, retired petty officers or Chelsea pensioners with a disability such as a wooden leg. They had the reputation of being the most useless person on board. But they had their own privileges and powers. The greasy scum at the top of the pot of boiled salt meat was considered unhealthy while in fact it might have been a useful, though disgusting, addition of essential animal fat to the seamen's diet. The cook did a brisk trade selling the fat scum to the crew to smear on their bread or to make oatmeal pudding; the rest he saved for the return to port when he sold it to the grease dealers. This fatty 'Slush' was also used to grease the masts and to waterproof hats and boots. The smell must have been terrible.

As on E. J. Mather's fishing boat in the North Sea, cooking on naval vessels was done in one huge ship's cauldron. Each mess, or group of six to eight men, had their food boiled in a bag with a button or tally to identify it. The 'mess' cook collected the food and the biscuit ration doled out by the steward's assistant, who was known as 'Jack the Dust'. Biscuits stamped with a broad arrow, the royal mark, were stored in barrels and canvas bags in the bread room. This was lined with either tin, or in the better class ships, with mats or deal planks, and was well caulked to keep it as dry as possible. But old hardtack still crumbled to dust and the bread room was more often a dirty, dusty, weevil-infested hole. Sailors used to tap the biscuit on the table to knock out the weevils, but the lightest tap could reduce it to dust. 'Every biscuit is like a piece of clockwork, moved by its own internal impulse, occasioned by the myriads of insects that dwelt within.'

Likewise the cheeses, if not rock hard, were often poorly preserved and would quickly rot. Soon they would, it was said, 'walk themselves out the door' they were so full of heaving maggots. One solution with weevils was to spread the infested bread on tarpaulins in the hot sun, or even better rebake them. This not only killed the weevils but also cooked them into the bread thus providing some additional protein. The taste of weevil was said to be bitter whilst maggots or 'bargemen' were spongy and tasted 'cold'. An ingenious way to entice the maggots out of salt meat was to put a fresh fish on top of a pile of meat. The black headed maggots, knowing the fish would be more nutritious than the meat, crawled out to the fish bait.

Throughout the naval victualling system fraud and malpractice were rife. Contractors supplying the preserved foods bribed purchasing officials to buy short weights and old and poor quality foods. The 'sell-by date' was unheard of. Food was commonly preserved years before it was stowed into a ship's hold when it would already be old and tainted. Salted meat was not hung and dried as it was for sale on land but left stored in the brine in barrels until it was uneatable. Bakers on the Thames supplying ship's biscuit, the mainstay of the seaman's diet, were also making their fortunes by adulterating the flour and cheating over the weight. Biscuits forty years old are known to have been issued.

The Admiralty victualling authorities were supposed to carefully calculate and properly supervise the provisioning of ships in order to prevent graft and ensure adequate food for the crews. The man who came between a seaman and his food most, however, was the purser who was responsible for the provisions issued by the Victualling Board. The ship's purser, who held a very powerful position, constantly short-rationed the men in ways that everyone not only knew about but accepted as part of 'traditional practice'. The purser was personally accountable for the entire value of the ship's stores, so to protect himself, he had to keep careful and complex accounts of every detail of provisions stowed on the ship and every portion of it doled out to the cook and the men. It became a regular practice for the purser to give sailors short rations in order to make up his losses through food deterioration. This meant that a mess of five men received only the daily allowance for four men, a practice known as 'four over five'. No provisions were ever allowed to be thrown away however bad their state except for the cheese, which when putrid could make such a stench that the whole ship was permeated. In 1740 a survey of provisions showed that 'Eighteen hundred and ninety five pounds of cheese' had been condemned that year.

However revolting the seaman's rations may seem to us, they were in fact far better fare than the diet of most country people in sixteenth- to eighteeenth-century Europe. A pound of salt meat, 1 lb of biscuit and a gallon of beer a day was far more than a hardworking single peasant, or even a whole family, could expect to eat every day. Many country men willingly joined up and did not complain. But the dreadful hardship and extremely tough physical work required of them, combined with an inadequate diet, took a very heavy toll. William Hodges, writing in 1695, calculated that for every man who died in action, ten died because of bad or insufficient nourishment. Scurvy, the scourge of naval ships, was equally feared by fishermen and crews of all vessels that by the sixteenth century 'littered the seas'.

The symptoms of scurvy were first described by Magellan on his 1519–21 voyage around the world on the *Victoria*. Lacking fresh food, the crew had been thrown back on their decayed biscuit supplies and were reduced to eating leather and rats. 'As a result of this bad nourishment, a strange disease fell upon us. The upper and lower gums swelled so greatly as to cover the teeth, so that the sick man could take no good.' They had found that the surviving men recovered with great speed once they were able to take on board fresh coconuts, yams and sugar cane.

In 1535 a French captain, Jacques Cartier, searching for a new route to the Spice Islands, was trapped over a terrible winter in the Gulf of St Lawrence where his men became ill: 'Their legs swell, their sinews black as any coal.' Cartier noticed that when the native people showed similar symptoms they were quickly cured with a brew of the leaves of a 'certaine Tree' probably *Sassafras officinale*. Cartier made his crew drink the infusion, which they found disgusting, but they 'were delivered of that sickness'. One or two other ships' crews were similarly saved by taking the local cure such as leple leaves or scurvy grass, and sailors of long experience such as the Vikings, Chinese and Dutch already knew about the value of taking cranberries, ginger plants, sauerkraut, winter cresses, young spruce and pine shoots, horseradish, sorrel, seaweed and the scurvy grasses on their long voyages. While these remedies may have helped save men in smaller boats on shorter voyages, the increasing size of ships and time spent at sea meant it was impossible to provide fresh food for long. Even the most enlightened ships' captains were unable to understand what caused scurvy.

James Lancaster was the commander of the first English expedition to the East Indies, which set out in February 1600. The four ships of the expedition did not reach land until the following summer by which time many of the men had already succumbed to scurvy. But in one ship, James Lancaster's, there were very few cases. The reason was that the Commander had brought with him bottles of lemon juice, of which he gave three spoonfuls every morning to each man. The newly formed East India Company was so impressed that they arranged for supplies of lemon-water to be taken on all its ships. Despite his apparent breakthrough, however, Lancaster persisted with the most commonly held belief that scurvy was caused by a diet of salt meat. Other theories were advanced. Scientists continued to refer to an 'overflowing of black bile' and a 'corruption of the humours' caused by 'unwholesome air'. The physician to the English fleet at the end of the seventeenth century wrote that scurvy was a consequence of 'an idle life, and a feeding on salt beef and pork'. Even the type of salt used in curing was examined as a possible source of evil.

A Dutchman, Dr Johannes Backstrom, wrote a small book in 1734 that claimed that scurvy was caused by a deficiency of fresh vegetables. He coined the word 'antiscorbutic' and he advised that seamen should lay up a greater store of vegetables than of salt meat and that soldiers under siege should plant seeds of antiscorbutic plants on the ramparts, indeed he declared, as modern nutritionists still do, that everyone should eat more vegetable matter for a healthy life. But Backstrom's contemporaries would have none of it and some even blamed scurvy on the Dutch method for refining salt.

As a consequence, by the middle of the eighteenth century 'sea scurvy' was as bad as ever, and was still feared by every naval commander and every man in his crew. In England in 1747 a naval surgeon, Dr James Lind, was ordered by the Admiralty to investigate the disease. He carried out careful experiments, including treating twelve sick seamen with different remedies. Two men were given cider daily, two had drops of elixir of vitriol (concentrated sulphuric acid), two had vinegar, two had sea water, two were treated with a mixture of garlic, mustard seed, horseradish, balsam and gum myrrh and another two were given orange and lemon juice. The pair fed with orange and lemon juice recovered quickly, the ones given cider improved more slowly. The others made no improvement at all. Lind published a long account proving to the navy how it could rid itself of scurvy. But all his advice about citrus fruit and other remedies for scurvy were disregarded by the Admiralty because of the extra expense. They argued that it would be difficult to supply in large enough quantities in a way that would keep for long voyages and ignored Lind's suggestions for preserving fruit juices and greens. Meanwhile the useless and dangerous oil of vitriol and vinegar continued to be issued to sick seamen. Of the 185,000 men raised for 'sea-service' during the Seven Years' War (1756–63) no fewer than 130,000 are reported to have died as a result of scurvy.

In the 1770s Captain Cook successfully protected his men on several voyages with a regime of hygiene, fresh vegetables whenever possible, doses of malt and the 'rob', or boiled essence of lemons or oranges plus large helpings of sauerkraut 'which does not spoil by keeping'. He was awarded a medal by the Royal Society for 'having conquered scurvy'. But Cook's ships were not ships of war and the Admiralty remained unmoved by the evidence, even claiming that any effort to change or improve the diet of the English tar was impossible due to his extremely conservative nature. 'Our seamen are so besotted in their beef and pork that they had rather adventure on all the calentures [fevers] and scarbots [scurvies] in the world than be weaned from their customary diet or the least bit of it.'

Nearly 200 years after Captain Lancaster had successfully dosed his crew with lemon juice the Admiralty finally accepted that it was the best antiscorbutic for treating sick seamen. But they preferred to buy cheaper limes from the British colonies rather than lemons from the Mediterranean, believing that the two fruits were the same. The juice of the lemon is in fact two to three times richer in antiscorbutic vitamin C than that of the lime. Americans were soon nicknaming British sailors 'limers' or 'limeys'.

Another problem was how to preserve fruit juice for long voyages. James Lind's method was to evaporate juice gently in bowls set in almost boiling water for several hours until it became a thick syrup, like portable soup or veal glue, which he then tightly corked under a layer of olive oil. This method would have reduced the vitamin activity but not destroyed it. Other less effective methods included boiling and then bottling with airtight stoppers or the addition of brandy or rum. The labels on modern bottles of Rose's Lime Juice Cordial record that by the 1860s Lauchlan Rose had a thriving business importing lime juice from the West Indies. Rose had devised a method for preserving juice without alcohol and the label claims 'he invented the world's first concentrated fruit drink'. By 1895 both naval and merchant shipping was ordered to serve one ounce of lemon or, more often, lime juice to every member of crew after the ship had been at sea for ten days. This was in fact far below the necessary daily amount needed but was probably just sufficient to prevent serious outbreaks of scurvy.

'Perhaps one of the most bewildering aspects of the history of scurvy,' J. J. Keevil wrote in *Medicine and the Navy* in 1957, 'is the manner in which a cure was repeatedly found, only to be lost again because of a wrong theory of its manner of operation, or because some uncontrollable factor offered a preferable explanation when it came to accounting for deaths . . .' By the end of the eighteenth century, the authorities were still blaming the 'distemperature of the aire', the 'vapours of the sea', the cold, the heat, the stagnant water, the filth on the ships or the men's morals, their laziness or indiscipline. They continued to blame the predominant diet of salt meat, thinking that it contained the seeds of the disease. In fact it was what it did not contain – vitamin C – that was the real problem. Nevertheless, by focusing the authorities on improving the meat supplies, the ravages of scurvy were to lead directly to a revolution in food preserving.

Navies had assumed critical military importance in the long wars between France and England. Both the French and British navies had radically increased in size – Nelson's *Victory* had a crew of 900 men at the Battle of Trafalgar – requiring more and better provisioning. Even when the fleets were not voyaging for long distances, ships had to stay at sea for up to six months holding blockades against the enemy. Ill health and nutritional diseases continued to decimate the crews and eventually even the Royal Navy began to realise that if its ships were better and more effectively provisioned, with food preserved with improved methods, they would have a greater fighting chance in war.

Both the French and British navies let it be known that they were searching for a new miracle food. The solution would have to be found in new inventions and better techniques for preserving food, discoveries that would eventually transform everyone's diet forever.

CHAPTER ELEVEN

FROM COOKS TO CHEMISTS

Tell me what you eat: I will tell you what you are.
Brillat Savarin, *Physiologie du Gout*, 1825

The endless search for the perfect healthy diet continues to dominate Western magazines and television as they churn out 'new' information about anti-oxidants, fat-free diets, high-fibre diets, five fruit and vegetable diets, vegetarianism and the Mediterranean diet. As a result, many of us are now fairly well versed in the language of nutrients; vitamins, minerals, fats, fibres and carbohydrates. We may not completely understand what they are, nor exactly how they work, but we are not alone. Chemists, physicians and dieticians are still exploring the known and researching the new. We have, after all, only tried eating a fraction of the potential edible resources on the planet.

The idea that our food intake can influence our health is a very ancient one, although it was for a long time coupled with the belief that food determined not just health but also social status. Development of medical science and ideas about nutrition were dominated by the teachings of Aristotle, Hippocrates and later, the Greek physician Galen, who drew up a dietary 'regimen of health' that remained unchanged and unchallenged for centuries. In the second century AD, Galen declared that an individual's diet should take into consideration their age, sex, 'humoral disposition', state of health and occupation, as well as climatic, seasonal and environmental factors. It was believed these could have an impact on the individual according to his 'qualities' and 'humours'. For example, small children and the elderly were believed to be full of water and phlegm and should therefore eat 'hot' foods. Lamb, which was very moist and 'phlegmatic', was therefore unsuitable for old men or babies who already had too much phlegm. By the same principle, a choleric man would need to eat less hot and dry foods, such as cabbage, and more cool foods, such as lettuce. Galen's classification of foods bears little relation to their true nutritional content, whether they are starchy, fatty, acid and alkaline foods. But perhaps the most controversial and damaging rule was for fruit, which Galen classified as 'cold' and considered a cause of disease. He even claimed that his father lived to be a hundred years old because he never ate fruit.

From what is known today, the Galen diet, if rigidly pursued, could have been nutritionally quite dangerous. Fortunately, few people have ever stuck rigidly to a diet. The rules for the 'regimen' were as complex, time-consuming and detailed as any modern slimming regime. Originally created for wealthy and important members of society, the rules were designed for those who had the time to analyse his or her 'qualities' and 'humours', as well as the wealth to afford both quantity and choice of foodstuffs. To 'eat according to ones qualities' was a maxim that has been practised by the rich for centuries. While it may have improved their standing amongst their peers, these diets did little to improve their nutritional health. Yet for hundreds of years, no one dared to question it.

Even more extraordinary were the so-called scientific theories on the natural order of the world that determined a parallel status for foods with those who ate them. Just as they were taught that food consisted of the same elements as themselves, people also believed that plants and animals held a place in the social order. The value of a food could be determined by its place on this ladder of 'natural' society. Roots were particularly low in status since they were buried under the earth. Common greenstuffs that grew at ground level were also thought lowly and fit only for people of low social groups. Leeks, turnips and onions, along with the common 'greens', were left to the lowly peasant to eat. Fruits that grew high in trees and birds that flew in the air were deemed more attractive and beneficial food for the 'high born'.

The early medieval nobleman in Europe covered his table with huge quantities of food, in particular meat. By the fifteenth and sixteenth centuries, the wealthier classes were less concerned with manly pursuits of hunting and war and were more interested in courtly and diplomatic business. Consequently, they preferred a creative table of quality rather than one overloaded with food. Feasts became an elaborate visual theatre and an excitement to the palate rather than a filling of the stomach. Banquets grew more and more inventive in their menus. The ability to serve fresh foods in any season continued to be a great source of social standing. At the same time, expensive, refined foods were considered good for wealthy, refined stomachs, while coarse and common foods were deemed sufficient for the common, poor stomach. An Italian physician predicted sickness for those who ate foods inappropriate to their social status. Rich people, it was argued, should not eat heavy soups made with pulses, vegetables or offal for they were not 'nutritious or easy to digest'.

These dietary theories often led people to give up nutritious foods in favour of unsuitable ones. In addition, until the sixteenth century, agricultural practice remained undeveloped and quite primitive and traditional food preserving techniques, as well as having practical drawbacks, were not always capable of retaining the vital nutrients in the food. All these factors helped contribute to the widespread dietary diseases that were the scourge of both rich and poor.

Many country people knew enough about their food and about medicinal herbs to counter the worst effects of a poor diet, but as soon as people moved to towns and had less control over their food provision, the problem worsened. The difficulties of bringing large supplies of foods to feed urban workers meant an increasing reliance on preserved and portable foods and until transport could be improved, urban dwellers, with no kitchen garden or access to country herbs, often ate less well than their rural cousins. The town dwellers lived on bread, pickled or salt herrings and cheese, with occasional cheap cuts of fresh meat such as sheep's heads or pig's trotters. When money was short or prices were high, meat had to give place to cheese or broths made with dried peas and beans. Furthermore, urban dwellers who considered themselves to be moving up the ladder were less inclined to eat poor country fare such as vegetables. It was commonly believed that vegetables were 'windy' and unfit to be eaten except in broths, or occasionally, well seasoned with oil, in salads. Fresh fruit was sometimes eaten as a dessert by the wealthy though it was still believed to cause fevers and other ailments.

As a result, scurvy and other scorbutic illnesses were rife, not only on the seas but in the towns as well, particularly in northern climates and amongst people confined to poor institutions. Hundreds of thousands died from scurvy and many countless thousands more suffered poor health and low resistance to other diseases because they were in a 'scorbutic' state. In 1940 Professor Drummond wrote in *The Englishman's Food* that children in Scandinavia were found to have mild scurvy at the end of the winter, which rapidly improved as soon as they ate fresh food in the spring. With people subsisting over the intervening centuries on a winter diet of salted meat and pickled fish and rye or wheat bread, scurvy was a common problem across northern Europe, Russia and even in parts of China. During the 1850s some 10,000 California gold seekers died of scurvy, though many others survived by eating winter purslane known as 'miners' lettuce'.

Many other dietary diseases were rife. 'Night blindness', a common and potentially serious eye condition, was the result of vitamin A deficiency. When the peasant diet was lacking in eggs, milk, animal fats or green vegetables (usually in the winter months) they were particularly prone to this disease. Cooked liver, if it could be got, was known to provide a quick cure. The fishermen who went on long sea voyages provisioned only with flour, salt meat and fish, often found their sight deteriorating in poor light, their eyelids becoming swollen and sore. Recognising the early symptoms, they would immediately cook and eat some cod's liver and were soon well again. Xerophthalmia is still found in Egypt, India, Sri Lanka and in parts of China where a cereal diet dominates and little or no meat or vegetables are eaten. Vitamin A deficiency also causes stones in the bladder, a painful condition that was often described by wealthy gentlemen in their diaries. Perhaps this was partly because the affluent thought that butter, offal and green vegetables, all rich in vitamins, were foods fit only for the poor.

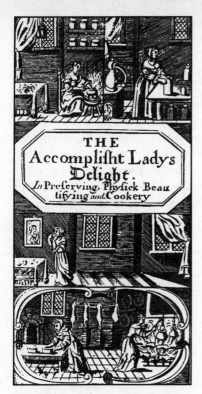

All over the world these and other dietary deficiencies were affecting both rich and poor who, with no knowledge of vitamins, were unaware of the causes. But they were beginning to discover how to treat them. In the seventeenth century, wealthy households that could afford oranges and lemons added the juice to older, traditional recipes for medicinal syrups made with scurvy grass, brooklime and watercresses 'to make an excellent syrup against the scurvy'. As late as the eighteenth century in England people still curdled blue (watered down) milk with the juice of scurvy grass or some verjuice or cream of tartar to make a concoction 'very good to drink in the spring for scurvy'. But fruit and vegetables were usually heavily overcooked reducing their vitamin C content and, as we have seen, many of the traditional preserved foods were failing to provide a whole host of necessary nutrients.

Preserving, cooking and preparing medicines and cosmetics were essential skills for accomplished ladies. Hannah Woolley's book was published in 1685

The nineteenth century saw many revolutions and one of the most significant was in food technology. Cooks and cookbooks, scientists in their laboratories, the poor diet of the sailors, soldiers and the urban poor, and problems with supplying food to the burgeoning cities all conspired to foster this revolution. Many of the ideas on which it depended were slowly being developed back in the seventeenth century without, however, anyone understanding the underlying principles. Nevertheless, the greatest minds of the age were turned towards improving food preserving and, for a while at least, cooks turned into chemists and chemists into cooks. Eventually in 1861 came the breakthrough discovery of Louis Pasteur that organisms were in the air and were not spontaneously generated. He demonstrated that liquids, especially wine, could be preserved safely by heating in sealed containers to at least 60°C (140°F) and keeping them there for thirty to forty minutes. This procedure, later called pasteurisation, killed any pathogens present and most spoilage organisms as well. In the meantime, however, experimentation continued and empirical knowledge grew. New techniques were tried, but as many were based on incorrect scientific premises, it was to be a long, erratic and sometimes frustrating journey.

> So great a universitie
> I think there ne'er was any,
> In which you may a scholar be,
> For spending of a penny.
>
> Coffee house rhyme, Anon, 1667

According to John Aubrey, who briefly recorded many important lives of the seventeenth century, Francis Bacon, philosopher and statesman, would often, for his health, ride out in an open coach in any weather. On one freezing cold, early spring afternoon in 1626, Bacon was out taking the air near Highgate with his companion Dr Witherborne. Deep snow still lay along the roadside and 'It came into my Lord's thoughts, why flesh might not be preserved in snow, as in Salt'. Physician and philosopher both became so excited by the idea that they decided to conduct an experiment at once. 'They alighted out of the Coach and went into a poore woman's house at the bottom of Highgate hill, and bought a Hen, and made the woman exenterate it, and then stuffed the body with Snow, and my Lord did help to doe it himselfe.' Bacon, by then an infirm old man of sixty-five, became so chilled himself that he was too ill to go home. Dr Witherborne instead took him to the Highgate home of the Earl of Arundel where Bacon was put into a damp bed. Within three days, he died. It is more likely, however, that it was the damp bed rather than the refrigeration experiment that ended his life.

Bacon was famous for favouring experiment and observation, rather than the old traditions and authorities. His interests were wide and varied and included preserving. Bacon's revolutionary spirit of enquiry and experiment lived on after him and in the same year that he died, another 'philosopher' was born. Robert Boyle, 'the father of chemistry', founder of the Royal Society and still famous for Boyle's Law, was to be the first man to take food preserving out of the kitchen and into the laboratory.

In one generation, in spite of the bloody Thirty Years' War and civil war in England, a great era of science, mathematics and physical experiment had arrived. According to Macaulay in his *History of England*, Bacon had sown the good seed so that 'During a whole generation his philosophy, had, amidst tumult, wars, and proscriptions, been slowly ripening in a few well constituted minds.' Men of class, fashion and learning began meeting in the new coffee houses opening up all over London, Paris and Amsterdam in the 1650s. They went daily to their own particular favourite place to gossip and learn the news and to discuss politics, the arts and philosophies with like-minded peers. Both the English and French authorities feared that these coffee houses, introduced from the Muslim world, were filled with subversives. They certainly attracted a wide range of custom providing a unique public place where people could gather without drinking alcohol. In addition, many of the houses provided special rooms for social or business meetings.

The young Robert Boyle, who had grown up during these exciting times, was already in touch with a circle of natural philosophers that became known as the 'invisible college'. These men, dedicated to new scientific enquiry and practical experiment, met regularly in coffee houses where they debated a wide and eclectic range of scientific ideas covering everything from mathematics to agriculture. Congregating every Wednesday or Thursday afternoon in Garraway's or Jonathon's coffee house in Cornhill, early members included John Aubrey, John Evelyn, botanist and numismatist, Samuel Pepys, John Locke, the statistician Sir William Petty, John Dryden, Sir Christopher Wren, Sir Kenelm Digby, Roman Catholic writer on recipes and domestic economy, Robert Hooke, mathematician and physicist and

A popular London coffee house in 1695 where gentlemen could read the news and discuss 'matters of importance'

Jonathan Goddard, one of the first English makers of telescopes.

But anyone who had paid a penny could sit by the fire and smoke as he listened or joined in debate with these able and inventive men whose insatiable appetite for knowledge was further fired by ideas flowing across the Channel from Europe. They even managed to conduct some experiments as they gathered round the warm fire and peered through the smoke into a home-made microscope or at some strange liquid in a bottle. Robert Hooke recorded in his diary 'Met with Metredony Speed. At Garaways with hime and discourses of wine and fermentation etc.' On another occasion he observed 'a hair worm and some miscroscopes shewd at Jonathans'. Women were occasionally tolerated as spectators. Pepys describes, with some reluctance, a visit by the Duchess of Newcastle, 'Several fine experiments were shown her of Colours, Loadstones, Miscroscope, and of liquors; among others, of one that did while she was there turn a piece of roasted mutton into pure blood . . .'

Gatherings also took place at Gresham College and it was at one meeting there in 1660, when Sir Christopher Wren gave a lecture, that an idea for a permanent institution to promote experiments in physics and mathematics was raised. After the Restoration of Charles II, the Royal Society received its Royal charter. Its motto was taken from Horace: 'The words are the words of a master, but we are not forced to swear by them. Instead we are to be borne wherever experiment drives us.' This showed a clear determination to move on from the rigid laws laid down by the early classicists Aristotle, Galen and Hippocrates. Meanwhile, a similar movement was growing in Paris where the Acadamie des Sciences was founded in 1666.

But the informal nature of the early days of the 'invisible college' remained unchanged. Essays, questionnaires and letters continued to be circulated and shared amongst both the London members and those on their country estates far from the city. A small number of aristocrats and gentry, obliged to stay on their estates during the Civil War and the Interregnum, had found time on their hands and begun to experiment with improving the fertility of their land, their crop yields, their livestock breeding and the traditional ways of preserving their estate produce. These men corresponded with each other, sharing ideas and the results of their investigations. Sometimes, however, there seems to have been some rivalry and secrecy concerning discoveries. Robert Boyle records that he has heard from '. . . an eminent Naturalist, a Friend of yours and mine, that hath a strange way of preserving Fruits, whereby even Goos-berries have been kept for many Moneths, without the addition of Sugar, Salt, or other tangible Bodies; but all that I dare tell you, is, that he assures me his Secret consists in a new and artificiall way of keeping them from the Air.'

There may well have been an element of personal rivalry as well, as the possibility of financial reward beckoned. John Aubrey writes that Boyle '. . . is charitable to ingeniose men that are in want, and foreigne Chymists have had large proofe of his bountie, for he will not spare for cost to get any rare Secret'. In fact Robert Boyle was busy experimenting and investigating a wide range of ideas, in particular the activity of gases and air, and it was this interest that first led him to experiment with new methods of preserving food. Boyle, like so many others until Pasteur's breakthrough, at first believed that air alone was the cause of putrefaction and that the ability to remove it from the food was the answer to successful preserving. He would have been aware that keeping food free from air was not a new idea and that people had been attempting to achieve it with varying success for centuries. More recently, the bottling of fruit and potting of cooked meats and fish had been creating considerable interest as new ways of preserving fresh meats and fruits 'beyond their wonted seasons of duration'.

But it may also be reasonable to assume that another reason that Robert Boyle and some of his colleagues spent so much time and energy on experimenting with ways to preserve food 'without the addition of Sugar, Salt, or other tangible Bodies' was more than simply academic. Fellow Royal Society member Samuel Pepys was for a time responsible for naval food supplies. He no doubt would have voiced the Admiralty's wish to find new ways to feed its men in the light of the then commonly held belief that salt meat caused scurvy. This was coupled with the recent challenge that fruit, which might offer an effective cure, had somehow also to be preserved for long voyages. The most effective methods known then involved sugar, which was expensive and as Boyle himself noted, too much sugar 'clogs most men's stomachs'.

Over half a century earlier, Sir Hugh Plat had tried unsuccessfully to interest the Admiralty in his many revolutionary preserving ideas, knowing that a contract would bring him considerable reward. 'But if I may bee allowed to carrie either roasted or sodden flesh to sea, then I dare adventure my poore credit therein to preserve for sixe whole monethes together; either Beefe, Mutton, Capons, Rabbits, etc. both in a cheape manner, and also as fresh as we doe now usuallie eat them at our Table. And this I hold to be a most singular and necessarie secret for all our English Navie; which at all times upon reasonable tearmes I will be readie to disclose for the good of my country.'

Boyle, too, was keenly aware of the importance of his work to seamen. He wrote, 'tis sufficiently known to Navigators, how frequently, in long Voyages, the Scurvy, and other diseases, are contracted by the want of fresh Meat, and the necessity of feeding constantly upon none but strongly poudred Flesh, or salted Fish; and therefore, he is much to be commended that hath first devised the way to keep Flesh sweet, without the help of those fretting

Salts.' Boyle conducted a number of experiments including preserving meat in alcohols, thereby keeping 'an entire Puppy of pretty bigness, untainted for many weeks' and preserving other foods with mixes of chemicals such as saltpetre, lime water and even urine. He also experimented with sealing fruit in airtight bottles without adding sugar and potting cooked meats under an airtight layer of fat, both ideas, as we have seen, that were already beginning to appear in contemporary cookery books. Boyle, however, was keen to take these processes further, in particular to find ways to preserve 'raw flesh itself . . . with things that do not so much fret it, nor give it so corrosive a quality, when eaten, as our common Salt doth.' Much of the food being sealed into containers retained some air, unwittingly sealing the problem in. Boyle tried removing all the air by creating a mechanical vacuum pump to draw out any remaining or trapped air and he invented a manometer with which to measure air pressure. In 1667 he wrote: 'I have also lately put into practice another thing, about which I must earnestly desire your secrecy . . . the thing I pretend to do, in short is this; to seal up glasses hermetically, when without the help of heat (for it is done by the engine) they are more exhausted of air.'

Boyle still favoured the exclusion of air over the use of heat. However, a number of experiments over succeeding years gave varying degrees of success and these results clearly showed him that while air had a role in food spoilage and removing it helped the preservation, it was not the whole cause of spoilage nor the complete answer to preserving. He also experimented with using steam to create a vacuum in food containers, which often brought him close to realising the importance of the use of heat in preserving. Boyle worked closely with Samuel Hartlib who had been the focus of a large part of this group actively trying, amongst many other experimental activities, to improve food production and preservation, and with Robert Hooke and Antony van Leeuwenhoek, who both developed simple microscopes revealing minute creatures and 'animalcules', blood corpuscles and milk-fat globules. Boyle also conducted experiments with another colleague, a French physicist Denys Papin, who had taken refuge in England to escape religious persecution and is still famous for his 'Digester of Bones'. The forerunner of the modern pressure cooker, Papin's contraption boiled bones down to a gelatin in which food could be preserved. Papin later took over many of Boyle's experiments with food and, using his Digester, began to heat food such as gooseberries in airtight containers. At last he reached the critical breakthrough that had eluded Boyle: 'Heating under vacuo doth hinder them from fermenting.' But the heat process Papin used was very mild; it involved putting glass containers of fruit in cold water in a *bain-marie* and bringing the water to the boil, a process that seemed to preserve without using sugar for some acidic fruits, but was not effective for raw meat. From this Papin did come to another important conclusion, that different foods reacted in different ways and might require different treatment or degrees of treatment for successful preserving.

Papin's huge Digester could cook up to 10 lb of meat and he experimented with cooking meat jellies, which he believed could solve the pressing problem of scurvy. However, like portable soup and potted foods, meat jellies were expensive and difficult to make in any quantity and none was ever made for use at sea. Papin continued to work closely with Boyle and members of the Royal Society, reporting back regularly on his findings, successes and failures, which the eminent men were required to taste and possibly even to risk some upset stomachs. In 1687 Papin produced some peas that he had preserved in vacuo ten months previously; 'I have put some butter, pepper and salt to season part of them, that the Royal Society may be pleased to try how they will taste.' In the minutes of the meeting it was observed that the peas had 'contracted something of a rancid Tast, but were otherwise well preserved', and in 1687, the Society reported that Papin had succeeded in preserving 'Great quantities of Fruit with their Tast without any sugar or other alteration than what can be made with a little boiling'.

> The Way is this; he shuts up the Fruits in Glass Vessels
> exhausted of the Air, and then puts the Vessel thus
> exhausted in hot Water, and lets it stand there for some
> while; and that is enough to keep the Fruit from the
> Fermentation, which would otherwise undoubtedly happen . . .

This description, which involved heating food in sealed containers, might sound familiar to anyone used to bottling fruit or vegetables. In fact, it came tantalisingly close to the method finally developed for canning 100 years later.

In 1691 Robert Boyle died, Denys Papin had moved abroad and Thomas Porter and John White were granted a patent for 'Preserving all Kinds of Foods'. Neither man was a member of the Royal Society and there is no record of their preserving method, but it was significantly the first commercial patent for food preserving and shows that there was by then considerable interest in developing and marketing new kinds of processed foods for sale. By now both the French and British navies had been receiving a steady stream of submissions for new food-preserving processes from enthusiastic inventors. They were sent a strange assortment of pots of meat, dried cakes of soup, purées and concentrates, dried vegetables and pastes, and new types of biscuit. Only a few of the ideas proffered were given sea trials. None, so far, were considered better or cheaper than salt meat and hardtack.

But then, in the wake of the French Revolution of 1789, the French government offered a reward to anyone who could develop a new method of preserving food. The stipulation was that the end product should be easily transportable, economic to produce and provide a better diet than salt meat. It was this French initiative that found the man who produced the solution.

⌒ CHAPTER TWELVE ⌒

CANNING

Nicolas Appert was not a chemist but a professional cook — a chef and confectioner who later became a skilled food technologist. Appert was born in 1750 in the small French provincial town of Châlons-sur-Marne, situated on the edge of the Champagne region, where his father was a brewer and innkeeper, first at the White Horse Inn and later the Palais Royal Hotel. No doubt Nicolas was helping his father from an early age. He wrote that he was brought up and trained 'In the pantries, the breweries, storehouses, and cellars of Champagne, as well as in the shops, manufactories, and warehouses of confectioners, distilleries and grocers'. By the

Nicolas Appert, aged about fifty

time he was twenty-two years old, Appert had become 'No ordinary cook, but a highly skilled chef and a connoisseur of good food and tempting dishes'. He soon found employment with the Prince Palatinate Christian IV, followed by a post as chef for the Duc des Deux Ponts and later the Princess of Forbach.

Appert was clearly a very intelligent, gifted and ambitious young man and, having mastered running the kitchens of the aristocracy, he chose to move on to be master of his own business. At thirty-one he set himself up in business as a confectioner in Paris in the

Rue des Lombards, where he started to experiment with conserving sweets and fruits with sugar and then gradually became obsessed with other ideas for preserving all kinds of food. Appert was, of course, familiar with traditional preserved foods, but he believed that eating them was not always either a pleasant or healthy business. He observed that drying took away the aroma, changed the taste of the juices and hardened the fibres making the food difficult to chew. Salt gave food an unpleasant acerbity and made it tough and indigestible. He was not to know then that many of the vitamins and other nutrients were destroyed or lost as a result of the long and severe treatment foods underwent at that time during salting, drying or smoking. Appert was determined to find a way to keep food successfully without spoiling either its flavour or texture. At first he experimented with champagne bottles, of which no doubt he had plenty, and then with wider necked bottles. These he filled with fruit, vegetables or meat and stood in baths of hot water.

Appert was to spend the best part of ten years experimenting, always with meticulous care and great attention to detail, working his way through trial and error through every aspect of his new method. In the meantime Paris was erupting with political ferment and food riots. Protests were held complaining at the rocketing price of sugar, which may be the reason why Appert moved in 1795 to Ivry-sur-Seine, four miles outside Paris, where he began to spend even more of his time on his food preserving. He also found time to fulfil his responsibilities as mayor of the town, where he was becoming quite an esteemed figure, well known for his industrious, if rather mysterious, activities. By now he felt confident enough of his ideas to produce some examples on a small scale, which he sold locally, possibly to test the village palate. He also delivered to the French navy some bottles of his preserved soup, boiled beef in gravy and beans and peas, all of which he declared would be of great value in combating scurvy. In 1803, after three months of storage, the Préfet Maritime sent Appert's bottles of conserves for sea trials at Brest where the French fleet, under blockade by the Royal Navy, were no doubt grateful for some new food and fresh diversion. The report sent to the Navy Minister in Paris must have happily confirmed Appert's belief in his product. 'The broth in bottles was good, the broth with boiled beef in another bottle very good as well but a little weak; the beef itself was very edible. The beans and green peas, both with and without meat, have all the freshness and flavour of freshly picked vegetables.'

This was the culmination of all that had been tried by cooks and chemists for many centuries, from the Romans, who heated fruit and wine in jars, to the scientists Robert Boyle and Denys Papin, who experimented with extracting air by steam or heat. Contributing, too, were the English cooks and their recipe books, successfully bottling gooseberries and other fruits by immersion in warm water. It was a process that preserved food by simply heating it in a sealed container. Without apparently being aware of it, Appert had brought together the different discoveries of the past and was able to correctly declare, 'The application of fire in a manner variously adapted to various substances, after having with the utmost care and as completely as possible, deprived them of all contact with the air, effects a perfect preservation of those same productions, with all their natural qualities.'

However, it is unlikely that Appert consulted scientific reports, and although he was probably familiar with some bottling processes including wine, French cookery books, unlike the English, had very few fruit bottling recipes. Appert's discoveries were arrived at by a combination of empirical study and professional culinary experience.

France and England were still at war and while England was slowly adjusting to industrial revolution and a burgeoning urban work force, France was still coping with the aftermath of a bloody political revolution. The majority of its population was rural peasants suffering from repeated famines and fighting. Appert's own life, however, was probably relatively isolated and no doubt happy as he laboured in his little laboratory tucked away in the countryside. Free from distractions and other 'theories' Appert could fairly claim that, as far as he was aware, '. . . no author, either ancient or modern, has ever pointed out, or even led to the suspicion, of the principle which is the basis of the method I propose'. But word of Appert's work was inevitably spreading and he himself was not shy of advertising his wares to the influential and wealthy, as well as to government and naval officials. In 1804 Appert moved again, this time to the village of Massy, nine miles south of Paris. By now he was under the patronage of Grimod de La Reynière, a lawyer, journalist and gourmand, who published the *Almanach des Gourmands*, a kind of forerunner to the *Guide Michelin*. De La Reynière terrified food manufacturers, shops and suppliers with his habit of turning up unannounced, eating huge quantities of food without paying and then writing vitriolic reports in his almanac. He also demanded delicacies to be delivered to his home where he and his friends stuffed themselves and then declaimed on the merits or demerits of the foods. Described as the 'first modern gourmand and well organised parasite' de La Reynière nevertheless had enormous influence and chefs and food suppliers queued up for him to endorse their products. Appert, it seems, had not been afraid to submit his 'little bottles' of preserved foods to de La Reynière and was rewarded by his patronage and influence in selling his revolutionary new preserved foods. Furthermore, with his patron's help, Appert was now able to build new workshops to his own precise specifications.

There were four rooms: one held an enormous cauldron and other utensils and apparatus for preparing and cooking the fruit, vegetables and meat; the second room was used for preparing milk, cream and whey; in the third room, fitted with bottle racks, the bottles were corked and tied and put into canvas bags designed to protect the bottles and collect the shattered glass if one exploded, as sometimes happened; in the fourth stood three large copper boilers raised on bricks in which the bottles of food would be placed for sterilising. Each boiler was fitted with a wide tap, able to drain out the hot water quickly so that temperatures and timings could be carefully controlled. There were three further areas for preparing the vegetables, storing and preparing fruit and a cellar with more bottle racks for washing and storing bottles. Appert was extremely particular about the quality and design of both bottles and corks. He had the bottles specially made of toughened glass with wide necks and he made his own stoppers with layers of cork glued together with isinglass with the grain running horizontally to prevent air getting in. The food was placed in the glass jars, hermetically closed, secured by iron wire and sealed with pitch.

Appert believed in cleanliness and hygiene, not a particularly common concern in those days; he also strongly advocated the use of the freshest and best-quality foods for preserving. 'There should,' he declared, 'be . . . but one step from the garden bed to the water bath,' so he set his food processing factory within a sizeable market garden where he could supervise the growing of fresh vegetables and fruit, while meat and milk was brought in daily from the surrounding farms. The Appert establishment soon grew into a lively small business. '. . . In each bottle and at little cost is a glorious sweetness that recalls the month of May in the heart of winter,' eulogised de La Reynière. No doubt with help from his patron, Appert was able to find an outlet for his bottled foods at a shop in Paris and his little business soon grew into a sizeable industry employing up to forty women during the summer, kept busy growing, preparing and bottling the vegetables.

Meanwhile, naval shipboard trials of Appert's preserved victuals continued, with favourable reports from the ports of Brest and Bordeaux. In 1809 a special commission sent a report on Appert's preserved foods, including fruits, vegetables, juices, milk, whey, soup and some meat stew, to the Council of Administration of the Société d'Encouragement pour l'Industrie Nationale. The supplies of cane sugar to mainland Europe were cut off during the Napoleonic Wars and the French government was anxious to find a way of preserving food without sugar as well as reducing the import of foreign commodities. Appert heard of 'flattering rewards' being offered by the Société d'Agriculture for the 'composition of a work on the art of preserving, by the best possible means, every kind of alimentary substance', and he decided that he would offer the results of his own investigations.

Appert was invited to give a demonstration of his method to members of an official government commission. They returned a month later to taste the results, which were reported to have been in an excellent condition. The report, recognising the value of the results of his labours 'as the preservation of animal and vegetable substances may be of the utmost utility in sea voyages, in hospitals and domestic economy', awarded Appert 'un encouragement' of 12,000 francs, a fairly substantial amount of money at that time, on condition that he disclosed, in 200 copies, all the details and description of his invention. This Appert did, in a book entitled *L'Art de Conserver Pendant Plusieurs Années Toutes les Substances Animales et Végétales*, which was translated into several languages and eventually ran to four editions. The newspaper the *Courrier de L'Europe* was full of praise for Monsieur Appert who '. . . has found a way to fix the seasons; at his establishment, spring, summer and autumn live in bottles, like those delicate plants protected by the gardener under glass domes against the intemperate seasons'.

Appert, by now sixty years old, was still a 'dynamic and jovial little man despite his bald head and Mephistophelian eyebrows' and was by all accounts popular with his work force and respected by the officials with whom he dealt. Although he was himself a good business man he appeared to be content to make his methods common knowledge to anyone who wished to follow his process in their kitchens at home or even on a larger scale. Appert made it clear from the start that 'alimentary substances, in order to be preserved, should be, without exception, subjected to the application of heat in a water-bath; after being rigorously excluded from all contact with the air . . .' and he wrote that the details of his process consisted principally of:

> 1st. In enclosing in bottles the substances to be preserved.
> 2d. In corking the bottles with the utmost care; for it is chiefly on the corking that the success of the process depends.
> 3d. In submitting these inclosed substances to the action of boiling water in a water-bath (*Balneum Mariae*) for a greater or less length of time, according to their nature, and in the manner pointed out with respect to each several kind of substance.
> 4th. In withdrawing the bottles from the water-bath at the period described.

This deceptively straightforward process is the basis of industrial food canning and domestic bottling as we still know it today. But it was a process that could still not be explained and therefore remained open to misinterpretation and wrong explanations. The eminent French chemist Gay-Lussac, a member of the Société's

Food Preservation Committee, was commissioned to investigate Appert's methods. Gay-Lussac, like Robert Boyle, was pre-eminent in the study of gases and, not surprisingly, was a firm advocate of the air exclusion hypothesis. Gay-Lussac maintained that oxygen was responsible for putrefaction and that the success of Appert's process was in 'locking up' the oxygen. For many years Appert, keen to have his method approved, was prepared to concede to Gay-Lussac's authority and continued to put great emphasis on the exclusion of air both before and after heating, although he knew from later experiments that heat destroyed bacteria and any remaining air after careful sealing was therefore sterile.

The report made by the Special Committee in 1809 included two interesting comments. One refers to Appert's promise to be able to send French produce abroad and for foods from other countries to be equally successfully transported into France, thus recognising the potential importance the process would have for international trade in foodstuffs. The other significant observation was that while Appert's food products and antiscorbutic juices would be suitable for sick crew members, feeding the whole crew on a long voyage would entail shipping enormous numbers of breakable glass bottles. The Committee expressed its confidence that Appert would 'find means to obviate this inconvenience, by the choice of vessels less fragile and of a larger size'.

In 1810 Appert's book was published and he accepted the ex-gratia cash payment for publishing the details of his discoveries, thus foregoing any possibility of profiting commercially from a French patent. But only three months after the book first appeared, a London broker called Peter Durand was granted a patent in England, virtually identical to Appert's method, which he quickly sold to an engineer, Bryan Donkin for £1,000. Donkin, with his partners John Gamble and John Hall of the Dartford Iron Works, were soon producing food using Appert's method, but in tins instead of glass bottles, thus making them the first food canning business in the world.

Did Peter Durand take advantage of hostilities between France and England to steal Appert's ideas and profit from them as many have suggested? Is this another case of an inventor losing out to the entrepreneur? Accusations and theories surrounding this mystery have found their way into a number of publications. But recently Dr Norman Cowell, after much extensive and detailed research, has been able to uncover most, if not all of the truth. With his new evidence, a different story can now be told.*

The year 1809 was a busy one for Nicolas Appert. His long years of experiment had come to fruition and his conserving methods were at last receiving the attention and praise they deserved. It all seemed to be coming together with a generous payment to publish his work plus the possible prize of a profitable contract from the French navy. But it is unlikely that Appert had made much money whilst developing his ideas and what he did make was ploughed straight back into his laboratory at Massy, which was heavily mortgaged, while his tireless quest for improvement and innovation consumed his small sales profits. His relatively uneducated and humble origins also made him understandably hungry for recognition and respect for his achievements. He was therefore working hard giving demonstrations to committees, sending out samples to the navy and hurriedly writing his book. It now seems likely that Appert was also looking to further advance himself in England.

French inventors, frustrated by events in France, looked with envy at the rapid industrialisation in England. Unable to present their ideas to British manufacturers in person, some used agents to act for them. Peter Durand's food preservation patent states that it was an 'invention communicated to me by a certain foreigner'. A year later Durand took out another patent, this time for a French-designed oil lamp. The application included exactly the same statement, a commonly accepted term meaning that the patentee was not the inventor and that the invention was being introduced from another country. There were periods when hostilities between the two countries were relaxed and some

* The story as told here is the author's interpretation of Dr Cowell's findings and also uses material from other sources and does not necessarily represent his views. Copies of Dr Cowell's Ph.D. thesis 'An Investigation of Early Methods of Food Preservation by Heat', which includes new information about the story of M. Appert and the early canning industry, can be read at the Science Museum Library London and the University of Reading Library.

travel and contact was possible. The year 1810 was one such period and during the summer the Paris Chamber of Commerce sent a commission to London to try to renew trade between the two countries. Peter Durand was himself from a Huguenot family with relations on both sides of the Channel who dealt in food and wine and there could have been plenty of opportunity for Durand to communicate with Appert and other French client inventors. It is clear from contemporary and later records that Peter Durand and Donkin, Hall & Gamble knew that the patent was of Appert's invention. Appert's involvement, in contrast, is shrouded in mystery.

Appert was informed of his award from the Société d'Encouragement pour l'Industrie Nationale and its condition of publishing the details of his process on 30 January 1810. His completed manuscript was accepted by the Société on 19 April and the book was published in May with reviews appearing in the Paris press on 21 May. Peter Durand was granted his patent in England on 25 August. This did not leave a lot of time for a broker with knowledge of neither science nor cookery to plagiarise a complex book written in French. Moreover getting a patent at that time was a lengthy and costly operation. The application had to be fully written up covering every detail and possible variation and, once registered, could be further delayed by challenges from other recent patentees. It is therefore extremely unlikely that Durand could have both prepared and been granted his patent only three months after the publication of Appert's book.

The specifications in Durand's patent included a number of variances and alternatives to Appert's basic method, a usual ploy of the patentee to cover all possibilities, some of which Appert would not have approved. It listed the use of a wide variety of different containers made of glass, pottery and metal. It described Appert's special corks but also covered the use of other kinds of fitted or ground stoppers, screw caps, cocks, cross plugs or covers of various kinds of material such as bladders, cloth, parchment or leather. Methods of heating included not just Appert's water baths but ovens, stoves, steam baths 'or any other fit situation'. It also allowed the possibility of leaving the containers unsealed 'until the effect of the heat had taken place'. Appert knew he sealed his bottles completely, air and all, but, as we have seen, he had been too humble to challenge the authority of Gay-Lussac and others. In fact, by writing this theory into his patent, Durand ensured further decades of what was essentially poor practice derived from an erroneous and misleading theory. Most of the wording in the application was, however, exactly the same as that used by Appert in his book, which would suggest that Appert must have provided Durand with the manuscript before publication so that Durand, possibly with help from an English patent writer, could prepare the patent application. This might explain some of the curious anomalies that coincide more with methods associated with English fruit bottling. A patent application had to cover every possible variant and eventuality and Durand made sure that it did.

Assuming that Durand was acting for Appert, his next job would have been to sell the patent to a manufacturer who would develop it. John Gamble, who also had family connections with France, had previously developed a French patent for a paper- making machine with a colleague Bryan Donkin, an engineer who later became a Fellow of the Royal Society. Donkin had previously worked in John Hall's iron works at Dartford. Between them they had experience of working with and developing French inventions as well as access to tinplate manufacturing. According to a history written by John Gamble's son Frederick, they examined the details of Durand's patent and, 'After a series of experiments made by the patentees . . . they found that the system of preservation, as it was then constituted, was too defective and uncertain in its results, to be made the vehicle of any safe or profitable commercial enterprise. The porous nature of the corks used enclosing the bottles, on the one hand . . . and the fragility of the glass bottles, on the other, caused the process of perfect preservation to be too precarious a matter to allow implicit reliance to be placed on its uniform success . . . Both these defects were obviated by the use of tin.'

Whatever its other defects were, Donkin, Hall and Gamble must have been sufficiently convinced of the profitable nature of the process, as well as their ability to transfer it to tinned iron canisters, to justify the enormous investment necessary to buy the patent, develop it and build and equip a factory that would manufacture a new, untried technology. By 1813 everything was in place in a building they called a 'Preservatory' in Blue Anchor Road, Bermondsey.

Appert himself knew that there was still more work to be done to improve and develop his process. The French navy had expressed their concern about the glass bottles and Appert would have been investigating other possibilities including tinned iron canisters. This in itself was not new. Back in the seventeenth century Robert Boyle had reported that the Dutch were storing ship's biscuits in tin-lined casks. Later, in the 1770s, a Captain John Stedman, an English mercenary fighting in the Dutch colony of Surinam in South America, described eating roast beef packed in dripping in soldered airtight tinplate containers which had been sent out from the Netherlands. Around the same time Duhamel du Monceau, a Fellow of the Royal Society, published a work on fishing that included a description of Dutch fishermen potting salmon in a 'tin box' covered with an airtight layer of melted butter.

By the mid-eighteenth century the British were well ahead in tinplate production, whilst in war-torn France tinplate was of poor quality and lacked the same expertise in metal-working. For Appert to have developed tins as an alternative to glass, he would have had to import the metal and to have found extensive capital to set up workshops to produce the hand-made tins in which to preserve his food. In 1814, only two months after Napoleon had abdicated and been exiled to Elba leaving an exhausted and bewildered France and yet another Louis on the throne, Nicolas Appert made a visit to London. At this time his little factory had been requisitioned as a field hospital, France was in disarray and there were serious food shortages. Moreover, the French navy was refusing to honour its debts for contracts made under Napoleon. With no factory, bad debts and a shortage of raw materials, Appert may have felt it was time to visit England to see his agent, collect on profits due to him and to see how his methods had been developed by Donkin, Hall and Gamble using their tins. Appert may also have decided to investigate the potential use of steam and other technologies being developed in the more advanced world of British industry. He would have heard of the successful sea trials of tinned food by the Royal Navy in England and that a presentation of tins had been made to members of the royal family.

Appert may also have felt it was time to set the record straight and to be awarded some of the honours for himself and he made plans to submit samples of his own bottled food to the Royal Society hoping for official British commendation for his work.

One person we know Appert visited when he was in London was Sir Charles Blagden, a Royal Society Fellow who knew France well and spoke excellent French (it may be assumed that Appert spoke no English). In a cryptic entry in his personal diary for Friday, 24 June, Blagden makes a startling record of what Appert had said to him during their meeting:

> Appert came: brought me a letter from Baron Humboldt: It appeared clearly that he came for profit. I engaged him as to his preservation, to come to Soho Square on Sunday with further things on his method to have tasted. Learned that company (Donkin) had given Girard only £1000 (tho they gave anr £1000) for his patent. Girard's improvement was in the soldering so as to make tight by metallic security preserved in tin; and then varnish about with a brown varnish: factory J.G. & Co. given large orders.

On the basis of their conversation, Blagden was in no doubt that Appert came to London 'for profit'. He heard from Appert, who had only been in London a few days, that John Gamble and his partners had paid £1,000 to someone called Girard, plus, it seems another £1,000. Appert described to Blagden how this Girard had worked on improvements on tin making and soldering. Appert also knew that the company had been given large orders. Donkin was known to be quite secretive with his manufacturing and business dealings and Appert could only have known these details if he had spoken either to Peter Durand or one of the partners. There are some other mysteries arising from these brief notes. Did Appert's remark 'only £1000' mean that he regarded it as too low? Who was 'another payment of £1000' for? Immediately after Appert's London trip, Peter Durand's financial circumstances suddenly improved so much that he was able to become a Freeman of a City Livery Company, a Freeman of the City of London and a Licensed Broker – all of which cost money to achieve. And who was Girard?

On the 21 May 1810, Sir Charles Blagden had received a letter from Marcelin Claude Berthollet, the French chemist and statesman who first discovered calories in food, recommending to him a M. Girard:

> Je vous addresse, mon cher ami, Mr Girard artiste très
> ingénieux et très eclairé, auquel je prens [sic] beaucoup d'in-
> térêt: je vous serai très obligé des services que vous pourrez
> lui rende [sic] . . .

Berthollet was a generous patron of Appert and had helped him on many occasions. He later successfully petitioned the French government for finance to help Appert rebuild his factory. Phillippe Girard was indeed an ingenious and enlightened artist: he was also the inventor of a hydrostatic oil lamp, for which Peter Durand had taken out a patent in England in 1811. Appert and Girard, both protégés of Berthollet and authors of inventions patented by Durand clearly knew each other. The payment to Girard suggests that, possibly on Durand's or Appert's recommendation, Girard's knowledge of metalwork was being employed in making improvements to the tins that Donkin was busy developing as containers for Appert's processed foods. It seems possible that not only did Appert engage Durand to sell his patent to Donkin, Hall and Gamble but that he, like Durand, remained involved in the company's early stages of developing their tinned foods. At the time of Appert's visit, Girard was in a debtor's prison after being bankrupted by his 'expensive experiments' so Appert may have been concerned with collecting dues for both himself and his friend.

In the fourth edition of his book, published in 1831 when Appert was eighty-two and Girard, then living in Austria, was fifty-six, Appert mentions Girard as having had only 'very vague notions' of Appert's process, which is clearly untrue. Appert had been paid a considerable sum by the French authorities and in the early years his discoveries were regarded as a French military secret. It is very likely that his secrecy concerning his relations with English canning would have been to protect not only himself but any French colleagues also involved with him. He surely would not want it known that he had been selling his process to his country's enemy for profit.

The Royal Society archives have no record of a visit in 1814 by M. Appert. This is because he was only received informally at the home of Sir Joseph Banks, then President of the Society, on 24 June. Blagden, who was present, again records the visit in his diary: 'I talked a good deal with Appert, who exhibited his preparations. One glass of milk not good: the other well preserved but not fine. Plums very good. I did not stay for the meal . . .'

Appert's reception seems to have been lukewarm. Durand and Donkin, Hall and Gamble had already presented their tinned food to Sir Joseph Banks who had shown great enthusiasm, while Appert had only produced bottled foods. As far as the Royal Society was concerned, Appert had come with nothing that was either new or a technological advance. He was given a testimonial letter, which named him as the author of a pioneering book but not as either an inventor or manufacturer, and sent on his way.

Appert's London trip was a terrible disappointment. With characteristic snobbery and a degree of Francophobia, an article appeared in the *Edinburgh Review* while Appert was in London, which belittled both Appert's humble background and his small rural French 'laboratory'. It is not known whether he was able to collect any funds for either himself or Girard. Appert went home. His factory was in ruins and he was forced to leave Massy and return to Paris and find much smaller premises where, without all his equipment, he found it very difficult to continue with production or improving and refining his products.

It was not until after the restoration of the Bourbon monarchy that the French government declared Appert a benefactor of humanity and gave him financial assistance to set up in bigger and better equipped premises. There, he could pursue his researches, publish his latest results and produce preserved foods on a commercially viable scale. Appert was not a man to be easily defeated, despite his advancing years, nor was he too proud to adopt innovations that others had made. With financial help, he quickly recovered and soon began to develop the use of more robust, but at that time more expensive, tinned iron canisters for some of his foods, particularly for supplying the French navy. Characteristically in later editions of his book, Appert wrote of the need for the best possible tinplate, for refined and new lead solder and for good, reliable, conscientious tinsmiths, because rapid and accurate soldering was essential. But he continued producing food in glass jars for the domestic market. The French today still prefer to buy most of their preserved foods, especially delicacies, in glass containers. It was not long before Appert could produce accounts showing annual sales of over 100,000 francs and he also won several prizes for competitions to produce giant cans of preserved meat.

By the 1830s Appert, now into his eighties, with help from his nephew Raymond Chevallier-Appert, had built up his new factory and equipped it with specially designed machinery and utensils for the large-scale production of both bottles and cans. Many canning companies kept their processes secret but Appert always published details of new developments in his own factory. Much of his equipment was now mechanised. Meat was now cooked quickly under steam in specially designed large retorts (like pressure cookers). Cans were still sterilised in water baths heated over fires but the steam was also re-used to heat other food.

Appert's provisions continued to be used by the navy though only a few civilian French expeditions were keen to supply with them. One who did was Captain Freycinet who sailed on a three-year circumnavigation of the globe. He wrote to the Société d'Encouragement pour l'Industrie Nationale that 'M. Appert has completely resolved the problem of feeding sailors'. But Freycinet did also complain that the English, whom he angrily accused of stealing the idea from the French, kept supplies of tinned food in many of their fleet depots, while the French, who invented the product, still treated them as novelties which could only be bought in large sea ports of France.

Joseph Colin was an old friend and colleague of Appert. He, too, was a confectioner, and lived in Nantes on the west coast of France. Like many others, such as M. Quinton of Bordeaux, he may have been one of Appert's sales agents in the early years before setting up on his own. Colin was familiar with the old local tradition of packing sardines preserved in vinegar into large earthenware jars called 'oules' under butter or oil. The sardines were a popular regional delicacy, which Colin believed he could sell further afield. Captain Freycinet also tested Colin's canned sardines and in 1822 a local Nantes newspaper interviewed the explorer. Freycinet is reported to have said, 'At Colin's, in the rue de Moulin, a complete range of all preserved foods may be bought, including items which cannot be found in Paris, such as sardines in butter and in oil. They have come through all the tests to which I have subjected them in 38 months of navigation.' By 1824 Colin had set up his own sardine canning factory using Appert's now well-established methods as well as his support and encouragement. Whether Appert benefited financially is not known, but a report in 1836 shows that Colin was producing 100,000 cans of preserved food, only one third of which were sardines, which suggests that he was also producing large amounts of Appert's other food products under licence as a regional producer.

There were a number of others in the region who were to copy Colin and set up their own establishments. A restaurateur in Nantes called Millet converted his restaurant, which was situated in the centre of the town, into a sardine canning factory. There were soon complaints about the smell of frying fish and noise and Millet was forced to move to the outskirts of the town. The fish canning industry grew and flourished in Brittany. Good-sized sardines, freshly caught offshore, exactly fitted the cans. They were beheaded and gutted, lightly fried in oil and packed into the cans, which were then welded and sterilised. Before the sardine abandoned the coast of Brittany, there were nearly thirty small fish canning factories and more to come until by 1880 the region was producing nearly fifty million cans of sardines, which were sent all over the world. A 'box of sardines', like the tin of baked beans, became the great food standby in stores, cupboards and as 'dust gatherers' on forgotten shelves to be joined later by tins of salmon and tuna.

Appert's small grant, which had barely financed his experiments, apparently left him with little to live on in spite of running a thriving business. Elizabeth, his long-suffering wife, had left him and he finally retired, handing over his business to his nephew who renamed the company Chevallier-Appert. In June 1841 Nicolas Appert died aged ninety-one, apparently forgotten and abandoned. Why he was buried in a common grave with a pauper's funeral remains a mystery. Perhaps events overtook him as so often happens to pioneers and inventors. Or maybe the French authorities got wind of his foreign dalliances and he fell out of favour. Either way, his name was all but forgotten until he was commemorated on a postage stamp in 1955. Now, however, Appert is remembered as the true pioneer of the heat processing used in canning. Whether Appert sold to the enemy or not, his tremendous energy, enthusiasm and skill, along with his openness and co-operation in the dissemination and continuing development of his ideas, ensured that tinned foods and the great benefits that they brought, arrived sooner rather than later.

In November 1812, before the company of Donkin, Hall and Gamble had actually been formed or their factory built, and while they were still carrying out their own investigations and experiments on Appert's process, Durand persuaded a Captain George King to take some samples of their tinned meats and soups on board his ship, the *Mary & Susannah,* on a round trip to Jamaica. Captain King came home in July 1813 with four unused tins, which he duly returned with a message saying that '. . . the meats and soups I opened during the voyage, were as good as when first put up, and I have no doubt will keep in all climates'. The four returned tins with copies of this testimonial were immediately put to good use. The partners kept one and Durand sent another to the Duke of Kent, who responded by writing that the contents, once they were warmed up and 'with the addition of a little sauce and vegetables, proved as excellent a dish as any one could desire to have at their table; which is another proof of the excellence of their mode of preserving meat without salt, for the purpose of a sea voyage or a campaign in the field'. The Duke then suggested that the third tin should be sent to the Prince Regent.

Durand then sent the remaining tin to the Commissioners for Victualling His Majesty's Navy. Their immediate response was to order trials of 'Messrs Donkin and Co.'s canisters of cured meat to be carried out in both the West and East Indies'. Reports were to be made as to the 'probable advantages to be derived by its being supplied for the use of the sick and convalescent on board His Majesty's ships on long voyages, or in tropical climate'. The

Royal Navy had finally found the victualling answer that it had sought for so long, and despite initially feeding tinned food only to its sick sailors, the diet for the ordinary seaman at last began to make small improvements. The navy became the principal customer of Messrs Donkin, Hall & Gamble and the company began to prosper.

Bryan Donkin, himself a gifted inventor, designed the tinplate canisters (which the English chose to call 'tins', while the Americans adopted 'cans'). These continued to be used for the best part of a century until they were replaced by machine-made tins automatically filled and sealed. In the early days every tin was made by hand by skilled workers and two men could make only 120 tins a day. A cut length of tinplate was bent round to form a cylinder and the edges were soldered together. There were two tinplate discs with raised flanges about one quarter of an inch deep designed to be fitted closely around both ends of the cylinder. One disc was then soldered on the base of every cylinder. A line of open-ended tins were then filled with the prepared food, usually cooked meat, but also soups and vegetables such as carrots and parsnips. Next, the top disc was carefully soldered onto the top. This top piece had a hole about half an inch in diameter with a raised corrugation around it and through this hole gravy or brine was poured until the tin was full. A cap, with a small vent hole to allow steam to escape, was soldered over the gravy hole and the tins were then heated in boiling water, sometimes for as long as six hours. After heating, a cold wet sponge was pressed onto each vent hole to stop steam escaping, the steam vent was quickly sealed up and the tins left to cool. Tins for sea stores were liberally coated with red lead paint to protect them from sea water, which would corrode the tin. Each tin lid was fitted with a ring for carrying and for hanging them up. In 1841 calcium chloride (or sodium nitrate) was put in the sterilising baths raising the temperature above boiling and greatly reducing the processing time, which often overcooked the food. Another innovation was the practice of continuing to heat the tins after the final sealing. This would have had nothing to do with air extraction but was invaluable in destroying any remaining bacteria and must have been empirically arrived at. Temperature was sometimes not adequately

Filling and soldering cans in a French canning factory, 1870 — possibly Chevallier-Appert

controlled and there was the occasional accident; one operator was described as having been 'killed most ridiculously and ignobly by a boiled turkey'. The canister containing the turkey was overheated and burst; '. . . the dead turkey sprang from his coffin of tinplate, and, killing the cook forthwith, made him at once a candidate for a leaden one.'

A solution to the problem of exploding tins was to heat them in an enclosed container called a retort or autoclave, using steam under pressure, rather like Papin's seventeenth-century Digester and our modern pressure cooker. In 1831 Appert had already designed an autoclave for cooking meat and his nephew later patented one for processing the tins as well. Retorting of tins was known in Britain in the 1830s and by the 1870s, autoclaves had been developed in America and Britain that successfully remained in use until the end of the nineteenth century.

Tins were produced in a variety of sizes ranging from the smallest (2 lb) to enormous ones weighing nearly 17 lb, which must have created huge problems with sterilisation. All the finished tins were tested in a chamber for a month where they were subjected to tropical temperatures to check they had been properly processed. If they had not, the tins would bulge out at the ends, and in the early days some even exploded. However, this was not a very sound method as some bacteria could not have been detected by this means.

Opening these tins presented quite a challenge. Most early tins were sold as military supplies and until the 1840s the instructions on tins called for the use of a hammer and chisel. The earliest domestic openers were made in the 1860s and were called Bull's Head tin openers, as they had a cast-iron handle shaped into a bull's head and tail and were sold with tins of bully beef. It could be a violent and messy business. The unfortunate Lady Mary Hodgson, caught up in the siege of Kumasi in west Africa in 1900, was trying to remain calm as she cut up tinned Bologna sausage. 'It was the last one of our stores, and had been saved up for this dreaded but expected moment. The sausage was in a tin which had in the hurry been badly opened, and it would not allow itself to be pushed out; the poor thing had a great wound in its side from the tin-opener, and every time I attempted to cut off a slice the sausage would recede.'

Nowadays canned food production is most often associated with the USA but it was an English immigrant, William Underwood, who first introduced canning to America when he arrived there in 1817. He had worked in the pickling business in England and started preserving 'after the manner of Appert' when he opened a factory in Boston. There he first bottled and later canned lobster and salmon, which he exported using the label 'Made In England', presumably to make the consumer feel it was a well-tried safe product from the old country and not something suspect from the 'new'. It was Underwood's book-keepers who first used the word 'can'. In 1819, another English immigrant, Thomas Kensett also started by preserving oysters and other seafood, first in glass jars and later in hand-made 'vessels of tin'. By 1825, Kensett, together with another canner, Ezra Daggett, had established a thriving cannery in Baltimore. Only eight years after taking out his first controversial English patent, Peter Durand resurfaced in America where he took out another patent for the same process; whether Appert was also part of this venture is not known.

America was initially slow to develop technical advances but the enormous success with fish canning soon resulted in a rash of factories springing up along both eastern and western coasts and progress speeded up. The American Civil War in 1861 created the first major demand for American canned food, especially pork and beans, condensed milk, oysters and green beans for the Union troops and a meat and vegetable stew known as 'burgoo' for the Confederates in the South, where there was widespread hunger. Despite the army sutlers reporting that the men preferred French canned sardines, salmon and peas, hundreds of soldiers returned to their homes with praise for this dependable, portable and storable food. Cans of corn, baked beans, hominy, pumpkins, sweet potatoes, succotash and seakale were soon filling shelves in the home and appearing at table in all kinds of dishes. With the newly built railroads, food producers were quick to seize on a new way of safely moving huge quantities of meat, fruits and vegetables produced in abundance and canned in one state to other states thousands of miles away where there might be shortages.

In 1849 a new machine for food canning was invented to make the tops and bases of the cans; this enabled two unskilled workers to produce as many as 1,500 cans per day. By 1865 improvements in canning production included the manufacture of cans made of thinner steel with a rim around the top of each can, which led to can openers being developed instead of the hammer and chisel. In 1866 a special can with its own key opener was introduced. By the turn of the century, America had succeeded in mechanising both the manufacture of cans and the canning process and the country had leapt to the front of the world canning industry. Europe and Britain imported vast quantities of US Pacific canned salmon and salmon canneries appeared at the mouth of almost every river as far north as Alaska. The cans were given a final coating of a mixture of red lead, turpentine and linseed oil. The resulting fiery red colour came to be associated with red salmon and some canned salmon today still has the characteristic red label.

By the 1870s America was packing more different kinds of food in far larger quantities than any other country. Canning in the US revolutionised the way people ate and cooked, leading the way to all kinds of factory processed and packaged foods. James Collins in *The Story of Canned Foods* wrote that: 'Canning gives the American family – especially in cities and factory towns – a kitchen garden where all good things grow, and where it is always harvest time. There are more tomatoes in a ten-cent can than could be bought in city markets for that sum when tomatoes are at their cheapest, and this is true of most other tinned foods. A regular Arabian Nights garden, where raspberries, apricots, olives, and pineapples, always ripe, grow side by side with peas, pumpkins, and spinach; a garden with baked beans, vines and spaghetti bushes, and sauerkraut bed, and great caldrons of hot soups, and through it running a branch of the ocean in which one can catch salmon, lobsters, crabs and shrimp, and dig oysters and clams.'

The first settlers to arrive at Sydney Cove in Australia in 1788 were provisioned for their long sea journey with salt beef, salt pork, flour, pease, ship's biscuit, butter and rice. They had no idea that they would have to live on these for many years, until the unyielding land, lack of water and harsh conditions that they first found were finally made to produce some fresh food. They had to rely on imported salt meat, and so that they could start salting their own meat, they had to recover the salt from bought salt meat. Later, the settlers made a bitter salt from boiled sea water, which they could use to salt meat and fish and for curing seal skins. But at that time there was not enough meat to preserve and so in 1801 shiploads of salt were sent to Tahiti where their plentiful pork was salted into barrels, and over the next twenty years thousands of tons of salt meat was imported into Sydney. By the 1820s, however, Australia had its own large herds of sheep and cattle that supplied a now thriving trade in salt meat, much of which was sent back to England.

Dr Keith Farrer, in his book *A Settlement Amply Supplied* about Australian food preserving, writes that 1835 was a watershed in Australia's history. It was 'the year in which the real story of Australia's progress began, for the twelve years which followed were the age of the squatters when men began feverishly to put their money, or their credit, into sheep, packed their belongings into drays, saddled their horses and drove their flocks North, South and West of the boundaries of the Nineteen counties'. The land filled with thousands of sheep until all the best areas were taken. But in the early 1840s disaster struck when the price of sheep fell to almost nothing. Farmers were reduced to boiling the sheep to render tallow, which they sent in casks to England. Portable soup and mutton hams were also made and exported along with the hides, wool, glue made from the hooves and fertiliser from the bones.

Australia had a glut of freshly butchered meat but the nearest large meat market was 10,000 miles away. So far away, in fact, that canning had to be rediscovered in Australia. Sizar Elliot was born in England in 1814, and went to live with an uncle in Australia in 1835. Elliot was appalled by the amount of good meat going to waste and 'knowing as I did that in the old country meat was preserved in tins, the idea struck me that the same thing could be done in the new'. Elliot first experimented in his own kitchen with salt water and then with baths of whale oil which could be heated to high temperatures. He built a small factory and 'continued from day to day to gain fresh knowledge and experience'. Elliot sold his tins of Beef and Vegetables, Mutton and Vegetables, Lamb and Green Peas and Oxtail Soup to captains of passing American merchant sailing ships, which resulted in several orders for more (English captains were suspicious of food preserved in the colony). But others were hard on his heels, men who had been to England to train in the English method before returning to open much larger concerns. Feeling swamped by much classier competition, Elliot sold his factory in 1851 and moved on to other challenges.

An outbreak of rinderpest raged in England in the 1860s decimating the local cattle and providing Australia with a perfect opportunity to ship enormous quantities of canned meat at much cheaper prices than home-produced canned meat. 'It gave,' wrote Professor Drummond, 'such a fillip to the production of canned meat in Australia that it was not long before these forms of beef and mutton were obtainable more cheaply than fresh meat.'

South America was another meat producer a long way from the

important food markets with no way of preserving their meat for export. The massive numbers of cattle roaming the pampas in Argentina and Uruguay in the mid-nineteenth century were initially intended to produce valuable hides for leather. The carcasses were left to rot or, like Australian sheep, were rendered down to make fat. As we have seen, some meat was dried to make jerked beef for home consumption but the success of von Liebig's factory producing meat extract encouraged the introduction of canning. Fray Bentos in Uruguay became famous for its cans of corned beef. It could be made from almost any quality of meat, which meant that the South American glut of cheap poor-quality beef could easily undercut French and British production. By the end of the century, many of the world's largest canneries were operating on the coasts of South America fulfilling huge orders from the military in Europe and the US.

But this panacea for armies and navies still had a long way to go before it was either sufficiently cheap or palatable to be accepted by the general public. In 1851 the Great Exhibition was staged in London in the specially built Crystal Palace, the '8th wonder of the world'. Prince Albert was the driving force behind it and his ambition was for the Exhibition to be the greatest show of 'the products, manufacturers, natural products and arts of all nations' with special emphasis on the wonderful achievements of Great Britain and the countries of her vast empire. Visitors passing through the Food Hall would have seen a colourful and exotic collection of foods from almost every part of the known world: cereals, pulses, hops, oils, pastas and bags of every conceivable variety of flour; dried fruits, spices, nuts, seeds and curiosities from every land. There were raisins from Malaga, almonds from Jordan, currants from Cephalonia, pickled fruits from the East Indies and dried banana from Barbados. Preserved peaches, pears and apples had been sent from the Cape Colony, plums from Wurtenberg and olives from Spain. Tea was on display from China and India, coffee from the British colonies and cocoa from the Antilles. The finest potted caviar had been shipped from Russia, sharks' fins from Malacca, isinglass from the East Indies and cod liver oil from Nova Scotia.

The heady aromas and strange tastes must have been almost

overpowering. Many of the marvellous and exotic foodstuffs were still unfamiliar to the British public, sent from places they had never visited nor barely knew of. Numerous samples of familiar traditionally preserved foods were exhibited as well, including plenty of dried, salted or smoked meats and fish, barrels of beef, pork and tongues, cases of smoked hams, bacons and sausages and kegs of butter and lard. Alongside these appeared cakes of dried blood, portable soups and concentrated meat jellies and pastes, gallons of preserved milk and some giant cheeses. There was even a whole preserved pig.

But the exhibits which excited particular interest were the canned foods, a process that was hardly new. (Donkin, Hall and Gamble, known by then as John Gamble, displayed a can made in 1813.) They had been largely distributed to the navy, army and the colonies. Some luxury canned foods had been available in quality stores such as Fortnum and Mason, but to the ordinary family enjoying their big day out, canned food was as much a novelty as the hundreds of other strange, exciting and foreign exhibits that they were to find. John Gamble's complete list of exhibited foods was extraordinary.

> Canisters of preserved fresh beef, mutton and veal; of fresh
> milk, cream and custards; of fresh carrots, green peas,
> turnips, beetroots, stewed mushrooms and other vegetables;
> of fresh salmon, codfish, oysters, haddock and other fish;
> and of real turtle soup, mock turtle soup, oxtail and other
> soups. Preserved hams for use in India, China etc., calipash,
> calipee and green fat for making real turtle soup, all
> preserved by the same process. Also soup and bouili, for
> emigrants and troops at sea. Pheasants, partridges etc.,
> preserved. The whole preserved so as to keep in any
> climate, and for an unlimited length of time.

The French, including Appert's nephew, sent some delicious sounding 'heated and hermetically sealed' foods such as petit pois and truffles, champignons, artichokes and flageolot beans. There were sardines in oil from Nantes as well as 'complete dinners . . . with gravy and sauces ready for use' preserved in boxes and 'intended for navy officers, sportsmen and travellers'. There were also numerous examples of canned foods from America and Australia, Germany and Switzerland. The public was enthusiastic, the press eulogistic, in the popular imagination canned foods were already a promising success. But just as the English public might have embraced this revolutionary new food, a severe crisis of confidence occurred, sending reverberations around the world.

In June 1846, the Admiralty had felt that the price of canned meat was sufficiently competitive that it could afford to add canned meat to every sailor's general ration. But it was decided that one way to reduce costs was to buy supplies of meat in very large cans, weighing up to 12 lb. In January 1852, just a few months after the Great Exhibition, *The Times* reported that navy depots were having to condemn huge numbers of cans which had 'gone off'. According to *The Times*, out of 2,707 canisters opened, only 197 were found to be fit to eat. The navy was obliged to admit that supplies of putrid canned meat had been discovered on several occasions in the past. Fuelled by the press, a major, well-publicised scandal blew up, which the government were quick to try to suffuse by setting up an enquiry.

Almost all the condemned cans had been supplied by Stephen Goldner, the man who had first patented the use of calcium chloride brine baths. Goldner had a factory in Moldavia where he was able to get cheap meat and labour. According to the press, the putrefied meat included 'Pieces of heart, roots of tongue, pieces of palate, coagulated blood, pieces of liver, ligaments of the throat, pieces of intestines – in short garbage and putridity in a horrible state . . .' Quite enough to put anyone off ever eating canned meat. The quality of the meat, poor supervision and malpractice were all investigated but the committee eventually came to the conclusion that, however poor the quality of the meat, it was in fact the large size of the cans that was causing them to 'blow'. Still labouring under the misapprehension that the expulsion of air rather than heating was central to preservation, they concluded that the cans were so big that a 'complete expulsion of air' was impossible. In fact, sufficient heating was not reaching through to the centre of the bigger cans, thus leaving pockets of bacteria to proliferate. But their conclusions were close enough to the truth for the Admiralty ordered smaller cans, as well as proper inspection of supplies. Stephen Goldner was never again allowed to supply canned meat to the navy.

But in the public eye, the damage was done. In Europe, Britain, Australia and America many people remained nervous of canned food and were reluctant to eat it. Now many also believed that it caused food poisoning. Indeed, after some disastrous shipments of charqui from South America the British public had become very much prejudiced against preserved meats in any form. Australian meat also came to be commonly termed 'charqui' for some time.

In addition, until the 1860s, canned food was always over-cooked, did not look or smell very appetising and was not cheap. Housewives wanted recognisable cuts of meat not blocks of flavourless, overcooked meat, described by the *Lancet* as 'done to rags'. Anthony Trollope bought some cans of Australian meat for his servants to try. He tasted some himself and found that: 'It was sweet and by no means unpalatable, but was utterly tasteless as meat. Whether it did or did not contain the nutritive qualities of meat I am unable to say. Servants in my house would not eat it,

A display of early tins. The largest and oldest, with a carrying handle, is the famous 1823 tin of veal returned from Edward Parry's expedition. It was later opened and tasted in 1938

because, no doubt they could get better. With such of the working classes as can afford meat themselves occasionally or in small quantities – as to whom a saving in the cost of meat would be a matter of the greatest consequence – I could never find that it was in favour. As the preserved meats are without bone, they may, at the price above named, be regarded as being half the cost of first class English meat. But I think that by most English workmen half a pound of English fresh meat would be regarded with more favour than a whole pound of Australian tinned meat.'

It was time to start 'selling' the product. The *Illustrated London News,* having led the press vilification of putrid canned meat, later published a detailed and complimentary description of a visit to a London cannery in an effort to restore confidence. Daniel Tallerman, an enterprising Jewish salesman from Australia, set up the Australian Meat Agency in London. He was determined to show that Australian meat was nutritious, cheap and good to eat. He organised a series of mass demonstrations to workers and their families where he served mutton pies, beef steak pies, beef steak puddings, mince collops, stuffed rolls of mutton, brawn sausages and dumplings; all good traditional English working-class fare made with cheap meat brought all the way from Australia. Tallerman instituted 'penny dinners' of Irish stew or soups with bread and supplied meat to ragged schools and dinners for working men and their wives at 3 pence each. *The Times*, with predictable condescension, observed that 'The penny dinners are vulgar things, but they assuage a good deal of suffering.' Tallerman also received a letter written on behalf of Queen Victoria: 'It will be very gratifying to Her Majesty if the colonists of Australia are able to furnish a supply of wholesome animal food at a price within the reach of the poorer classes of this country, and her Majesty will watch with interest the progress of such an undertaking.' The indefatigable commercial traveller even tried to sell Australian meat at the French court of Napoleon III.

The growing urban populations of Europe and America increased the demand for cheap, transportable food and produced a more educated and confident working class. Through development of trade unions and self-help organisations like the Co-operative Societies, ordinary working people were gradually beginning to demand better conditions and better food both at work and at home. The Co-operative stores helped to introduce the cheaper canned meats from Australia and South America to the domestic market. Advertisements for canned food began to fill the popular press with glowing testimonials, scientific awards, wild nutritional claims, collectible cards and colourful illustrations of well-fed children and contented housewives, suggesting the freshness and naturalness of the product (just as they do today). Advertisements for Heinz cans of baked beans showed a working man in overalls spooning up beans which, it was claimed 'carry three times the nourishment of beef'. Labelling was also a fine art of deceit and conceit. The 'My Lady' and 'Little Duchess' brands of tinned fruits were clearly aimed at the better class of housewife. 'Jack Tar' and 'Sailors' Savouries' were for the more rugged type and Wilson's Corned Beef was for the snob. By 1880 Great Britain was importing sixteen million pounds of canned meat.

But, mirroring the earlier impact of the American Civil War, it was the vast mobilisations of the First World War that finally brought canned food to the European masses. British soldiers fighting in the Boer War had been issued with the first composite emergency ration packs containing two tins to be used only in 'extremity'. One had held 4 oz of beef concentrate and the other 5 oz of cocoa paste. The great mainstay of the British army in both World Wars was, however, corned beef, which was found to be ideal for soldiers on the move who could eat it cold straight from the can. The Tommy called it 'Bully beef', a name derived from the French 'bouilli' (boiled) beef, which had been fed to the French army in the Franco-Prussian War of 1870. Behind the front line in the First World War, huge depots were filled with stores of tinned spam, corned beef, tinned jam, hard cheese and even prepared meals.

By the Second World War, every soldier was issued with tiny personal stoves called tommy-cookers, which used fuel tablets to warm up drinks or these tinned meals. Instructions on compo tins such as 'simply stand in boiling water for 30 minutes' often seemed cruel to the soldier hunkered down with damp matches and his little cooker after marching long hours in freezing, drenching rain. In the desert, burning petrol-soaked sand produced a good heat for cans. But the desert heat was itself a problem and sometimes the cans became too hot to handle. In *The Sharp End*, John Ellis writes, 'When opened, they spewed out their contents, a revolting oily liquid containing a few strings of gut-like meat. Again the manufacturers instructions were not without a grim irony, cautioning the diner to "chill before serving".'

The demands of the military, as ever, fuelled improvements to the basic can design. During the Second World War self-heating cans were developed with a tube in the centre with a quick heating element lit by a wick. They proved popular if one could get them. John Foley described how his men were caught in a snowstorm and were able to keep warm with self-heating tins of tomato soup. They lit the wicks with the lighted ends of cigarettes and '. . . in a matter of seconds we were drinking hot soup and bringing down blessings on Mr Heinz and the shadowy figures of I.C.I. who were jointly responsible for this salvation'.

The eventual success of canned or tinned food relegated most traditional food preserving to quaint practices of undeveloped regions. Today, for both the necessities and comforts of life, Americans consume more than 200 million cans of food and drink each day. The 'tin can civilisation' has reached into every remote corner of the globe. Every path that man has taken through jungle, mountain or desert is now littered with empty cans and ring pulls.

CHAPTER THIRTEEN

GREAT JOURNEYS

From Greenland's icy mountains,
To India's coral strand . . .'
Hymn by Bishop Heber, 1823

Travellers' Fare

When people put down roots, built homes and created a set-tled and ordered life, there were always some, a few, who could not keep still. In the Middle Ages there were pilgrims, scholars, poets and artists searching for wider horizons and new experiences. There were also carriers, merchants, tinkers, magis-trates, inspectors and diplomats, each carrying his goods and some provisions on his back or in a saddle bag. Royalty, nobility and gentry moved between their far-flung estates in large wagons or carriages with vast retinues of servants, along with attendant rob-bers, footpads and highwaymen. Wealthier travellers on the main highways relied on monastery guest houses, hospices or inns whilst others exploring unknown or untrodden places had to insure them-selves against hunger by taking supplies of the traditional preserved and travelling foods of their own culture. Portable food had, of course, to be light, compact and nutritious to supplement what-ever they could buy from farms or markets. Preserved foods were also useful where religious or dietary rules forbade the traveller to eat the local food.

Dried food was the first choice because it was light and com-pact. The Chinese traveller in the Han period always carried the dried grain foods known as 'pei', 'hou' or 'ch'iu', dried fruit and cured fish plus some dried meat such as snake or duck. Indians took strips of dried bummelo fish (Bombay duck) and thick cakes of ghee along with small bags of rice. In the mountains, Tibetan travellers made a concoction of tea leaves and yak butter, which was stuffed into a length of thick bamboo, stoppered and carried over their shoulders. European travellers would provision with salt beef or pork, pickled herring, hardtack, tea and dried fruit; later, if they had a large wagon or pack animals, they could load up with potted meat or fish or, even later, with the heavier tinned foods. In the southern Mediterranean, the Greeks carried paximadi, and in Afghanistan people had bars and cakes made from dried fruits such as mulberries and nuts, honey and parched flour – rather like the cereal bars of today. In North America they had pemmican, jerky, 'Johnny' or 'journey' cakes and dried cornmeal, bundles of smoked fish, bags of dried beans and small flitches of bacon. In eastern Europe they took dried fermented milk products, skins of clarified butter, dried meat and gourds filled with yoghurt, and in the deserts of North Africa they had dates and dried milk.

There seemed plenty to choose from, but there was rarely enough. Every traveller experienced hunger and worried about the next meal. Women travellers, not surprisingly, were often better organised in their planning. Elizabeth Justice, who travelled in Russia in 1739 wrote that when her family went on a journey, 'They have what they call a travelling Waggon; in which they put their Beds and Bedding. They can either sit upright, or lie along, as they shall think convenient. They generally take good store of Liquor, Tongues, Hung-Beef or anything that is potted; for there is but bad Entertainment upon the Road.' Mary Schaffer, who explored the Canadian Rockies in the 1880s in her pursuit of wild flowers and animals, became quite an expert on the best provisions to take on a journey, such as 'granulose' as a lighter substitute for sugar, dried milk and dried eggs. But 'Each of the three has its limitations,' she wrote, 'and to this day I wonder if that dried milk had ever seen a cow, or if any hen would acknowledge the motherhood of those dried eggs.' Above all she warned fellow travellers to 'Beware of the dried cabbage; no fresh air in existence will ever blow off sufficient of the odor to let it get safely to the mouth.' She did, however, rely on plenty of beans, rice, dried potatoes and dried fruits and vegetables of 'little weight and wonderful nuturant qualities . . .' Ella Sykes, who travelled through Persia on a side-saddle in 1898, took with her a large store of Swiss condensed milk and some tins of egg powder,

'A combination of the two making capital custard puddings. Dried plums, peaches, apricots and figs had been laid in at Kerman, and were invaluable in a country almost destitute of fruit and vegetables at the best of times and of course completely so during the month of February in which we were travelling. Tins of "Chollet's Compressed Vegetables" [a dried vegetable cake developed during the Crimean War] were a great standby for our soup, and when I mention that we carried "jelly packets" with us, my readers will see that we travelled in real luxury!'

Every opportunity to acquire food had to be grasped. A willingness to eat whatever was available, regardless of its appearance or taste, was a prerequisite for survival for solitary travellers, many of whom brought back journals filled with fascinating information about new, foreign foods. Isabella Bird was an indefatigable, fearless, independent-minded and incurable traveller. Born in 1831 with a spinal complaint, she was a sickly child and finally a doctor suggested that travel might help take her mind off things. He probably meant nothing more than an Atlantic cruise with plenty of invigorating sea air and warm sunshine. But Isabella never really kept still again. She travelled to Hawaii via Australasia and from there to the United States where she rode, alone on her pony, Birdie, thousands of miles around the Rocky Mountains. After a brief marriage to a doctor in England, Isabella, now well known as a result of her book *A Lady's Life in the Rocky Mountains*, again took to the road and travelled through India and Persia, Korea and Japan. Her travels through the interior of Japan, described in her book *Unbeaten Tracks in Japan*, were even more extraordinary as she insisted on going into parts of the interior where no European, let alone a European woman, had ever ventured before. Concerned friends in Yokohama, where she stayed before setting out, warned her of the dangers and the discomfort and continually discussed the 'Food Question'. 'Foreign ministers, professors, missionaries, merchants, all discuss it with becoming gravity as a question of life and death, which by many it is supposed to be,' Isabella reported. Hotels or inns in Japan were called *yadoya* and like European inns, they varied widely in quality. On Isabella's 'unbeaten tracks', the only food she was likely to find in the peasant-run inns was rice, tea, pickles, eggs, 'an occasional elderly chicken', black beans and boiled cucumbers, plus vegetables 'rendered indigestible by being coarsely pickled'. 'Food,' Isabella was told, '*must* be taken, as the fishy and vegetable abominations known as "Japanese food" can only be swallowed and digested by a few, and that after long practice.' Having rejected all sensible European advice, Isabella set out on her epic journey with a small supply of von Liebig's meat extract, 4 lb of raisins, some chocolate, both for eating and drinking, and some brandy 'in case of need'. She travelled in a *karuma*, a sort of small dogcart pulled by running coolies. They set off at a brisk pace, sometimes stopping for rest and refreshment at a roadside tea house called a *chaya*, where the coolies could eat rice, pickles, salt fish and soup, while Isabella stuck to tiny cups of tea.

She found most of the *yadoya* dreadfully uncomfortable – the fleas, beetles and flies 'played carnival' in the dark, and the local people were no less irritating as they poked holes through the paper walls of her room in order to peep in at the first foreign woman to pass their way. She must have felt as though she was in a booth of a side show. In one particularly unpleasant *yadoya*, Isabella describes a stand on which stood large brown dishes with food for sale: 'Salt shellfish in a black liquid, dried trout impaled on sticks, sea slugs in soy, a paste made of pounded roots, and green cakes made of the slimy river confervoe [a green algae] pressed and dried – all ill-favoured and unsavoury viands.' Later that afternoon she watched a man 'without clothes' treading out on a mat a paste of coarse flour and buckwheat, which was then cut into strips and boiled. More palatable snack food for the day's journey might be light wafers made of white of egg and sugar, chewy balls made of sugar and barley flour, sugar-coated beans, bricks of fine flour kneaded with sugar and 'yokan', a delicate sweet made with beans and sugar, rendered firm by a gelatinous substance obtained from seaweed and then shaped into oblongs and kept in dried leaves.

Isabella eventually arrived in the city of Niigata where she found several shops selling European tinned meats, condensed milk and other 'travelling requisites'. She bought a tin of Gail Borden's 'Eagle' brand of condensed milk and, on opening it she found a substance like pale treacle, 'with a dash of valerian'. A bottle of

Smith's essence of coffee, bought for a high price, when opened revealed a 'sticky and bitter paste'. Even the travellers' soap, looking luxuriously semi-transparant, produced a livid skin rash. Isabella discovered many poisonous frauds and forgeries in bottles with highly reputable makers' names such as Bass, Martell, Guinness and Cross and Blackwell that contained 'vile and unwholesome trash'. However, she did manage to buy a new, improved mosquito net plus some sago and two tins of genuine condensed milk, a tin of biscuits, some chocolate and quinine. Thus re-equippped, Isabella plunged back into the interior.

Travellers, especially English ones, were notoriously prejudiced about the unfamiliar 'foreign' foods on which they were obliged to survive. Despite the fact that for a European, Japanese food might have seemed a particularly challenging example, Isabella Bird did not confine her observations to the mostly preserved staple foods which seemed barely to sustain the very poor people living in the remote areas where she travelled. She also wrote a special chapter describing the 'range of Japanese eatables'. These included over ninety kinds of sea and river fish eaten boiled, broiled or raw: highly salted whale meat or bonito fish, dried salmon, sea slug, cuttle-fish, clams and oysters, which were often eaten raw with soy sauce. This sauce, she recorded, was made from fermented wheat and soybeans with salt and vinegar and a dash of sake to heighten the flavour. All kinds of wild fowl were also described including goose, duck, heron, cranes and storks. Isabella also noted numerous varieties of vegetables and fruits that were eaten fresh, pickled or salted. These included fourteen kinds of beans, peas, buckwheat, maize, potatoes, squash, garlic, chillies, yams and the celebrated 'daikon' (turnip radish) 'from which every traveller and resident suffers . . . it has made many a brave man flee'. Preserved daikon root is slightly dried and then pickled in brine with rice bran. It is very porous and absorbs much of the pickle and then 'has a smell so awful that it is difficult to remain in a house in which it is being eaten. It is the worst smell that I know of except that of a skunk!' They also dried mushrooms, persimmon fruit and seaweed which was eaten everywhere. 'I have scarcely seen a coolie make a meal of which [seaweed] is not a part, either boiled, fried, pickled, raw, or in soup.' There were many kinds of soup including one containing dried snails, which Isabella described as a 'broth of abominable things'. But there were also many others made with combinations of more appetising, if just as exotic-sounding ingredients, such as salt pheasant, dock root, lettuce, sea perch, sea slug, jellyfish, lobster and boiled crane. She also noted the popularity of 'sashimi', the now famous thin-sliced raw fish dishes to enjoy with soy sauce and sake.

Isabella's contemporary observations about Japanese food reveal how much was preserved in so many ways. She noted the great divide between the cities and the rural poor: 'In the cities the essential elements of the diet of an ordinary Japanese are rice, fish and pickled daikon; in the interior rice, or in its place millet, beans, or pease and daikon. A coolie's average consumption of rice daily is two lbs. Of the luxuries of which I have written I never saw any on my northern tour – game never, and poultry and fresh fish very rarely.' She suggested that the traveller interested in good Japanese food should visit the better class of *yadoyas* in cities such as Osaka, Kyoto and Yokohama.

In 1896, Isabella travelled through parts of China and on her return to England, wrote *The Yangtze Valley and Beyond*. In 1901, her itchy feet took her on one final journey, this time to Morocco. She died peacefully in her bed in Edinburgh in 1904.

Heading West

Unlike Isabella, for the majority of women in the past, life itself was journey enough with few diversions from the demands of family and home. But sometimes circumstances made it necessary for them to literally take up their homes and families and make long and perilous journeys in search of safety or a new life. When the persecution of the Mormon settlements in the eastern states finally erupted into violence in June 1844 with the lynching of their leader Joseph Smith, the Mormons were forced to leave, 'every last saint'. They took a thousand wagons onto the Oregon trail and headed out for a promised land in the west. Ursalia Hascall joined the Mormon trail more out of a sense of adventure than spiritual fervour. Her letters to friends are filled with lists, inventories and housewifely pride in making a perfect little home on wheels. Her provisions were probably better than most of the other brethren lined up around her: 'Three yoke of oxen with flour enough to last us one year, ham, sausages, dry fish, lard, two cans hundred pounds of sugar, 16 of coffee, 10 of raisins, rice with all the items we wish to use in cooking.' Ursalia's menus and inventories continue throughout the trail. There would be coffee for breakfast, milk and hasty pudding for dinner, and perhaps a piece of one the fat calves that the company killed every now and then and divided up. Sometimes they were able to gather some wild food as they went along and even preserve it for keeping. Her first letter from the wilderness tells us that there were black walnuts '. . . in abundance, hundreds of bushels of grapes, orchards of wild plums, fifty bushels in a place, you never saw anything better [to] make pies and preserves'.

While the Mormons were being harried and forced to move on, there were others, mainly farmers but townspeople as well, who also seemed far from settled in the east. They too started heading west to find a piece of free land or to strike it rich in the gold and silver mines and many were tempted by stories of fertile, golden lands, flowing with milk and honey, bathed in a balmy climate. 'He told of the great crops of wheat which it was possible to raise in Oregon, and pictured in glowing terms the richness of the soil and the attractions of the climate, and then with a little twinkle in his eye he said "And they do say, gentlemen, they do say, that out in Oregon the pigs are running about under the great acorn trees, round and fat, and already cooked, with knives and forks sticking in them so that you can cut off a slice whenever you are hungry."' How many people on the trail, in the last stages of starvation and sickness, might remember this hallucinatory image of a juicy stuck pig and curse that particular story teller?

They went as family groups in trains of between twelve and forty-two wagons and would cover between five and twenty miles a day. Usually the journey would last from four to nine months. They had to travel more than 2,000 miles crossing vast deserts, scaling high mountains and crossing flooded rivers. At the same time, they would have to endure driving rain and thick mud and risk being caught in snowstorms. Unless they arrived before autumn they would be forced to stay in winter camps and face starvation, disease and freezing cold. None of them could hope to survive the journey without proper and sufficient provision, which included large quantities of preserved foods.

Special wagons were built to withstand the terrible conditions and filled with food, tools, clothing and all their worldly goods. The men cut and kiln-dried oak for the wagons, prepared hickory wood for axles, fired up the forges to beat out tires and chains, and twisted hemp in the long rope-walks. They rounded up live-stock and bought some pack mules, horses, milk cows and oxen to draw the wagons. The women sewed tents, wagon covers and sacks for flour and crackers. It was all a very expensive business. *The Emigrant Guide to Oregon and California 1845* recommended that each emigrant be supplied with '200 pounds of flour, 150 pounds of bacon, 10 pounds coffee, 20 pounds sugar, 10 pounds salt'. In preparation for the long journey the women dried squash and fruits such as apples and peaches, baked 'journey' cakes or biscuits, salted and cured pork, filled sausages and packed crocks with pick-les and sauerkraut. They also cooked up jams and preserves, and made cider and vinegar. Meats were either smoked, dried or salted, and dried vegetables and fruit were hung on strings in the wagon. Additional supplies included barrels of crackers, cornmeal, smoked or chipped beef, rice, tea, coffee, raisins, sugar, lard, sal-eratus (baking soda), mustard and tallow.

Some, like Ursalia, could afford a few luxuries such as 'Huge barrels of buttermilk stored for drinking and making biscuits . . . sauerkraut, jerked deer and buffalo tongue, bear bacon all stored away'. Canned goods, apart from sardines, were still expensive and not common but luxuries might include a gallon of wild plum and crab-apple preserve, a barrel of cranberries, a bottle or two of whisky, some honey or blackberry jam, good bacon, hams, bologna sausages, whole cheeses, barrels of both white and brown sugar and great cakes of maple sugar. Most wagons stocked some basic medicines such as quinine, opium, medicinal alcohol, hartshorn for snake bites and citric acid used as an antidote for scurvy. 'A little of the acid mixed with sugar and water and a few drops of essence of lemon made a fine substitute for lemonade.'

But even the best-stocked wagon, which would be feeding up to a dozen people every day, could not sustain them on the entire journey without supplementing the provisions with fresh meat and wild green stuffs. The men hunted buffalo, deer, mountain sheep, even the loathed jackrabbit, and sometimes caught catfish in the streams. Draught animals, horses and cows died in huge numbers on the route, were lost through stampede or stolen by marauding Indians. Towards the end of the journey, fresh meat became extremely scarce.

Train after train of wagons pulled out, lined up and headed west, like entire villages on wheels. In 1853 Amelia Stewart Knight set out with her husband and seven children (an eighth would be born on the way) and she saw ahead 'three hundred or more wagons in sight as far as the eye can see'. With their long, sturdy frames and high white canopy, the wagons came to be known as 'prairie schooners' looking like a stately line of great white ships moving slowly through the waving sea of prairie grass.

For the women, daily life in the wagons was in some ways not much different from back home. Food had to be cooked, clothes mended and laundered, babies and small children cared for. They learned to churn butter by the rocking movement of the wagon and to raise their bread on the move so it was ready to bake when they stopped and made up an oven of baked earth and clay. Life was particularly trying when it rained: the wagons and tents were drenched and everything began to rot including the dried foods. 'All the clothes remain wet. Even the babies'.' Charlotte Stearns Pengra noted in her diary, 'I hung out what things were wet in the wagon, made griddle cakes, stewed berries and made tea for supper. After that was over made two loaves of bread, stewed a pan of [dried] apples, prepared potatoes and [dried] meat for breakfast . . . and mended a pair of pants for Wm. pretty tired.'

The diet was monotonous but the women tried to keep up standards. One man invited to eat in a neighbouring wagon early on in the journey described the meal as 'Hot biscuits, fresh butter, honey, rich milk, cream, venison steak, and tea and coffee – and there were green peas gathered that day from the wild vines along the trail'. One can only hope that the woman who prided herself on 'setting a good table' did not later lose her milk cow nor be too generous with her provisions so early on.

'For six months and three days we lived in our wagons and travelled many a weary mile,' wrote Lydia Waters, but despite the terrible, monotonous diet, the sickness and the Indian attacks, 'there were', she noted, 'many things to laugh about'. The women visited sick friends and exchanged gossip, they helped each other and socialised as Georgia Rea described: 'Knitting, tatting, crocheting, exchanging receipts for cooking beans or dried apples or swapping food for the sake of variety kept us in practices of feminine occupations and diversions. We did not keep late hours but when not too engrossed with fear of the red enemy or dread of impending danger, we enjoyed the hour around the campfire, the men folk lolling and smoking their pipes and guessing, or maybe betting, how many miles we had covered during the day. We listened to readings, storytelling, music and songs and the day often ended in laughter and merrymaking.'

The women's voices can still be heard through their lists of provisions, and their courage and adaptability still impresses. Many did not survive the journey, and alongside the trail were numerous shallow graves of men, children, mothers and new-born babies. But between 1840 and 1870 over a quarter of a million men, women and children successfully crossed the continent to Oregon and California in what was considered one of the greatest migrations of modern times. The Great Trek in South Africa in 1836 hardly bears comparison. The Boers probably numbered less than one tenth of the American migrants and travelled generally less than half the distance. There is no evidence that the Great Trek had any influence upon the American migration, yet there are numerous similarities, not least in the hardships both Boers and American migrants stoically faced and in their ability to prepare and carry quantities of preserved foodstuff into unknown territory. Without it, it is arguable that neither great movement of people could have happened at that time.

The Captain's Table

For people travelling by sea, conditions were often little better than those suffered by the naval ratings of the time. In the early days, sea travel was a long, dangerous and at best uncomfortable business not to be undertaken lightly. Cabin passengers were not commonplace until the eighteenth century. Apart from merchant and naval sailors and fishermen, the majority who crossed the seas before that time were government agents, missionaries and explorers. Food supplies were a continuing preoccupation and even the best-supplied ships could run dangerously low. Christopher Columbus found just such a situation on his fourth voyage in 1502. His son Ferdinand, who travelled with him, wrote, 'And what with the heat and the dampness, even the biscuit was so full of worms that, God help me, I saw many wait until nightfall to eat the porridge made of it so as not to see the worms.' The Pilgrim Fathers barely managed to stay alive on the 'poorly provisioned' *Mayflower* on a diet of 'salt horse', hardtack, smoked bacon, dried fish, grains and dried peas, mouldy cheese and beer in ironbound casks.

The perils of eating at the Captain's table in the early eighteenth century. The East Indiaman Clyde *in heavy seas*

Voyages to the tropics presented special problems. A report to the Royal Society in 1667 described how, on a voyage to Jamaica; 'the steams of the Sea [were] found to be of such a nature, that our sweet-meats rotted; Sugar of Roses, and other Lozenges grew moist; notwithstanding that there was no reason to attribute it to any rainy weather. The Pies and Gammons of Bacon which had kept well before, after they had been once exposed to the open Air, decayed more in a day or two than in six weeks before.' Honey, juniper and pine tar were smeared onto hams and bacon to help protect them in tropical conditions. In 1463, the *Mary Talbot* stowed 200 honeycombs to sweeten the salt meat, stockfish, beer and oat cakes. It is curious how little honey is mentioned in ships' stores as it would seem an ideal food both nutritionally and for storing at sea.

Occasionally, though, special food was taken for 'banketting on shipboard of persons of credite'. Notes were written to trading captains with advice on how to keep their passengers well fed and happy: 'First the sweetest perfumes to set under hatches to make ye place sweet against their coming aboord.' There follows a long list of delicacies, clearly designed to withstand the damp conditions at sea. 'Comfets of divers kinds made of purporse by him, that is most excellent, that shall not dissolve,' such as marmalade, sucket, barrelled figs and raisins of the 'sunne', prunes, dried pears, walnuts, almonds and olives and special apples that 'dureth two yeeres'. No common ship's biscuit for these important passengers but 'Excellent French vinegar, and a fine kind of Bisket stieped in the same do make a banketting dish, and a little sugar cast in it cooleth and comforteth, and refresheth the spirits of man.'

Few dishes have been devised specially for sea-goers but Hannah Glasse, in *The Art of Cookery*, written in 1747, devoted a special chapter for ships' captains. Some of her recipes seem rather unrealistic for the rigours of sea passage and she has a delightful passion for 'Artichoke Bottoms for sea Captains', for which she gives recipes to dry, fry, ragoo and fricassee. Various puddings, using rice, oatmeal, suet and peas sealed in crusts or pudding bags would have been practical and portable and easy to boil in a ship's cauldron. Moreover, ketchup to keep twenty years and a fish sauce 'to keep the whole Year' would certainly have been useful, and anyone contemplating a really long and hungry voyage might have been tempted by her recipe for Sea Venison which begins, 'When you kill a sheep, keep stirring the Blood all the time till it is cold . . .' It is a lengthy and complex business but eventually the cooked mutton pieces are marinated in wine and vinegar for twelve hours or more, salted for a further week or ten days and finally end up in a rich, gravy-filled pie.

Longer journeys demanded more inventive ways to improve the ship's rations. In 1815, some of the first cans produced by Donkin, Hall and Gamble were tested on a long voyage to the Bering Straits and the South Seas, along with supplies of dried meat and vegetables picked up in St Petersburg. The captain, Otto von Kotzbue, wrote that the soup made from the Russian food tasted disgusting and that in order to 'take away the bad taste of the soup, I had two boxes of English patent meat opened; these contain fresh meat boiled in steam, and are soldered together with so much care that not the least air can penetrate; on which account the meat, even after years, cannot be distinguished from quite fresh'. On non- military ships, some efforts were even made to provide fresh food including a variety of livestock. A milking nanny was often taken on sailing ships, as Cobbett notes: 'When sea voyages are so stormy as to kill geese, ducks, fowls and almost pigs, the goats are well and lively – when a dog of no kind can keep the deck a minute a goat will skip and leap about on it as bold as brass.' Charles Dickens recalls the terrible tedium of meals aboard ship on his journey to America on the Messenger in 1842. 'There are three meals a day. Breakfast at seven, dinner at half-past twelve, supper about six. At each there are a great many small dishes and plates upon the table, with very little in them; so that, although there is every appearance of a mighty "spread", there is seldom really more than a joint: except for those who fancy slices of beet-root, shreds of dried beef, complicated entanglements of yellow pickle, maize, Indian corn, apple sauce, and pumpkin.'

Dorothy Hartley's aunt, who kept detailed journals of her travels, was one of the first women to sail around the West Indies, a voyage that even by the 1850s still took several months. 'We took goat's milk and hens for eggs and pigs and sheep,' she remembered. 'The butcher looked after all the animals and they were all eaten by the end of the voyage.' But even then the daily diet still consisted mainly of 'salt meat, dried peas and beans, and forms of beans and bacon. We also had boiled salt beef with dumplings, carrots and root vegetables'. By then, scurvy was better understood. Watercress plants, rich in iron, were commonly taken on board growing in jars of water, eggs were greased in hot lard and packed in sawdust, butter salted down in kegs, eating apples conserved in jars, and redcurrant juice. In addition, there would be salves and ointments such as broom buds, cod's liver oil and blackhog's lard. The ships provided lemons against scurvy and for the cabin passengers' punch. English watercress roots, carelessly discarded in ports and estuaries around the world, have subsequently thrived, causing serious ecological problems.

The captain of a passenger-carrying ship was often expected to supply extra luxuries for passengers who dined with him. He in turn, not surprisingly, expected his passengers to bring hampers of provisions on board to help stock his larder if they wished to dine at the captain's table. Dorothy Hartley's aunt did, and 'always took a ham as a present to the Captain, as we sat at his table, we cooked it specially with cider and cloves. The cloves helped keep it. We used to take poultry, potted in tubs and potted trout and salmon done in vinegar, and potted meat in jars. We grew to be very clever! It was our pride.' She also managed to take potted cold roast fowls to sea and boiled down her own portable soup.

As sea passage became faster, passenger ships grew into liners and cruise ships capable of carrying a huge range of fresh, canned and, later, frozen foods. On-board meals improved immeasurably. A young emigrant going out to New Zealand in the 1880s could describe eating rather well. They were issued with beef, pork, preserved meats, suet, butter, biscuits, oatmeal, peas, rice, potatoes, carrots, onions, raisins, tea, coffee, sugar, treacle, mustard, salt, pepper water, mixed pickles, some fresh fruit and the now compulsory lime juice. She and her friends also brought with them a large tin containing 2 lb of good tea, sugar, figs, meat extract and a bottle of strong home-made calves-foot jelly for seasickness.

Great Expeditions

By the end of the nineteenth century, much of the world had been explored. Great expeditions had crossed Australia and mapped the wilds of America. In 1801, Captain Meriwether Lewis and Captain William Clark explored the American northwest carrying 193 lb of portable soup, 20 barrels of flour, 14 barrels of parched corn, 42 barrels of salt pork, 200 lb of beef tallow and 50 lb of pig lard stored in whisky barrels. They also carried sacks of beans, dried apples along with quantities of sugar, coffee, salt and hardtack biscuits. There were many difficulties in planning and provisioning such a long expedition with a large team of men heading into unknown territory. They would be unlikely to be able to buy much food or other necessities for a number of years. They therefore needed to be able to hunt wild animals, to know about the nutritional qualities of plants and herbs, where to find water and how to feed their pack animals. To achieve this even partially, they would have to take a large amount of provisions and equipment. The more they took, the more people and animals they would need to carry and guard them. On some expeditions, the preserved provisions were carried more as a backup as they tried to 'live off the land' and this could be successful if the natives were friendly. For others it would be the only food available for months or even years.

Lewis and Clark both knew that discipline and rationing were going to be essential if they were all to survive. 'The day after tomorrow lyed corn and grece will be issued to the party, the next day Poark and flour, and the day following indian meal and poark . . .' Like the Cape trekkers, they often made jerky when they had excess meat from a hunt. They shot bear, elk, moose and racoon in the summer and gathered wild berries, grapes and roots. In the autumn, they caught beaver, geese, deer and turkey. They often traded with the Native Americans, who were on the whole friendly, and they learned how to live off the land and how to make pemmican. They saw great quantities of salmon drying on scaffolds and watched as 'half dry' fish were gently cooked in water heated with hot stones from the fire. They described how the Indians prepared and dried fish for market and how they ate pounded dried fish 'a disagreeable food which occasioned so much sickness among the men'. The Clatsop Indians showed the men how to trap sturgeon in the rivers and they watched the Indian women as they dried deep purple huckleberries in the sun or in kilns and then pounded them and baked them into huge loaves. Lewis was particularly impressed with this bread, which, he wrote, 'keeps very well during one season and retains the moist jeucies of the fruit much better than by any other method of preservation'. Lewis and Clark's expedition took two years and five months; the team survived near-starvation through terrible freezing winters, yet only one man died.

Exploration in the eighteenth and nineteenth centuries was important to the prestige of the great nations yet too many expensive and ambitious expeditions sent out in the search for new trade routes still failed because of an inadequate diet. Long journeys overland and voyages at sea were put in jeopardy by the explorers' inability to carry the right provisions to sustain them. While some expeditions were able to supplement their provisions with local food supplies, survival in the inhospitable conditions of polar exploration was quite another prospect. But it was thought that perhaps with the arrival of canning and other new preserving methods, the problem had at last been solved.

Winter Quarters
British Antarctica Expedition
October, 1911

Dear Sir,

I have pleasure in informing you that your 'Golden Syrup' has been in daily use in this hut throughout the Winter and has been much appreciated by all the members of the expedition.

I regard it as a most desirous addition to necessary food . . . of a Polar Expedition.

Yours faithfully,
Captain R. F. Scott

Scott wrote this letter to Messrs Tate and Lyle sitting cosily in his base camp while his men enjoyed a hearty hot breakfast of fresh bread, marmalade, porridge, scrambled 'Truegg' a 'dehydrated yellow powder out of catering-size tins', coffee and tea. He was unaware that only a few days before, the Norwegian Roald Amundsen and four companions had set off for the South Pole, all expert skiers travelling with lightly loaded sledges pulled by well-trained dogs who could whip them along over the ice, covering up to seventy miles a day. For many years it had been Scott's ambition to be the first man to reach the South Pole. To this end he had raised huge sums of government money and equipped himself with ponies and large numbers of men, all of whom would have to be fed. He also had expensive motor sledges, vast quantities of equipment and mountains of food – tinned, dried, salted, frozen and even fresh. They had set up a base camp with officers on one side of a wall of tea chests and men on the other. For dinner, the cook boiled pemmican into hot 'hoosh', while the steward laid the officers' table.

Scott and his men had been preparing the final assault for months, and had set up a line of provision dumps. They practised sledging over the ice and snow to familiarise themselves with the ever-present dangers of crevasses and 'sastrugi', hidden icy-hard ribs of snow that can upset a sledge. But by the time Scott and his team finally set out, Amundsen had already planted the Norwegian flag at the South Pole. Even before Scott's team reached the great Beardmore Glacier, his motor sledges had been ditched and the ponies were dead. The men were reduced to pulling the sledges themselves, a slow, freezing, gruelling journey that burned up their energy and left them exhausted and severely frost-bitten. Reaching the Pole after Amundsen was a dispiriting experience and they turned wearily for home. Eleven miles short of the One Ton Depot, one day after Captain Oates had been a gentleman and disappeared into the whiteness, Scott, Wilson and Bowers expired in their tent, clinging together in their last hours for some warmth and comfort. It is generally agreed that they died as a result of malnutrition and exhaustion. Despite all the expense, the planning, the men and equipment and the stores of foods, Scott had failed to take adequate nutrition for his needs.

Many Arctic explorers encountered a strange 'amphibian' life when their ships were held fast in the winter polar ice. Perhaps the strangest story was that of Captain John Ross and his nephew James Clark Ross, who were after the prize of £20,000 offered by the British government to anyone who could find the legendary North West Passage. In 1818 John Ross was the first man to find himself on the right course to the Pacific amongst the maze of Arctic islands to the north of America, but was forced to turn back. His lieutenant, William Parry, frustrated by Ross' early retreat, himself undertook three voyages and, without realising it, discovered most of the route for the North West Passage.

For his third attempt in 1824, Parry could shop around a number of British food canning suppliers who by then ran well-established businesses. Parry's expedition took over twenty-six tons of tinned meats, vegetables and soups and he was the first to take tinned provisions as the principal food supply. But on this voyage, Parry's ship, the *Fury,* became trapped in pack ice off Somerset Island. Parry unloaded all his equipment and food supplies including the vast quantities of tinned food, which he left sitting on the Arctic ice. After watching helplessly as the *Fury* was crushed and ground apart, the crew struggled away over the ice on the long journey to safety.

John Ross's Arctic expedition camped on Somerset Island where they survived on William Parry's abandoned cache of tinned foods

In 1829 John and James Ross organised yet another attempt on the prize and persuaded the gin magnate Felix Booth to fund it. John Ross, like Scott, was fascinated by modern machinery and experimented with steam power. Convinced that his new technology would revolutionise Arctic exploration, Ross fitted his ship, the *Victory,* with a steam engine, confident that she would plough easily through the polar ice. The 'crude, clanking, ill-fitted engine' was abandoned before they even reached Arctic waters. Cursing the 'execrable machinery', Ross realised too late that it had taken up so much space on the ship that he had only provisioned adequately for a brief exploration. Fortunately for Ross and his crew, they reached Somerset Island where they discovered Parry's treasure trove of food untouched during the previous five years and still in perfect condition. 'I need not say,' wrote Ross, 'that it was an occurrence not less novel than interesting, to find in this abandoned region of solitude and ice and rocks, a ready market where we could supply all our wants . . . all ready to be shipped when we chose, and all free of cost.' Ross loaded the *Victory* with tins of meat and vegetables, canisters of flour and sugar and kegs of butter, though 'all we could stow away,' he wrote, 'seemed scarcely to diminish the piles of canisters'. One of the boiled mutton tins made it back to London to appear as the star exhibit on the stand of John Gamble & Co. at the Great Exhibition of 1851. This unopened tin, exhibited as a marvel of longevity, was to keep for another eighty-seven years before it was opened by Professor Jack Drummond in 1938. The contents were found to have suffered little nutrient loss despite some iron and tin contamination.

If fortune smiled on this ill-organised expedition, it did so in strange ways. The *Victory* sailed on through the pack ice in a fruitless search for a way through. By September, they were preparing to winter in a bay they called Felix Harbour after their patron. Many Arctic voyagers had wintered over in the ice before and Ross felt confident now that he had Parry's food supplies. He wrote ecstatically about the visual splendours of the Arctic, describing icebergs 'like castles and towers and mountains, gorgeous in colouring, and magnificent, if often capricious, in form'. His crew took a more jaded view of their winter wonderland, even though they were not yet to realise that the *Victory* would never find open water again and was doomed to remain in her prison of ice forever. But in the three years that they endured life trapped on the *Victory*, valuable lessons were learned. The ship became a sort of research station, perhaps the forerunner of the many scientific and meteorological bases that now squat in the snow around both Poles. John Ross became fascinated by the Inuit, who had a winter camp of 'ice houses' nearby. The Inuit had never seen a white man before and believed that the *Victory* was a creature with wings. 'Sure that they were alone in the world' the Inuit were perfectly at home in their polar landscape, snowy hunting grounds and ice houses. The Inuit both amazed and appalled Ross but he noted that they were healthy and did not suffer from scurvy or other diseases. Despite his view that they were 'gourmandising savages who devoured their food in a primitive frenzy', he realised that if he could persuade his crew to eat Inuit food, they might also escape the diseases to which so many half-starved explorers had in the past succumbed. Ross believed that 'all experience has shown that the use of oil and fat meats is the true secret of life in these frozen countries', and so coerced his unwilling men to eat fox meat, Arctic salmon and seal blubber. This was bought from the Inuit along with whale, reindeer, fish, sea fowl and seals. Ross also made his men cut down on their consumption of gin of which, thanks to their sponsor, they had more than plenty.

But by the spring of 1832, the Inuit had left, the preserved provisions were almost gone, and Ross believed that they could no longer survive. They were sick of the sight of snow.

> These are the objections to a snow landscape . . . the gale is
> a gale of snow, the fog is a fog of snow . . . when the
> breath of the mouth is snow, when snow settles on the hair,
> the dress, the eyelashes, where snow falls around us and fills
> our chamber, our beds, our dishes . . . where our sofas are
> of snow, and our houses are of snow: when snow was our
> decks, snow was our awnings, snow our observatories, snow
> our larders, snow our salt; and when all the other uses of
> snow should at last be of no avail, our coffins and our
> graves were to be graves and coffins of snow.

They attempted to escape in the longboats, but got no further than back to Somerset Island, where at least they could build a winter shelter and live off the remains of Parry's cache of tinned food. They barely survived the fourth winter in the Arctic. Some men began to suffer from scurvy and 'the hopeful did not hope more, and the despondent continued to despair'.

In July 1833 they finally escaped to open sea and were rescued by whalers. Ross and his crew had survived four and a half years in the Arctic living on preserved food supplemented, for a short but important period, by the Inuit diet. They returned home with valuable scientific information and important lessons in survival for future Arctic explorers, lessons of which few took heed.

Polar fever was to keep hold its grip on the explorer's imagination and the dream of a North West Passage was to claim many more lives. Sir John Franklin made several attempts and the third, in 1845, was the most expensive and lavishly equipped expedition ever mounted by the British Admiralty. His stores included 20 tons of tinned provisions. He commanded the ships HMS Erebus and HMS Terror, both of which had recently returned from a gruelling but successful expedition to Antarctica under James Clark Ross. Franklin sheltered the ships for the winter in a harbour on Beechey Island, discovered and named by William Parry. Franklin and his crew of 134 officers and men then vanished into the Arctic ice. There followed numerous private and public rescue expeditions including one sent by the US navy in 1850. The medical officer, Elisha Kent Kane, who had been summoned from the Gulf of Mexico and had never before been to the Arctic, described how the freezing conditions affected their food. 'Dried apples became one solid breccial mass of impacted angularities . . . Dried peaches the same.' Fruit stored in barrels had to be 'cut up both fruit and barrel . . . with a heavy axe' then defrosted so that wood and fruit could be separated. The 'sauerkraut resembled mica . . . Sugar formed a very funny compound' and required a saw to cut it up, while butter and lard, less affected, only required a 'chisel and mallet' to remove it. Flour changed very little and molasses at -32.2°C (-28°F) could be 'half cut by a stiff iron ladle'. 'Pork and beef are rare specimens of Florentine mosaic' requiring a 'crowbar and handspike, for an axe will hardly chip them'. And for dessert 'ices come, of course unbidden'. 'Some sugared cranberries, with a little butter and scalding water, and you have an impromptu strawberry ice' served on the shaft of a hickory broom used as 'a stirrer first and a fork afterward'. Metal spoons and mugs were a real danger as they 'might fasten to your mouth'. 'Thus much for our Arctic grub. I need not say that our preserved meats would make very fair cannon-balls, canister shot!!'

It was not until 1859 that the fate of the Franklin expedition became known. One hundred and forty years later, theories about the cause of the disaster are still being explored. A recent and popular 'story' is that the men were poisoned by the lead solders used to seal the tinned food provisions. In 1984, a Canadian forensic anthropologist disinterred the graves of three sailors who had been buried in the permafrost on Beechey Island. The post-mortem revealed excessive traces of lead, which the Canadian team concluded had been ingested by eating tinned food contaminated with lead. For the new wonder food to have turned out to have had a killer sting in its tail would have been cruel irony. However, the Australian food scientist Dr Keith Farrer (along with a number of other colleagues) believes that this simply wasn't possible. One explanation for the lead found in the sailors' remains was the high levels of environmental lead already present in many parts of nineteenth-century Europe. For example, water pipes were made of lead, beer was stored in lead-glazed tanks, there was lead acetate in cider and wines, tea chests were lead lined and some kinds of food containers were lead-glazed, often resulting in lead contamination particularly in the preparation of acid foods such as lemon juice and vinegar pickles. These were all food and drink products regularly consumed by ships' crews (in 1830 there had been an outbreak of lead poisoning in the French navy from the ships' water supply). The sailors who were examined died early on in the expedition when it was the practice to eat fresh food first, though if they had been in the sick bay they would have had more tinned food as 'sick comforts' than their healthy fellow sailors. However, it takes a considerable time for lead levels to build up in the body and high levels could not have suddenly appeared after only a few months of eating preserved meat products supposedly contaminated with lead. Lead has been used for soldering cans of food since they were first made in 1810 but only tiny amounts could be absorbed into tinned meat and vegetables because lead is protected electrolytically from the solution by the tin and iron. Whether or not the three seamen were suffering from overt lead poisoning, which Dr Farrer suggests is unlikely, the lead could not have come from the tinned provisions.

Not surprisingly, the journals of many explorers are obsessed with food and hunger. The Australian Sir Douglas Mawson, who explored the Antarctic, wrote in 1912, 'I will always remember the wonderful taste that the food had in those days. Acute hunger enhances the taste and smell of food beyond all ordinary conception . . . Cocoa was almost intoxicating and even plain beef suet, such as we had in fragments in our "hoosh" mixture, had acquired a sweet and aromatic taste scarcely to be described.' Frederick Whymper, an Englishman who took part in the 1866 Alaska Survey (just before the United States bought Alaska from Russia for $7.2 million), describes surviving in their survey station in temperatures down to -44°C (-49°F). 'The effect of intense cold on our stores in the magazine was a very interesting study; our dried apples were a mass of rock and had to be smashed with an axe, our molasses formed a thick black paste, and no knife we had would cut a slice of ham from the bone till it was well thawed in our warmer room. Our preserved meats would, with a continuation of those times, have been preserved forever.' The grouse and hares they bought from the Inuit were immediately frozen and 'there was no fear of them getting "high" in that climate'. Later, in August, when the weather improved, Whymper and his team moved on, stopping briefly at an empty research station in Plover Bay where the men found a keg of specimens preserved in alcohol left by 'one of our Smithsonian collectors'. The long winter of alcohol deprivation proved too much and the men drank the alcohol and were 'visibly affected thereby'. 'They thought it a pity to waste the remaining contents of the barrel, and, feeling hungry, went on to eat the lizards, snakes, and fish which had been put up for a rather different purpose! Science was avenged in the result, nor do I think they will ever repeat the experiment . . .'

Francis Spufford wrote in his recent book *I May Be Some Time – Ice and the English Imagination* that all expeditions dumped some signs, the detritus of their passage. 'The lavish equipment with which the grand expeditions set out made each a travelling storehouse of contemporary arts and technologies, a Crystal Palace afloat, crammed with stuff ranging from steam organs to electroplated cruets. It also made for diverse garbage, especially if things went wrong. Empty tins, broken oars, perished cloth, spoiled food, and domestic impedimenta were all abandoned in the snows. Where they were not crushed by ice, or dropped into the sea, the climate preserved many of them. Thoreau, ending *Walden* with a fantasia on exploration, did not forget them either: "explore your own higher latitudes", he urged his readers, "with shiploads of preserved meats to support you, if they be necessary; and pile the empty cans sky-high for a sign."'

CHAPTER FOURTEEN

REFRIGERATION AND FREEZING

Yonder the harvest of cold months laid up,
Gives a fresh coolness to the Royal Cup;
There Ice like Christal, firm and never lost,
Tempers hot July with December's frost.
Edmund Waller (1606–87)

Almost the best part of a picnic on a hot summer's day is that moment when the bottles of drink are retrieved from the cool water of a running stream, the silt of a shady river bank or a rocky pool washed by the sea. Cool boggy moss, wet sand or a breezy outcrop can also serve to cool the drinks, prevent the milk turning and the butter oozing. More sophisticated picnickers can now take thermos flasks filled with crushed ice and insulated food bags packed with pre-chilled food, kept cool with packs of frozen chemicals.

Storing food and drink in low temperatures is an ancient practice. The cold air of a natural cave or the cool environment of a well-insulated underground pit or chamber worked as natural refrigerators for grains and root crops. Furthermore, just as hunters on the arid plains found that their kill would dry out in the sun, so hunters of the ice-bound regions must have discovered that meat left in the snow or freezing, icy winds would also keep, at least until it thawed.

Keeping food cool slows down bacterial action in food thereby helping keep the food stored safely for longer, a process now known as refrigeration. Micro-organisms do not like the cold. It slows down their metabolism and makes them sluggish, unable to reproduce and less keen on their putrefying activities. As soon as the food becomes warm the organisms become active again.

Cooling or refrigerating food extends the storage life, while freezing preserves food for much longer periods. But, unlike any other preservative process, freezing does not actually destroy the organisms, it merely puts them into a chilling limbo until they and the food they inhabit are defrosted.

While the hunter may have temporarily lost some meat in the freezing snow, he might also have buried some 'overkill' of meat or fish in the ground to hide it from predators or rival hunting parties. If the burial was deep enough and the ground sufficiently cold, the flesh would have been protected for a while. Sometimes, where the right conditions were available, the technique developed of freezing food to preserve it. Peruvians living in the Andean Mountains grow hundreds of different varieties of potato. It is here, in fact, that the potato originated. For centuries they have preserved some of these potatoes by a unique freezing and drying process. The potatoes are dipped in water and spread out on the ground and left overnight in the freezing night air. Next morning, everyone gathers to tread out the moisture by crushing the crisply frozen tubers underfoot – a painfully cold experience. This process is repeated every day and night for four or five days until the potatoes are blackened and desiccated and ready to be stored. The end result, 'chuno', is still very important in the local diet. A variation of this technique, when the pulp is dried in the dark, produces a white chuno called 'tunta', which is made into flour.

The Dolganes, a nomadic tribe related to the Inuit, still roam across the far north of Siberia. They live in tents, miles from any civilisation, moving huge distances on home-made skis. Using packs of dogs, they hunt for meat, mostly bear and reindeer. They pack the meat into snow where it keeps frozen until they return for it. The Inuit themselves have always known about the mammoths deep frozen in their prehistoric ice cemeteries; they make ivory ornaments from the tusks and may even use their meat in hard times. In Lapland where nearly all food is commonly frozen and game is already frozen when it is taken from the trap, the most popular dish is 'poronkaristys', a kind of reindeer hash traditionally made by cooking shavings of frozen reindeer meat.

In these northern regions, food became frozen unavoidably and the fact that the food was preserved was a fortunate, but unsought side-effect. In Russia, long hard winters with temperatures well below freezing are commonplace and people are accustomed to buying 'frozen' food in the markets in winter. H. G. Muller in *Waste Not Want Not* quotes a description of the so-called frozen market in St Petersburg in 1880: 'There were partridges from Saratoff, swans from Finland, heath-cocks from Lavonia and Esthuria and geese from the steppes where Cossacks had killed them from horseback with their whips. All these birds were frozen, packed into chests and sold in the market. The freezing was so rapid that snow hares were frozen in an attitude of flight, with ears pointed and legs outstretched. Frozen reindeer or mighty elk with hairy snout stretched upon the ground and antlers raised majestically into the air, disappeared piece by piece as saw or axe separated them for distribution amongst the customers.' Today one can still go to the open air markets in Russia and buy icy blocks of fish chopped apart with an axe before being weighed for customers and milk frozen on sticks and sold like large 'popsickles'.

In warmer regions, ice was only used for cooling, although people have enjoyed chilled drinks and cooled food in the most unlikely places. Ice pits and ice houses were known to have been built in Mesopotamia almost 4,000 years ago and the powerful and wealthy men and women of Persia, Egypt, Rome and Greece were accustomed to being served cold drinks and chilled fruits in even the hottest weather. Alexander the Great ordered trenches to be dug at Petra, filled with winter snow and covered with oak branches so that his soldiers could drink cooled wine in summertime. As well as chilling drinks, snow and ice were also used by physicians to treat patients with fever, inflammation and stomach complaints. So all around the Mediterranean, snow was collected from the mountains and carried down to the cities were it was sold daily or stored in ice houses. The snow was packed hard into pits and covered with branches, straw, leaf mats or coarse cloth.

The Chinese, too, were harvesting and storing ice by at least 1100 BC as a verse, offered to their Goddess of Cold in the famous 'Shih Ching' or 'food poems', describes:

> In the days of the second month, they hew out the ice with harmonious blows;

And in the third month they convey it to the ice houses
Which they open in those of the fourth, early in the
morning,
Having offered in sacrifice a lamb with scallions.

Sometimes the ice had to travel many miles. Thirteenth- and fourteenth-century Egyptian royalty had their ice shipped from the mountains of Lebanon all the way to Cairo. Canon Pietro Casola of Milan while on a pilgrimage in 1494 was presented with a sack of snow when he landed at Jaffa. 'It was a great marvel to all the Company,' he wrote, 'to be in Syria in July and see a sack of snow.' In 1574 the Spanish physician Nicolas Monardes wrote that 'From Flanders much ice is carried to Paris, a distance of 60 leagues.' Like sugar, ice became a part of the fabulous sparkling jewellery of banquets, with centrepieces of elaborate ice sculptures, sugar trionfi, chilly jellies, iced sherberts and glass or silver bowls of ice-encrusted fruits – a magical spectacle to delight both eye and palate on hot midsummer nights.

By the sixteenth century numerous palaces, estates, chateaux, abbeys and monasteries throughout Europe, the Middle East and China had their own ice houses. Soon, anyone with aspirations to elegant living had ice or snow houses built and by the eighteenth century many of these had acquired architectural pretensions, with Gothic arches or Grecian pillars. Some were constructed on a huge scale with several insulated doors edged with leather or covered with sheepskin to make airtight seals. The basic construction, however, changed little up to the nineteenth century, by which time there were over 3,000 in Britain alone, some of which were still being used through the Great War. But ice was not just the preserve of the rich; in some parts of Europe the peasants erected simple ice stacks made from branches, heather and peat near to ponds, flooded meadows, lakes and slow-moving rivers that froze in wintertime.

Although ice houses were principally used for storing ice rather than for preserving food they gradually came to be seen as useful refrigerators for food. The architect John Papworth wrote in 1819 that 'The icehouse forms an excellent larder for the preservation of every kind of food liable to be injured by heat in summer; thus fish, game, poultry, butter, etc., may be kept for a considerable time.' The food was either buried in the ice itself or laid on boards or shelves on top of it. In some ice houses food was hung in baskets on pulleys or hooks in the cold air above the ice. Fruit was often stored in this way chilled in the hottest weather by an artificial winter that

> Exerts his art to deck the genial board:
> Congeals [freezes] the melting peach, the nectarine smooth,
> Burnished and glowing from the sunny wall;
> Darts sudden frost into the crimson veins
> Of the moist berry; moulds the sugared hail;
> Cools with his icy breath our flowing cups;
> Or gives the fresh dairy's nectared bowls
> A quicker zest.
>
> Anna Letitia Barbauld (1743–1825)

But building, filling and running ice houses remained expensive and arduous. A second-century record of the personnel roster of a Chinese royal palace includes amongst the vast army of kitchen servants no fewer than ninety-four 'ice men'. As recently as 1913, estate workers at Buckland House in Oxfordshire still faced the gruelling annual task of filling the ice house from the pond. Two men in a punt broke the ice and grappled it with long poles with iron spikes on the end, pulling huge pieces to the shore where two more men broke them up with wooden mallets. Six men with wheelbarrows carried the ice up the hill to the ice house and tipped it in. Four more men stood in the ice house shovelling and ramming the ice down into the pit, levelling it out and covering it with water, which froze and solidified it, and laying on sawdust or straw to insulate it. This was a cold and miserable task that took many days, and workers needed to be revived with warmed beer, brandy or rum.

Collecting ice from smaller ponds or ditches, however, did not produce ice clean enough to consume. The increasing demand for clean, good-quality ice opened an important new market. In Europe, when a mild winter failed to produce ice, people had to look north, to Greenland and Norway. Whalers had long been accustomed to chop large chunks of ice off passing icebergs for their own use (there had even been experiments in towing small icebergs home) and now they could get a price for it. In nineteenth-century Paris and London, cooks, confectioners, butchers, fishmongers and wine merchants all rushed to buy from ships bringing cargoes of ice from the 'Greenland seas'. Ice harvesting was a dangerous business in those seas of fog and freezing temperatures, but large quantities of ice from the north were shipped as far afield as India and Australia. Despite the ice being 'remarkable for its purity and transparency', competition from quite a different source soon began flooding the market.

The first overseas cargo of American ice was shipped from Boston to Martinique in 1806 and the Shakers, experts in all kinds of frugality and preserving, had already built very complex, heavily insulated ice houses everywhere they had settled. Despite the fact that about three-quarters of the ice harvested was lost in transport, many thousands of tons of ice were exported from the clear ponds and lakes of Massachusetts, the most famous being Wenham Lake. The Wenham Lake Ice Company sent hundreds of shipments of ice to Britain and the rest of Europe and soon sent its rivals packing with an aggressive sales drive that included sending a large block of ice to the Queen at Windsor and exhibiting a massive and deceptively permanent looking (but regularly renewed) block of ice in the window of its grand Strand headquarters. The company introduced 'miniature ice houses' or, as they were termed, refrigerators or ice boxes for household use. They claimed that the ice came from pure mountain lake water that was safe to use in food and drinks and was crystal clear. Wenham Lake stores opened all over Britain with horse-drawn carts delivering to houses every day. In the wealthy cities of Europe the ice trade flourished with ice arriving from Norway and from Russia as well as the US.

By the late eighteenth century the use of natural ice had become invaluable in many food and drink trades, in restaurants and the brewing industry. But the most significant was the development of the use of ice in the fishing industry, which was to have a far-reaching influence on the history of food preserving.

* * *

Dr John Bell, a Scottish physician visiting Peking in 1720, was sent a Christmas present of a large sturgeon from the Amur river, 1,000 miles north of Peking, 'preserved,' he noted, 'by being kept frozen among the snow'. Another Scot, Alexander Dalrymple, a hydrographer attached to the British East India Company, was working off the Chinese coast in the 1780s where he often observed how the fishermen carried ice on their boats in order to preserve the fish at sea. Just as Dutch and French fishermen had realised the importance of salting fish on board ship, Chinese fishermen were taking ice to sea and packing freshly caught fish in it. The ice was stored in ice houses built on the flat estuaries on the coast around the city of Ning-Po. In 1786 Dalrymple returned to England and was kept busy writing up reports in East India House in Leadenhall Street, London. There, one day, he met George Dempster, a Scottish MP who worked tirelessly to improve Scottish agriculture and fisheries – the ideal person to whom to report the novel activities of the Chinese fishermen of Ning-Po.

In 1784 Dempster had made a tour of inspection of the Scottish Islands and had been horrified by the effect the salt taxes had had on Highland fisheries. Salt for curing was supposed to be free of import duty but the bureaucracy surrounding exemption was complex and the penalties 'so high as infallibly to ruin any of those who, thro' forgetfulness, casual accidents, or ignorance, omit in any case to comply with the letter of the Law with the most scrupulous punctuality'. Despite having some of the finest catches of fish, which London shops were keen to buy, the fishermen and their families lived in appalling poverty in hovels built of loose stones or mud covered with turf or straw. 'A pot for boiling potatoes constitutes the principal part of their furniture.' George Dempster took up their cause and vigorously pressed in Parliament for changes and improvements.

The problem of conveying fresh, uncured fish from Scotland to the English markets seemed insurmountable, yet when Dempster, a man of vision and initiative, heard from Dalrymple how the Chinese fishermen used ice, he was so excited by the potential for the Scottish Islands that he immediately took pen and ink, and 'on the spot' wrote an account of the conversation to a salmon merchant he knew in Scotland called Richardson. At Dempster's urging, Richardson packed some freshly caught salmon in boxes filled with crushed ice and sent them to London by sea. After a journey of six days, the fish arrived in perfect condition.

It seems extraordinary that it had taken so long for the British to adopt the use of ice as a way of keeping fish fresh in transit. Mr Richardson admitted in a letter to the *Scots Magazine* in October 1786 that he 'made the experiment rather in consequence of Mr. Dempster's earnest manner of writing, than in expectation of any good', but that it 'answered beyond expectation'. As a result of the success of this first experiment, Richardson and others were soon sending south regular shipments of salmon packed in ice from the River Tay, from Aberdeen, Montrose and Inverness. Neither Richardson nor Dempster could have possibly foreseen what a vast industry would eventually grow from this experiment but Richardson did acknowledge that his own success and the resulting benefits to Scottish fishing communities was due to 'that patriotic gentleman Mr Dempster'. Mr Richardson also gave a present of £200 to buy a piece of plate for Mrs Dempster, which suggests that his own profits were very considerable. The observant Alexander Dalrymple, however, later 'died of vexation after being unjustly deprived of his office in the Admiralty', where he was then employed, a blow he never recovered from.

By the turn of the century there were ice houses at all the main salmon fisheries. These were supplied with ice from ponds, rivers and lochs, from shiploads of Wenham Lake ice or supplies from Norway. By 1814 the *Edinburgh Review* reported that icing was 'the mode of preserving fish now adopted on all the eastern rivers and coasts of Scotland (and the West country), and we believe, in some parts of Ireland, by which means salmon is conveyed fresh to the capital of the empire . . . its adoption has been to many a source of great private emolument, and productive of much material benefit . . .' In 1817 well over 7,000 100 lb boxes of iced salmon from the Dee and the Don were sent to London. By 1838 regular steam boats whisked the frosted fish to Edinburgh and London in perfect condition in even the warmest weather. Herrings, a much more difficult fish to keep, were also sprinkled with salt and packed in boxes of ice and successfully sent by fast-sailing smacks from Berwick to London. Towards the end of the century the combined benefits of railways, steam and ice were to revolutionise the fish trade and bring affordable, refrigerated fish to both rich and poor tables.

While ice revolutionised the business of transporting fresh fish from ports to towns, its potential had yet to be seen by the fishermen themselves. It was a young Scotsman named Samuel Hewett who, no doubt having seen the benefits of ice for the fish merchants of Scotland, not only took ice to sea but found a way to make it himself. Hewett and his father had set up a thriving fishing fleet at Barking in Essex and along the east coast from Greenwich, Gravesend, Brixham to Yarmouth. It was known as the Short Blue Fleet after the flag the smacks flew. Fishing was either by lining or trawling and most of the fish was brought back in well-smacks, specially designed fishing boats with wells of sea water built amidship with watertight bulkheads. Holes in the hull below the water-line allowed the sea water to enter and circulate. Live fish, caught on lines (trawled fish were often damaged or suffocated), were fed into the well from a narrow hatch. On their return to port, the live fish were transferred to smaller 'hatch boats' and quickly sent upriver to Billingsgate fish market. A major problem with meeting the increasing demand for fresh fish was the difficulty of sending the fishing fleets further afield to find the more abundant fishing grounds. Well-smacks were unsuitable for rough seas, were very slow and when the boats pitched and rolled about the fish were damaged or died. Samuel Hewett came up with the idea of 'fleeting', a system whereby every day the fastest smack in the fleet would collect the catches of all the other boats and race back home to port. Fleeting meant that the trawlers that had previously operated alone could fish together in groups and stay out in fishing grounds for longer. Gradually trawlers and fishing gear were adapted to suit deep sea fishing conditions and as the fleets grew in number, so fleeting became more efficient until boats could stay at sea for six weeks or more. Many of the fishermen complained this kept them away from home for too long. And there were still considerable problems with transferring and transporting fish in good condition from the distant fishing grounds back to port.

Samuel Hewett had shown great skill and initiative in discovering new fishing grounds, creating bases for building and repairing his ships and developing the fleeting system and transport to markets. He had already brought great benefits to the fishing industry and helped the supply of cheap good-quality fish, but he was still looking for new ideas that would enable him to take the Short Blue Fleet into more distant and richer fishing grounds.

In 1843 Robert Fortune, the famous plant collector, was on an expedition for the Royal Horticultural Society in northern China. The First Opium War was over, the Treaty Ports were opening to foreigners and Fortune had already discovered many new plants such as the fragrant lilac-pink *Rhododendron fortunei*. In August 1845 Fortune wrote a letter to the *Gardener's Chronicle* describing the ice houses of Ning-Po, first seen by Dalrymple some sixty years earlier. He gave details of how the houses were constructed, being simpler and cheaper than those built in Britain, and highly efficient despite being exposed to the heat of 'a sun, very different in its effects from what we experience in England'. The warmth, he wrote, 'would try the efficiency of our best English ice-houses as well as it does the constitution of an Englishman in China'. Fortune repeated Dalrymple's story about fish being transported inland packed in ice and, more significantly, how fishermen took it to sea in their boats. He also observed that unusually, the Ning-Po ice houses were only used for preserving fish, the local peasants having no time for cooling drinks or making ices. Fortune then revealed an important piece of information that Dalrymple had failed to mention, namely how the ice houses were supplied.

> The Chinaman, with his characteristic ingenuity, manages also to fill his ice-houses in a most simple way, and at a very trifling expense. Around the house he has a small flat level field connected with the river. This field he takes care to flood in winter before the cold weather comes on. The water then freezes and furnishes the necessary supply of ice at the very door. Again in spring these same fields are ploughed up and planted with rice, and the water which drains from the bottom of the ice-house helps to nourish the young crop.

Perhaps Samuel Hewett took the *Gardener's Chronicle* and read Fortune's description of the low-lying Ning-Po estuary. The picture he drew, with the sails of little fishing boats seeming to flit through the fields, might have sounded very familiar to someone intimate with the sight of ships sailing through the Norfolk Broads or the estuaries of Dagenham and Barking. Like George Dempster before him, Hewett was eager to take up new ideas and put them quickly into practice. He realised that the Chinese had not only found a cheap way to produce their ice but they had also used it to benefit fishing both on land and at sea. Within a few weeks of the publication of Fortune's letter, Hewett had started building an ice house on the Essex marshes, filled it with Norwegian ice and sent shiploads of it out with the fishing fleet. With his considerable powers of persuasion, Samuel Hewett then encouraged the local farmers to flood their fields in the winter and when they froze, to collect the ice and store it in his new ice house. As many as 3,000 men, women and children were employed to gather in this winter crop, which for most local farmers was a profitable harvest further supplemented by hiring out some frozen areas to ice skaters. On the first high tide of the autumn, the sluice gates in the sea-wall protecting the Dagenham marshes were opened, flooding huge areas of marshland. At that time farmers could rely on frosts as early as November with the bulk of ice being cut after Christmas. There were queues of carts outside the ice houses waiting to unload their ice, a sight which Henry Mayhew, author of the survey 'London and the London Poor', described on a visit to Barking on a freezing cold winter's day: 'The whole population seemed astir collecting ice. Women and boys were breaking it, numbers of men were throwing or lifting it into carts, and even wheelbarrows, for all kinds of vehicles were in requisition, and some of the roads were all but impassable from the number of ice carriages of every kind. The ice was carried to the ice houses of the fishing-smack proprietors, where it was to be reserved for the warmer seasons. It is sent out in the smacks and the fish is packed in it – such as is not brought alive – to be the better preserved.'

Hewett built many more huge ice houses, which he filled with Essex ice stored ready to load into fast cutters designed to carry the ice out to the fishing fleet and return with boxes of chilled

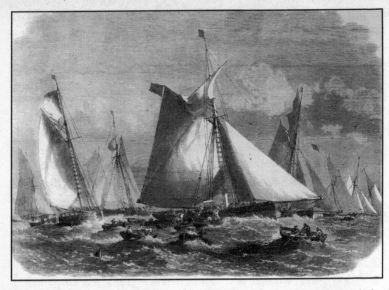

The drawing made for the Illustrated London News of a carrier collecting fish from the Short Blue fleet of trawlers

fish. In September 1864 the *Illustrated London News* sent a writer and an artist out to sea to bring back a report of the 'largest fleet engaged in the deep-sea fisheries of Great Britain – that of Messrs Hewett of Barking'. When a carrier arrived, wrote the journalist enthusiastically, 'a more exciting scene can hardly be imagined than when a carrier-cutter hoists her flag to take in cargo for market. The boats of the fishing fleet immediately throng around her with their boxes and hampers, rowing many a hard race to see which will reach her first. They hang on to her from bow to stern like a swarm of bees and packages after packages are literally rained upon her deck, until sometimes she has to make sail and force a passage away from them; for the hardy fishermen have an idea that a carrier never can be overladen and accordingly pile their packages on board until it sometimes becomes absolutely dangerous.' Up to 1,000 boxes of fish were in the hold between thick layers of ice using nearly 18 tons of ice to chill as much as 40 tons of fish. On the return voyage to the fleet the carrier picked up fresh ice at Barking or Gorleston, and in later days when fast steamers were used, ice-lugs would take ice out to steamers so they could restock without even entering harbour. With their use of ice the Hewett family had transformed the British fishing industry and ensured that affordable fresh fish could be eaten by everyone.

In the years when the Essex ice harvests failed and they were forced to buy expensive Norwegian ice, the Hewetts decided it was time to turn their attention from collecting natural ice to making it artificially. In 1863 the first artificial ice making plant or 'ice engine' in England was installed at Barking by Samuel, and Robert soon set up a plant at Barking. Samuel traded under the name the New Ice Company and Robert as the British Ice Making Co Ltd. The Hewetts, however, were not alone in the search for new ways of making cold.

Making Cold

. . . 'tis fixed as in a frost.
Alexander Pope (1688–1744)

For most people their supply of ice was dependent on their own climate or the ability to buy natural ice brought from elsewhere. The Persians, however, living in one of the most parched areas of the ancient world, were not to be deterred by their lack of ice. Even in the desert, they found a way to make it themselves. In 1620 the Italian traveller the Marquis Pietro Della Valle wrote a description of the ancient 'ice-manufactories' around Isfahan. On the vast plains outside the city where the sun burns down in the day and nothing prevents the freezing north winds from howling through, they built enormous walls up to 50 feet in height with adjoining wings at right angles at each end. The flat side of these 'shade walls' faced due south and the winged side faced north thus creating a permanent shade within the shadow of the wall yet allowing the north wind free access. Within this dark and cool enclosure they dug a large, deep trench. Out on the exposed plain near to the wall during the short, sharp winter months they made a number of small furrows lined with tiles. These were flooded in the evening and during the nights, under the frigid clear skies, the shallow channels of water, 'not more than four fingers in depth' became frozen. Before dawn the ice was collected, broken up and packed into the trench set behind the 'shade wall' where water was thrown onto it. 'Thus all the pieces garnered meld into one solid mass reaching from end to end of the trench and of more or less thickness according to the quantity taken from the channels.' This was repeated every night throughout the winter months and the ice was stored in perpetual shade in the deep trench covered in straw to be collected when required. Wealthy Persians liked to travel in great luxury and their passion for iced drinks and chilled fruit was well satisfied on even long journeys by special ice boxes called 'yaktan'. They were made of wood or cloth and lined with felt or leather. Filled with chipped ice for the journey, they were then strapped to one side of the horse's saddle.

But man-made ice using the elements, however ingeniously they were harnessed, was only the beginning. Serious efforts to produce manufactured ice began towards the end of the sixteenth century. By then it was known that bottles of liquid could be cooled by shaking and turning them in saltpetre and snow or cold water to distribute the cold. Salt reduces the temperature of ice or snow to below freezing point, so that a container of water packed inside a mixture of ice and salt will eventually turn to ice. Saltpetre and nitre have a similar effect. Wealthy Italians who learned of this method had their liquors cooled by rotating long-necked bottles in saltpetre dissolved in water. The use of saltpetre and nitre to reduce temperature spread through Europe, where they were already being used to manufacture gunpowder.

Francis Bacon, who put to the test numerous preserving techniques, was interested, as we have seen, in cold as one form of preserving. He observed how meat and drink kept better in winter or in cold environments and he showed how common salt 'increased the activity of cold'. Bacon was the first person to recognise the potential for freezing food in ice chambers and he suggested that the serious enquirer into nature should take advantage of the 'conservatories of ice and snow', then used for delicacies and to cool wine in summer. This, he felt, was 'a poor and contemptible use' of a valuable scientific resource.

Bacon was present at a demonstration made by the Dutch

inventor Cornelius Drebbel for King James I one hot summer day in the Great Hall at Westminster. Drebbel had brought with him an air cooling device that used salt or nitre added to snow to lower the temperature. Apparently the Dutchman's machine was so successful that the King and his courtiers fled shivering outside to warm up. Although artificial freezing was not properly understood, these first ice makers were slowly discovering the 'trick of calling back winter in midsummer'. But enquiring into nature was one thing, attempting to recreate it was another, and man's attempts to make ice was regarded by most people as an ungodly and unnatural act. Even as late as the nineteenth century some European and American Puritans still regarded artificial ice making as a God-provoking exercise.

Robert Boyle, a founder of the Royal Society, experimented with producing artificial cold and found that other salts, such as sal ammoniac (ammonium chloride), reduced the temperature even more quickly and successfully. Like Bacon, Boyle was fascinated by the extremes of heat and cold. He wrote in his *History of Cold* in 1665 '. . . there may be very differing wayes (and some of them seemingly opposite) to make many things outlast their Natural periods of Duration.' With the benefit of newly invented early thermometers Boyle could experiment with the preservative effects of low (and freezing) temperatures on food. In 1666 he tried to 'produce cold without snow, ice, hail, wind or nitre'. He also froze ox gall, sheep's blood, milk, eggs, eels in vinegar, oranges, lemons, onions and other foods, as well as making notes about the expansive force of freezing liquids. However, during the sixteenth and seventeenth centuries experiments in producing ice or cold air were regarded more as a form of entertainment or luxury for the rich than as something of real practical and scientific significance. Apart from Bacon's experiment with freezing his chicken, few showed much interest in actually preserving in ice food for consumption.

The 'discovery' that ice could be formed by evaporation was first made in 1775 by Dr William Cullen, Professor of Medicine and Chemistry at Glasgow and Edinburgh. He gave a public lecture on 'Cold Produced by Evaporating Fluids' and produced a very small quantity of artificially made ice by creating a freezing temperature with ether evaporated in a partial vacuum. Cooling by evaporation occurs because the warm molecules at the surface of a liquid escape and the temperature of the remaining liquid progressively falls. The use of evaporative cooling is a technique that actually dates back to biblical or even earlier times. The Egyptians cooled water by putting boiled water into shallow earthenware jars on the roofs of their houses exposed to the night air. Slaves were kept busy wetting the outside of the jars and the resulting evaporation cooled the water within.

Many other eighteenth- and nineteenth-century inventors and scientists studied the mysteries of making cold, including the French scholar of thermodynamics, Nicolas Carnot. Robert Salmon and William Worrell received the first British patent in 1819 for the production of cold, and in 1828 the American-born Jacob Perkins patented a machine in London for producing low temperatures by the compression and subsequent expansion of a vapour. This form of refrigeration depends on the fact that when a gas is compressed it gets hot and when it expands it cools down. If a compressed gas is cooled by, say, cold water, expanded, compressed, then cooled and expanded progressively, the temperature will fall to refrigeration temperatures. In 1828 Richard Trevithick, the Cornish inventor who had built the first working steam locomotive in Great Britain, experimented with artificial refrigeration and gave a lecture on the 'Production of Artificial Cold'. He described a design for a machine for simultaneously making ice and cooling air. But Trevithick died before he could finish it. The French brothers Edmund and Ferdinand Carré also made many experiments on the production of cold and Ferdinand made the first ammonia absorption unit. Ammonia dissolves readily in water but is just as readily driven off when the solution is heated. In an ammonia absorption unit the gas is cooled, liquefies, and is then blown into an evaporator. As the ammonia evaporates, the temperature falls. In practice, the evaporator is the bank of cooling coils often visible, covered with ice, in cold rooms. Ferdinand Carré showed this invention at the Great Exhibition in 1851 and it was later used extensively in America.

But for many centuries the predominant use of natural ice and snow remained simply for cooling drinks, fruits and desserts and for use against fevers and other ailments. Food was not generally thought to be preservable with ice except for short periods. Instead scientists and inventors fashioned these early freezers either to produce cold air or to make ice. However, the increasing demand for ice in commercial food production and trading, and in brewing, coupled with the considerable price for purchasing and storing ice in large enough quantities, made its manufacture potentially highly lucrative. Trevithick, when he heard that £100,000 was being spent on Greenland ice, wrote, 'A thought struck me at the moment that artificial cold might be made very cheaply . . .' What's more, if fresh fish could be brought home in ice from distant fishing grounds, surely so could meat from those great meat producing lands of Australia, New Zealand and Argentina? The goal was to be able to relieve over-producing countries of their vast surplus of meat and deliver it to the masses of Europe as real joints, rather than the overcooked pieces of indistinguishable meat in cans.

There comes a point in time when an idea, which has been gently simmering, suddenly comes to the boil, not with one man crying 'Eureka' in one place, but a number of people at roughly the same time unwrapping different parts and it all slowly falling into place. In the case of the story of the development of refrigeration and freezing, in particular of meat, it was once again the French who led the field only to let it go. In 1876 Charles Tellier, a French engineer, wagered that he could send a leg of mutton across the Atlantic Ocean in perfect condition. A steamer, appropriately named the *S.S. Frigorifique*, (a name specially coined for the occasion and now adapted by the French to *frigo* meaning a refrigerator) was fitted out with three of Tellier's vapour compression refrigerating engines and cold rooms insulated with powdered cork and chaff. The *Frigorifique* sailed from Rouen on 19 September and arrived at Buenos Aires on Christmas Day. On arrival some of the French meat was reported to have had dark spots and, when cooked, had an unpleasant flavour. The ship set out on its return voyage to Rouen on 14 August 1877 loaded with local beef. After a voyage of 104 days the refrigerated Argentine meat was unloaded and 'a careful selection had to be made' because much of it had arrived in a poor condition. The turf used as ballast was later blamed for the unpleasant flavour. A Paris newspaper patriotically, if rather prematurely, declared that the problem had been solved. If it was not entirely successful, the cargo of the *Frigorifique* was nevertheless the first shipment of chilled meat to be brought through the tropics.

In the same year a French shipping company installed Carré's ammonia-compression machine instead into one of their ships, the *S.S. Paraguay*. The ship sailed from Buenos Aires in October with 5,000 carcasses of mutton kept at a temperature of -27°C (-17°F), sufficient to freeze the meat so that it was 'petrified, as hard as a stone'. Her journey home was delayed by an accident that forced the ship into St Vincent for four months of repairs, yet she arrived at Le Havre in May 1878 with meat still in 'tip-top condition'. The local press wrote that 'the congealing [*congeler* is French for 'to freeze'] completely destroys the germ of putrefaction', which is, of course, sadly incorrect. Eighty tons of the hard frozen mutton were defrosted, cooked and served up to the garrison troops while another, smaller consignment was said to have been served for a whole week at the Grand Hotel in Paris.

Neither the *Frigorifique* nor the *Paraguay*, with their very different machines for making cold (the former chilling the meat and the latter freezing it), ever sailed with cargoes of chilled or frozen meat again. The *Frigorifique* was sold and made to take the retrograde step of carrying a cargo of dried meat before colliding with a bridge on the river Seine. The *Paraguay* was prepared for a second voyage with a much bigger cargo but according to Dr Bergés, who wrote a history of Argentina's meat industry in 1908, '. . . the project was never realized, and this new industry of the freezing of meat was abandoned by the French'. Bergés later wrote that 'As has happened in the history of industries, it has been the French who have made the discoveries, and the English who have turned them to account to their profit. The refrigerating industry belongs to this number.' He would no doubt also have had the canning industry on his list.

If nineteenth-century French businessmen lacked the necessary foresight and courage to back their inventors' achievements, there were many others who had both the vision and the capital to invest in the dream of bringing the overproduction of meat in the New

World to the meat-starved tables of the Old. The great Australian pioneer and later newspaper proprietor James Harrison was the Scottish-born son of a salmon fisherman. He noticed that the ether used to wash printing type had a cooling effect and this spurred him to pursue ideas for using this to create refrigeration. He experimented with an ether compression machine and despite its hazards he succeeded in producing ice artificially. In 1850 he built an ice factory but it failed to produce enough ice to be profitable; he did, however, sell his idea to a brewery, which installed a machine of his design, the first of its kind. Harrison was losing money fast but he was so enthusiastic about his invention that he went to England and applied for a patent. He also discussed his work with James Faraday and John Tyndall of the Royal Institution and others who shared his enthusiasm, but could produce no finance to back him. Harrison had a bigger machine made, which he installed in a larger factory, but there was little call for Australian home-made ice and Harrison was in trouble. In 1862 he had to sell his Sydney Ice Company to rivals who wanted to suppress his machine in favour of one invented by the French engineer Eugene Nicolle that, like Carré's, used the ammonia absorption process.

Harrison's rivals were Augustus Morris, a wealthy Australian farmowner who had tried to raise funds amongst farmers to offer a substantial bonus to the first person to ship fresh meat from Australia to Europe using artificial refrigeration, and Thomas Sutcliffe Mort, a wealthy wool broker who was also concerned about the Australian meat business and had shipped a few casks of salted beef to England as early as 1846. Although he did not become involved in the canning industry Mort later became fascinated with the 'diabolical idea' of freezing meat for export. Morris introduced Mort to Nicolle. They joined forces and started to conduct experiments with Mort supplying the capital and passion and Nicolle the engineering skill. After taking over Harrison's company, Nicolle and Mort set about finding the best method of shipping frozen meat and by 1875 they had established in Sydney the first freezing works in the world that used ammonia compression. Their company became the New South Wales Fresh Food and Ice Co. with a slaughtering works in the Blue

Mountains supplying the Sydney markets. Three hundred guests attended the inaugural lunch where they feasted on meat that had been frozen for nearly sixteen months. In his speech Mort announced that 'Before long France and England will look to us almost entirely for their supply of food.'

By now Mort had spent more than £80,000 on his freezing experiments and in 1876 he was finally ready to fulfil his dream. He chartered a ship, fitted it with Nicolle's freezing machine and loaded it with meat. But the ship never sailed with its precious cargo because the pipes carrying the liquid ammonia leaked over the meat and destroyed the experiment. This failure was such a great disappointment to Mort that he died shortly after.

Meanwhile Harrison's finances had recovered sufficiently for him to try once again to achieve his dream of sending frozen meat by sea to England. By this time North American meat traders were sending frozen and chilled beef, using natural ice and salt, across the Atlantic to London's Smithfield market in fairly good condition but the far longer voyage from Australia through the tropics could not be done by simply packing meat on ice. Harrison conducted numerous trials with his machine until he was able to convince enough farmers to send some carcasses on a trial shipment. The *S.S. Norfolk* left Melbourne in July 1873 with 20 tons of frozen mutton and beef but the refrigerant tanks leaked during the voyage and the meat went bad. Broken by his failure, Harrison, now almost bankrupt, retired to London to pursue his scientific studies. He died in Australia in 1893. Another man's fortune was gone and another inventor's spirit crushed. But these determined men had made important contributions both scientifically and in helping pioneer the inexorable drive towards the success of an industry that 'hung on the slender piston-rod of a refrigerating machine'.

By the mid-1870s inventors and businessmen around the world had still failed to solve the problem despite 'considerable spirit and enterprise having been devoted to working out new processes for meat preservation more efficient than those already in use'. The Royal Society of Victoria in Australia had received patent applications for a range of ideas yet none seemed as effective as the 'well-known method of Appert'.

However, in 1879 another ship was ready to take its place in the history of the frozen meat trade. The *S.S. Strathleven* was chartered by Andrew McIlwraith and fitted with a new steam-powered air compression refrigerating machine developed by Bell and Coleman in Glasgow. She sailed from Sydney on 29 November 1879 and arrived safely in London on 2 February with 40 tons of frozen beef and mutton in excellent condition 'frozen quite hard and covered in an artificial rime'. One hundred and fifty people sat down to a celebratory dinner on board ship eating dishes made from frozen beef and mutton. The Queen and Prince of Wales were sent a carcass of frozen lamb and expressed their 'satisfaction'. The press, after publishing the usual verbose noises of praise declaring that *Strathleven* meat when cooked could not be distinguished from freshly killed English meat, raised doubts nonetheless regarding its commercial viability. But the beef, sold at 4½ pence and 5½ pence per pound and the mutton, at 5½ pence to 6 pence per pound, were competitive with both English and American meat. Like other pioneering ships before her, the *Strathleven* was later stripped of her machinery and insulation and returned to her trade run in the Atlantic where she was lost in a storm in 1901. But her epoch-making journey led to many more voyages bringing to Europe not only meat but butter and cheese from Australia, New Zealand, South America and North America.

During shipment and storage, chilled or frozen food had to be kept at constant low temperatures until it was sold (meat was never sold frozen in those days). Freezing and refrigeration plants were built at slaughterhouses, cold stores at ports and defrosting halls at meat markets where meat could be hung before being sold. In London meat was taken upriver in insulated barges to the vast cold meat stores at Smithfield market. There were considerable risks in working with freezing machinery. The men who worked in market freezing rooms had to wrap their hands and faces in old newspaper or rags. Rheumatism was a common ailment and few packing house workers lasted longer than five years. Captain Whitson nearly froze in the machine room of the *S.S. Dunedin* and was saved by his first mate crawling in behind him and attaching a rope to his legs and hauling him out.

Bringing farm produce to market in good condition had always presented great problems especially over the huge distances and difficult climates in America. In 1810 Thomas Moore, a farmer from Maryland, Virginia invented a portable refrigerator to carry his butter to market. An insulated ice box (like that of the ancient Persian travellers), the invention consisted of an oval cedar tub with an inner sheet-metal container surrounded by crushed ice. Rabbit skins were stretched across the top. Moore also developed a home refrigerator with a 6 foot storage chamber and ice box above. 'Every housekeeper,' he declared, 'may have one in his cellar, in which, by the daily use of a few pounds of ice, fresh provisions may be preserved, butter hardened, milk, or any other liquid preserved, at any temperature.' The first commercial slaughterhouses were built in rural areas near the farms and the meat was salted into barrels or heavily smoked and sent on to market. But the increasing need to transport huge quantities of food meant there would have to be a solution as equally revolutionary as refrigerated ships.

When the Union Stockyards were built in 1865 in Chicago, where the railroads met from both east and west, it suddenly became possible to ship carloads of live animals direct to the slaughter yards, which soon became the centre of the US meat trade. Gustavius Swift, who came from a family of farmers in Cape Cod, revealed his business acumen early on. He bought a heifer for $20 from his father and sold it for a profit of 50 per cent. He then began buying pigs and steer and took the carcasses to the Cape where he sold them. He was said to be a great judge of livestock but he soon realised that it was far more profitable to transport dead meat than live animals to the eastern markets. The railroads, which were equipped for shipping live cattle, were not so keen on taking butchered meat. Live animals were heavier, which meant larger freight charges, and there were other associated businesses feeding and watering livestock that also had an interest in keeping the live transit. But Swift went ahead and invented and built his own refrigerated railcars. In 1869 his first shipment of chilled beef was sent from Chicago to Boston. This was not a success but Swift persisted until one day in 1877 he took his wife and six children down to the freight yards. As the first train equipped with effectively refrigerated cars filled with tons of freshly butchered meat pulled out, Swift turned to his wife with a smile and said 'There are gigantic days in every man's life Annie.' Glowing with pride he added, 'This is one of mine.' Swift went on to create a vast business of his own private refrigerated car lines, quickly followed up by a fleet of refrigerated steamships that carried his meat across the Atlantic. It is said that he probably crossed the Atlantic twenty times before he achieved success with establishing his name and his frozen meat at Smithfield meat market. With his relentless energy and enthusiasm Swift captured an important share of the meat trade and made himself both famous and fabulously rich.

Despite its success both British and European consumers remained nervous of frozen meat, many still believing that it could cause food poisoning. Before 1914 no respectable working-class wife would have been seen in a butcher's shop that only sold imported 'frozen' beef and mutton. Market research, then in its infancy, gave one housewife a nasty shock when in 1888 she found, pushed up alongside the bone in a leg of mutton (which she had bought as English at 9 pence a pound), a small piece of paper on which was written 'Where did you buy this leg, and what price did you pay? inform J. C. Ashburton Christchurch, N.Z.' For some reason the Belgian and French authorities insisted on frozen carcasses with the lungs still attached. The French, who were virtually self-supporting in food, could afford to be choosy and were indifferent to the idea of frozen meat, preferring fresh meat including horse. Germany was in the throes of her own industrial revolution and farmers were anxious to keep imported meat out. Despite this reluctance to buy foreign frozen meat vast amounts were arriving in England and threatening to flood the market. Frozen meat was sent to British military garrisons in Malta, Egypt, Gibraltar, Hong Kong, Singapore and the new American garrison in the Philippines. Soldiers in the Boer War also benefited from deliveries of Australian frozen meat. But it was not until the period of mass unemployment between the wars that working people in Europe began to accept frozen food.

Some of the resistance to this new way of preserving resulted from problems known as 'burn' and 'drip'. Refrigerated air is intensely dry and 'freezer burn' was the name given to the areas of meat that had become so dehydrated that they had the appearance of a burn. The meat from carcasses with burn was unsightly though not dangerous, but the damaged parts were inedible and had to be cut out. Burn was off-putting to meat merchants and shoppers and reduced profits. It was later solved by encasing the carcasses in muslin, cotton or stockingette.

More serious, however, was the slow rate at which foodstuffs were frozen. This could result in large ice crystals forming, which ruptured the cellular structure of the meat and destroyed much of the texture, flavour and natural juices as well as reducing the vitamin content. 'Drip' was the name given to the unpleasant blood-stained serum that dripped from thawing carcasses of meat that had been slow-frozen. However revolutionary and successful the technology was in bringing huge quantities of foods long distances, if it did not look or taste good, the housewives of the developed world would not buy it.

The Father of Frozen Foods

The 'Father of Frozen Foods' did not invent quick freezing. With characteristic modesty he said there was 'Nothing very remarkable about what I had done . . . The Eskimos had used it for centuries, and scientists in Europe had made experiments along the same line I had. What I accomplished, with the co-operation of many other men, was merely to make packaged quick frozen food available to the public.' Actually, he did rather more than that.

Clarence Birdseye (Bob to those who knew him) was born in Brooklyn, NY in 1886. His father was a lawyer and legal scholar. Birdseye may have inherited his father's precise and enquiring mind but he early on developed his own quite different lifelong interests in natural history and food preserving. At the age of five he gave his mother a perfect little mouse skin he had preserved; his growing proficiency in taxidermy led him later to put an advertisement in a sporting magazine offering instruction in the art, and he created a stir at high school by enrolling in the cookery class. Family summers were spent on a farm in Long Island where he tramped through the fields studying wildlife. He also loved to go hunting and he longed for a gun of his own. The family was not well off and his ability to raise funds by ingenious means was soon called upon. He trapped some of the muskrats that overran the farm and sold them to a breeder for $1 a piece. Soon he had enough to buy a gun.

Following the family tradition, Birdseye went to Amherst College in Massachusetts. He dreamt up many imaginative schemes to meet his college expenses, including selling frogs, caught in the college fields, to the Bronx Zoo for snake food, and live-trapping specimens of rare black rat that he found in a shed behind the Amherst butcher's shop and selling them to a Columbia University geneticist. On one summer vacation in the southwest he made a $600 profit selling bobcat and coyote skins. But it was not enough to get him through college and finally forced to drop out, he was unable to graduate.

Instead, Birdseye got a job in Washington as an assistant naturalist with the Biological Survey of the US Department of Agriculture. But it was a desk-bound, low-paid job and he soon had itchy feet. Against the advice of all his friends, he chucked in the job and returned to fur trapping. Eventually he had enough money under his belt to be able to propose to Eleanor, the daughter of a founder of the National Geographical Society and a remarkable woman in her own way. She would prove to be a considerable influence and helper to him in their long life together.

Clarence and Eleanor returned to Labrador in northeastern Canada where he could continue with his lucrative trading in furs. They lived in a tiny three-roomed shack, 250 miles from the nearest store or doctor. While Clarence travelled with his dog sled, Eleanor tended the winter traps and their baby son, Kellogg. For food they caught fish and game and kept the food outdoors, exposed to the Arctic winds until they were ready to use it. Birdseye observed that these foods, when frozen in winter temperatures as low as -50°C (-58°F), were more flavourful than similar foods frozen in spring and autumn. He cut paper-thin slices from the frozen foods and discovered that the quick-frozen flesh was firm. The meat of rabbits, ducks and caribou, if frozen quickly at these very low temperatures, seemed to retain its freshness indefinitely. The couple also caught fish through holes in the ice during the sub-zero winter and froze them.

When cooked weeks later, they were as firm and fresh as if they had just been caught. Greenstuff was a greater problem. The only fresh vegetables were those occasionally brought in by ship and they were eagerly awaited. In order to make them last as long as possible, Birdseye experimented with putting them in barrels filled with salt water where they froze very quickly. Whenever they wanted cabbage, they would simply hack one out. Even the baby's wash tub was filled with frozen vegetables and so they had 'fresh' greens all winter.

Fired with enthusiasm for this 'freezing business', Clarence and Eleanor started all kinds of trials at home. These kitchen experiments were to continue for many years, despite Eleanor's increasing irritation with finding preserved foods all round the home. Her son Kellogg later recalled one occasion when 'Mother was not at all pleased to find pickerel flipping around in the bath tub.' But these simple, crude experiments confirmed that quick freezing avoided the problems associated with the traditional, slower methods, in particular the formation of ice crystals within the food.

In 1917 Eleanor and Clarence returned to the US, where Birdseye embarked on an eight-year struggle to find a commercially practical method of quick freezing, a mechanical way to 'reproduce the Labrador winters in New England'. With a capital investment of $7 to buy an electric fan, buckets of brine and cakes of ice, Birdseye set up in a borrowed corner of an ice-cream plant in New Jersey and started experimenting with mechanical freezing. His first success was with fillets of haddock, frozen brick-hard in square containers made from old candy boxes. The following year he set up a company to sell frozen fish and quickly went broke. No one was ready for it.

Birdseye knew, however, that he had discovered the basis for an entirely new type of freezing operation. So confident was he that Eleanor and he 'hocked' their insurance, took out their savings and pooled their resources in order to be able to design and build the first automatic freezer and set up a new company. This was ambitiously called the 'General Seafoods Company', in 'anticipation' of being, like General Motors and General Electric, an industry leader. In order to be nearer fresh supplies of fish, the Birdseyes moved to the fishing port of Gloucester, once

Clarence Birdseye experimenting in his workshop in the 1920s

famous for its great salt cod industry. With his usual enthusiasm, energy and persuasive powers Birdseye was able to raise some finance from a small group of colleagues and with it establish a laboratory for research and development. There, he struggled on until he had perfected his process. He called it 'quick freeze'.

His unique method, which he quickly patented, involved chilling metal plates in calcium chloride brine down to -40°C (-40°F) and then pressing packets of food between them. Direct contact with these plates froze food faster than any method tried before. By 1928 Birdseye was able to quickly freeze meat, poultry, fish and shellfish in commercial quantities. His fascination with the idea of food freezing was not only avid, but wide ranging. There was not a frozen food item that he did not experiment with. He tried all kinds of foods including baked goods and even complete cooked dishes, always tasting everything himself. He built a double belt contact freezer, in which the food was frozen on two sides simultaneously, using two hollow metallic belts filled with cold brine. After that, he made multi-plate freezers and mounted them on trucks to make mobile machines to freeze vegetables as soon as they were picked.

But commercial success still proved elusive. His was a small concern and he was a cut-and-try experimenter on a small scale. He had faced many obstacles, much resistance and numerous discouragements. But he it never occurred to him to lose faith in the soundness and potential of his process or to give up. The only missing ingredients for success were capital and the ability to sell to a public that remained obstinately wary of frozen food.

Eventually, it was a frozen goose that laid the golden egg. Marjorie Merriweather Post, the daughter of the founder of Postum, a large food processing company, was enjoying a yachting holiday off the coast of Massachusetts. The yacht called into Gloucester harbour for reprovisioning and Marjorie sat down that evening to a dinner of roast goose. This she found so tender and with such an unusually good flavour that she asked her chef where it had come from. To her amazement the chef told her that the goose had been frozen for several months and that he had bought it from a small shore plant where the 'eccentric' owner had the novel idea of freezing food quickly to preserve it.

Marjorie immediately sent her husband ashore to interview Birdseye about his process and became determined to persuade the board of directors of the Postum company that they must buy the tiny struggling business and put it on its feet. Three years later she was successful and the Postum company changed its own name to General Foods Corporation. Birdseye was paid a staggering $22 million, the largest sum then paid for a single process. He remained an important member of the company working on improvements, inventions and fresh ideas. The patents came thick and fast and the frozen food industry had really begun.

Birdseye's restless pursuit of new challenges continued, but at least he now no longer had to struggle financially. Gone were the days of selling rats or skins and the hard life in the frozen north. A colleague reported that one day when they were going out to a slap-up business lunch, Birdseye 'drove us to the hotel in a Model A Ford coupe, and then phoned his wife to bring down the Packard 8. After lunch he drove us along the shoreline and pointed out a beautiful lot on the ocean'. With great glee Birdseye had said to him 'All my life I have desired a Packard 8 car and that property. Now I have them.' With their new-found wealth the Birdseyes built a beautiful and very grand house on Eastern Point where Eleanor could indulge her passion for gardening. Birdseye, too, became fascinated with botany and in later years the couple wrote a number of books on horticulture. He specially loved to go fishing in his power launch the *Sealoafer* and to go out with his gun and his dogs. Birdseye also continued to experiment and design, producing an efficient fish filleting machine, a reflector and infra-red heat lamps and a kickless harpoon gun for hunting whales. He was fascinated by hydroponic farming and believed that it would be possible to grow enough food on the rooftops and in the cellars of New York City to provide three square meals a day for 'every inhabitant of that immense city'.

But the cautious inhabitants of New York and the rest of America took some persuading before they would embrace frozen food let alone anything more futuristic. One of the major early problems in inducing people to accept quick frozen foods was a widespread aversion to 'cold storage' foods, which were often associated with unpredictable off-flavours and inferior quality generally. General Foods soon launched the term 'frosted foods' to suggest something new and improved. How, they wondered, could you convince the conservative housewife that quick frozen food can be entirely fresh, even though it is frozen hard as marble? And while the consumer was cautious, the retail food shop was even less enthusiastic about paying out capital for a freezer cabinet in which to display these dubious wares.

In Springfield, Massachusetts there was one grocer who, with ten others, was prepared to be a 'missionary' to convert an eating public that had been brought up on fresh and canned foods. On 6 March 1930, Joshua Davidson first opened his new freezer cabinet, designed by Birdseye, supplied by General Foods and filled with an alluring range of 'frosted foods'. On offer were June peas and spinach, frozen raspberries, loganberries and Oregon Bing cherries with their stalks on, plus a 'really superb selection of prime meat and fish products'. This became the 'miracle' that produced fresh foods out of season and changed eating habits so radically that there are generations today who no longer know what fresh peas in the pod taste like, indeed they might not even like them. Frozen peas are processed far nearer to picking than the fresh pea can be bought in the shop. Even when frozen, the enzymes continue to slowly produce sugar from starch, which makes frozen peas much sweeter than fresh.

In an article in the trade magazine *Quick Frozen Foods* published thirty years later, the grocer Davidson recalled that 'The food customer of 1930 was prejudiced against frozen foods. She felt foods were frozen because they were low grade or spoiled and had to be frozen to be salvaged.' As part of the campaign to create an image, the General Food Corporation changed its name to Birds Eye, as it has famously remained ever since. Birds Eye lady demonstrators visited these pioneering stores to explain to the public how 'frosted foods' were made and how they could be cooked. There was one woman customer whom Davidson never forgot. Unable to understand their explanations, she returned every day with more questions, but she never bought anything. Eventually she brought in her son whose job was to take the information back to his father. 'It seems her husband wouldn't permit her to buy any frozen foods until he understood the method of preparation.' This was a story that was to be repeated many times over until customer resistance gradually diminished and they even began to ask for new products and make suggestions, such as the woman who once asked why they didn't put the vegetables and meat together as an entire meal. Even more prophetic was an advertisement launching Birds Eye frozen food range in the *Ladies Home Journal* in 1930 in which it was claimed that frozen food would completely change the way people shopped. The advertisement predicted that there would be a new kind of store in the future which was 'not a grocery store or a meat market or a fish market or a delicatessen, but all four rolled into one. It is a food store in the broadest sense of the word'.

Birdseye's achievements included, therefore, the beginning of the frozen food chain. One of the reasons, possibly the main one, why frozen foods took so long to become established was the time it took to ensure that food stayed frozen until it reached the consumer who could thaw and prepare it. The danger was that micro-organisms present initially, would become active when the food was thawed. Birdseye not only solved the problems associated with slow freezing, he also developed freezers which could be used for freezing on site, for display in shops and finally the domestic freezer for the home.

Birdseye never stopped inventing and experimenting and going 'around asking a lot of damn fool questions and taking chances'. He developed a process for dehydrating foods, the next step forward in food preserving. His last challenge was in 1955 when he went on a trip to Peru in order to experiment with crushed sugar cane stalks known as 'bagasse', which he believed could be converted into paper pulp. The heart attack he suffered there was probably brought on by the high altitude. Clarence Birdseye was taken home to New York where he died a year later aged sixty-nine.

Birdseye had requested that instead of flowers at his funeral, people made a contribution to a scholarship fund in order that impoverished students could attend Amherst College and actually manage, unlike him, to graduate.

CHAPTER FIFTEEN

DEHYDRATION AND BEYOND

Starvation destroys an army more often than does battle, and hunger is more savage than the sword.
Vegetius *On Military Science*, fourth century AD

It has been said that one reason why the Americans failed in Vietnam was because the Viet Cong were able to live on a very light portable diet whilst the Americans relied on huge amounts of supplies. In his book *The Things They Carried*, Tim O'Brien describes how each US soldier was equipped to be prepared for war in the jungle: 'Among the necessities or near-necessities were P-38 can openers, pocket knives, heat tablets, wristwatches, dog tags, mosquito repellent, chewing gum, candy, cigarettes, salt tablets, packets of Kool-Aid, lighter, matches, sewing kits, Military Payment Certificates, C rations and two or three canteens of water. Together these items weighed between 15 and 20 pounds, depending upon a man's habits or rate of metabolism.' In complete contrast, O'Brien describes how 'A 15-year-old VC corpse was found to be carrying a pouch of rice, a rifle, and three magazines of ammunition.'

As we have seen, canned and even in some situations, frozen food was invaluable in feeding troops stationed in one place, such as in the trenches during the First World War. Soldiers on the move, however, are more often successful when they are supplied with lightweight, portable provisions. In 1280 Marco Polo described how the Mongol army set out on their long expeditions carrying solid blocks of dried milk which they mixed with water for a nourishing drink '. . . they will ride a good ten day's journey without provisions and without making a fire'. When the Scots invaded England in 1327, Jean de Froissart wrote that they travelled quickly on horseback without baggage-carts. They were so well trained and self-sufficient that they could subsist for a long time on half-cooked meat from cattle they found and cooked in the animals' hides so that they did not even need cooking pots. The only provisions they took with them were a small bag of dried oatmeal strapped to the saddle plus a large, flat stone, which they used to bake a small cake like a wafer. 'Hence it is not surprising that they can travel faster than other armies.'

In the nineteenth century, while developments in early canning and freezing were being explored, experiments with other new preserving methods seemed to be returning to the ancient principles of drying food. Army victuallers were particularly interested in more efficient methods of reducing certain foods to storable and portable dry grains or powder. In 1841 Downes Edwards, a Surrey farmer, obtained a patent for 'the Preserving of Potatoes and other Vegetable Substances'. Edwards soon dropped his interest in 'other vegetables' and concentrated on the potato. Dried potato, which retains much of its vitamin C, proved to be fairly effective against scurvy, it kept well in most conditions and, unlike canned vegetables, it was easily portable. For these reasons it was taken on many of the great expeditions of the time including the ill-fated Franklin expedition to the Arctic. The product was enthusiastically adopted by both the army and naval forces and it was also taken in convict and emigrant ships to Australia. In 1844 the *Nautical Magazine* published pages of testimonials from around the world including twenty from the army, eighteen from the merchant navy and eleven from the Royal Navy, which together 'prove its value, and should remove all prejudice and open the hearts of all caterers of officers' and other messes'.

Edwards' process involved boiling or steaming well-washed potatoes until their skins began to crack. They were then peeled and pushed into a cylinder of tinned iron 'closely pierced' with holes about one eighth of an inch in diameter. A piston forced the potato through the holes forming small threads, which were then spread evenly onto hollow steam-heated trays of tinned iron. As they dried, the extruded potato was raked over and the temperature gradually reduced from 71°C to 37.8°C (160°F to

Edwards also produced convenient and 'delicious' dessicated dishes for the family at home

100°F) during the twelve hours that it took to dry out. When the potato was fully dry and looking like rice grains, it was packed into casks 'or otherwise', such as metal cases that could hold up to the equivalent of 5 hundredweight of potatoes. After only a year of production, Edwards confidently claimed that his dried potato would keep for twenty years in the right conditions. Dried potato was also believed to be a suitable base for puddings, for bread with or without wheaten flour, and for cakes and pastry. One naval surgeon described the new preserved potato as 'wholesome, palatable, and nutritious, portable, easily prepared, and with common care will keep uninjured in any climate, and I believe for any length of time'.

Attempts were also being made to dry other foods using similar processes. By 1847 a patent had been taken out to manufacture dried foods such as 'Symington's Dessicated Soups', which were sent out to beleaguered British households all over the empire and remained popular until the end of the century. In 1850 the Frenchman Etienne Masson patented his process for compressed dried vegetables. The vegetables were dried in wicker trays in a current of hot air (24°–62.8°C/75°–145°F) using either lime, calcium chloride or a partial vacuum to speed up the process. The desiccated vegetables were then compressed into hard cakes, marked with grooves so they could be easily broken into portions, wrapped in tinfoil and sealed into tins. Gradually the method was improved until the moisture could be removed at a lower temperature thus better preserving the vitamin C. In 1886 an Australian introduced the first mechanical method for dehydrating apples on a rotating belt using a current of hot air. In 1884 a Swiss miller, Julius Johannes Maggi, introduced large-scale manufacture of powdered soups under the name of Maggi & Co., and he later made meat concentrates in a granulated form known as 'bouillon' cubes.

In 1855 the flamboyant, brilliant and highly efficient French chef Alexis Soyer went out to the Crimea to advise the military leaders of the allied armies, who seemed unable to satisfactorily feed their men, despite the fact that the troops were not on the move, nor cut off from supply lines. Hygiene was almost non-existent in the camps and in the hospitals. Scurvy and other dietary diseases were rampant, contributing to the numerous deaths from contagious diseases such as cholera. Thousands of men died for no reasons other than lack of planning, proper administration of adequate and nutritious food, warm protective clothing, proper shelter and efficient transportation of sick men out of the lines and provisions into them. The Russian soldiers were no better off and lived on a daily ration of a bowl of cabbage soup, $1\frac{1}{2}$ lb of bread and a portion of dried meat called 'tchi', usually made from beef, but in desperate times even the meat of crows was used.

As soon as he arrived, Soyer set up his famous stove that will 'boil, stew, bake and steam'. A similar design was still in use during the Gulf War using bottled gas or petrol instead of coal or wood. Soyer brought order to the chaos of the camp kitchens, reorganised men's rations and instructed soldiers in simple, but nutritious cooking methods. He made hearty soups and stews economically, using all the parts of freshly butchered animals and leaving nothing to waste. He baked special nutritious 'bread-biscuits' with flour and pea meal that could be dunked in soup or tea and were superior to the tough, unbreakable British hardtack, and he wrote special recipes for the mass production of meals for soldiers. He inspected the provision stores and judged the tinned meat to be of very low quality and the dried vegetables sent from England to be too highly dried having 'lost their aroma as well as their nutritious qualities'.

Soyer immediately sent off to Paris (by the newly invented and installed telegraph) for large consignments of pressed, dried vegetables made by a firm called Chollet. Chollet-cakes, when reconstituted, made a reasonably tasty and nutritious substitute for fresh vegetables but Soyer ordered his own special cakes for the army in the Crimea, which he called 'coarse julienne'. Each hundredweight of dried vegetables was to consist of 'twenty pounds of carrots, twenty pounds of turnips, ten of parsnips, fifteen of onions, twenty of cabbage, five of celery, and ten of leeks; with one pound of aromatic seasoning, composed of four ounces of thyme, four of winter savoury, two of bayleaf, four of pepper, and an ounce of cloves; the whole to be pulverised and mixed with the vegetables'. Each dried vegetable cake served 100 men.

After the successful storming of Sebastopol, Soyer was asked to provide a special lunch that the French, British and Russian generals would attend together to celebrate the end of hostilities. He decided to produce one huge dish which he called *The Macedoine Lüdersienne à l'Alexandre II* in honour of the defeated Russian commander, General Lüder. He used up every last bit of preserved food that he could find in the officers' camp store and the list of ingredients is a fascinating insight into the preserved provisions available to officers while their men had barely survived on their meagre rations. This monster dish was composed of:

12 boxes of preserved lobsters
2 cases of preserved lampreys
2 cases of preserved sardines
2 bottles of preserved anchovies
1 case of preserved caviar
1 case of preserved sturgeon
1 case of preserved tunny
2 cases of preserved oysters
1 pound of fresh prawns
4 pounds turbot clouté
12 Russian pickled cucumbers
4 bottles pickled olives
1 bottle mixed pickles
1 bottle Indian ditto
1 bottle pickled French beans
2 bottles pickled mushrooms
½ bottle pickled mangoes

2 bottles of pickled French truffles
2 cases of preserved peas
2 cases of preserved mixed vegetables
4 dozen cabbage lettuces
100 eggs
2 bottles preserved cockscombs

The gap between conditions for army officers and their men did, however, slowly close as improvements in the transport and supply of more nutritional rations were made. Around the turn of the century nutritional analysis of rations began to get more sophisticated as the properties of vitamins, minerals and carbohydrates gradually became better understood. Over the following years a number of special nutritional studies and reports were made in Britain. In 1941 the Army Catering Corps was set up to organise military kitchens, train army cooks and introduce the regular use of composite rations, which were to combine the advantages of both tinned and dried foods. The first 'compos' were sufficient to feed twelve men with three meals for a day. They were made up of tinned meat and puddings, biscuits, cheese, chocolate, tea, sugar, blocks of dried vegetables and milk powder. The shortage of metal for tins during both World Wars and the need to save shipping space with more compact food supplies led to a greater reliance on dehydrated meat and vegetables. German soldiers, for example, continued to eat preserved sausages rather than tinned meat and they carried quantities of crisp bread and dried vegetables including sauerkraut, which was compressed into blocks and wrapped in aluminium foil or cellophane.

The sudden huge demand for dehydrated foods in the 1940s led to a frantic scramble to build factories equipped to carry out mechanical drying, especially a new form of tunnel drying whereby small diced cubes of vegetables travelled on trays along a tunnel towards a huge fan blowing hot air over it. The food moved slowly from the cooler to the hotter end of the tunnel ensuring a gradual drying process that resulted in a product with only 3 per cent moisture. This could be either packed into cans purged with nitrogen, or compressed under pressure into individual blocks. These foods were lightweight, compact, long lasting and retained almost all of their original nutritional value.

For the Normandy landings in June 1944, British troops had ration packs of dried food totalling 4,000 calories. Douglas Allenbrook, in his memoir *See Naples*, described US 'compo' rations as: 'smallish oblong boxes wrapped in waterproof paper containing concentrated food; dried beef with carrot chips, thick crackers resembling compressed cardboard, rounds of processed cheese, lemonade or coffee powder and always, thanks to the American tobacco industry, little packs of cigarettes. Constipation was the order of the day with D rations.' 'C rations', by contrast, still relied on canned food such as pork and beans and were said to have the opposite effect and 'erred on the side of looseness'.

The static nature of much of the fighting in Europe meant that regular fresh supplies were fairly reliable. Soldiers were only at the front for short periods before being relieved and returned to the rear where they could eat hot meals instead of compo rations. But in the Middle East things were very different, as supply to front-line troops was very poor and most men had to survive on a staple diet of dried food blocks, bully and biscuit. John Ellis quotes one officer who complained of '. . . a diet which had been mainly bully beef, biscuits, rice and tea. Even if one added the etceteras, the morning porridge, the sausage, the oleo-margarine, the occasional "meat and vegetable" compound which took the place of bully, the menu was hardly elaborate . . . There had been none of those delicacies which the home papers tell us we have enjoyed.'

Poor provisioning meant a monotonous diet but British ingenuity ensured that some soldiers cooked up some strange concoctions of their own. As ever the British Tommy was resourceful with his cooking and all kinds of ingredients were mixed up together and strongly flavoured with the addition of curry or chilli powder, Tabasco sauce, Bisto, Oxo or Marmite. The biscuits were so hard they had to be smashed up and mixed with tinned condensed milk or treacle to make a thick mass popularly known as 'burgoo' or mixed with water to make porridge or a crude pastry. Perhaps the greatest example of culinary and technological initiative should go to two American airmen stationed in Britain who were missing their ice-cream back home so much that they decided to make their own. The US government had classified ice-cream as an 'essential foodstuff' and the Secretary of War considered it to be indispensable to the morale of the US army. The airmen discovered a unique way of adapting the processes necessary for making ice-cream – freezing temperatures and constant movement. Before each sortie they prepared the dried ice-cream mixture and put it in a large can anchored to the rear gunner's compartment of a Flying Fortress. Well shaken up, it was nicely frozen over enemy territory at high altitudes. This enterprising recipe was printed in 1943 in the *New York Times* in an article entitled 'Flying Fortresses Double as Ice-cream Freezers'. One hopes that the US Secretary of War approved.

As was often the case, a number of new food technologies developed out of military needs and increasingly sophisticated methods of drying were developed. Liquids such as milk were originally drum dried by dribbling or spraying onto the surfaces of hot, slowly rotating drums from which the solids were removed by knives. This method was replaced by drying atomized sprays of liquid in streams of hot air. Freeze drying, which involves the food being frozen and subjected to a high vacuum, although expensive, is the most effective way of dehydrating food so that it retains its flavour, colour and nutrient value and can be reconstituted almost immediately by simply adding boiling water.

Each war brought some new innovation. Some of the soldiers worst off for their chow were those isolated in Burma, whose only relief from bully and biscuit was when they were sent some experimental synthetic soya-link sausages, which were quickly thrown out. Freeze-dried coffee was first sent to soldiers in the Korean War. More recent technologies have produced extruded dried foods, heat tabs to heat food and flameless ration heaters such as chemical pads activated by salt water, which can heat a meal in five minutes. New kinds of packaging were developed including 'Alucans', which are heat sealed, semi-rigid aluminium containers lighter than conventional cans. The Gulf War was an opportunity to test a number of new ideas such as the introduction of T-rations or Tray Packs for front-line American troops, which were 'thermetically processed shelf-stable foods, packaged in hermetically sealed, half-size steam-table containers which serve as package, heating pan and serving tray'. These had a shelf life of three years if kept in the right conditions. More controversial were the 'Meals Ready-to Eat Individual' (MREs), plastic 'retortable' pouches of a single meal for one man. Each MRE consisted of an 'entrée', such as meat balls in BBQ sauce or chicken in chilli sauce, crackers with a choice of cheese, peanut butter or jelly spread, a dessert plus a packet of coffee, cream substitute, sugar, salt, chewing gum, matches, toilet tissue, towelette, a plastic spoon and the occasional treat of cakes or freeze dried fruits. US Desert Shield troops were told they '. . . should not worry about the effect of MREs on sex drive or on the digestive system . . . No chemicals are added to lessen libido and the meals do not cause constipation'. MREs were not, however, popular with American soldiers, who tried to offload them onto British troops who also preferred their tinned food and compo rations and found no difficulty in resisting the offers of MREs. Also tested in the Gulf were 'Lunch Buckets', which were simply plastic cups containing dehydrated soup or pasta requiring the addition of boiling water, rather like the instant 'pot noodles' found in supermarkets.

Many of the latest innovations in food preserving technology involve hi-tech packaging and some of the most valuable discoveries for these were first made by our venture into space.

Gastronauts

Baby whales and astronauts face a common problem – how to eat in an extremely difficult environment. For a baby whale, suckling liquid milk under water would mean a loss of milk leaking into the sea and the baby gulping in sea water whilst suckling. Maternal whales solved the problem by producing a thick milk, as solid as blue cheese with 49 per cent fat, which is squeezed like toothpaste from the teat into the baby's mouth. Other sea mammals, such as seals, also produce a solid rather than liquid milk. Eating in the weightless environment of space presents similar difficulties. In conditions of zero gravity, food and drink will not remain on plates, in open cups, on spoons, nor in the astronaut's open mouth. It would fly around causing havoc, damaging sensitive instruments and contaminating the spacecraft's atmosphere with disease-producing bacteria, viruses and toxins.

The first food challenge for NASA was therefore to get food into the astronaut's mouth. Like the mother whale, scientists came up with semi-solid foods such as puréed meats, vegetables and fruits. Sealed into tubes made of aluminium, the food could be squeezed directly into the mouth. 'Food management', they stated, was about the 'control of errant food debris'.

In 1962 Lt. Col. John Glenn became the first American to orbit the Earth. Only five hours after being rocketed into space and completing three orbits, the spacecraft Mercury splashed safely down in the Atlantic Ocean. It was a successful and historic trip, but so short that it was not felt necessary to supply in-flight meals. The food sent up was for experiment, to find out if an astronaut could actually swallow in space. Happily, it turned out that they could and for many successive space flights astronauts were made to feed on semi-liquids forced into their mouths from toothpaste-

like tubes and to chew on bite-sized cubes of freeze-dried foods. Many complained about the awkward tube squeezing. They also found the food unappetising and they had trouble with rehydrating the freeze-dried cubes and capturing the escaping crumbs.

Astronaut Loren Shriver demonstrates how food acts in microgravity while eating candy coated peanuts on a shuttle mission

According to NASA, the primary objective in designing food technology for space travel is to provide food that is safe and nutritious, lightweight and compact for storage. It must be packed in a convenient form that allows it to be used safely and easily in the weightless environment of a spacecraft. In the later Gemini missions things did begin to improve. The aluminium tubes used on Mercury flights were replaced because the tubes weighed more than the food inside. Bite-sized chunks of dried foods were coated with an edible gelatine to reduce the crumbling problem and rehydratables were encased in an improved plastic container. Dried food was rehydrated by injecting cold water into the pack. After kneading the contents for about three minutes, the food became a purée, which the astronaut then squeezed through a tube into his mouth. Great attention was paid to nutritional values and to hygiene. After each 'meal' germicidal pills were put into the empty food bags to prevent fermentation and gas formation. The bags were then rolled and stowed in special waste disposal units.

None of this sounded much like proper eating and, as flights became longer, spacemen demanded better, pleasanter ways of feeding themselves. Tempting 'menus' were prepared and before lift-off the men could choose such home comforts as shrimp cocktail, chicken and vegetables, butterscotch pudding and apple juice. On the later Apollo flights, the added luxury of hot water was available to rehydrate the food into hot meals, which did much to improve the flavour of some dehydrated foods. Apollo crewmen also had newly introduced 'spoon-bowl' packages for rehydrating foods. They also had 'retort pouch' meals or 'wet packs' containing thermostabilised (heat preserved) foods that needed nothing more than heating up and had the enormous advantage of tasting like real food. These innovations helped make eating a rather more normal, if still not a particularly tasty experience. One problem with eating in space is that food does in fact taste different. As gravity tends to pull body fluids down towards the legs, the sinuses get congested and the taste experience is similar to when you have a heavy cold. For this reason most astronauts choose highly flavoured or very spicy foods.

Food on the relatively short Mercury, Gemini and Apollo flights were mainly clever adaptations of the survival foods used during the Second World War. Culinary considerations were not a priority in planning for space travel. Skylab and the Space Shuttle would, however, present more long-term feeding challenges. Thirty-day Shuttle missions with up to seven crew require large amounts of food and water. Food had to be designed to survive for that period and to withstand the temperature and pressure changes, acceleration and vibration of a much longer flight. The amount of water required for rehydration is also a constraint. But it was also time to improve not just the technology of the food, but also the living and eating conditions for men spending an increasing amount of time in space.

In 1967 NASA appointed the designer Raymond Loewy, famous for creating the Heinz soup label, the Coke bottle and the 1951 Studebaker, to be their 'Habitability Consultant'. Not surprisingly, Loewy was less interested in the food itself than the eating environment. He believed that a happy space crew was one able to replicate home life as much as possible even if his food wasn't quite as 'Mom' might have cooked it. Loewy designed a galley where the packaging, storage and preparation of food was better organised and easier, with an arrangement of table and chairs in a triangle so that the crew members could face each other sociably whilst enjoying a 'proper meal'. While they ate, the food containers were held in a tray attached to the table or by Velcro taped to the astronaut's lap. Mealtime could now be something to look forward to, a time to get together, to relax, talk and enjoy the meal as they hurtled through space.

Conventional ovens and eating utensils helped create an air of normality. Interestingly, microwave ovens cannot be used in space because of the dangers of escaped radiation. But freezers were introduced on Skylab and frozen foods are now available to today's astronauts. Scientists are still working on the business of keeping space travellers well fed. More imaginative menus are planned, with food now being irradiated and packaged using the latest technology and sent to NASA for Space Shuttles and to Star City in Russia for crewmen in the MIR Space Station and future long-haul space missions.

When Senator John Glenn was again fired into space in 1998, he ate and drank from the newly developed Chill Can, which uses carbon dioxide, made from waste industrial processes, stored at low pressure. Simple heat exchangers remove heat from the drink or food when the gas is released. Claimed to be more efficient and thus environmentally friendly than Earthbound cool-drink vending machines, self-chilling cans are expected to be part of the food technology of the future. Food irradiation, once hailed as the miracle food preserver, involves bombarding food with gamma rays to kill bacteria. The process evolved at the beginning of the twentieth century (X-rays were first discovered in 1895) when soft fruits were irradiated, prolonging their freshness and even, it was claimed, making them taste sweeter. It can certainly extend the shelf-life of soft fruits and the tropical fruits expensively imported by supermarkets by denaturing the enzymes that hasten the ripening process (which is why these kinds of exotic fruits rarely taste 'ripe'). Irradiation also kills some (but not all) micro-organisms in various types of foods. Irradiation does not, however, make food radioactive because the doses are so small, and irradiated food has been successfully used in hospitals and to feed astronauts for many years. However, despite the fact that we are already surrounded by low-level radiation from mobile phones, microwave cookers, computers and televisions, public fears fuelled by the appalling outcome of nuclear disasters such as Chernobyl have made consumers extremely hostile to the idea of food irradiation. Although it is legal in most countries, food irradiation seems for most too great a risk and the jury is still out on whether it will ever be considered acceptable for commercial use.

Nevertheless an enormous amount has been learned from space travel and the benefits to people at home on Earth are already being grasped. The science of space food preserving and nutrition has already helped in the development of food for people in hospitals, nursing homes and for the elderly at home. In America, a project called Meal System for the Elderly uses NASA's nutritional expertise to improve the diet of many people who might otherwise be unable to eat easily.

As more experience in space flight is gained, food preserving for space travellers and others travelling into the farthest reaches of land, sea and air will continue to benefit. No doubt there will be many further endeavours to find ways to preserve foods to sustain life on future missions into unfamiliar territories. Most of these 'space-age' foods are still very expensive and only well-funded adventurers, the military and the space projects can afford to use them. But some of the processes have gradually become cheaper to execute and the results have found their way onto the supermarket shelves. Amongst those preserved foods developed or improved as a result of space travel are instant noodle meals in plastic pots, freeze-dried coffee, 'cook and chill' meals and vacuum-packed foods. The lightweight, easily transportable 'retort pouches' are now familiar to shoppers in the form of flexible packages of food that combine the advantages of the metal can and the 'boil in the bag' packaging. Foods preserved in them retain their natural flavours, minerals and vitamins, and can be stored for long periods without refrigeration.

There are now businesses that specialise in supplying preserved, lightweight packaged foods to travellers, adventurers, the military, nervous home owners and homeless refugees. These companies usually produce a range of both dry and wet rations supplied with lightweight heating facilities. They are packed to protect against insects, strong enough for air dropping and robust enough for long transportation. For example, BCB International in Cardiff send military combat rations to NATO troops and refugee relief rations to Bosnia and Kosovo. Their ready-to-eat, easy-to-prepare preserved rations, called MRS, consist of freeze-dried and vacuum-packed wet foods, made up into carefully designed and nutritionally balanced meals. These are now also bought by campers, balloonists, trans-Atlantic sailors, climbers and the few individuals still tackling one of the Poles. MRS meals have been taken to the top of Everest, across oceans, over Arctic wastes and through jungles and deserts, anywhere, in fact, that people still feel the urge to go to.

CHAPTER SIXTEEN

FEAST OR FAMINE

In the light of the progress in food preserving made thanks to steps forward in space travel, it is worth remembering that the twentieth century, for many, also involved several severe steps backwards. We have seen how warfare has often been a catalyst for improvements in food preserving, but when we look at preserving on the home front in Britain during the Second World War, we see it sometimes tells a rather different story.

In April 1940 the Germans invaded Denmark and Norway, in May they entered Holland, Luxembourg and Belgium and by the end of June they had occupied most of France. British food supplies from these countries were effectively cut off. Over half the nation's bacon and ham, eggs, butter, condensed and dried milk was stopped and when Italy entered the war in June, foods coming through from the Mediterranean were also restricted. Even onions and tomatoes ceased to come from the Channel Islands. Moreover during bombing raids vital ports such as Bristol were damaged and warehouses filled with food stocks were also destroyed. Finally, when Japan entered the war in 1941, Britain's sources of rice, sugar and tea, as well as rubber and tin – so important for preserving – were cut off.

Most damaging of all, however, were the German submarines circling the British Isles laying mines and sinking the merchant ships bringing in essential supplies, including food. Soon the British people found themselves in a virtual state of siege. Food shortages inevitably meant food rationing. This was first introduced in January 1940 for bacon, sugar and butter and by the end of that year, meat, tea, margarine, cooking fat and cheese were also rationed. In 1941 the distribution of fresh milk and eggs was controlled and jam, marmalade, treacle and syrup joined the ration list. Points rationing, a German idea, was introduced in 1941 for tinned meats, fish and vegetables. The points system allowed people more choice to shop around, to save for a treat or something special as well as giving the shopper a bit more control over their meal planning. Food rationing was not finally ended until 1954, nine years after the end of the war.

Before the war Britain had been importing nearly 30 million tons of food, over half its total annual consumption, but by the end of the war it was importing less than 10 million tons. Yet no one starved, indeed the British people as a whole were said to have been better fed than ever before. The iron rations of war replaced the poverty diet of the 1930s and most were healthier as a result. Wartime meals may have been monotonous and not very tasty but they were well balanced, ensuring the simple, minimum nutritional requirements – something that a large percentage of the population had not benefited from previously. The Ministry of Food under Lord Woolton (immortalised by 'Woolton Pie', made entirely of patriotic home-grown root vegetables) set up a Food Advice Division that created Food Advice Centres around the country. These were staffed by home economists who gave advice and demonstrations in markets, factory canteens and stores advising people about rationing and how to cook and keep their families well fed. Cookery and nutrition leaflets were distributed, BBC radio broadcast 'Food Facts for the Kitchen Front' while 'Food Flashes', which were shown in the cinema, attempted to teach the British people how to cook and eat better. A Vitamin Welfare Scheme ensured that children and pregnant women had cod liver oil plus preserved concentrated orange juice specially imported from America. Factories and schools were expected to provide canteens serving inexpensive, unrationed meals and restaurants were not allowed to charge more than 5 shillings for a meal, no matter whether they were Joe's Caff or the Savoy. Top restaurants were, however, permitted to charge as much as they liked for service and wine in order to make up their profits, a practice enthusiastically continued to this day.

Some of the disappearing food imports – bananas, citrus and tropical fruits – however much they were missed, were luxuries that people could do without. Reductions in the supply of tinned and frozen meat and tinned fruit and vegetables from New

Zealand, Australia and the US were harder to cope with. Those boats that did get through tended now to carry dried fruit to save space, whilst meat carcasses were boned and cut up before packaging also to save weight (a practice which became commonplace after the war). Dehydrated foods were not at all popular with the English housewife, however. 'Putting food into battle dress', as it was known, may have helped the shipping problem, but it often left the housewife with unrecognisable and tasteless pieces of food. At least pickles, sauces and spreads were unrationed and still available to put back some flavour.

There was always a way round a lack of an ingredient. 'Mock', meaning 'a substitute', appeared in many wartime recipes. Mock marzipan used soya flour, onion salt replaced onions, and there were various chemical substitutes for sugar, milk and eggs. There were mock oysters made of sardines and artichokes, mock burgers made of dried mashed potato and mock plum pudding with grated carrot, mashed potato and chopped prunes instead of mixed dried fruits and breadcrumbs. Oxo, Marmite and Bisto, still valuable contributors to cooking today, were used to flavour almost every savoury dish including mock goose, mock chops and mock sausages. The scum from jam making was used to make chewy fruit sweets and as icing sugar was strictly forbidden, brides had to be content with cardboard wedding cakes. But good cakes still got made including the excellent keeping Trench Cake that needed no egg. There is a story of how a slab of Trench Cake was sent to the front in France; after ten weeks of travelling all round the country constantly missing the recipient Tommy, the cake was eventually returned to England where it was found to be still in perfect condition. So it was sent out again, this time successfully, and was reported to have been greatly enjoyed.

Possibly the worst aspects of wartime food was the monotony of the diet and the endless, bossy nannying and finger wagging about not wasting anything, making the best of things, tightening your belt and doing your bit on the 'kitchen front'. It was one thing to accept spartan and boring daily fare, but the enforced cheerfulness must sometimes have been the last straw. Women, who were under increasing pressure to relieve men for the Forces by taking on war work, still had to run the home, often as the sole adult coping with the extra challenges in the kitchen and managing the complicated arithmetic of rationing coupons and points. Shopping became a battle of nerves, waiting in long queues outside shops for food (sometimes not even knowing what they were queuing for) and daily worrying about feeding their families. At the same time women were working long hours in factories or driving lorries or ambulances. Women had to 'keep smiling through' while the Ministry of Food issued even more cheery posters along the lines of 'Let Your Shopping Help Our Shipping'.

During 1941 conditions on the home front deteriorated. In the first three months of the year over $1\frac{1}{2}$ million tons of merchant shipping was sunk. In early spring the US pledged financial and material help to beleaguered Britain. The American Lend-Lease scheme was introduced boosting the number of warships available to escort convoys, and quantities of American canned fish, fruit, vegetables and strange canned meats such as Spam (Supply Pressed American Meat), Prem, Tang and Mor (a spiced sugared ham) did reach the hard-pressed British housewife. The Americans also sent over welcome supplies of cheese, bacon and lard, dried eggs, dried or evaporated milk, beans and soya flour.

Nevertheless, by March 1942 shortages of every kind were commonplace and food suggestions were becoming increasingly bizarre: 'Why not experiment with unrationed sheep's heads?' 'Why not give baby the turnip water for his vitamin C?' 'Why not use cormorants' eggs for making cakes?' Horseflesh was sold ostensibly for pets but was consumed by many pet owners. New kinds of food supplies made it necessary to teach people how to cook with unfamiliar preserved foods like dried eggs, dried skim milk and dehydrated vegetables and to persuade a public, normally conservative about its food, to accept some strange new foods, some tasty like dried bananas, which were chewy and very sweet, and some rather less mouth-watering.

Snoek was planned to be the saviour of the fish problem. Fishing in Britain had become a very dangerous business even close to shore. The coastline was covered in barbed wire, mines and booby traps so that beaches, estuaries and inland waters became very hazardous places for fishing. The best boats from the fishing fleets were commandeered by the navy and fresh sea fish became another luxury. In response, the government began issuing new kinds of preserved fish along with some old ones. The more familiar tinned sardines, salmon and mackerel were joined by salt cod, on which the British had never been keen. Brought in from Iceland, it was heavily salted and was described as being 'like boiled flannelette'. Tinned pilchards were unfamiliar and frozen or tinned whalemeat like 'fishy liver', which even the dogs refused to eat, was completely alien. Even the government was stumped by snoek, a relative of the tunny or mackerel that lives in the southern hemisphere where it is known as Australian barracuda . 'I have never met a snoek,' said one Minister, 'so I cannot tell you much about it.' Nevertheless, eleven million $\frac{1}{2}$ lb cans of snoek were imported to be sold cheaply. Once tasted, most of the canned snoek was left on the shelves. Quantities of salted snoek also arrived which was even more inedible. The Ministry of Food, desperate to shift the snoek, published recipes for snoek sandwiches, snoek paste and snoek piquant. According to Australian gourmets the snoek, when eaten fresh or smoked, has a delicate and delicious flavour. But for the wartime British housewife tinned and salted snoek was too great a challenge. Yet she was still expected to put a brave face on it and serve some of the strange new varieties of fish.

> When fisherfolk are brave enough
> To face the mines and foes for you
> You surely can be brave enough
> To face a fish that's new!

Courage in the face of snoek was, however, too much for most people.

While the Ministry of Food controlled the manufacture and distribution of nearly all foods, the Ministry of Agriculture and Fisheries was in charge of growing it. Since the beginning of the war, the government had realised that Britain would have to go back to producing most of its own food. The 'Dig For Victory' campaign started with a massive ploughing of nearly two million acres of pasture land and grasslands. Gardens large and small, allotments and city parks were all dug up to grow vegetables and fruit.

Livestock, which required a lot of pasture and feedstuff, was reduced, resulting in less meat and increased meat rationing. But dairy cows were kept for milk and chickens for eggs while pigs, which would eat anything, including food scraps, were back in the 'cottagers' back yards' along with a few hens and the odd duck or rabbit. Poultry, rabbit and pig clubs were encouraged with neighbours joining together and workers contributing their waste food from the canteen to feed one or two animals, which were later shared. An enterprising group of refuse collectors in Tottenham used special equipment to steam the separately collected kitchen waste under pressure (all pig swill had to be boiled for an hour to destroy organisms). Their concentrated pig swill was known as 'Tottenham Pudding' and the idea was quickly adopted for use by the 4,000 pig clubs that had formed by the end of 1942.

Home-raised pigs were due to be slaughtered from November to February but most people now had no idea how to deal with the carcass. Encouragement and advice about home food production was swiftly followed up with information about how to preserve surplus product. Instructional leaflets were produced showing how to cut up home-produced meat and how to salt it. Refrigeration in the home was extremely rare and expensive (in some of the grander houses Victorian ice houses were restocked) and most people still used food safes or cold cabinets and cool stone-lined larders. Housewives were urged to preserve every ounce of their home-grown food for the winter. In the years of shortage old skills and learning had to be renewed and relearned, or for the older generation, simply remembered. Even the most prosperous housewives, now servantless, were forced to learn the old techniques as well as how to depend on more modest food supplies. The younger city and suburban women learned traditional ways to make sausages, faggots, brawn and pork pies and homes with old-fashioned hearths once again hung up the cured meat to smoke it – just like the old days.

The Food Research Station of Bristol University advised the government about home preserving techniques and contributed instructions and recipes to the 'Growmore' and the 'War Cookery' leaflets. Housewives were shown how to dry apples, mushrooms, plums, onions and herbs; how to salt string beans, dry haricot beans, and to make jams, fruit cheeses, pickles and chutneys; how to bottle and, where the equipment was available, how to tin food. There were also leaflets about how to preserve eggs. Fresh eggs known as 'shell eggs' to distinguish them from dried eggs, were particularly valued. 'Eggall', the powdered egg used during the First World War, had given dehydrated eggs a bad name and the Ministry of Food had to work hard to convince the public that dried egg processing had improved. Certainly, American spray-dried eggs were an improvement on earlier versions. Eggs were not only important suppliers of protein, but also essential aerators and emulsifiers in a whole range of traditional cookery from light sponge cakes and cheese soufflés to mayonnaise and white sauces. Skill and ingenuity in dealing with dried egg became a popular subject of advice and of pride.

Whole shell eggs could be preserved between March and May when hens were laying at their best. The easiest and most popular method was to lay them gently in a bucket filled with waterglass (sodium silicate solution). The alkali retarded the growth of micro-organisms and the silicate made a protective coating on the shell to keep out contaminants. Another chemical solution was called OTEG, which could be bought from the chemist, into which the eggs could be carefully dipped using a pair of tongs. When it dried, it formed a coat of varnish on the shell sealing the air out. Some women even rediscovered the art of butter making using the cream from the top of their milk bottles and butter substitutes for potting were suggested in various recipes printed in the leaflets, including Potted Cheese using melted margarine and stale cheese and Potted Hard Roe Butter with pounded herring roe and margarine pressed into little pot or jars. Fruit and vegetable drying was an easy and cheap method of preserving. Apples and pears, even windfalls could be dried.

Much of the wartime sugar demand was met from home-grown crops of sugar beet rather than imported cane sugar. Little cane sugar was being refined in England and the Thames refinery of Tate and Lyle turned instead to dehydrating vegetables while another refinery concentrated on producing golden syrup, which was much in demand. Sugar rationing was very strict but extra was allowed for anyone preserving fruit. The Long Ashton Food

FOOD FACTS

HARVEST HOME

Apple pudding on wintry days? Runner beans for dinner in December? This is the time to make sure you will have these dishes later on. Preserve every ounce of home-grown food you can spare for the winter. You are on a *fighting food standard* now. Nothing must be wasted. Gather in the garden harvest now, so you can enjoy your 'Harvest Home' in the winter.

ELDERBERRY AND APPLE JAM

Ingredients: 3 lb. elderberries, 3 lb. apples, 5 lb. sugar. *Method:* Remove berries from stalks and wash. Warm them to draw juice. Simmer for ½ hour to soften skins. Core apples and simmer until quite soft in another pan with very little water, pass through sieve or pulp well with wooden spoon, add apples to elderberries, reheat and add sugar. Stir until dissolved and boil rapidly until jam sets. Make first test for setting after 10 minutes.

Salting Beans

Salting is the best way of preserving runner or French beans. Use young fresh beans. Take a lb. of cooking salt to 3 lb. of beans.

Wash the beans, dry, string them and, if large, break into pieces. *Crush* the salt with a rolling pin. *Put a* layer of salt about 1 inch deep into the bottom of a crock or jar (any large jar will do). *Press* in a layer of beans, then another layer of salt ½ inch deep, and so on. The secret of success is to pack the salt well down on the beans. *Finish* with a layer of salt 1 inch deep. *Cover* with a cloth or paper and tie with string. *Leave* for a few days for beans to shrink.

Don't worry if contents become moist. *Just add* more beans and more salt until jar is full again. If beans are well covered with salt it doesn't matter how moist they are. *Re-cover*. Store in a dry cool place.

Before use, wash beans thoroughly in hot water, then soak for 2 hours in warm water. Cook in the usual way, but without salt.

RECIPE of the WEEK No. 20

Marrow Surprise

Cooking time: 20 minutes. **Ingredients:** 1 medium sized marrow, 4 oz. grated cheese, ½ pint household milk and vegetable stock, 2 tablespoonfuls flour, 1 oz. margarine, ½ lb. carrots, 1 cup sliced beans, salt, pepper. **Quantity:** Four helpings. **Method:** Peel marrow, unless garden fresh, remove seeds, slice beans and carrots, cut marrow into large pieces. Put carrots and beans in one saucepan with a little boiling salted water. Cover and cook till almost tender. Add marrow, cook for five minutes. **Cheese Sauce:** Melt margarine in a saucepan, blend in flour, cook for a few minutes, add milk and vegetable stock to make thick sauce, stir until smooth, add grated cheese. Pour sauce over marrow, carrots, beans. Brown under grill. Serve with potatoes.

Apple Rings

Here's a way of keeping apples that can be used for windfalls or blemished fruit. Wipe the apples, remove the cores and peel thinly. Cut out any blemishes. Slice into rings about ¼ inch thick. Steep the rings for 10 minutes in water containing 1½ oz. of salt to the gallon. Thread the rings on sticks or canes to fit across the oven or spread on trays. Dry very slowly until they feel like chamois leather. The temperature should not exceed 150° F. Turn once or twice during cooking.

Pears can be treated in the same way, but they must be cut in halves or quarters and spread on the trays.

DRYING HERBS

Parsley, mint, sage, thyme, marjoram and bay leaves can be dried and stored for the winter. Gather the leaves on a dry day. Wash small leaved herbs such as thyme, tie in muslin bags and hang by the fire to dry. Large leaved herbs such as bay leaves should be tied in muslin, dipped in boiling water. Then dried in a cool oven, this takes about 1 hour.

FREE — Ask at any of the Food Advice Centres or Bureaux for a free copy of the *Hedgerow Harvest* leaflet, or send a postcard to the Ministry of Food, London, W.1. The leaflet contains many useful recipes for preserving wild fruits and berries.

THIS IS THE 2nd WEEK OF RATION PERIOD No. 2.

How are you? **FIGHTING** *fit, thanks!*

Learning to preserve home-grown food for winter. One of a series distributed by the Ministry of Food during the 1940s

Research Station, which advised the Ministry, discovered that the addition of bicarbonate of soda reduced the acidity of fruit to be preserved, lessening the amount of sugar required, particularly with fruits such as gooseberries, blackcurrants, raspberries, plums, loganberries and rhubarb. Half a level teaspoon of bicarb to 1 lb of fruit reduced the sugar needed by a third.

Kilner jars and other special preserving jars were highly prized possessions carefully looked after, for if rubber rings deteriorated they could rarely be replaced and waxed paper soon ran out. One government leaflet even suggested corking the jars securely and painting over the corks with melted paraffin wax, or tying them down with a soaked bladder, as had been the practice centuries before. Almost every household got together to make jams, jellies and chutneys using home-grown fruit as well as produce from neighbours and farms. A big surplus in the late summer and autumn months required many hands to ensure that nothing was wasted. The great plum glut of 1940 galvanised the National Federation of Women's Institutes into setting up Fruit Preserving Stations, run by women volunteers, across the country, in church halls, kitchens of stately homes, school canteens and empty warehouses, using a wide assortment of equipment from small primus stoves to huge Aga ranges. Anyone could sell their surplus crops of home-produced fruit and vegetables as well as the hedgerow harvests of elderberries, sloes, blackberries, bilberries, rose-hips and rowanberries. Although the preserving centres were allowed to buy special rations of sugar, they were encouraged to use substitutes such as glucose, honey, saccharine with added gelatine and syrup made from sugar beet. Lemons were replaced in the preserving recipes with citric or tartaric acid or pectin-rich fruits. Vegetables were often used to bulk up and give colour to jams: marrow gave body and cooked beetroot gave a rich colour while grated carrot could pass for peel in a jar of 'marmalade' or could be thickly chopped to look like apricots. Rhubarb was added to strawberry and blackcurrant preserves. Fruit pulp from damsons, medlars and quinces was made into fruit cheeses. These, apparently, improved with keeping and 'should never be eaten under six months'. The 'scum' from jelly making was always kept to sweeten and flavour puddings or was boiled down to a syrup to be used in stewing fruit. There were plenty of recipes for Carrot Jam, Green Tomato Jam, Vegetable Marrow and Ginger Jam and even Parsley Honey.

Bottling and canning were also encouraged but with some caution. Bottling vegetables could only be done by trained women because of the risk of contamination with soil organisms, one of which causes botulism, a nowadays rare but deadly kind of food poisoning. Even quite recently there had been a number of nasty outbreaks of botulism in both Europe and America caused by improperly home pickled and bottled vegetables. But bottled fruit, including tomatoes, was a very popular way to preserve some of the better quality produce from people's gardens. The wartime leaflets gave four different methods that did not use sugar. The pulp of stewed fruit with its concentrated natural sugars could be simply bottled and sealed; fruit, packed into jars, could be heated in the oven and then covered over with boiling water; or jars of fruit could be sterilised by standing them in a deep pan of water and simmering for the correct amount of time. These three were based on methods that had been practised successfully since the eighteenth century. A fourth, newer method, was called the Camden Method named after Chipping Camden in Gloucestershire where food preservation research laboratories had first developed it. This rather drastic-sounding process involved packing fruit into a jar and covering it with a solution of sulphurous acid. It was said to be particularly suitable for preserving plums, greengages and apples. It was so popular that chemists produced the acid in tablet form for sale to the public. The recommended 'recipe' was one tablet to 10 fl oz of cold water to cover 1 lb of uncooked fruit in a preserving jar. The metal lids had to be smeared with Vaseline or covered with paper to protect them from the sulphur before the jars were sealed. When the fruit was required, it had to be boiled for fifteen minutes in order to remove all the sulphur dioxide. Canning, which was less common, could only be done if either the American 'Dixie' or pre-war, English-manufactured portable canning machines were available. The cans were very expensive although they could be re-used by cutting them down by about an inch after each use until they eventually became too small. Sterilisation had to be done with particular care to obtain the correct temperatures for the right length of time – in just the same way as Nicolas Appert would have done 140 years before.

By the end of 1940 the Women's Institute and its army of helpers had produced 3 million lb of jam, 150 tons of canned fruit and 160 tons of pulped fruit and chutney. They had been so successful that the Ministry of Food joined in, introducing strict rules and regulations. Each centre was visited to check the quality and that the amount of sugar allocated matched the amount of jam made – 6 lb of sugar was meant to make 10 lb of jam, considerably less than the 1 lb sugar to 1 lb of fruit that is nowadays considered usual. WI members were no longer able to buy back their jam at wholesale prices and they found themselves working hard for no reward other than to feel they were doing their patriotic duty for the war effort. Fruit prices and harvests fluctuated and enthusiasm wavered but they stuck it out and were

In almost every village members of the Women's Institute made huge quantities of jam from locally grown fruit.

rewarded in 1941 when their compatriots, the American Federation of Business and Professional Women, provided four mobile kitchens mounted on Ford V8 chassis. These were driven all over the countryside collecting orchard and wild fruit, which was quickly canned and sterilised in the kitchens producing an extra 1,000 tons of canned fruit. Despite the hard work, most of the women remember the preserving centres as having provided great entertainment and a useful training. Jennifer Davies in *The Wartime Kitchen And Garden* quotes a young housewife who recalled that she '. . . learned more from the jam-making centre than I would ever have done left to my own resources'.

Food shortages after the war lasted far longer than anyone expected. In fact they became worse rather than better as the international stocks of food were sent to parts of the world where people had suffered far worse than in Britain. There were very real fears of a world famine and grain stocks were so low that bread had to be rationed in 1946. Shipping could, however, once again move safely across the seas with supplies of tinned, dried and frozen foods.

The people who struggled out of the years of post-war austerity fell in love with the benefits brought by convenience foods, nylon sheets and Formica tops, and who could blame them? Succeeding generations began to acquire the trappings of greater wealth and more leisure time and the reasons for preserving and storing food in the home slowly changed and became more complicated. Once, it had simply been a need to conquer the seasons and accumulate a sufficient stock of preserved foods to fill the cellars and store-rooms in order to guard against the fickleness of nature and the threat from enemies and disease. But preserving for self-sufficiency, once an ideal in the thrifty mentality of peasant people, would soon no longer be worth the effort.

The great exodus from the countryside to the towns and cities in the nineteenth century had spelled the beginning of the end of self-sufficiency and bulk home preserving, yet farm life in most rural areas of Europe and North America had changed very little even as late as the 1950s. Mixed farming still provided the bulk of the household needs and they could be partly, if not completely, self-sufficient. It was a source of pride not to have to buy from the village shops or town markets. However, by the 1950s a few farms lucky enough to have electricity installed deep freezers and in some regions of Germany and Holland, giant freezers were communally shared to freeze butchered farm livestock. From this point on, the increasing specialisation on farms and the decline of the small, family-owned farms meant that it was no longer possible for country people to provide for all their needs themselves. The new home freezers began to be partly filled with industrially frozen food and partly with home-grown produce. Freezing, which requires little preparation, reduced the length of time farm women spent on preserving and preparing food and left them with spare time, which many used to go out to work in the local town. Like urban women who had no garden or livestock, rural women now earned cash to buy food to put in their freezers. Modern food retailing appeared on the horizon and grew with astonishing speed, bringing variety and cheap mass-produced food. The way people bought their food was transformed.

It wasn't really so long ago that we shopped in some of the last food stores in English towns staffed by people who still sliced the bacon, weighed the butter, cut the cheese, filled blue or brown paper bags with loose biscuits, tea, rice and pulses, and sent the bill winging over your head in metal tubes to a lady seated in a wooden booth by the door. By the late 1970s most of them had finally closed their doors and re-emerged as boutiques or hair-dressers' salons. These small food shops had first sprung up on street corners wherever new housing was built. For the city poor, food remained a constant preoccupation and a daily worry about how to pay for it. Grocery stores in middle-class areas were well stocked with 'fancy' foods and fresh meat and vegetables but they remained unknown commodities in the poorer urban areas. There, the corner shops could not afford to stock up with fresh food every day and the bulk of produce on their shelves was preserved in some way. Tins of meat and vegetables and packets of dry goods, smoked or cooked meats, salt or smoked fish, flour and dried peas and beans, pickles in barrels or jars, sauces and vinegars, jams, black treacle, loose biscuits, sugar, tea and dried fruit were all delivered to the shop in bulk and weighed and packed individually to order. There was tinned brawn, corned beef, pickled herrings, bloaters, kippers or 'digbies' and Finnan haddock. Tins of condensed milk, fruit and salmon were the luxuries, while boiled ham on the bone was for special occasions and funerals. Later, newer products were put on the shelves, like margarine or 'Maggie-Ann', then a symbol of a poverty diet. Adulteration of food (an ancient practice) was rife and hygiene was very poor. Milk was illegally dosed with formaldehyde to prevent souring, eggs were often cracked or bad and without a refrigerator the shopkeeper had to keep a careful eye on meat and cheese in hot weather. Often rancid meat was washed with charcoal water and the rotten parts were cut away and some shopkeepers even sold the putrefied trimmings.

But by the 1960s and 1970s enormous improvements in industrial food production and modern farming methods brought cheaper, better quality and safer foods, even if some of the modern techniques sound as unappetising as many of the traditional preserving methods described in this book. For example, 'mechanically recovered' bits of meat and fish, once known as 'slaughterhouse waste' is mashed and formed into frozen burgers, fish fingers and pies. These processed, but no doubt nourishing foods are cheap and bought by the less well-off, as was dried meat and salt fish in the sixteenth century. Sugar and salt are now used in even greater amounts than ever before to flavour and preserve food, along with numerous modern chemical sweeteners, colourings, flavouring agents, additives and preservatives. Sadly, industrial preserving tries unsuccessfully to emulate the most popular preserved flavours and specialities on the 'deli' counter. Many smoked meats, for example, are given a 'smoke flavour', added as a liquid solution or a 'natural gaseous smoke' concentrated into a liquid form. 'Farmhouse cheeses' are made in a factory with milk from many different sources so that there are none of the inherent characteristic flavours one associates with regional cheese names. Food labels have always been designed to make the consumer feel that they are eating something that is fresh, natural, healthy and wholesome. The word 'style' we see on so many labels means that the product is not made in the region named but is made by the methods used in that region.

When shopping for food took over from food production in the home it removed people from the realities of food sources and from the experience of food production and processing. Slaughtering, butchering, gutting and plucking, once natural parts of preserving at home, are all activities few would now undertake with any confidence. Sowing, manuring, growing and harvesting are less offensive but still considered better left to the experts. Many city children do not know where milk, eggs or bread come from nor have seen animals on a farm or vegetables growing in the ground. For many people their only contact with food is with reheating and eating it. With fast food came fast eating and a decline in the social importance of mealtimes. Eating is gradually becoming a fast intake of fuel rather than a social or sensual experience.

But it is the seasonality of food that has been most profoundly changed by our modern systems of supply and distribution. Our eating habits were once based on the annual rhythms of harvests. The time for slaughtering, growing, storing and preserving our food was all planned seasonally. As Massimo Montanari wrote in *The Culture of Food* in 1994, 'The high-handedness of the food industry has unquestionably upset many of the traditional rhythms and habits of life, and created, together with many benefits, both health concerns and considerable cultural disorientation.' Preserving is no longer about conserving the seasonal surplus harvest for leaner times. In the West, supermarkets have almost done away with seasons altogether by displaying, year round, produce on the shelves. However, the pros and cons of selling out-of-season foods were, it seems, being argued as long ago as the fourth century BC when Aristophanes wrote *The Seasons*:

A: 'You will see, in midwinter, cucumbers, grapes, fruit, wreaths of violets, roses, and lilies . . . The same tradesman sells thrushes, pears, honeycomb, olives, beestings, haggis, celandine, cicadas, embryo-meat. You can see baskets of figs and of myrtle-berries together covered in snow, and what is more, they sow cucumbers at the same time with turnips, so that nobody knows any longer what time of the year it is . . . A very great boon, if one may get throughout the year whatever he wants.'

B: 'A very great evil, rather! For if they couldn't get these things, they wouldn't be so eager for them and spend so much money on them. As for me, I would supply these things for a brief season and then take them away.'

In 1980 Elizabeth David also argued for a seasonal approach to food when it is fresh and 'at its best, most plentiful and cheapest'. She hated tinned and frozen foods and wrote that 'frozen peas with everything not only marginalises the pleasure of eating those delicate, fresh, sugary green peas but also homogenises the rhythms of the year. We lose the sense of place and feel of the seasons'. She was not, however, against the traditional preserving practices that produced honest food with character, texture and flavour.

Today we not only want our food to be fresh, we also expect a huge variety of foods from every part of the world to be available to us throughout the year. Just as the wealthy nobles and royal palaces in the past searched for ingenious ways to produce fresh and exotic foods, we now look to technology to produce foods not only out of season but also from distant countries and cultures. In the past the old traditional food-preserving techniques were the 'poor' methods for cheating the seasons and fresh and perishable foods were luxuries reserved for the few. The Roman

Emperor Gallienus 'ate melons in the dead of winter' and wealthy families picked fresh fruit from their heated greenhouses, which were serviced by an army of servants and gardeners. And it was not only food out of season that denoted power and wealth, food from outside the locality or region was also worth showing off. The Chinese enjoyed 'paws of bear and various other wild animals which arrive salted from Siam, Cambodia or Tartary'. Bartolomeo Stefani, chef to the Gonzaga court in the seventeenth century, could supply his masters with both fresh and foreign luxuries, for with 'good horses and a good purse' he knew that he could find in all seasons 'all those ingredients I call for'.

Fast and efficient transport for food, always an important factor, has in recent decades become almost more valuable than preserving. Wealthier consumers can now eat 'fresh' produce grown in distant parts of the world and flown into their shops in a matter of hours. Taste, however, is often the first casualty, with texture losing out a close second. Most of us have been tempted to buy rosy-looking peaches, bunches of purple grapes and golden apricots for winter treats only to find them hard and woody in texture and virtually without taste. This is because they are often harvested long before the natural ripening and sweetening from the sun. How much nicer to chew on succulent sun-dried apricots and peaches, dates and raisins – the traditional, seasonal preserved foods of Christmas.

The alluring, foreign, out-of-season foods, which fill supermarket shelves, are not then a new phenomenon. In the West the privileges of wealth have simply been extended to vastly greater numbers of people, while those who cannot afford fresh buy tinned, dried, frozen 'pre-formed' and 'ready-to-eat' foods. Other parts of the world are not so lucky. In many regions so much of the land is used to grow food for export that little is left on which families can grow their own traditional foodstuffs and they are forced to import industrially processed foods to the detriment of their diet and their ability to feed themselves. For thousands of years people living in the Pacific Islands have experienced periods both of plenty and of hunger. They survived by preserving and eating their indigenous food products. Over the years, the traditional ways to preserve and store local food were forgotten and today, when there is a drought or a hurricane, the islanders are forced to buy imported tinned and dehydrated foods, white rice and flour, often provided by overseas aid agencies. Islanders have come to rely on and acquire a taste for these foods, but they cause obesity and health problems and are far more expensive than the local produce. As a result, a training project was set up by the University of the South Pacific to encourage islanders to rediscover the skills and practices of their own preserving traditions. Pacific foods such as breadfruit, figs and mangoes, they argued, have a higher food value and people will get more nutrition from fermenting, drying and smoking the foods grown in their own countries than from imported industrially preserved foods.

Even the poorest countries in the world could be capable of feeding themselves reasonably well for most of the time. But increasingly many have come to rely on processed food imports that must be paid for with scarce foreign currency. In many cases the ability of the poor country to control its own food supply has been lost and any crisis, be it natural or human, immediately returns it into a cycle of famine and malnutrition, disease, debt and increased dependence on wealthier nations.

Industrial food production may have ended traditions of self-sufficiency but hoarding and stockpiling still appear to have a place in even the wealthiest countries. As we have seen, kings and military leaders always felt more secure when their granaries were full and their castles and fortresses were well stocked with long-lasting foods. Well-filled cellars and store cupboards and generous hospitality are matters of great pride in any culture. No one, after all, wants to be caught out with no food in the house. Centuries of famine, disease and war are ingrained in the memory of mankind and the fear of hunger is as strong as ever. Even within living memory, much of the world has been in the grip of war and seen countless numbers die of malnutrition and starvation. Millions of people have become refugees, have lost their homes and been forced to make new lives elsewhere. Those who stayed behind have had to retreat to a primitive, almost hand-to-mouth existence where traditional forms of food preserving are once again vital to survival and preserved food is stored, hidden or used as barter for other essentials. It was not so long ago that a bankrupt Russia was paying its soldiers in pickled cucumbers and in the months following Chernobyl uncontaminated dried milk powder was hoarded in huge quantities. For those who still live on the knife edge of survival as well as those who live in the lap of luxury, stockpiling food still helps people at least feel prepared for the worst.

One can find on the Internet an extraordinary range of advertisements for companies selling preserved provisions for stockpiling. These claim to be able to provide the food products needed for sustainable living in the face of the threat of natural and man-made disasters such as earthquakes, floods, tornadoes or hurricanes – even nuclear war. For example you can buy dehydrated, freeze-dried, vacuum- and perma-packed or canned foods from 'Safe Haven', 'Survive America', 'Food Reserves', 'Mayday Industries', 'Quake Pac', 'SOS Food Lab', 'Peace of Mind Essentials' and 'Just In Case Foods'. The names reveal much about the fears and concerns of Americans (for whom they are mostly intended) who live across a vast continent covering different climates and different lifestyles and who have not forgotten the fear of hunger. As recently as the 1930s, during the Great Depression, the US government set up rural reconstruction programmes to try to improve the living conditions and nutrition of the rural poor. Agencies were instructed to help local familes to build their own home freezing units, smokehouses and better storage places.

More recently there has been a return to home food production, not for reasons of frugality, but out of a wish to be in control of food, to know where it came from and how it was prepared and processed. More than ever before, people are concerned about whether their milk came from a cow and their eggs from a hen. Fear of hunger is in many areas being overtaken by a fear of obesity and disease caused by eating the wrong food. Many people now long for more natural 'home-made' comestibles and one reaction to the growth of industrial food processing, which is filling shelves with bland, anonymous food, is a new interest in home preserving, and magazines have started to give old-fashioned 'Grandma's tips' for preserving in the traditional way. Some call it 'boutique' or 'gourmet' preserving; now no longer a necessity but a leisure activity. In the US in particular traditional cooking and preserving are still celebrated. For example, Polish communities still make 'kolbas' sausage, 'rakia' pickled cabbage and home-made chilli in oil and garlic. As one Polish-American puts it, 'Before we had ceilings there were always sausages and hams hanging up in the rafters, but we still make them for the memory and the taste, an affirmation of who we are and where we come from.'

Home preserving, however, still carries as many risks and dangers as it always has. Botulism and other less deadly forms of food poisoning still lurk in the kitchen, smokehouses and store-rooms of the unwary or inexperienced. Freezing and refrigeration is now a valuable additional aid to old-style traditional preserving by keeping the produce fresh before the preserving is started. It is also a safer way to store preserved products than some older, less hygienic means. Delicatessens and speciality food shops now offer luxury preserved foods from many different cultures – smoked, dried and cured fish and meat, hams, sausages, fermented pickles and sauces, strong tasting cheeses, dried herbs, spices and crystallised fruits and conserves – old-fashioned foods using traditional methods but with modern hygiene regulations (which are not always in sympathy with the true spirit of the food as the French, who love to get round regulations, will never tire of telling you).

An Italian 'deli' in Bedfordshire in the 1950s, filled with preserved specialities giving immigrants a taste of home and introducing new foods to postwar Britain

The French more than any other culture have continued to produce their own preserved foods simply because they taste better than anything else. In many regions of France, in particular the southwest, the majority of their 'produits régionaux' are preserved delicacies: hams and 'saucisse sèche', pots of foie gras and pâté, cans of 'confit de canard', 'tripoux d'Auvergne', 'truffes', 'anchoid Perigourdin', packets of 'pruneaux d'Agen', 'marrons glacé', jars of preserved fruits and vegetables, olives of all kinds and hundreds of other delicious things. These are not just sold to enthusiastic tourists but are found in every household where French regional cooking is still consumed and respected. In France many rural people still regularly preserve their produce, some still kill a pig or two, while other households pickle, pot or bottle their fruits and vegetables. They cook delicious soups, confit and cassoulets, which they take down to the co-operative or local supermarket to have sealed in the canning machine. They do this because they choose to eat well and they prefer to retain control over the quality and taste of their food. Unlike the English high street, where few quality food stores have survived the competition of supermarkets, the French can still shop for their favourite foods in the local *charcuterie*, *boulangerie*, *boucherie* and *pâtisserie*.

Food is part of our identity. Wherever we have moved and whomever we have assimilated with, what we eat remains central to our culture. Traditional food preserving has travelled with migrants and refugees, and come to be enjoyed in new parts of the world. Cheaper travel has opened up a new and wider world of tastes and experiences for people to discover. Perhaps the most valued aspect of preserved food is not that it feeds us in hard times, allows us to travel and prevents waste, but that it gives us pleasure; it creates unique foods of taste and texture. Food preserving is part of our culture, cuisine and memory – it is there in our feasting and celebrations, and we should continue to preserve and enjoy all of those rich and delicious traditions.

Select Bibliography

This book is intended to appeal to a broad readership and so I have not used footnotes in the text. I have named important contributors where appropriate though some minor quotes are not sourced. A complete bibliography for a book as wide-ranging as this one would be far too long; many works are obscure or very old and can only found in specialist libraries. This select bibliography lists publications broadly covering food history and some aspects of the social history covered in the book. A few are currently in print and most can be found in good libraries. I would be happy to reply to any queries about sources and to receive readers' criticisms, comments and corrections via Headline Books, 338 Euston Road, London NW1 3BH. E-mail: headline.books@headline.co.uk.

Alan Davidson's definitive and invaluable *Oxford Companion to Food* arrived in the shops just as I had finished this book and I would recommend it to anyone interested in food and its history. Readers wishing to try some preserving at home will find Oded Schwartz's colourful and mouth-watering *Preserving* a pleasant antidote to some of my less attractive ethnographic descriptions.

Abdalla, Michael 'Traditional Methods of Food Preservation Used by Modern Assyrians' in *Food Conservation* (Prospect Books, 1988)

Aka, Christine 'The Change in Rural Food Storing in a Village in North-West Germany' in *Food Conservation* (Prospect Books, 1988)

Alcock, Joan 'The Travels of the Hon. John Byng Through England and Wales in the 18th Century' in *Food on the Move* (Prospect Books, 1996)
'Food in Tibet' in *Disappearing Foods* (Prospect Books, 1994)

Allen, Brigid *Food: An Oxford Anthology* (OUP, 1994)

Amery, C. et al *American Heritage Cookbook* (Simon & Schuster NY, 1964)

Anderson, E. N. *The Food of China* (Yale Press, 1988)

Apicius *De re Coquinaria/culinaria* (trans. Barbara Flower & E. Rosenbaum as *The Roman Cookery Book*) (Harrap, 1958, reprinted 1974)

Appert, Nicholas *The Art of Preserving all Kinds of Animal and Vegetable Substances for Several Years* (trans. London, 1812)

Aresty, Esther B. *The Delectable Past* (Allen & Unwin, 1965)

Ashley, Maurice *England in the Seventeenth Century* (Pelican, 1952)

Aubrey, John *Brief Lives* ed. Oliver Lawson Dick (Penguin, 1976)

Aykroyd, W. R. *Sweet Malefactor: Sugar, Slavery & Human Society* (Heinemann, 1967)

Bacon, Josephine 'A Meal in a Piece of Pasta' in *Food on the Move* (Prospect Books, 1996)

Bayne-Powell, R. *Housekeeping in the 18th Century* (John Murray, 1956)

Beaman, Sylvia *The Icehouses of Britain* (Routledge, 1990)

Beattie, Owen & Geiger, J. *Frozen In Time: The Fate of the Franklin Expedition* (Bloomsbury, 1987)

Barr, Pat *A Curious Life for a Lady* (Penguin, 1985)

Barrow, John (ed.) *Captain Cook's Voyages of Discovery* (Everyman Library, 1967)

Bergon, Frank (ed.) *The Journals of Lewis and Clark* (Penguin, 1989)

Bernal, J. D. *Science in History* (four volumes) (Watts, 1969)

Bird, Isabella *Unbeaten Tracks in Japan* (John Murray, 1880)

Bitting, A. W. *Appertizing or the Art of Canning: Its History and Development* (San Francisco, 1937)

 Canning and How to Use Canned Foods (Washington, 1916)

Black, Maggie *A Taste of History: 10,000 Years of Food in Britain* (English Heritage, 1993)

Boswell, James *Journal of a Tour to the Hebrides with Dr Johnson* (1786, Everyman, 1912)

Boyd-Orr, D. *Feeding the People in Wartime* (Macmillan, 1940)

Bradley, Robert *The Country Housewife and Lady's Director* (1739, Prospect Books, 1981)

Braudel, Fernand *Capitalism and Material Life 1400–1800* (trans. Miriam Kochan) (Weidenfeld & Nicholson, 1973)

 The Structures of Everyday Life : Civilization & Capitalism, 15th–18th century (Collins, 1981)

Brears, Peter *Traditional Foods in Yorkshire* (Edinburgh, 1987)

 'Pots for Potting: English Pottery and its Role in Food Preservation in the Post-mediaeval Period' in *Waste Not Want Not* (Edinburgh University Press, 1991)

Brillat Savarin, J. A. *La Physiologie du Gout* (1825) (trans. A. Drayton as *The Philosopher in the Kitchen*, Penguin, 1970)

Brothwell, Dan & Patricia *Food In Antiquity: A Survey of the Diet of Early Peoples* (Thames & Hudson, 1969)

Brown, Catherine *Broths to Bannocks: Cooking in Scotland 1690 to present day* (John Murray, 1990)

Bryant, Arthur *Samuel Pepys: The Saviour of the Navy* (Cambridge University Press, 1928)

Burnett, John *Plenty and Want: A Social History of Diet in England from 1815 to the Present Day* (Routledge, 1968)

Buxbaum, Tim *Icehouses* (Shire Publications, 1998)

Calder, Angus *The People's War: Britain 1939–45* (Cape, 1969)

Campbell-Platt, G. *Fermented Foods of the World: A Dictionary and Guide* (Butterworth, 1987)

Carpenter, K. J. *The History of Scurvy and Vitamin C* (Cambridge University Press, 1986)

Cato *De Agricultura* (On Farming) (trans. A. Dalby) (Prospect Books, 1998)

Chamberlain, Lesley *The Food and Cooking of Russia* (Allen Lane, 1982)

Chang, K. C. (ed.) *Food in Chinese Culture – Anthropological and Historical Perspectives* (Yale University Press, 1979)

Cheke, Valerie *The Story of Cheese-making in Britain* (Routledge, 1959)

Cobbett, William *Cottage Economy* (Peter Davies, 1929)

 Rural Rides (two volumes) (Everyman, 1967)

Collins, James H. *The Story of Canned Foods* (New York, 1924)

Columella *On Farming* (Loeb Classical Library, 1955)

Cowell, Norman D. 'An Investigation of Early Methods of Food Preservation by Heat' (Unpublished Ph.D. Thesis, University of Reading Department of Food and Science Technology, September 1994)

Critchell, J. T. & Raymond, J. *A History of the Frozen Meat Trade* (Constable, 1912)

Curtis-Bennet, Sir N. *The Food of the People Being the History of Industrial Feeding* (Faber, 1949)

Cutting, Charles L. *Fish Saving: A History of Fish Processing from Ancient to Modern Times* (Leonard Hill, 1955)

Dalby, Andrew *Siren Feasts: A History of Food and Gastronomy in Greece* (Routledge, 1996)

David, Elizabeth *Harvest of the Cold Months: The Social History of Ice & Ices* (Penguin, 1995)
Spices, Salt and Aromatics in the English Kitchen (Penguin, 1975)
An Omelette and a Glass of Wine (Penguin, 1986)

Davies, Jennifer *Wartime Kitchen and Garden* (BBC Books, 1993)

Davies, R. W. *The Roman Military Diet* (Britannia, 1969)

Defoe, Daniel *A Tour through England and Wales* (1727, Everyman, 1928)

Dembinska, Maria *Food and Drink in Medieval Poland* (University of Pennsylvania, 1999)
'Methods of Meat and Fish Preservation in the Light of Archaeological and Historical Sources' in *Food Conservation* (Prospect Books, 1988)

Densmore, Frances *Chippewa Customs* (Minnesota Historical Society Press, 1979)

Déry, Carol A. 'Food and the Roman Army: Travel, Transport and Transmission' in *Food on the Move* (Prospect Books, 1996)

Derry, T. K. & Williams, T. I. *A Short History of Technology from the Earliest Times to AD 1900* (Clarendon Press, 1960)

di Schino, June 'Queen Christina of Sweden and the Triumph of the Baroque Banquet in Italy' in *Food on the Move* (Prospect Books, 1996)

Dirar, Hamid A. *The Indigenous Fermented Food of the Sudan* (CAB Wallingford, 1993)

Doerper, John 'Salmon, the Food that Travels' in *Food on the Move* (Prospect Books, 1996)

Driver, Christopher *The British at Table, 1940–1980* (Chatto & Windus, 1983)

Drummond, J. C. & Wibraham, Anne *The Englishman's Food: Five Centuries of English Diet* (Jonathan Cape, 1959, reprinted Pimlico, 1994)

Dudley, Donald *Roman Society* (Penguin, 1978)

Ellis, John *The Sharp End: The Fighting Man in World War II* (Pimlico, 1980)

Farrer, K. T. H. *A Settlement Amply Supplied: Food Technology in 19th-Century Australia* (Melbourne University Press, 1980)

Fei, H. T. *Peasant Life in China: A Field Study of Country Life in the Yangtse Valley* (Routledge, 1939)

Fenton, A. *Scottish Country Life* (Edinburgh, 1976)

Feldman, A. & Ford, P. *Scientists and Inventors* (Bloomsbury, 1989)

Fellows, Peter (ed.) *Traditional Foods: Processing for Profit* (IT Publications, 1997)

Fenton, Alexander 'Sequences in the Preservation of Milk Products in Scotland' in *Food Conservation* (Prospect Books, 1988)

Fenton, A. & Kisban, E. (eds) *Food in Change. Eating Habits from the Middle Ages to the Present Day* (Donald, 1986)

Fergusson, James (ed.) *Letters of Sir George Dempster to Sir Adam Fergusson 1756–1813* (Macmillan, 1934)

Finau, Sitaleki & Goodwillie, Dianne (eds) *Storing and Preserving Pacific Island Foods* (University of the South Pacific, 1990)

Firth, C. H. *Cromwell's Army* (Methuen, 1921)

Fisher, M. F. K. *With Bold Knife and Fork* (Pimlico, 1993)

Fitzgibbon, Theodora *A Taste of Scotland* (Pan Books, 1970)

Forbes, R. J. *Studies in Ancient Technology* (Brill Leiden, 1955–8)

Forster, Margaret *Rich Desserts and Captain's Thin* (Vintage, 1997)

Fortune, Robert *Three Years Wanderings In the Northern Provinces of China 1847* (Garland Press NY, 1979)

George, M. Dorothy *London Life in the Eighteenth Century* (Penguin, 1966)

Ginzberg, C. *The Cheese and the Worms* (trans. J. Tedeschi) (Routledge, 1980)

Glasse, Hannah *'First Catch Your Hare' The Art of Cookery Made Plain and Easy* (1747, A Facsimile of the first edition with biographical introduction, Prospect Books, 1995)

Goody, Jack *Cooking, Cuisine and Class* (Cambridge University Press, 1982)

Grigson, Jane *Charcuterie and French Pork Cookery* (Penguin, 1967)
     Fish Book (Penguin, 1993)

Grigson, Sophie & Black, William *Fish* (Headline, 1998)

Hakluyt, Richard *Voyages and Documents* (OUP, 1965)

Hardyment, Christina *Home Comfort: A History of Domestic Arrangements* (National Trust, 1992)

Haroutunian, Arto der *North African Cookery* (Century, 1985)

Harris, M. *Good to Eat: Riddles of Food and Culture* (Allen & Unwin, 1986)

Harris, M. & Ross, E.V. (eds) *Food in Evolution*, (Temple University Press, 1987)

Hartley, Dorothy *The Countryman's England* (Batsford, 1930)
     Food in England (Macdonald, 1954)

Hartley, Dorothy (ed.) *Thomas Tusser: His Good Points of Husbandry* (Country Life, 1931)

Hawgood, John *The American West* (Eyre & Spottiswood, 1967)

Herodotus *The Histories* (Penguin, 1971)

Hippisley Coxe, Araminta & Antony *The Book of Sausages* (Gollancz, 1994)

Hobhouse, Henry *Seeds of Change* (Sidgwick & Jackson, 1985)

Hope, Annette *A Caledonian Feast* (Mainstream, 1989)

Hosking, Richard *A Dictionary of Japanese Food* (Charles Tuttle, 1997)
     'The Fishy and Vegetable Abominations Known as Japanese Food' in *Food on the Move* (Prospect Books, 1996)
     'Some Japanese Food Rarities' in *Disappearing Foods* (Prospect Books, 1995)

Hudgins, Sharon 'Feasting with the Buriats of Southern Siberia' in *Food on the Move* (Prospect Books, 1996)

Hunter, Lynette 'Nineteenth and Twentieth Century Trends in Food Preserving: Frugality, Nutrition or Luxury' in *Waste Not Want Not* (Edinburgh University Press, 1991)

Iddison, Philip 'Arabian Travellers' Observations on Bedouin Food' in *Food on the Move* (Prospect Books, 1996)

Isitt, Verity *Take a Buttock of Beef:17th-Century cooking* (Ashford Press, 1987)

James, T. G. H. *An Introduction to Ancient Egypt* (British Museum Publications, 1979)

Jobse-van Putten, J. 'Development of Food Preservation [in Holland] in the Past Hundred Years' in *Food Conservation* (Prospect Books, 1988)

Jones, Evan *American Food: The Gastronomic Story* (The Overlook Press, Woodstock, 1990)

Karlansky, Mark *Cod: A Biography of the fish that Changed the World* (Jonathan Cape, 1998)

Keevil, J. J. *Medicine and the Navy* (E. & F. Livingstone, 1958)

Kelsey, Mary Wallace 'Exploring North West America, 1804–6' in *Food on the Move* (Prospect Books, 1996)

Kisbán, Eszter 'Domestic Conservation of Fat in Hungary' in *Food Conservation* (Prospect Books, 1988)

Köck, Christoph 'Preserving Food at Home or Buying it to Hoard' in *Food Conservation* (Oslo, Prospect Books, 1988)

Kowalska-Lewicka, A. 'The Pickling of Vegetables in Traditional Polish Peasant Culture' in *Food Conservation* (Prospect Books, 1988)

Kremezi, Aglaia *The Mediterranean Pantry* (Artisan NY, 1994)
'Paximadia: Food for Sailors, Travellers and Poor Islanders' in *Food on the Move* (Prospect Books, 1996)

Kuper, J. (ed.) *The Anthropologist's Cookbook* (Routledge, 1977)

Kurti, Nicholas 'Space, Time and Food' in *Food on the Move* (Prospect Books, 1996)

Lathan, R. (ed.) *Samuel Pepys: The Shorter Pepys* (Penguin, 1987)

Le Roy, Ladurie E. *The Peasants of the Languedoc* (University of Illinois, 1976)

Leeming, Margaret *A History of Food From Manna to Microwave* (BBC Books, 1991)

Leipoldt, C. L. *Leipoldt's Cape Cookery* (W.J. Flesch & Partners, 1976)

Levenstein, H. A. *Revolution at the Table: The Transformation of the American Diet* (OUP New York, 1980)
A Paradox of Plenty: A social History of Eating in Modern Times (OUP New York, 1993)

Levy, Paul *The Penguin Book of Food and Drink* (Penguin, 1997)
Out to Lunch (Chatto & Windus, 1986)

Lloyd, C. *The British Seaman 1200–1860: A Social Survey* (Collins, 1968)

Lloyd, C. & Coulter, J. S. *Medicine and the Navy* (volume three) (Eyre & Spottiswood, 1961)

Lord, F. A. *Civil War Sutlers and their Wares* (Thomas Yoseloff NY, 1969)

Luard, Elizabeth *European Peasant Cookery* (Bantam Press, 1986)
The Barricaded Larder (Bantam Press, 1989)

Manley, J. J. *The Age of Tin* (William Tweedie, 1872)

Martin, Martin *A Description of the Western Islands of Scotland c.1695 and A Late Voyage to St. Kilda 1698* (ed. D. J. McLeod) (E. Mackay, 1934)

Mason, Laura & Brown, Catherine *Traditional Foods of Britain: An Inventory* (Prospect Books, 1999)

Mayhew, Henry *The Morning Chronicle Survey of Labour and the Poor* (Caliban Press, 1982)

McGee, Harold *On Food and Cooking. The Science and Lore of the Kitchen* (Harper Collins, 1991)

Mennell, S. *All Manners of Food: Eating and Taste in England and France from Middle Ages to the Present* (University of Illinois Press, 1995)

Merlin, A. & Beajour, A. Y. *Les Mangeurs De Rouergue* (Duculot, 1978)

Minns, Ruth *Bombers and Mash: The Domestic Front 1939–45* (Virago, 1985)

Miroslava, Ludvíková 'Old Food Preserving Methods Practised in Moravia' in *Food Conservation* (Prospect Books, 1988)

Montanari, Massimo *The Culture of Food* (Blackwell, 1994)

Morgan, J. *On a New Process for the Preservation of Meat for Food* (Journal of the Society of Arts vol. XII, 1864)

Muller, H. G. 'Industrial Food Preservation in the Nineteenth and Twentieth Centuries' in *Waste Not Want Not* (Edinburgh University Press, 1991)
'Marching on their Stomachs: The Soldier's food in the Nineteenth and Twentieth Centuries' in *Food For The Community* (Edinburgh University Press, 1993)

Newby, Eric *A Book of Travellers' Tales* (Collins, 1985)

Newman, L. (ed.) *Hunger in History* (Blackwell, 1990)

Nugent, A. (ed.) *Lummi Elders Speak* (Washington, Lynden Tribune, 1982)

O'Brien, Tim *The Things They Carried* (HarperCollins, 1991)

Oyler, Philip *The Generous Earth* (Hodder & Stoughton, 1950)

Passingham, W. J. *London's Markets* (Sampson Low, 1935)

Perry, Charles 'The Horseback Kitchen of Central Asia' in *Food on the Move* (Prospect Books, 1996)

Philippon, H. *Cuisine Du Quercy Et Du Perigord* (De Noël, 1979)

Plat, Sir Hugh *Delightes for Ladies* (Introduction by G. E. Fussell) (Crosby, Lockwood & Son, 1948)

Pliny the Elder *Natural History* (Penguin, 1991)

Polo, Marco *Travels* (trans. Ronald Latham) (1958)

Pope, Dudley *Life in Nelson's Navy* (Allen & Unwin, 1981)

Porter, Roy *English Society in the Eighteenth Century* (Pelican, 1982)

Radeva, Lilija 'Traditional Methods of Food Preserving among the Bulgarians' in *Food Conservation* (Prospect Books, 1988)

Rahola, Jaakko 'Kalakukko: Food for the Home and Travel' in *Food on the Move* (Prospect Books, 1996)

Revel, J. *Culture and Cuisine: A Journey through the History of Food* (trans. Helen Lane) (Doubleday, 1972)

Richardson, A. *The Old Inns of England* (Batsford, 1934)

Riddervold, Astri 'On the Documentation of Food' in *Food Conservation* (Prospect Books, 1988)

Robertson, Una *Illustrated History of the Housewife 1650–1950* (Sutton 1997)
'The Introduction of Tinned Food into the Diet of the Royal Navy' in *Food Conservation* (Prospect Books, 1988)

Robinson, E. F. *The Early History of Coffee Houses* (Keegan Paul, 1893)

Robinson, R. K. *The Vanishing Harvest: A Study of Food and its Conservation* (Oxford Science Publications, 1983)

Rodger, N. A. M. *The Wooden World: An Anatomy of the Georgian Navy* (William Collins, 1986)

Root, Waverley *Eating in America: A History* (William Morrow NY, 1976)

Rousset, H. *Conserves Alimentaires* (Desforges, Girardout & Cie, 1925)

Sabban, Françoise 'The Problem of Preservation by Fermentation in 6th Century China' in *Food Conservation* (Prospect Books, 1988)

Saberi, Helen J. *Noshe Djan: Afghan Food and Cookery* (Prospect Books, 1986)
'Travel and Food in Afghanistan' in *Food on the Move* (Prospect Books, 1996)

Sambrook, Pamela & Brears, Peter *The Country House Kitchen 1650–1900* (National Trust, 1996)

Schlissel, Lillian *Women's Diaries of the Westward Journey* (Schocken Books NY, 1982)

Schuchat, Molly 'Camping Food in America' in *Food Conservation* (Prospect Books, 1988)

Sen, Colleen Taylor 'The Portuguese Influence on Bengali Cuisine' in *Food on the Move* (Prospect Books, 1996)

Seymour, J. S. *Self Sufficiency – the Science and Art of Producing and Preserving Your Own Food* (Faber, 1973)

Schwartz, Oded *In Search of Plenty: A History of Jewish Food* (Kyle Cathie, 1992)

Shibberbottom, Roy 'Hard Rations' in *Food on the Move* (Prospect Books, 1996)

Smith, Alan *Science and Society in the Sixteenth and Seventeenth Centuries* (Thames and Hudson, 1972)

Smith, R. & Christian, D. *Bread and Salt: A Social and Economic History of Food and Drink in Russia* (Cambridge University Press, 1984)

Soyer, Alexis *Soyer's Culinary Campaign* (London, 1857) (Introduction by Bathorp & Ray, Southover Press, 1995)

Spedding, J. *An account of the life and times of Francis Bacon* (two volumes) (Trubner & Co., 1878)

Spufford, Francis *I May Be Some Time – Ice and the English Imagination* (Faber, 1996)

Spurling, Hilary *Elinor Fettiplace's Receipt Book* (Penguin, 1986)

Stead, Jennifer 'Necessities and Luxuries: Food Preservation from the Elizabethan to the Georgian Era' in *Waste Not Want Not* (Edinburgh University Press, 1991)
'Navy Blues: The Sailor's Diet 1530–1830' in *Food For the Community* (Edinburgh University Press, 1993)

Stegner, Wallace *The Gathering of Zion: The Story of the Mormon Trail* (University of Nebrask, 1964)

Stevenson, J. & Davidson, P. (eds) *The Closet of Sir Kenelm Digby Opened* (Prospect Books, 1997)

Stobart, Tom *The Cook's Encyclopaedia* (Batsford, 1980)

Stolicnâ, Rastislava 'The Ways of Food Preservation in Slovakia' in *Food Conservation* (Prospect Books, 1988)

Stratton, Joanna *Pioneer Women: Voices from the Kansas Frontier* (Simon & Schuster, 1981)

Strang, Jeanne *Goose Fat and Garlic* (Kyle Cathie, 1991)

Steinkraus, K. *Handbook of Indigenous Fermented Foods* (Decca, 1996)

Swinburne, Layinka 'Ship's Biscuit and Portable Soup' in *Food on the Move* (Prospect Books, 1996)

Tannahill, Reay *Food In History* (Penguin, 1988)

Theodoratus, Robert 'Salmon's Rise from Poor Man's Food to Gourmand's Delicacy' in *Food Conservation* (Prospect Books, 1988)

Thévenot, Roger *A History of Refrigeration throughout the World* (International Institute of Refrigeration, Paris, 1979)

Thorne, Stuart *The History of Food Preservation* (Kirkby Lonsdale, 1986)

Toussaint-Samat, M. *History of Food* (trans. Anthea Bell) (Blackwell, 1992)

Trager, James *The Food Chronology: A Food Lovers Compendium of Events and Anecdotes from Prehistory to the Present* (Henry Holt NY, 1995)

Tristram, W. Outram *Coaching Days and Coaching Ways* (Macmillan, 1901)

Unruh, John D. *The Plains Across: Overland Emigrants and the Trans-Mississippi West* (University of Illinois Press, 1979)

Van Der Post, L. *First Catch Your Eland* (Hogarth Press, 1977)

van Duyn, Jeanette *Canning, Preserving, Pickling and Fruit Desserts* (Durban, 1921)

van Winter, Johanna 'Preserved Food in Medieval Households in the Netherlands' in *Food Conservation* (Prospect Books, 1988)

Viser, Margaret *Much Depends on Dinner* (Penguin, 1986)

Vries de, A. *Primitive Man and His Food* (Chandler Book Co., 1952)

Watteville de, H. *The British Soldier: His Daily Life from Tudor to Modern Times* (J.M. Dent, 1954)

Willings, Heather *A Village In The Cevennes* (Gollancz, 1979)

Williamson, Kenneth *The Atlantic Islands* (Collins, 1948)

Wilson, C. Anne *Food and Drink in Britain* (Penguin, 1973)
Waste Not Want Not (ed.) (Edinburgh University Press, 1991)
'Preserving Food to Preserve Life: The Response to Glut and Famine from Early Times to the End of the Middle Ages' in *Waste Not Want Not* (Edinburgh, 1991)
The Book of Marmalade (1985) (Reprinted Prospect Books,1999)

Woolrich, W. R. *The Men Who Created Cold* (Exposition Press NY, 1967)

Yates, Lucy *The Country Housewife's Book* (Country Life, 1934)

Yule, Sir Henry *The Book of Ser Marco Polo the Venetian* (John Murray, 1903)

Picture Credits

Page 3: Mammoths found in Jamalm Peninsula, *Mary Evans Picture Library*; 6: Kublai Khan distributing grain; 10: Eighteenth-century kitchen from E. Smith, *The Compleat Housewife* 1742; 20: Salmon from Olaus Magnus *Historia de Gentibus Septentrionalibus* 1555, *theartarchive*; 31: Stillhouse from N. Bailey, *Dictionarium Domesticum* 1736; 43: Italian kitchen scene from *Cuoco Secreto de Papa Pio Quinto* 1570; 52: Catching geese and dressing poultry after a tomb painting at Thebes; 65: Measuring salt in France 1528, *theartarchive*; 68: Beached whales from Conrad Gesner, *Historia Animalium* 1551; 95: Gordon and Dilworth's Catsup, *Robert Opie Collection*; 106: Curing food in French Guyana, nineteenth-century engraving, *theartarchive*; 111: Herring factory from Du Hamel Du Monceau, *Traité Général des Pesches*, 1769; 126: Katsuobushi at Tosa, Shikoku from *Nihon Sankai meisan* zue 1799; 129: Chinese banquet scene; 143: Cheese making from Denis Didérot Encyclopédie 1760, *Mary Evans Picture Library*; 152: Nineteenth century dairymaid; *Royal Collections*; 155: Advertisement for marmalade, *Robert Opie Collection*; 162: Boiling house for sugar from R. Bridgens, West India Scenery 1836, *theartarchive*; 175: Advertisement for Bovril, *Robert Opie Collection*; 178: Ploughman's lunch; *Mary Evans Picture Library*; 195: Sailors at mealtime after George Cruikshank c.1800, *Peter Brears*; 211: *The Accomplisht Lady's Delight* 1677; 214: Seventeenth-century London coffeehouse, *theartarchive*; 221: Nicolas Appert from Louis Figuier, *Merveilles de l'Industrie*, *Mary Evans Picture Library*; 239: French canning factory from Louis Figuier, *Merveilles de l'Industrie*, *Mary Evans Picture Library*; 247: Tinned food for William Parry's expedition, *Science Museum / Science and Society Picture Library*; 261: Dinner on board ship from nineteenth-century aquatint; 268: Ross's camp on Somerset Island from his book 1834, *Mary Evans Picture Library*; 286: Trawler fishing from *Illustrated London News* 1864, *The Illustrated London News Picture Library*; 301: Clarence Birdseye, *Corbis-Bettmann / UPI*; 309: Advertisement for Edward's soups; *Robert Opie Collection*; 316: A snack in space, *NASA*; 328: Food facts leaflet, *Imperial War Museum*; 331: Jam making with the Women's Institute, *Hulton Getty*; 339: Italian delicatessen, *Hulton Getty*.

Every effort has been made to trace and contact the copyright holders of all material reproduced in this book. The author and publisher will be glad to rectify any omissions at the earliest opportunity.

Index